A generation of feminist research has explored the extent to which the roles – and expectations – of women and men vary across cultures. In this volume, leading anthropologists reflect on the evidence and theories, broadening the conventional field of comparison to include female/male relationships among non-human primates and introducing fresh case studies which range from lemurs to hominids, from Japanese peasants to male strippers in Florida, from skeletal remains of a Korean queen to mother/child conversations in Samoa. They document the rich and often surprising diversity in sex and gender hierarchies among both human and non-human primates.

D0877804

Sex and gender hierarchies

Publications of the Society for Psychological Anthropology 4

Editors
Robert A. Paul, Graduate Institute of the Liberal Arts, Emory University, Atlanta

Richard A. Shweder, Committee on Human Development, The University of Chicago

Publications of the Society for Psychological Anthropology is a joint initiative of Cambridge University Press and the Society for Psychological Anthropology, a unit of the American Anthropological Association. The series has been established to publish books in psychological anthropology and related fields of cognitive anthropology, ethnopsychology and cultural psychology. It will include works of original theory, empirical research, and edited collections that address current issues. The creation of this series reflects a renewed interest among culture theorists in ideas about the self, mind–body interaction, social cognition, mental models, processes of cultural acquisition, motivation and agency, gender and emotion. The books will appeal to an international readership of scholars, students and professionals in the social sciences.

Sex and gender hierarchies

Edited by

Barbara Diane Miller

Department of Anthropology
University of Pittsburgh

Published by the Press Syndicate of the University of Cambridge
The Pitt Building, Trumpington Street, Cambridge CB2 1RP
40 West 20th Street, New York, NY 10011–4211, USA
10 Stamford Road, Oakleigh, Victoria 3166, Australia

© Cambridge University Press 1993

First published 1993

Printed in Great Britain at the University Press, Cambridge

A catalogue record for this book is available from the British Library

Library of Congress cataloguing in publication data applied for

ISBN 0 521 41297 8 hardback
ISBN 0 521 42368 6 paperback

CE

Contents

LIBRARY
ALMA COLLEGE
ALMA, MICHIGAN

Figures

Contributors

Marigene Arnold
Department of Sociology and Anthropology
Kalamazoo College

Sharon Bennett
Department of Anthropology
State University of New York College at Plattsburgh

Gerald D. Berreman
Department of Anthropology
University of California at Berkeley

Caroline Bledsoe
Department of Anthropology
Northwestern University

Mark Nathan Cohen
Department of Anthropology
State University of New York College at Plattsburgh

Elizabeth Colson
Department of Anthropology
University of California at Berkeley

Marvin Harris
Department of Anthropology
University of Florida

Brigitta Hauser-Schäublin
Institute of Ethnology
University of Basel

Gilbert Herdt
Committee on Human Development
Department of Behavioral Sciences
University of Chicago

Eleanor Leacock (deceased)
Department of Anthropology
City University of New York

Maxine L. Margolis
Department of Anthropology
University of Florida

Barbara Diane Miller
Department of Anthropology
University of Pittsburgh

Sarah M. Nelson
Department of Anthropology
University of Denver

Elinor Ochs
Department of TESL/Applied Linguistics
University of California at Los Angeles

Rayna Rapp
Department of Anthropology
New School for Social Research
New York

Joan B. Silk
Department of Anthropology
University of California at Los Angeles

G. William Skinner
Department of Anthropology
University of California at Davis

Melford E. Spiro
Department of Anthropology
University of California at San Diego

Patricia Chapple Wright
Department of Anthropology
State University of New York at Stony Brook

Adrienne L. Zihlman
Anthropology Board
University of California at Santa Cruz

To the memory of Eleanor Leacock,
pioneer in the anthropology of gender

Preface

There is little need these days for another general collection of anthropological essays on sex and gender. But this volume is important because it comprises chapters from all of anthropology's four fields – archaeology, physical anthropology, social/cultural anthropology, linguistics – and is explicitly motivated by the goal of creating a stronger discipline and better understanding of gender through cross-field comparisons and sharing. Another distinguishing feature of these essays is their focus on hierarchy between and within groups of males and females. Rather than merely documenting male–female differences our concern is with analyzing systematic relationships of inequality based on sex and gender.

The authors of this volume met in Mijas, Spain, in January 1987 for several days of intensive discussion. The financial and organizational help of the Wenner-Gren Foundation for Anthropological Research, Inc., made our meeting possible and supported the preparation of the published papers. The conference occurred at the confluence of Lita Osmunden's and Sydel Silverman's leadership of the Wenner-Gren Foundation, and this project has benefited from the wisdom and guidance of both people.

The Graduate Group in Demography at the University of California-Berkeley (1987–8), the Population and Development Program, South Asia Program, and Department of Rural Sociology at Cornell University (1988–90), the Department of Sociology and Anthropology at the State University of New York at Cortland (1988–9), the Department of Anthropology at Ithaca College (1989–90), and the Department of Anthropology at the University of Pittsburgh (from 1990 on) provided pleasant and stimulating settings as well as institutional support during this book's preparation. A small grant in 1986 from the Appleby-Mosher Fund of the Maxwell School of Citizenship and Public Affairs at Syracuse University supported background library research.

Richard Shweder, co-editor of the Society for Psychological Series, possesses an unusual breadth of intellectual vision and therefore appreciated the diversity of views presented in this book. My editors at Cambridge University Press provided superb guidance throughout the production process: Jessica Kuper saw the value of the book and helped keep it on course in many ways, Frances Brown was a keen-eyed and conscientious copy-editor, and Jayne Mathews was patient yet firm about turnaround. Near the end, my friend Alf Hiltebeitel provided pertinent advice about why one should not prepare an authors index.

The manuscript was word-processed by Esther Gray, of the Metropolitan Studies Program of Syracuse University, in her highly professional way and Colleen Mylan and Cecelia Dugan, of the Department of Anthropology at the University of Pittsburgh, word-processed the index with care. The figures were prepared by Marie J. Zeidler, and the artwork was funded by the Asian Studies Program and the Department of Anthropology at the University of Pittsburgh. My thanks to all these institutions and individuals.

One editorial goal for a collection of essays is that the chapters will speak in "one voice" stylistically, and I hope this unified stylistic voice has been achieved. But in terms of the content and perspective of each chapter, unique voices ring out loud and clear. Each author has his or her own purposes, and each pursues that purpose in a different way. In organizing the Mijas conference, I sought no unified vision of anthropology but instead chose authors representing diversity in their theoretical approach, empirical foundations, and analytic technique. This is not to say that all bases are thereby covered. Any such process of selection must unfortunately involve omissions. The book does provide a rich menu of studies from a variety of contexts – both human and non-human, ancient and contemporary, pre-industrial and post-industrial. A range of topics are explored – mothering and child care, work, health, eroticism and sexuality, intra-family relationships and power, public power, ritual and belief, and change in all of these.

The Mijas conference was in many ways risky and experimental. It convened scholars whose ideas are so diverse and sometimes antagonistic that they may not otherwise have ever sat at the same table to discuss their views. The meeting involved its own hierarchical dynamics based on the culture of human interaction at an academic colloquium and often clearly tied to gender. Were we authors to meet again, our discussions would be different because we have benefited immeasurably from lessons gained at Mijas. At a second meeting, we would be better able to bridge gaps between the fields and see the crossovers, linkages, and contrasts that at first came only with some difficulty. We have learned much from this project about the discipline of anthropology as a whole, and we hope this book will contribute to the growth of anthropology and its role in promoting understanding of gender hierarchies in all their complex and changing manifestations.

Barbara Diane Miller

A note on the discussions at Mijas

Elizabeth Colson

I am concerned here with certain implications of what was said at Mijas, rather than with the contents of the conference papers. We were asked to consider how the exploration of a particular subject, gender hierarchies, could contribute to, first, the development of better theory and methodology in anthropology in general, and second, the pulling together of physical anthropology, archaeology, linguistics, and social/cultural anthropology, on the assumption that those working in each subdiscipline would come to recognize the relevance to their own research of knowledge generated in the other fields.

Gender hierarchies were a good choice for such a discussion. We found commonalities that concerned all four subdisciplines. At the same time we were also made aware of the difficulties that lie in the way of communication or collaboration: differences in vocabulary, methodology, and theoretical assumptions.

"Gender" caused relatively few problems as a concept with which all could work, although primatologists may well prefer to use "sex" rather than "gender," given their concentration on biological phenomena. Even so, Zihlman and Wright convinced me that using "gender" and "gender relations" does not distort the reporting of primate behavior, given that so much of primate social life appears to be constructed.

"Hierarchy" was more problematic and raised a number of issues which we touched on, but did not fully explore. The primatologists preferred to talk in terms of dominance and submission, for these are terms which can be used to rate particular encounters and refer to the situational nature of their observations. Hierarchy implies something institutionalized which governs relationships over time between individuals who consistently accept placement in a system of ranking. It was noticeable that Zihlman and Wright appeared more willing to use hierarchy when describing intra-sex relationships among non-human primates, apparently because such relationships are more stable over time than inter-sex relationships because males and females, much of the time, may go their separate ways and have no need of consistent ranking.

Hierarchy, in fact, has connotations that have consequences for any methodology adopted, because of the kinds of evidence that must be collected if hierarchies are to be demonstrated. This kind of evidence is denied to the primatologist, the prehistoric archaeologist and the sociolinguist involved with the observational study of language learning. On the other hand, these three subdisciplines have a basic methodology in common, for their methods are those of the natural historian. Wright and Zihlman, as primatologists, and Ochs, as a sociolinguist, rely upon detailed observation of sequences of actions and interactions, either physical or vocal, but have no direct access to the meanings the actors impute to what they do. They look and listen but are unable to question those they observe. While archaeologists are precluded from observing behavior, and so have different methods and different problems from the primatologists and linguists, they too work in the tradition of natural history and obtain their data without the intervention of the screen of meaning thrown up by actors other than themselves and their fellow professionals. Nelson, who deals with an era when writing already supplements the archaeological record, found it possible to speak of hierarchies, whereas Cohen could not.

If hierarchy is more than dominance based on physical strength, if it involves legitimation as well as pecking order, then the term commits the primatologists, prehistoric archaeologists, and sociolinguists concerned with language acquisition to extrapolating well beyond their data. Nelson, as an archaeologist who can rely upon what actors said as well as upon the refuse born of their activities, could look in the written record for evidence of how men and women viewed each other in early Korea. She could query whether the centralization of power, with its implication of marked inequalities of rank, necessarily also implied that gender relationships were structured hierarchically. Cohen, as a prehistoric archaeologist, preferred to deal in less abstract terms, asking about specific evidence that males and females at particular times in history were subject to different deprivations or advantages: differential access to food, greater vulnerability to violence, differential exposure to specified sources of stress.

Linguists, however, provide a link between the concerns of primatologists and social/cultural anthropologists. Both groups found immediate relevance in Ochs' ability, as a sociolinguist, to provide linguistic cues for the rating of the presence or absence of dominance and subordination in particular encounters, and for pinpointing the initiator of attempts to shift control. The prehistoric archaeologists, debarred as they are from contact with their actors' discourse, found less relevance in this contribution of the linguist, but Nelson could see the relevance for interpreting the early written records.

Unlike their colleagues in the other three subdisciplines, the social/cultural anthropologists rely strongly upon questions put to actors: what are you doing, why are you doing it, what do you think will happen as a consequence, how do you categorize yourself and your fellow actors, including those invisible to the observer, etc., etc. Inevitably the number of variables multiplies.

Representatives of the other three subdisciplines demanded greater precision in definition, in the setting out of criteria on which the presence or absence of hierarchy could be empirically determined. The social/cultural anthropologists responded that what happens includes the actors' definitions, their sets of criteria, and these cannot be known in advance. Herdt, Hauser-Schäublin, and Spiro added that to understand what is happening one also needs to consider the individual historical experience that empowers meaning with emotion. Margolis and Rapp pointed to how what one sees takes meaning from the larger social context in which, for example, gender relationships are set. Newly introduced forms of technology, and any other form of activity, become quickly permeated with existing meanings. They spoke to the interconnectedness across whole ranges of activity, showing how particular actions can come to stand for larger systems of relationships. Therefore, we do not observe events circumscribed in time since situations have a past and future, and meaning in part refers to that continuity.

Berreman, Spiro, Herdt, and Hauser-Schäublin were particularly concerned with the way this interconnectedness serves to stabilize gender relations into hierarchies. The last three dealt more with how the hierarchy is legitimized through ideology and ritual. To Berreman, any form of hierarchy or institutionalized inequality is a form of domination which can be maintained only by the exercise of force: therefore, legitimacy is the ideology created by the oppressors and is always transparent to the oppressed. Those who may interact can and do impute very different meanings to what is happening.

In less extreme form this was a recurrent theme: hierarchy is not a unitary phenomenon in any society because its meaning shifts according to placement in the system and, for that matter, actors may also disagree about placement. If much of the existing ethnographic description tends to speak for some omnipotent representative culture bearer, so much the worse for that ethnography. As Sapir pointed out in the 1920s, each experiencing individual exists within a unique cultural world. When we reached this point, however, Harris and Leacock reminded us that whatever meanings individuals may attribute to what they do, they must act within institutionalized frameworks which determine opportunities and limit action, and these frameworks are subject to historical processes. As technology changes, so does the possibility for accumulating and exerting political power, and this process in turn affects other fields of relationships, including those of gender. Myths arise to explain the distribution of power and have their own ability to generate action. Spiro suggested that these myths can then spread, even to regions with very different economies and political organization.

Wright tried to engage the social/cultural anthropologists in the examination of variations in gender relationships according to such variables as ecology, population size, indices of political centralization, degrees of specialization of labor. By and large they did not respond, although in the papers before us we had a demonstration of the difficulties of such an exercise. Spiro, Berreman, Herdt, and Hauser-Schäublin reported the existence of a complex of ideas about gender which includes the belief that women are polluting and males vulnerable since semen can be depleted, and consequently that males need to be segregated and purified from female contacts. This pattern is found among state societies of high complexity, such as India and Burma, and in much of Papua New Guinea, where hierarchical political control was minimal; in temperate and tropical climates, where division of labor was elaborated and where it was minimal; in areas with highly developed priesthoods, and again where priesthood barely existed. Moreover, the complex existed both where in fact women were subject to real exclusions and subordination, and where women had much freedom and exercised dominance over household affairs, as in Burma.

In other words, although we can predict many things about a society if we know a few things about technology, centralization of political power, and the basic units of kinship, we cannot predict from these how men and women will regard each other, or how they will deal with one another. And, despite the persuasiveness of Spiro and Herdt, I doubt that we can predict such relationships from knowing how children are treated in infancy – equally dependent infants grow into very different kinds of adults.

Bledsoe and Leacock suggested some of the reasons for our difficulties in dealing with gender hierarchies as static phenomena for purposes of comparison when they focused on the way humans develop strategies for coping with such systems of social relations as they find, seek to alter these to their own advantage, and in doing so change the system. They left open the question of the relationship between ideologies and strategies, the degree to which ideologies can control when in fact advantages have shifted. One could also ask whether many people care about what others think if this does not interfere with what they themselves wish to do, a question that Spiro raised and left unanswered.

The conference suggested some interesting lines on which to work in examining degrees of freedom, although this left the archaeologists somewhat unhappy since they can extrapolate most freely if behavior is highly predictable. Recent research on primates indicates that sexual behavior is more variable among chimpanzees than among other non-human primates, that among them dominance/submission patterns are less consistent across genders, and that behavior in general is more variable. Zihlman emphasized flexibility and situational opportunism as characteristics of our closest primate kin. These are also the mark of the human species and have given it evolutionary advantage. Highly specialized, rigid behavior has its costs. Evolution, if it favors diversity, implies choice, and therefore the unlikelihood of long-term functional adjustments. Ideology, or myth, then is always out-of-date and always an extreme statement of an untenable position. Perhaps this is why it is enunciated so passionately by those who are given the leisure through the division of labor to elaborate it.

Part 1

Overview and theoretical perspectives

1 The anthropology of sex and gender hierarchies

Barbara Diane Miller

The fact of being born "female" or "male" in all human and non-human primate societies carries with it a specific behavioral assignment.[1] From lemurs to humans, there is no known primate society in which members are not differentiated by sex. Differences between males and females in primate societies, human and non-human, permeate every domain of life: reproduction, production, thought, and communication. Our human lives are influenced by gender differences every day, whether or not we realize it.

Social/cultural anthropologists make much of "cultural universals," features such as language and incest taboos that are found in every culture, because they provide clues about the nature of human adaptation. Gender-specific behavioral assignments are universal, but they are more than a cultural universal: they are an "order universal" in that they are found throughout the order Primates. Among all primates, males, not females, produce semen and females, not males, bear offspring, but that is as far as the cross-order universal in female–male differences extends.

Beyond those two biological facts, group-by-group variations in appropriate roles for females and males arise among both non-human and human primates. But variations are more complex among humans because humans have several cultural institutions that non-human primates lack: verbal and written language, religion, art, music, literature, and a sense of history.

Turning from differences (which can exist between equals) to hierarchies (which can exist only between unequals), we may ask if sex and gender hierarchies are universal in the order Primates. The perspective I take on this issue, not a completely agreed-upon stance no doubt, is that sex and gender hierarchies are not a primate-wide universal. Depending on how one defines a "society," it is possible to point to groups among both humans and non-human primates within which neither males dominate females nor females dominate males.

Assessing the existence and extent of sex and gender hierarchies demands that we look more closely than the level of "society." Complex,

3

socially stratified human societies may be characterized as a whole as being male dominated, but a socially disaggregated view may reveal much variation by class, social status, ethnicity, religion, and life-cycle stage. Variation by domain also exists, with females sometimes dominating in the domestic realm and males in the public realm. Sensitivity to subgroup and context-based variation existing within more general patterns provides a richer picture of sex and gender hierarchies than a society-wide view. But do not think that I mean that the wider generalizations should be abandoned; instead they should be tested against, reformulated, and enriched by more localized insights.

The chapters in this book explore variations across the order Primates, over time, cross-culturally, and intra-culturally. They demonstrate the extensive range of variation in sex and gender hierarchies. Keeping that variation in mind, we must also recognize that a survey of all human societies in the 1990s would probably reveal a preponderance of male-dominated (as defined one way or another) societies. But such a pattern has not characterized human society throughout its long history, or non-human primate societies past and present.[2]

Sex and gender

Why use two words, sex and gender? Our discussions at the Mijas conference confronted early on a dilemma caused by the connotations of these terms. Much feminist scholarship on humans distinguishes between sex, based on biological characteristics, and gender, based partly on biological characteristics and partly arbitrarily (for an early presentation of this distinction see Oakley 1972 and for a recent update see Johnson 1990:202–7). In this book, we also distinguish between sex and gender, using such terms as femininity and masculinity, woman and man, as (human) gender-related designations. The terms male and female can refer either to biological sex distinctions or cultural gender differences. Authors in this volume use the terms sex, gender, maleness, femaleness, and sexuality in contextualized ways, not always in agreement with one another's approaches. Such divergencies reflect the flux in anthropology and other disciplines as scholars and activists attempt to understand, and sometimes change, these complex words and their meanings.

The attribution of sex, among human and non-human primates, tends to rely primarily on genital conformation. Among humans, a new-born baby is immediately defined in most (if not all) cultures as a boy or a girl on the basis of its genitals. Scientific innovations now allow testing for sex through chromosome analysis. For example, the sex of athletes competing in the Olympics is determined through a chromosome test. Genitals and chromosomes, as sex determinants, do not vary from culture to culture or group to group: a penis is a penis whether it is possessed by a orang-utan, a Yanomamo, or a New Yorker, and the same goes for XX and XY chromosomes. Given some chromosomal material and training in how to read it, one does not need to know anything about a particular group to distinguish XX from XY chromosomes, in that group or any other, and to use that information in labeling the bearer's sex as either male or female. Not so with gender.

We cannot surely predict, on the basis of either genitals, chromosomes, or hormones what an individual's gender configuration will be in a particular group. Only two things can be known with certainty: that XY people may produce semen, and that XX people may bear children. Beyond that we cannot go. One might argue that XY people universally inseminate XX people, but that is only generally true, as evidence from New Guinea indicates (Herdt, this volume and his references): XY people also "inseminate" other XY people. Another potential case of universal behavior is that of mother (or mother-surrogate) care of young offspring among humans (Levy 1989). But the universality of that practice is disallowed by the cases, among others, of the Efe (Tronick, Morelli, and Winn 1987) and the Alorese (DuBois 1941), placing "mother or mother-surrogate care of young offspring" at the level of a generality, widely diffused, rather than a universality.

In some societies, people with XX chromosomes do the cooking, in others it is the XY people who cook, in others both XX and XY people cook. The same goes for sewing, transplanting rice seedlings, worshipping deities, and speaking in public. Even the exclusion of women from hunting and warfare has been reduced by recent studies from the level of a universal to a generality. While, it is generally true that men hunt and women do not, and that men fight in wars and women do not, important counter cases exist (see Harris, this volume).

Most primatologists feel that gender, like other complex symbol systems, is limited to humans.[3] Illustrations of the difficulty in using culture-laden terms for non-human primates can be found in the domain of reproductive relationships. While North American academics comfortably refer to both a human and a non-human primate who has just given birth as a "mother," they might not feel comfortable saying that both mothers have borne a "daughter" or a "son." In the case of the non-human primate mother, North American academics use the terms "female offspring" or "male offspring." These different lexicons reflect emic perceptions of the meanings involved in being a son or daughter versus a female offspring or a male offspring. North Americans who conversationally refer to a human baby as "offspring" would be suspected of coolness toward children or of having a somewhat twisted sense of humor (as in the television show Saturday Night Live term "parental units" for mom and dad). Other examples abound. Consider mating versus making love and pair-bonding versus marriage, distinctions that in English encode culture for humans and non-culture for non-humans.

The immense capacity of humans to symbol and to understand symbols clearly distinguishes us from our non-human primate relatives. But that is not to say that non-human primate societies evince no behavior that is arbitrary, distanced from sheer biological necessity, and learned inter-generationally. As the reader will see from Wright's chapter in this book on non-human primates, even primary offspring care cannot be univer-sally predicted on the basis of chromosomes or genitals because, among some non-human primates, males are responsible for the primary tasks of offspring care. Nor are non-human primate males universally the aggres-sive sex and females non-aggressive, or males dominating and females dominated (Zihlman this volume, and Hrdy 1981).

But not all human thought and behavior is culturally based with no biological foundations. The degree of difference, however, in the power of culture versus nature in modeling the behavior of human and non-human primates is vast. When I compare human and non-human primate behav-ior, I do so not in a strictly comparative sense, since the units are not equal. Rather I use the material in an analogous way: saying that "A" is like "B" indicates that the two are not identical but share similarities in form or function. Tasks for the future include more careful specification of those similarities and differences and attention to the degree of closeness of any analogy being considered.

The Mijas conference was not convened with the explicit goal of comparing human and non-human primates, but several contrasts between them in sex and gender differences and hierarchies emerged along the way. One difference between human and non-human sex assign-ments is that non-human animals cannot choose to be either male or female; instead their assignment is unchangeable. Among many human societies, an individual can opt for a different assignment and move across genders. Wikan's study of gender assignment transfers in Oman is an illustration (1977). Third gender roles, neither quite "male" nor quite "female," are another option available in some human societies (see Blackwood 1986). Transsexualism is, however, not an option in non-human primate societies.

Another difference between humans and non-human primates regarding sex and gender hierarchies is in the area of dissent. Dissatis-faction with one's gender assignment, questioning of the gender division of labor, and attempts to change gender roles can and do happen among humans. So far there is no evidence (and probably never will be) of dissatisfaction or reaction against sex role assignments among non-human primates. While human cultures have provided seemingly intractable gender roles and hierarchies, they also offer the ability to question and reject and reform them.

Hierarchy

According to a major English language dictionary, "hierarchy" is "any system of persons or things ranked one above another" (*The Random House Dictionary of the English Language*, 2nd edition, 1987). A hierarchy always involves more than one person or thing, or primate or other animal, that must be related to each other systemically, one above the other. The concept of hierarchy, added to sex and gender studies, is important. It forces us to think relationally, to consider the links between individuals and groups, and to examine the nature of those links and relationships. Are they open or closed, strong or weak, dynamic or static?

Implied in the phrase "one above the other" is a notion of dominance and control by the top party over the lower party. An example of a hierarchy among humans is the organization of the Catholic church: at the top is the Pope, in supreme command, beneath the Pope are archbishops who are above bishops who are above priests who are above lay people. The person on top controls the person beneath. But that is an ideal and static version of reality. In social hierarchies, individuals in lower positions can seek to influence those in upper levels through various means, or they may try to topple the system. Struggle between occupants of different niches may bring about repositioning, or the mere passage of time may bring a promotion. Studying hierarchies involves learning about both ideal structures and actual dynamics.

An added difficulty arises in studying complex human societies because male–female hierarchies vary depending on which sphere of activity is being considered. Early on in the anthropological study of gender, Friedl (1967) made the important point that women's status may be low in the public domain in most societies, but it may be high, even dominant, relative to males in the domestic domain.

Another problem is that valid definitions of differential status, or dominance, that apply across human societies are difficult to formulate (those who study non-human primates seem to be more agreed on appropriate definitions of dominance). Brown noted in the mid-1970s that there was no operational definition of "women's status" (1975:37, note 1), and not much improvement has been seen in the intervening years. Scholars still disagree as to which "measures" are most relevant. Control of important resources, including food and territory, access to tools and technology, power and authority, deference from others, and patterns of communication have all been considered.

Complications in assessing human gender inequalities arise from several directions, most notably from the distinction between "etic" measures devised by social analysts and "emic" measures valid only to the participants within a particular culture. Attempts at devising etic, cross-culturally relevant measures of male–female status are numerous. An early listing appears in Schlegel's (1972) cross-cultural study of matri-lineality and its effects on women's domestic status; her consideration of factors like deference behavior and the presence or absence of wife-beating focused on intra-household dynamics. Brown (1970) examines the division of labor by sex. Michaelson and Goldschmidt (1971) consider several facets of peasant life including subsistence roles and inheritance. Whyte (1978) includes variables from both the domestic and the public domains in his cross-cultural study of the "status of women": inheritance rights, labor participation, preferred marriage forms, and the ritualized separation of men and women. Sanday's (1981) analysis takes a more emic approach as she incorporates indicators of status taken from myth and folklore.[4] In non-human primate studies, all measures are etic since any emic realm among non-human primates cannot be accessed through current research methods. In this volume, approaches to assessing male–female status differentials and dominance vary from author to author; one purpose of this collection is to bring into scholarly juxtaposition such variation, not to control or suppress it.

Historically in the anthropological study of sex and gender, attention to biological measures of male–female inequalities, such as nutrition, health, and longevity, has been less developed among social/cultural anthropolo-gists compared to primatologists and paleoanthropologists. Since neither skeletal remains nor non-human primates can talk, researchers who work with them necessarily do things like measure bone length and content, weigh specimens, count incidences of aggression, and gather other kinds of explicitly etic data on welfare and survival patterns.

There are some exceptions. For example, female infanticide has been studied as an indication of low female status and male dominance in pre-state societies (Divale and Harris 1976). Related analyses indicate that where male dominance is strongest in northern India, intra-household son preference and daughter neglect act to bring about higher mortality rates for girls than boys (Miller 1981, 1987). Harris and Ross (1987) provide an evolutionary perspective on human population regula-tion mechanisms, such as female infanticide, abortion, and warfare. Such positivist analyses consider empirical evidence of gender-based discrimination, its variations, and outcomes, which are often at odds with textual/religious statements and other emic data.

But no matter how male–female hierarchies among humans are gauged, most scholars would agree that in the statistical sense, patriarchy or male dominance of some sort characterizes the bulk of human societies today. The whys and wherefores of the social evolution toward increased patriarchy among humans should be at the forefront of the anthropological research agenda (see Harris, this volume). Research on non-human primate societies should be increasingly informative about the evolution of gender hierarchies as well (see Zihlman, this volume), as they have changed over the millennia and as they may be changing in contemporary times owing to pressures on primate habitats and confinement in study centers.

From the human perspective it seems that change that has occurred in the past few centuries and is occurring in the present brings increased levels of male dominance and a decline of egalitarian or female-dominant systems. Such a trajectory, however, may turn out to be only a small digression on the vast path of human development yet to come. Centuries from now the trend toward patriarchy may be reversed, as some would claim has already begun in parts of Europe and North America, and a move toward greater egalitarianism made. In either case, we must not lose sight of alternatives to patriarchy that have existed in the past and that exist today among humans and our non-human primate cousins; thus examples of sex and gender equality or "attenuated" patriarchy (see chapters by Wright and Skinner, this volume) merit special attention.

The evolution of sex and gender studies in anthropology

Social/cultural anthropology

The 1960s and 1970s produced a growing awareness, particularly among feminist scholars who were mostly but not all women, that anthropology has been and still remains to a large degree a male-biased discipline (for a good early discussion see Schrijvers 1979). This period, which brought empirical enrichment to the study of women in anthropology, was motivated by the desire among social/cultural anthropologists to reveal the "invisible" world of women that had been ignored by previous ethnographers. It was a time of great discovery – the discovery was that half the world's population was almost completely unstudied. Of course, the roots of gender studies in anthropology extend further back in time than the 1960s and 1970s. Margaret Mead must be named as a major founding figure; her books remain classics in the field (especially 1935, 1949). Phyllis Kaberry's work is also of fundamental importance in developing the anthropology of gender (1939, 1952). In the next few paragraphs I cite some of the major social/cultural books on gender published between the 1960s and early 1980s (examples from the periodical literature, also vast, are not comprehensively reviewed here).

Many edited volumes appeared, including works by Ardener (1978, 1981), Bourguignon (1980), Rohrlich-Leavitt (1975), Caplan and Bujra (1978), LaFontaine (1978), Ortner and Whitehead (1981), Schlegel (1977), Etienne and Leacock (1980), Dahlberg (1981), Hirschon (1984), Vance (1984), Hoch-Smith (1978), MacCormack and Strathern (1980), Matthiasson (1974), Rosaldo and Lamphere (1974), Raphael (1975), Reiter (1975), Humphreys (1983), and Young, Wolkowitz, and McCullagh (1981). Some of these books examine specific topics for humans and non-human primates, while others look cross-culturally at women with regard to sexuality, gender symbolism, and the effects of colonization, for example.

Volumes of essays on women in particular regions also proliferated: Albers and Medicine (1983) on Native American women, Wolf and Witke (1975) on China, Gale (1970) on Australian Aborigines, Hafkin and Bay (1976) on Africa, Beck and Keddie (1978) on Muslim women, Allen and Mukherjee (1982) on India and Nepal, O'Brien and Tiffany (1984) on the Pacific, and Oppong (1983) on West Africa. Case studies of particular cultures have added much in-depth information on women. Some examples are: Strathern (1972) on New Guinea, Dwyer (1978) on Morocco, Lee (1979) on the !Kung, Murphy and Murphy (1974) on the Amazon, Spiro (1979) on Israel, Maher (1974) on Morocco, LeVine and LeVine (1979), Sacks (1979), and Bledsoe (1980) on Africa, Chiñas (1973) and Elmendorf (1976) on Mexico, Price (1984) on Surinam, Weiner (1976) on the Trobriands, Goodale (1971) and Bell (1983) on Australia, Hall and Ismail (1981) on the Sudan, Pellow (1977) and Bukh (1979) on Ghana, Poewe (1971) on Zambia, Ginat (1982) on Arab women in Israel, Loveland (1982) on Central America, Wikan (1982) on Oman, Makhlouf (1979) on Yemen, Atiya (1982) on Egypt, Roy (1976) and Jeffery (1979) on urban India and Sharma (1980) and Miller (1981) on rural India, Kerns (1983) and Massiah (1983) on the Caribbean, Smith and Wiswell (1983), Bernstein (1983), and Dalby (1983) on Japan, Johnson (1983) on China, Wolf (1972) and Kung (1983) on Taiwan, Skjønsberg (1982) and Risseeuw (1980) on Sri Lanka, Martius-von Harder (1981) on Bangladesh, Potter (1977) on Thailand, and Bennett (1983) on Nepal. During this period also, four textbooks on the anthropology of women were published: Friedl (1975), Kessler (1976), Martin and Voorhies (1975), and a reader edited by Tiffany (1979).

The overriding concern of most social/cultural research on gender of this period was to "correct" the male bias in traditional anthropology. But these studies were more than "compensatory" because they did more than just replicate for women what had been studied previously about men. Several studies questioned previous interpretations (Singer 1973; Weiner 1976, 1979; di Leonardo 1979; Mathews 1985). New directions emerged, spurred by the differences of women's lives compared to men's.

One impetus, prompted initially by Friedl's paper (1967), was to direct attention inward to the workings of the household, the "private domain," an area which few male anthropologists had penetrated. Recent examples of intra-household analysis include LeVine, Correa, and Uribe (1986) on marital morality in urban Mexico; Rohner and Chaki-Sircar (1988) on child treatment in West Bengal, India; Swartz (1982) on power relationships among the Swahili; and Sharma (1986) on household decision-making in urban North India. Strange as it may seem for the discipline of anthropology, of which one of the core subjects is marriage and the family, their internal dynamics were not much studied before an explicit focus on women developed, though notable exceptions exist (Whiting and Whiting 1975; Broude and Greene 1983).

This newly born interest in the domestic scene continues to develop. Reproductive practices, especially reproductive decision-making (Scrimshaw 1978), childbirth (MacCormack 1982; Jeffery, Jeffery and Lyon 1989), and child treatment (Scheper-Hughes 1987), have begun to attract research attention, a phenomenon linked to the growth of interest in medical anthropology in the 1980s. Martin's study (1987) of American women's knowledge of reproduction and experience of menopause is an important empirical analysis of a conceptual domain previously unexamined by anthropologists. A new interest in the analysis of the cultural amplification of motherhood (Zihlman 1978b; Poole 1984; Margolis 1984; Schrijvers 1985) promises to expose both its material bases and ideological buttresses.

The early period of development of anthropological gender studies in the 1960s and 1970s saw the publication of several key analyses of why males "universally" dominate females. Rosaldo's work was a leading force in this area (1974), as was Ortner's symbolic equation of females with "nature" and males with "culture" (1974). Related theories include Reiter's focus (1975) on patriarchal property rights and Harris' approach (1977) involving population regulation. An important counter-movement to the study of male dominance and female oppression appears in work devoted to revealing bases of women's power and autonomy. Illustrative work in this area includes analyses of Oaxacan women's secret knowledge about reproduction (Browner and Perdue 1988), power through "submission" in Greece (Danforth 1983), baptismal sponsorship as a source of Oaxacan women's power (Sault 1985), women's ritual roles in rural India (Wadley 1975), the relationship between power and economic change among the Nandi of Kenya (Oboler 1985), women shamans in Korea (Kendall 1985), women's political participation in rural Nepal (Molnar 1982), and marital arrangements and land ownership in matrilineal groups in Malaysia (Peletz 1987, 1989). These and other studies provide insights about the varying nature of women's power bases within contexts of greater and lesser male dominance. One must always keep in mind that the "power of the oppressed" is just that and cannot be equated with the power of those in dominant positions. Nevertheless the former may provide important supports for survival and even some tempering of the power of the dominant elements.

Sexuality (Shapiro 1979; Gregor 1984; Ember and Ember 1984) and sexual antagonism (Swartz 1958; Poole and Herdt 1982; McGilvray 1988) have also arisen as subjects of study. Interest in "third gender" roles has increased (Levy 1971; Miller 1982; Nanda 1986; Williams 1987). Homosexuality (Herdt 1982, 1984; Blackwood 1986; Lancaster 1988), blurred or transitory gender roles, and their relationship to gender hierarchies constitute yet another growing domain of research and one that can usefully be approached from anthropology's four-field front. Intra-gender relationships and hierarchies are a topic of interest that spans the fields as well (see Tiger and Fowler 1978; Hrdy 1981 on non-human primates; Dobkin 1967 on human females in Turkey). Key questions are to what extent and why intra-sex or intra-gender hierarchies differ from or resemble those across sex or gender.

Analyses of gender symbolism continue to proliferate (see the chapters in Ortner and Whitehead 1981 for early examples). Studies of gender symbolism and notions of gender are often derived from textual evidence, more or less linked with empirical data (see, for diverse examples, Taggart 1979; Keyes 1984; Kirsch 1985; Silverblatt 1987; Wadley 1976; Kemper 1980; Edwards 1982). Rituals also provide data for anthropologists interested in clues to subjective interpretations of gender differences (Werbner 1986). Symbolic analyses tend to be pervaded with structuralist conclusions; dualities reign supreme and oppositions abound. There are virgins and mothers (Hershman 1977), virgins and clowns (Werbner 1986), weavers and writers (March 1983), and other paradoxes (Strathern 1978). The influence of semiotics is felt in this area, and we even have a semiotic analysis of hominid sexuality (Rancour-Laferriere 1985). Too little of the work in this area links symbolic systems with other aspects of society: more often scholars overlook the empirical realities of gender inequalities in the pursuit of structural niceties. Bridging the ever-widening gap between symbolic approaches and more positivist studies is a daunting task. Some scholars, however, seem able to accomplish a fusion of attention to symbol systems and empirical gender hierarchies. Taggart's study of Nahuatl stories (1979) and Watson's analysis of the Chinese naming system (1986) are excellent examples, as are some of the chapters in this book (see especially Rapp and Spiro).

One important result of the interest in women has been the feedback of women's studies concerns into "men's studies." A healthy surge of research now examines males as males rather than generic representatives of a "culture." Specific topics being analyzed are fatherhood (Murphy 1983), "the making of men" great or otherwise (Godelier 1985; Herdt 1982; Harding 1985; Raphael 1989), competition and identity (Herzfeld 1985), power and belief (Sharp 1988), male sociability (Driesson 1983), and masculinity in folklore (Brandes 1980).

The early feminist assumption that enough (or too much) is known about men and that to understand women's status we must focus entirely on women errs in a disregard of the standard of measurement: men's status. Studying women's status can only be done in relation to something else and that is usually some foggy notion of men's status. Prefeminist generic studies no doubt neglected the female part of the equation, let us say, the numerator in the ratio, but also provided inadequate, unrefined information on "men." Is "men's status" a universal standard against which women's status of any place and any time can be assessed? The answer must be no, but our knowledge of variations in men's status is poor, though improving, thanks to studies like those mentioned above.

The other three fields

What about anthropology's other three fields? As a social anthropologist I am skating on thin ice in the following discussion, but I think it is worth the risk in order to bring forward the question of the differential development of sex and gender studies in the major subdisciplines.[5]

Much work in physical anthropology is concerned with gender differences, though one would not say that this field is fully gender-integrated. The study of human evolution is still male-biased as evidenced, among other things, by the use of male skeletal remains as the standard measure and the great preponderance of male primate skulls kept in museums (McCown 1982). In the area of human evolution, well-known work on the subsistence contribution provided by female gathering has helped balance the previous overwhelming priority given to male hunting by scholars (Hiatt 1970; Zihlman 1978a, 1981; Zihlman and Tanner 1978; Dahlberg 1981).

The study of sexual dimorphism, among both non-human primates and humans, looms large in the physical anthropology literature (a collection of studies on the subject is provided in Hall 1982), but scholars pay less attention to how sexual dimorphism (by whatever measure – height, weight, etc.) is associated with dominance. Does dimorphism favoring males lead to male dominance or vice versa (see the essays in Hall 1982 for diverse approaches to this question, and Silk, this volume, on dimorphism and mating among non-human primates).

The evolution of non-human primate sexuality (Lancaster 1979; Symons 1979) and human sexuality (Caplan 1987; Frayser 1985) is another important issue, and one that bridges physical and social anthropology. A related area of study in physical anthropology involves reproduction; major contributions have been made toward understanding non-human primate sex roles and parent/offspring relationships (see Altmann 1980; Taub 1984; Small 1984). Reproductive strategies in relation to primate evolution have also been usefully re-examined from a critical feminist perspective (Hrdy 1981). Topics as disparate as differential maternal treatment of infants on the basis of sex (Wheeler 1982) and group conflict resolution (de Waal 1989) necessarily involve the assessment of male–female dominance. Such areas of study parallel recent developments in social anthropology.

Compared to physical anthropology, there is a striking paucity of activity in studying gender in the field of human prehistory. The relative disinclination of archaeologists to work on gender questions may stem in part from the same problem that promoted the "man the hunter" model in human evolution: that which is hard – stone tools and weapons particularly – remains in the fossil record and tends to be associated by analysts with males, correctly or not (Conkey and Spector 1984). Whatever prehistoric males and females may have done that was "soft" is invisible because it has largely not been preserved, so the understanding of prehistoric gender roles may be further biased. Thus women in the fossil record are made even more invisible than they are in the ethnographies of many living cultures, and men, perhaps, rendered excessively visible.

Two serious problems in working with skeletal remains daunt those who study gender in prehistory: the difficulty in accurately determining the sex of many of the remains and the small number of usable fossil remains at any site from which dependable generalizations can be made concerning sex or gender differences, much less hierarchies. Fortunately, progress is apparent in spite of the data limitations (see Cohen and Bennett, this volume).

In anthropological linguistics, gender studies are a prominent endeavor. The topic of gender-differentiated language among humans, and its relationship with gender hierarchies, came into the anthropological mainstream in the 1970s. Harris, for instance, in the 1975 edition of his text, *Culture, People and Nature*, provided a subsection on "Obligatory Elitism and Sexism" in the chapter on language. Lakoff's (1973) classic article was a major impetus in the investigation of women's language use by anthropologists. Borker (1980) provides a useful review of the early anthropological literature on women and language; highlighting the relationship between language and gender hierarchy and how it varies cross-culturally. An excellent recent collection of essays pushes this tradition of inquiry in new directions, such as gender in children's speech (Philips, Steele, and Tanz 1987).

It is now generally accepted in anthropological linguistics that the language of dominant social strata works often to denigrate, or render invisible, members of dominated social strata. Humphrey (1978) documents this truth for Siberian nomads among whom daughters-in-law are restricted in the use of language to a degree far beyond that imposed on any other members of society, a restriction commensurate with their extremely low household status. Kuipers' (1986) work on the division of labor in language and society in eastern Indonesia addresses the issue of how linguistic inequality between the genders relates to inequality in other domains in a patrilineal society. Recently, the term "subordinate discourse" has entered the anthropological lexicon to describe gender inequalities in language (for example, Messick 1987).

The four fields of anthropology have evolved along varying paths in the study of sex and gender differences and hierarchies. The pattern of women-focused, "compensatory" research of the 1960s and 1970s is most characteristic of social/cultural, physical, and linguistic anthropology since prehistory and archaeology never experienced a real surge of interest in gender. Within social/cultural anthropology, much attention has been paid to economic roles, political roles, and the symbolism of gender, with intra-household dynamics more recently emerging. A revitalized and redesigned study of men is a new development in the field. Within physical anthropology, the study of sex roles in human evolution underwent revision as a result of the attention drawn to the inadequacy of the "man the hunter" model. In the realm of non-human primate studies, it seems that females have always been equally important (if not more so) to research as males. In the everyday life of non-human primates, culture does not enter the scene to restrict, disguise, or deny the importance of females as it tends to do in most human societies. Their role in food gathering and child care is prominent and not rendered invisible through language, and non-human primate censuses do not count only what males do as "work."

During the small percentage of time that humans have lived on earth, only an even smaller share of that history can be characterized as "patriarchal." Prehistorians have a major role to play in furthering our understanding of the transformations that evolving culture brings to human gender hierarchies. Ethnohistorians, following the lead of Eleanor Leacock, can help in reconstructing past gender structures with a more critical eye as to how human tendencies recreate the past in the shape of the present.

Challenges

The challenges of the 1990s in the anthropology of sex and gender hierarchies are several. Basic questions such as the causes, correlates, and consequences of various kinds of sex and gender arrangements have yet to be addressed satisfactorily. Attention to inequality in all its degrees still lies ahead. We must begin to specify what kind of male dominance/patriarchy is present in any given context: is it total, extreme, and even "lethal" to women (Miller, in preparation)? Or is it limited (Skinner, this volume), contradicted in certain domains (Spiro, this volume), or benign in its effects on women? We also need to examine the costs of patriarchy to men in terms of psychological stress that those in dominant positions experience, or other "costs" in the maintenance of dominance such as the negative impact of competitiveness and the "macho" male image on the health of men themselves (see for example Waldron 1983). Counter-cases to male dominance deserve focused attention. Where do more egalitarian societies emerge and what are their internal dynamics? Why does "development and change" often bring the downfall of the more egalitarian by the less egalitarian? Are there counter-cases to this grim generalization?

Beyond further knowledge generation, continued progress must be made in incorporating that knowledge into the heart of the discipline of anthropology and preventing its peripheralization (Papanek 1984). In addition, fragmentation within anthropology must be countered by greater communication among scholars working in its different fields.

Sex and gender hierarchies examined

Given the overload of books and articles to read and conferences to attend these days, scholars in one field often know little about advances in the others. Growth of the discipline of anthropology during the twentieth century increased the strength of each field but decreased communication across the fields. Each field has its own annual conference, its own scholarly journals, and therefore its own increasingly separate evolution.

An improved anthropology and an improved understanding of global patterns of sex and gender hierarchies can and must come from cross-field sharing. That is not the end of the line, of course, for interdisciplinary transfers provide lifeblood to any study as well. But anthropology is preeminently the comparative study of thought and behavior across human cultures, through time, and across human and non-human primate societies, and so it is in a key position relative to other disciplines. If we move ahead, so will others.

The book begins with theoretical overviews of sex and gender differences and hierarchies among non-human primates and humans, through time. The following chapters proceed along a life-cycle path from conception and birth to adulthood and death. Then there are several chapters addressing issues of complexity and change in human gender hierarchies. This linear organization does not capture completely the rich thematic reverberations between chapters; cross-referencing helps override some of that forced lineality.

Adrienne Zihlman's chapter offers a framework for looking at the evolution of sex differences among non-human primates. Focusing on three analytical fronts – the sexual division of labor, dominance and aggression, and sexual dimorphism – Zihlman argues that in each instance no convincing evidence exists either among non-human primates or in the human fossil record for biologically related bases of sex differences and possible gender hierarchies among humans. The need for critical analyses of the available data rather than a hasty adoption of a theory on the basis of over-crude generalizing is a key point of the article. Work roles and differential power, as examined by Zihlman, are the crux of many of the following chapters as well.

A theoretical exposition on the evolution of human gender hierarchies is provided in Marvin Harris' chapter. Building on a materialist-positivist approach to analyzing gender structure and change, he places warfare and plow agriculture in determinant roles with patriarchy and low female status as measurable outcomes. The examples in Harris' chapter document a strong association between male violence toward external enemies and extreme gender hierarchies, with females devalued and debased, within society.

Brigitta Hauser-Schäublin amasses data from Papua New Guinea cultures to demonstrate how, in the patriarchal framework there, basic biological facts about women having to do with blood – menstruation and parturition – are co-opted symbolically by men's rituals. Any power or status that women might accrue as reproducers is appropriated by men, leaving women as little more than reproductive vessels. In a comparative glance at some less patriarchal cultures in East Africa, she finds that the use of blood in rituals there creates solidarities among men rather than dominance over women.

Just as blood rituals in Papua New Guinea attach men to women's reproductive role, the "new reproductive technology" which includes prenatal testing (amniocentesis, chorionic villi sampling) removes reproductive power and decision-making from American women. Rayna Rapp's analysis of this situation in New York City is testimony that new reproductive technologies do not empower women, especially poor non-Anglo women, but work to increase the control of technology and technologists over women. "Advances for women," touted as such in North American society, are often the path to decreased power and health for women. The Dalkon shield and the birth control pill are prime examples. Studies such as Rapp's which pay attention to the entire power structure of medical behavior, from the research priorities of the medical sciences and the top technologists to the poorest "consumers," provide insights useful in promoting programs that might instead empower the consumers.

Fine-grained data gathered from recording hours of mother–child "conversations" in Western Samoa and white middle-class America provide the basis for Elinor Ochs' comparative analysis of the variable visibility of motherhood. Ochs finds that in America, mothers constantly render themselves invisible in dialogues with children, but not so in Western Samoa. Her presentation goes far beyond this insightful contrast, including such topics as differences in maternal accommodation to children in the two cultures. A resounding concluding point is a warning to anthropology itself: mothers as a category of women have been the most ignored by researchers of any social category, probably because mothers are themselves ignored in mainstream American culture. As Schneider (1984) has noted, people cannot help but see other cultures through their own cultural lens; anthropologists seek to overcome the limitations of their own frameworks through constant and careful comparison.

Variations in male–female involvement in offspring care among non-human primates are the subject of Patricia Wright's chapter. Comparisons of power between mates among numerous types of non-human primates yield three basic patterns: female dominant, male dominant, and co-dominant. Wright traces the relationship of these "domestic" dominance types to offspring care patterns and finds widely varying degrees of paternal care of infants not explainable in terms of paternal certainty as sociobiological theory predicts. Her comparative analysis of several species yields the conclusion that context-dependent adaptations are at work in creating diverse behavioral patterns. Generalizations relevant to humans are proposed in the areas of division of labor, sexual dimorphism, child care, mating receptivity, and predation pressure.

Themes of reproductive interests and child treatment take on a new edge in Caroline Bledsoe's study of child fosterage strategies among the polygynous Mende of Sierra Leone. Here female–female competition is sharp as co-wives vie for resources from the husband for their children and struggle to place their children in good fosterage situations to enhance their future status through educational opportunities. A blended consideration of gender hierarchies, social stratification, and the dynamics of economic development in Sierra Leone provides a holistic view of this system of intra-gender hierarchies that pivot around a central male resource (the husband) and children as future resources.

The cultural formation of boys' sexual and gender identities in Sambia culture, Papua New Guinea, is addressed in Gilbert Herdt's chapter. Among the Sambia, boys are inducted into a cult of ritual homosexuality, producing a hierarchy of adult males dominating young boys. Intra-gender bonding among males is coincident with male sexual antagonism toward women and the entire patriarchal structure of Sambia society. Herdt associates this type of cultural construction in Papua New Guinea with warfare in the past, echoing the larger political materialist themes explored in Harris' chapter.

G. William Skinner analyzes data from Tokugawa Japan to provide insights about the demographic outcomes – gender differences in child survival and adult longevity – of conjugal power structures. The Tokugawa population included in his study has a bilineal kinship system and male–female roles that are only slightly patriarchal, with the division of labor allocating equally important roles to men and women. Skinner finds evidence of infanticide, but not only female infanticide. Among the Tokugawan villagers, sex of the infant killed depended on the particular configuration of family power. Age differences between spouses and the presence or absence of the ascending parents in the household both affect patterns of survival in Tokugawa Japan.

Another male–female difference that can be the basis of inequalities, at least among non-human primates, is sheer size. Joan Silk reviews data on male–female size differences among non-human primates and links that data with information on pair-bonding patterns. She finds that size dimorphism between the sexes is a good indication of "domestic" organization – that is whether pair-bonding or multi-mate bonding prevails – but that dominance relationships across species are highly variable. One key finding is that regardless of size dimorphism and mating system, all non-human primate females have a substantial amount of autonomy: they choose their own mates and no such thing as forced mating exists. Moving from non-human primates, Silk considers the relevance of size dimorphism as a predictor of gender hierarchies among humans. At the societal level, no correlations are revealed, and the author concludes that cultural attributes more than the physical attribute of size are the bases of inequalities among humans. In America, short, slim men can buy guns just as easily as tall, heavy men, and the same goes for women. Culture can override physical size in determining hierarchies among humans.

Cohen and Bennett review the findings of many skeletal studies, gleaning insights about gender roles and hierarchies in prehistory and, particularly, change before and after the introduction of agriculture. Given the limitations of the data available and the small number of published studies that report on gender, Cohen and Bennett nevertheless are able to indicate an array of variations in male–female health status, productive workloads, and reproductive patterns among prehistoric people. Change is complex with no general formula apparent from the data. Again, local context leads to highly variable adaptations, yet the possibility that the intensification of agriculture brings greater benefits to males than females, or at least creates greater disparities than previously, has been documented in several cases.

Eleanor Leacock's analysis of change in gender hierarchies in Samoa takes an historical perspective, that she argues forcefully must be taken and which thereby debunks Derek Freeman's critique of Margaret Mead's work. Her exposition presents information on Samoan gender roles and relations in three historic phases: colonialism, missionary involvement, and recent economic development. Leacock demonstrates, as she has in her previous work, the impossibility of assuming that gender hierarchies today are the same as they were, even in the recent past. Her unfailing attention to historic detail is a great contribution to the anthropology of gender hierarchies.

Sarah Nelson examines another major question in the analysis of changing gender hierarchies: the role of the state. Her work on evidence from a Korean royal burial site documents the case of a state that developed without gender inequality as a prerequisite. As an example of a counter-case to a preconceived universal theory, the queens of Silla should take a prominent place in the anthropological record. The nonconformity of Silla poses questions about why Silla was different, where archaeologists might search for similar evidence (perhaps Japan), and where in the published literature reinterpretation of previous findings might be justified.

As Nelson compared evidence of possible gender inequalities in different domains such as ritual, politics, and work roles, Spiro's analysis of Burmese gender hierarchies also exposes cross-domain variation. Spiro distinguishes between the "cultural domain" (ideology) and the "social domain" (everyday interaction at the household and village levels). He finds dissonance in the gender hierarchies in each: culturally males are dominant, socially females are. His interpretation benefits from a psychoanalytic perspective which suggests that the cultural domain is a male artifact, created as a defense reaction to women's everyday dominance. This approach should be taken to other social contexts, where ideology and action may be found to be either congruent or not. The psychologies of the people involved in hierarchies, both male and female, invite further study cross-culturally.

A nearly reverse situation to the gender hierarchy dissonance in Burma is found in the case of male strippers in a Florida town, as analyzed by Maxine Margolis and Marigene Arnold. Here everyday life is characterized by male dominance while the rhetoric of male strip show advertising implies otherwise. Advertisements tell potential women customers that seeing a male strip show is their chance, their night out, presumably a reversal of traditional gender roles in which women perform and men ogle. At the strip show, the women customers are treated like juveniles, controlled by the situation, and symbolically humbled in relation to the dancer. Here is one more example of an "innovation" for women that instead reduces women to controlled consumers, comparable to what Rapp finds concerning reproductive technology. Change comes for women, but not of a liberating sort.

A systemic analysis of gender hierarchy trends in India is provided in Gerald Berreman's chapter. India is a complex civilization comprising an array of sociocultural variants and gender hierarchies ranging from extremely patriarchal to egalitarian. Berreman takes as his starting point a description of the traditional (1960s) gender hierarchy in the Himalayan region where he has worked, a region characterized by a relatively gender-balanced system contrasting with the extreme patriarchy of upper-caste groups in the adjacent plains. He shows how change, largely modeled on cultural patterns in the plains, has contributed to the decline of women's status in the Himalayas and an erosion of the entire social system there. Throughout India, the patriarchal system of the northern upper castes and classes is encroaching on other systems. Why and how patriarchy comes to predominate over other options are questions begging for future thought.

Constants and variables in sex and gender hierarchies

If we take a long and wide view of sex and gender hierarchies, we can see a vast range of diversity among primates and over time in the degree and distribution of male-dominated, female-dominated, and egalitarian contexts. Genitals and chromosomes are not varied over space and through time; they are constants. A simple rule of science is that variables (sex and gender hierarchies) cannot be explained by constants (genitals and chromosomes). Variation and change in sex and gender hierarchies operate under non-biological principles, among humans almost completely, and among non-human primates to an undetermined but demonstrable degree. If something is cultural and not natural, then it may be amenable to human influence.

As humans we can object to the gender hierarchies within which we live. As anthropologists we can provide examples of alternate gender scenarios and blueprints for improvements in our lives. This book is a statement against absolutes, biological determinism, and eternal inequalities in our lives.

We must not forget that human gender hierarchies are one of the most persistent, pervasive, and pernicious forms of inequality in the world. Gender is used as the basis for systems of discrimination which can, even within the same household, provide that those designated "male" receive more food and live longer, while those designated "female" receive less food to the point that their survival is drastically impaired. Worldwide, evidence shows that generally slaves, the poor, and females – not always exclusive categories – lead less comfortable and healthy lives than others. Thus, our study of gender hierarchies penetrates a domain of deprivation which overlaps with the study of other systems of inequality. As we here attempt to link the four fields of anthropology in looking at sex and gender hierarchies it is with the hope that our work will shed light on all institutionalized inequalities that are life-endangering and life-depriving.

NOTES

My thanks to Marvin Harris for comments on this chapter.

1 I use the term "assignment" to incorporate the concept of "role" for both humans and non-human primates. This use diverges from gender "assignment" as employed by Kessler and McKenna (1978:8), meaning the determination of a human baby's sex at birth.

2 A parallel exists between the contemporary majority of male-dominated societies and the minority of egalitarian societies, and that of industrialized nations in relationship to the dwindling population of foragers. The latter cases are relatively small in number but the lessons to be learned from them large.

3 How strictly this distinction is drawn varies from analyst to analyst. Zihlman (this volume) argues for a strict distinction. On the basis of evidence of variations in offspring care (Wright, this volume) and mating patterns (Silk, this volume), one might argue that some non-human primate behavior is "arbitrary" and "learned," that is, social if not cultural.

4 One difficulty with most cross-cultural analyses is that they assume social homogeneity within a given ethnographic site which is not appropriate for stratified villages in complex societies such as India and China where different classes have highly contrasting gender hierarchies.

5 I am not the first to raise the issue of four-field variation in the integration of gender into anthropological research, writing, and teaching. A panel entitled "Worlds in Collision" at the 1982 American Anthropological Association meetings was devoted to the question.

REFERENCES

Albers, Patricia and Beatrice Medicine, eds. 1983 *The Hidden Half: Studies of Plains Indians Women*. Washington, DC: University Press of America.

Allen, M. and S. N. Mukherjee, eds. 1982 *Women in India and Nepal*. Columbia, MO: South Asia Books.

Altmann, Jeanne 1980 *Baboon Mothers and Infants*. Cambridge, MA: Harvard University Press.

Ardener, Shirley, ed. 1978 *Defining Females: The Nature of Women in Society*. New York: John Wiley and Sons.

1981 *Women and Space: Ground Rules and Social Maps*. New York: St Martin's Press.

Atiya, Nayra 1982 *Khul-Khaal: Five Egyptian Women Tell Their Stories*. Syracuse, NY: Syracuse University Press.

Beck, Lois and Nikki Keddie, eds. 1978 *Women in the Muslim World*. Cambridge, MA: Harvard University Press.

Bell, Diane 1983 *Daughters of the Dreaming*. Winchester, MA: Allen and Unwin.

Bennett, Lynn 1983 *Dangerous Wives and Sacred Sisters: Social and Symbolic Roles of High-Caste Women in Nepal*. New York: Columbia University Press.

Bernstein, Gail Lee 1983 *Haruko's World: A Japanese Farm Woman and Her Community*. Stanford, CA: Stanford University Press.

Blackwood, Evelyn, ed. 1986 *Anthropology and Homosexual Behavior*. New York: The Haworth Press.

Bledsoe, Caroline 1980 *Women and Marriage in Kpelle Society*. Stanford, CA: Stanford University Press.

Borker, Ruth 1980 Anthropology: Social and Cultural Perspectives. In *Women and Language in Literature and Society*. Sally McConnell-Ginet, Ruth Borker, and Nelly Furman, eds., pp. 26–44. New York: Praeger.

Bourguignon, Erika, ed. 1980 *A World of Women: Anthropological Studies of Women in the Societies of the World*. New York: Praeger.

Brandes, Stanley 1980 *Metaphors of Masculinity: Sex and Status in Andalusian Folklore*. Philadelphia: University of Pennsylvania Press.

Broude, Gwen J. and Sarah J. Greene 1983 Cross-Cultural Codes on Husband–Wife Relationships. *Ethnology* 22(3):263–80.

Brown, Judith K. 1970 A Note on the Division of Labor by Sex. *American Anthropologist* 72(5):1073–8.

1975 Iroquois Women: An Ethnohistoric Note. In *Toward an Anthropology of Women*. Rayna R. Reiter, ed., pp. 235–51. New York: Monthly Review Press.

Browner, Carole H. and Sondra T. Perdue 1988 Women's Secrets: Bases for Reproductive and Social Autonomy in a Mexican Community. *American Ethnologist* 15(1):84–97.

Bukh, Jette 1979 *The Village Woman in Ghana*. Uppsala: Scandinavian Institute of African Studies.

Burton, Michael L. and Douglas R. White 1984 Sexual Division of Labor in Agriculture. *American Anthropologist* 86(3):568–83.

Caplan, Patricia, ed. 1987 *The Cultural Construction of Sexuality*. New York: Tavistock.

Caplan, Patricia and Janet M. Bujra, eds. 1978 *Women United, Women Divided: Cross-Cultural Perspectives on Female Solidarity*. London: Tavistock.

Chiñas, Beverly L. 1973 *The Isthmus Zapotecs: Women's Roles in Cultural Context*. New York: Holt, Rinehart and Winston.

Conkey, Margaret W. and Janet Spector 1984 Archaeology and the Study of Gender. *Advances in Archaeological Method and Theory* 7:1–38.

Dahlberg, Frances, ed. 1981 *Woman the Gatherer*. New Haven, CT: Yale University Press.

Dalby, Liza Crihfield 1983 *Geisha*. Berkeley: University of California Press.

Danforth, Loring 1983 Power through Submission in the Anasthenaria. *Journal of Modern Greek Studies* 1:203–29.

de Waal, Frans 1989 *Peacemaking among Primates*. Cambridge, MA: Harvard University Press.

di Leonardo, Micaela 1979 Methodology and the Misinterpretation of Women's Status in Kinship Studies: A Case Study of Goodenough and the Definition of Marriage. *American Anthropologist* 78(3):521–38.

Dobkin, Marlene 1967 Social Ranking in the Woman's World of Purdah: A Turkish Example. *Anthropological Quarterly* 2:65–72.

Driessen, Henk 1983 Male Sociability and Rituals of Masculinity in Rural Andalusia. *Anthropological Quarterly* 56:125–33.

DuBois, Cora 1941 Attitudes toward Food and Hunger in Alor. In *Language, Culture, and Personality: Essays in Memory of Edward Sapir*. Leslie Spier, A. Irving Hallowell, and Stanley S. Newman, eds., pp. 272–81. Menasha, WI: Sapir Memorial Publication Fund.

Dwyer, Daisy Hilse 1978 *Images and Self-Images: Male and Female in Morocco*. New York: Columbia University Press.

Edwards, Walter 1982 Something Borrowed: Wedding Cakes as Symbols in Modern Japan. *American Ethnologist* 9(4):699–711.

Elmendorf, Mary L. 1976 *Nine Mayan Women: A Village Faces Change*. Cambridge, MA: Schenkman Publishing Co.

Ember, Carol R. and Melvin Ember 1984 The Evolution of Human Female Sexuality: A Cross-Species Perspective. *Journal of Anthropological Research* 4(1):202–10.

Etienne, Mona and Eleanor Leacock, eds. 1980 *Women and Colonization: Anthropological Perspectives*. New York: Praeger.

Frayser, Suzanne G. 1985 *Varieties of Sexual Experience: An Anthropological Perspective on Human Sexuality*. New Haven, CT: HRAF Press.

Friedl, Ernestine 1967 The Position of Women: Appearance and Reality. *Anthropological Quarterly* 40(3):98–105.

1975 *Women and Men: An Anthropologist's View.* New York: Holt, Rinehart and Winston.

Gale, Fay, ed. 1970 *Women's Role in Aboriginal Society.* Canberra: Australian Institute of Aboriginal Studies.

Ginat, Joseph 1982 *Women in Muslim Rural Society.* New Brunswick, NJ: Transaction Books.

Godelier, Maurice 1985 *The Making of Great Men: Male Domination and Power among the New Guinea Baruya.* New York: Cambridge University Press.

Goodale, Jane C. 1971 *Tiwi Wives: A Study of the Women of Melville Island, North Australia.* Seattle: University of Washington Press.

Gregor, Thomas 1984 *Anxious Pleasures: The Sexual Lives of an Amazonian People.* Chicago: University of Chicago Press.

Hafkin, Nancy J. and Edna C. Bay, eds. 1976 *Women in Africa: Studies in Social and Economic Change.* Stanford: Stanford University Press.

Hall, Marjorie and Bakhita Amin Ismail 1981 *Sisters under the Sun: The Story of Sudanese Women.* New York: Longman.

Hall, Roberta L. 1982 *Sexual Dimorphism in* Homo Sapiens: *A Question of Size.* New York: Praeger.

Harding, Thomas G. 1985 *Kunai Men: Horticultural Systems of a Papua New Guinea Society.* Berkeley: University of California Press.

Harris, Marvin 1975 *Culture, People and Nature: An Introduction to General Anthropology.* New York: Thomas Y. Crowell and Co.

1977 *Cannibals and Kings: The Origins of Cultures.* New York: Random House.

1984 Animal Capture and Yanomamo Warfare: Retrospect and New Evidence. *Journal of Anthropological Research* 40(1):183–201.

Harris, Marvin and Eric B. Ross 1987 *Death, Sex, and Fertility: Population Regulation in Preindustrial and Developing Societies.* New York: Columbia University Press.

Herdt, Gilbert H., ed. 1982 *Rituals of Manhood.* Berkeley: University of California Press.

1984 *Ritualized Homosexuality in Melanesia.* Berkeley: University of California Press.

Hershman, Paul 1977 Virgin and Mother. In *Symbols and Sentiments.* I. M. Lewis, ed., pp. 270–300. London: Academic Press.

Herzfeld, Michael 1985 *The Poetics of Manhood: Contest and Identity in a Cretan Mountain Village.* Princeton: Princeton University Press.

Hiatt, Betty 1970 Woman the Gatherer. In *Woman's Role in Aboriginal Society.* Fay Gale, ed., pp. 2–8. Canberra: Australian Institute of Aboriginal Studies.

Hirschon, Renée, ed. 1984 *Women and Property, Women as Property.* London: Croom Helm.

Hoch-Smith, Judith, ed. 1978 *Women in Ritual and Symbolic Roles.* New York: Plenum Press.

Hrdy, Sarah B. 1981 *The Woman that Never Evolved.* Cambridge, MA: Harvard University Press.

Humphrey, Caroline 1978 Women, Taboo and the Suppression of Attention. In *Defining Females: The Nature of Women in Society.* Shirley Ardener, ed., pp. 89–108. New York: John Wiley and Sons.

Humphreys, S. C. 1983 *The Family, Women and Death: Comparative Studies.* New York: Routledge and Kegan Paul.

Jeffery, Patricia 1979 *Frogs in a Well: Indian Women in Purdah.* London: Zed Press.

Jeffery, Patricia, Roger Jeffery, and Andrew Lyon 1989 *Labour Pains and Labour Power: Women and Childbearing in India.* London: Zed Press.

Johnson, Kay Ann 1983 *Women, the Family and Peasant Revolution in China.* Chicago: University of Chicago Press.

Johnson, Miriam M. 1990 *Strong Mothers, Weak Wives: The Search for Gender Equality.* Berkeley: University of California Press.

Kaberry, Phyllis M. 1939 *Aboriginal Woman, Sacred and Profane.* London: George Routledge and Sons.

1952 *Women of the Grassfields. A Study of the Economic Position of Women in Bamenda, British Cameroons.* London: Colonial Office, Research Publication No. 14.

Kemper, Steven 1980 Time, Person, and Gender in Sinhalese Astrology. *American Ethnologist* 7:744–58.

Kendall, Laurel 1985 *Shamans, Housewives, and Other Restless Spirits: Women in Korean Ritual Life.* Honolulu: University of Hawaii Press.

Kerns, Virginia 1983 *Women and the Ancestors: Black Carib Kinship and Ritual.* Urbana: University of Illinois Press.

Kessler, Evelyn S. 1976 *Women: An Anthropological View.* New York: Holt, Rinehart and Winston.

Kessler, Suzanne J. and Wendy McKenna 1978 *Gender: An Ethnomethodological Approach.* New York: John Wiley and Sons.

Keyes, Charles F. 1984 Mother or Mistress but Never a Monk: Buddhist Notions of Female Gender in Rural Thailand. *American Ethnologist* 11(2):223–41.

Kirsch, A. Thomas 1985 Text and Context: Buddhist Sex Roles/Culture of Gender Revisited. *American Ethnologist* 12(2):302–20.

Kuipers, Joel 1986 Talking about Troubles: Gender Differences in Weyéwa Speech Use. *American Ethnologist* 13(3):448–61.

Kung, Lydia 1983 *Factory Women in Taiwan.* Ann Arbor, MI: UMI Research Press.

LaFontaine, Jean S., ed. 1978 *Sex and Age as Principles of Social Differentiation.* London: Academic Press.

Lakoff, Robin 1973 Language and Woman's Place. *Language in Society* 2:45–80.

Lancaster, Jane B. 1979 Sex and Gender in Evolutionary Perspective. In *Human Sexuality: A Comparative and Developmental Perspective.* Herant A. Katchadourian, ed., pp. 51–80. Berkeley: University of California Press.

Lancaster, Roger Nelson 1988 Subject Honor and Object Shame: The Construction of Male Homosexuality and Stigma in Nicaragua. *Ethnology* 27(2):111–25.

Lee, Richard B. 1979 *The !Kung San: Men, Women, and Work in a Foraging Society.* New York: Cambridge University Press.

LeVine, Sarah Ethel, Clara Sunderland Correa, and F. Medardo Tapia Uribe 1986 The Marital Morality of Mexican Women: An Urban Study. *Journal of Anthropological Research* 42(4):183–202.

LeVine, Sarah and Robert A. LeVine 1979 *Mothers and Wives: Gusii Women of East Africa.* Chicago: University of Chicago Press.

Levy, Marion J. Jr 1989 *Our Mother-Tempers: Some Influences of Women on Society*. Berkeley: University of California Press.

Levy, Robert I. 1971 The Community Function of Tahitian Male Transvestism: A Hypothesis. *Anthropological Quarterly* 44:12–21.

Loveland, Christine A. 1982 *Sex Roles and Social Change in Native Lower Central American Societies*. Urbana: University of Illinois Press.

MacCormack, Carol P., ed. 1982 *Ethnography of Fertility and Birth*. New York: Academic.

MacCormack, Carol P. and Marilyn Strathern, eds. 1980 *Nature, Culture and Gender*. New York; Cambridge University Press.

McCown, Elizabeth R. 1982 Sex Differences: The Female as Baseline for Species Description. In *Sexual Dimorphism in* Homo Sapiens*: A Question of Size*. Roberta L. Hall, ed., pp. 37–84. New York: Praeger.

McGilvray, Dennis B. 1988 Sex, Repression, and Sanskritization in Sri Lanka? *Ethos* 16(2):99–127.

Maher, Vanessa 1974 *Women and Property in Morocco: Their Changing Relation to the Process of Social Stratification in the Middle Atlas*. Cambridge: Cambridge University Press.

Makhlouf, Carla 1979 *Changing Veils: Women and Modernization in North Yemen*. Austin: University of Texas Press.

March, Kathryn 1983 Weaving, Writing and Gender. *Man* 18:729–44.

Margolis, Maxine 1984 *Mothers and Such: Views of American Women and Why They Changed*. Berkeley: University of California Press.

Martin, Emily 1987 *The Woman in the Body: A Cultural Analysis of Reproduction*. Boston, MA: Beacon Press.

Martin, M. K. and Barbara Voorhies 1975 *Female of the Species*. New York: Columbia University Press.

Martius-von Harder, Gudrun 1981 *Women in Rural Bangladesh: An Empirical Study in Four Villages of Comilla District*. Fort Lauderdale, FL: Breitenbach Publishers.

Massiah, Joycelin 1983 *Women as Heads of Households in the Caribbean: Family Structure and Feminine Status*. Paris: UNESCO.

Mathews, Holly F. 1985 "We are Mayordomo": A Reinterpretation of Women's Roles in the Mexican Cargo System. *American Ethnologist* 12(2):285–301.

Matthiasson, Carolyn, ed. 1974 *Many Sisters: Women in Cross-Cultural Perspective*. New York: The Free Press.

Mead, Margaret 1935 *Sex and Temperament in Three Primitive Societies*. New York: William Morrow and Co.

  1949 *Male and Female: A Study of the Sexes in a Changing World*. New York: William Morrow and Co.

Messick, Brinkley 1987 Subordinate Discourse: Women, Weaving and Gender Relations in North Africa. *American Ethnologist* 14(2):210–25.

Michaelson, Evelyn Jacobson and Walter Goldschmidt 1971 Female Roles and Male Dominance Among Peasants. *Southwestern Journal of Anthropology* 27:330–52.

Miller, Barbara D. 1981 *The Endangered Sex: Neglect of Female Children in Rural North India*. Ithaca: Cornell University Press.

  1987 Female Infanticide and Child Neglect in Rural North India. In *Child*

Survival: Anthropological Perspectives on the Treatment and Maltreatment of Children. Nancy Scheper-Hughes, ed., pp. 95–112. Boston: D. Reidel Publishing Company.

  in prep. Let Her Live: Patriarchy and Public Health Programs in India. Unpublished manuscript.

Miller, Jay 1982 People, Berdaches, and Left-Handed Bears: Human Variation in Native America. *Journal of Anthropological Research* 38(3):274–87.

Molnar, Augusta 1982 Women and Politics: Case of the Kham Magar of Western Nepal. *American Ethnologist* 9(3):485–502.

Murphy, Michael 1983 Emotional Confrontations between Sevillano Fathers and Sons: Cultural Foundations and Social Consequences. *American Ethnologist* 10:650–64.

Murphy, Yolanda and Robert F. Murphy 1974 *Women of the Forest*. New York: Columbia University Press.

Nanda, Serena 1986 The Hijras of India: Cultural and Individual Dimensions of an Institutionalized Gender Role. In *Anthropology and Homosexual Behavior*. Evelyn Blackwood, ed., pp. 35–54. New York: The Haworth Press.

Oakley, Ann 1972 *Sex, Gender and Society*. New York: Harper and Row, Publishers.

Oboler, Regina Smith 1985 *Women, Power, and Economic Change: The Nandi of Kenya*. Stanford: Stanford University Press.

O'Brien, Denise and Sharon W. Tiffany, eds. 1984 *Rethinking Women's Roles: Perspectives from the Pacific*. Berkeley: University of California Press.

Oppong, Christine, ed. 1983 *Female and Male in West Africa*. Boston, MA: George Allen and Unwin.

Ortner, Sherry B. 1974 Is Female to Male as Nature is to Culture? In *Woman, Culture and Society*. Michelle Zimbalist Rosaldo and Louise Lamphere, eds., pp. 67–88. Stanford: Stanford University Press.

Ortner, Sherry B. and Harriet Whitehead, eds. 1981 *Sexual Meanings: The Cultural Construction of Gender and Sexuality*. New York: Cambridge University Press.

Papanek, Hanna 1984 False Specialization and the Purdah of Scholarship: A Review Article. *Journal of Asian Studies* 24(1):127–48.

Peletz, Michael G. 1987 The Exchange of Men in 19th-century Negeri Sembilan (Malaya). *American Ethnologist* 14(3):449–69.

  1989 *A Share of the Harvest: Kinship, Property and Social History among the Malays of Rembau*. Berkeley: University of California Press.

Pellow, Deborah 1977 *Women in Accra: Options for Autonomy*. Algonac, MI: Reference Publications.

Philips, Susan U., Susan Steele, and Christine Tanz, eds. 1988 *Language, Gender and Sex in Comparative Perspective*. New York: Cambridge University Press.

Poewe, Karla O. 1971 *Matrilineal Ideology: Male–Female Dynamics in Luapula, Zambia*. London: Academic Press.

Poole, Fitz John Porter 1984 Cultural Images of Women as Mothers: Motherhood among the Bimin-Kuskusmin of Papua New Guinea. *Social Analysis* 15:73–93.

Poole, Fitz John Porter and Gilbert H. Herdt, eds. 1982 Sexual Antagonism, Gender, and Social Change in Papua New Guinea. *Social Analysis* 12 (special issue).

Potter, Sulamith Heins 1977 *Family Life in a Northern Thai Village: A Study in the Structural Significance of Women.* Berkeley: University of California Press.

Price, Sally 1984 *Co-Wives and Calabashes.* Ann Arbor: University of Michigan Press.

Rancour-Laferriere, Daniel 1985 *Signs of the Flesh: An Essay on the Evolution of Hominid Sexuality.* New York: Mouton.

Raphael, Dana, ed. 1975 *Being Female: Reproduction, Power, and Change.* The Hague: Mouton.

Raphael, Ray 1989 *The Men from the Boys: Rites of Passage in Male America.* Lincoln: University of Nebraska Press.

Reiter, Rayna R., ed. 1975 *Toward an Anthropology of Women.* New York: Monthly Review Press.

Risseuw, Carla 1980 *The Wrong End of the Rope: Women Coir Workers in Sri Lanka.* Leiden: Research and Documentation Centre, Women and Development, University of Leiden.

Rohner, Ronald P. and Manjusri Chaki-Sircar 1988 *Women and Children in a Bengali Village.* Hanover, NH: University Press of New England.

Rohrlich-Leavitt, Ruby, ed. 1975 *Women Cross-Culturally: Change and Challenge.* The Hague: Mouton.

Rosaldo, Michelle Zimbalist 1974 Woman, Culture, and Society: A Theoretical Overview. In *Woman, Culture, and Society.* Michelle Zimbalist Rosaldo and Louise Lamphere, eds., pp. 17–42. Stanford: Stanford University Press.

Rosaldo, Michelle Zimbalist and Louise Lamphere, eds. 1974 *Woman, Culture, and Society.* Stanford: Stanford University Press.

Roy, Manisha 1976 *Bengali Women.* Chicago: University of Chicago Press.

Sacks, Karen 1979 *Sisters and Wives: The Past and Future of Sexual Equality.* Westport, CT: Greenwood Press.

Sanday, Peggy R. 1981 *Female Power and Male Dominance: On the Origins of Sexual Inequality.* New York: Cambridge University Press.

Sault, Nicole L. 1985 Baptismal Sponsorship as a Source of Power for Zapotec Women in Oaxaca, Mexico. *Journal of Latin American Lore* 11(2):225–43.

Scheper-Hughes, Nancy, ed. 1987 *Child Survival: Anthropological Perspectives on the Treatment and Maltreatment of Children.* Boston, MA: D. Reidel Publishing Company.

Schlegel, Alice 1972 *Male Dominance and Female Autonomy: Domestic Authority in Matrilineal Societies.* New Haven, CT: Human Relations Area Files.

Schlegel, Alice, ed. 1977 *Sexual Stratification: A Cross-Cultural View.* New York: Columbia University Press.

Schneider, David M. 1984 *A Critique of the Study of Kinship.* Ann Arbor: The University of Michigan Press.

Schrijvers, Joke 1979 Viricentrism in Anthropology. In *The Politics of Anthropology.* Gerrit Huizer and Bruce Manheim, eds., pp. 97–115. The Hague: Mouton.

  1985 *Mothers for Life: Motherhood and Marginalization in the North Central Province of Sri Lanka.* Leiden: Eburon Delft.

Scrimshaw, Susan S. 1978 Stages in Women's Lives and Reproductive Decision-Making in Latin America. *Medical Anthropology* 2(3):41–58.

Shapiro, Judith 1979 Cross-Cultural Perspectives on Sexual Differentiation. In

Human Sexuality: A Comparative and Developmental Perspective. Herant A. Katchadourian, ed., pp. 269–308. Berkeley: University of California Press.

Sharma, Ursula 1980 *Women, Work, and Property in North-West India.* London: Tavistock.

1986 *Women's Work, Class, and the Urban Household: A Study of Shimla, North India.* New York: Tavistock.

Sharp, Henry S. 1988 *The Transformation of Bigfoot: Maleness, Power, and Belief among the Chepewyan.* Blue Ridge Summit, PA: Smithsonian Institution Press.

Silverblatt, Irene 1987 *Moon, Sun, and Witches: Gender Ideologies and Class in Inca and Colonial Peru.* Princeton: Princeton University Press.

Singer, Alice 1973 Marriage Payments and the Exchange of People. *Man* 8(1):80–92.

Skjønsberg, Else 1982 *A Special Caste? Tamil Women of Sri Lanka.* London: Zed Press.

Small, Meredith F., ed. 1984 *Female Primates: Studies by Women Primatologists.* New York: Alan R. Liss.

Smith, Robert J. and Ella Wiswell 1983 *The Women of Suye Mura.* Chicago: University of Chicago Press.

Spiro, Melford E. 1979 *Gender and Culture: Kibbutz Women Revisited.* Durham: Duke University Press.

Strathern, Marilyn 1972 *Women in Between: Female Roles in a Male World – Mount Hagen, New Guinea.* New York: Seminar Press.

1978 The Achievement of Sex: Paradoxes in Hagen Gender-Thinking. In *Yearbook of Symbolic Anthropology I.* E. G. Schwimmer, ed., pp. 171–202. London: C. Hurst.

Swartz, Marc J. 1958 Sexuality and Aggression on Romonum, Truk. *American Anthropologist* 60:467–86.

1982 The Isolation of Men and the Happiness of Women: Sources and Use of Power in Swahili Marital Relations. *Journal of Anthropological Research* 38(1):26–44.

Symons, D. 1979 *The Evolution of Human Sexuality.* New York: Oxford University Press.

Taggart, James M. 1979 Men's Changing Image of Women in Nahuatl Oral Tradition. *American Ethnologist* 6(4):723–41.

Taub, David Milton, ed. 1984 *Primate Paternalism.* New York: Van Nostrand Reinhold Company.

Tiffany, Sharon W., ed. 1979 *Women and Society: An Anthropological Reader.* Montreal: Eden Press.

Tiger, Lionel and Heather T. Fowler, eds. 1978 *Female Hierarchies.* Chicago: Beresford Book Service.

Tronick, E. Z., Gilda A. Morelli, and Steve Winn 1987 Multiple Caretaking of Efe (Pygmy) Infants. *American Anthropologist* 89:96–106.

Vance, Carole, ed. 1984 *Pleasure and Danger: Exploring Female Sexuality.* London: Routledge and Kegan Paul.

Wadley, Susan Snow 1975 *Shakti: Power in the Conceptual Structure of Karimpur Religion.* Chicago: Department of Anthropology, University of Chicago Studies in Anthropology.

1976 Women in the Hindu Tradition. *Signs* 3:113–25.

Waldron, Ingrid 1983 Sex Differences in Illness Incidence, Prognosis and Mortality: Issues and Evidence. *Social Science and Medicine* 17(16):1107–23.

Watson, Rubie S. 1986 The Named and the Nameless: Gender and Person in Chinese Society. *American Ethnologist* 13(4):619–31.

Weiner, Annette B. 1976 *Women of Value, Men of Renown: New Perspectives in Trobriand Exchange*. Austin: University of Texas Press.

1979 Trobriand Kinship from Another View: The Reproductive Power of Women and Men. *Man* 14:328–48.

Werbner, Pnina 1986 The Virgin and the Clown: Ritual Elaboration in Pakistani Migrants' Weddings. *Man* 21:227–50.

Wheeler, Rose Linda 1982 Infant Sex and Maternal Treatment Differences in Macaca Nemestrina. Ph.D. dissertation, Arizona State University.

Whiting, J. W. M. and B. B. Whiting 1975 Aloofness and Intimacy of Husbands and Wives: A Cross-Cultural Study. *Ethos* 3:183–207.

Whyte, Martin 1978 *The Status of Women in Preindustrial Society*. Princeton, NJ: Princeton University Press.

Wikan, Unni 1977 Man Becomes Woman: Transsexualism in Oman as a Key to Gender Roles. *Man* 12(2):304–19.

1982 *Behind the Veil in Arabia: Women in Oman*. Baltimore: Johns Hopkins University Press.

Williams, Walter L. 1987 *The Spirit and the Flesh: Sexual Diversity in American Indian Culture*. Boston, MA: Beacon Press.

Wolf, Margery 1972 *Women and the Family in Rural Taiwan*. Stanford: Stanford University Press.

Wolf, Margery and Roxanne Witke, eds. 1975 *Women in Chinese Society*. Stanford: Stanford University Press.

Young, Kate, Carol Wolkowitz, and Roslyn McCullagh 1981 *Of Marriage and the Market: Women's Subordination in International Perspective*. London: CSE Books.

Zihlman, Adrienne L. 1978a Women in Evolution, Part II. Subsistence and Social Organization Among Early Hominids. *Signs* 4(1):4–20.

1978b Motherhood in Transition: From Ape to Human. In *The First Child and Family Formation*. Warren B. Miller and Lucille F. Newman, eds., pp. 35–50. Chapel Hill: University of North Carolina Press.

1981 Women as Shapers of Human Adaptation. In *Woman the Gatherer*. Frances Dahlberg, ed., pp. 75–120. New Haven, CT: Yale University Press.

Zihlman, Adrienne L. and Nancy Tanner 1978 Gathering and Hominid Adaptation. In *Female Hierarchies*. Lionel Tiger and Heather Fowler, eds., pp. 163–94. Chicago: Beresford Book Service.

2   Sex differences and gender hierarchies among primates: an evolutionary perspective

Adrienne L. Zihlman

The search for understanding contemporary human patterns of behavior often delves into the ancient human past, as long as three to four million years ago, soon after our earliest ancestors separated from the apes and began their course along the human trajectory. Implicit in this search is the premise that the roots of human patterns of behavior lie in the evolutionary/biological, rather than in the more recent historical/cultural, domain. Therefore, the reasoning goes, we must look to human evolution and the anatomy and physiology of sex differences in order to explain human gender differences today.

The issue of gender hierarchies, and implied social inequality between women and men, is a central component in the debate about human gender differences.[1] This debate focuses on how the hypothesized differences in behavior between men and women might constrain the human way of life. By implication, though rarely spelled out, these (presumed) differences in behavior structure the relationship between women and men.

Rosaldo (1974, 1980) asserted that gender inequality and male dominance are universal in contemporary human societies. Although debatable, this view might seem consistent with the fact that men are somewhat larger in body size than women. If so, then men would seem "naturally" stronger, more aggressive and dominant than women. In seeking explanations for such a hierarchy, the hunting hypothesis has provided an apparent confirmation that gender inequality has a long evolutionary history.

This chapter addresses the issue of whether human gender differences or hierarchies have their roots in biology and evolution. In so doing, it examines anthropological assumptions surrounding three interrelated issues: a sexual division of labor, dominance and aggression, and sexual dimorphism. First, is the sexual division of labor in present-day human societies an outcome of an ancient hunting way of life or an extension of behaviors already existing in apes? The evidence for hominid hunting during human evolution and observed sex differences in foraging and feeding activities among chimpanzees provide a basis for addressing this question. Second, to what extent are dominance and aggression influenced or determined by biological sex? Finally, what problems are associated with characterizing sexual dimorphism in non-human primates, in modern human populations, and in the fossil record? What assumptions surround interpretations of sexual dimorphism in the fossil record? The issues are multi-faceted and must be approached with attention to their complexity.

The human sexual division of labor: an ancient pattern?

The sexual division of labor in human societies today has both economic and symbolic components. Economically, it is based on a system of reciprocal exchange, and rituals reflect the behaviors which are culturally defined as appropriate to women and men. In some societies a sexual division of labor may be associated with gender inequality. When did such a division first appear?

In the hunting hypothesis, a scenario of human evolution popular in the 1960s, hunting is *the* basis for the human way of life, an exclusively male activity and the central economic pursuit (Washburn and Lancaster 1968; Laughlin 1968; and the review of Zihlman 1987). Here, it is assumed that men controlled food provisioning and sharing, that men were leaders and "in charge" of and dominant over women and children. Gender inequality is implied in this interpretation of human evolution.

In a more recent interpretation of existing evidence an alternative, the gathering hypothesis, argues that women played a central economic role, by using tools to obtain and process plant foods. This scenario formulated for the earliest stage of human evolution draws on several lines of evidence. These include the discovery that women play an active role in subsistence activities in contemporary gathering/hunting societies (for example, Lee 1979; Estioko-Griffin and Griffin 1981; Estioko-Griffin 1986; Peacock 1985); that an omnivorous diet rather than one based only on plant material is characteristic of other primates, especially chimpanzees (Teleki 1975; Harding and Teleki 1981); and that the dentition of early hominids seems well suited to a diet containing considerable plant material (Wallace 1975). Although the diet of free-ranging baboons and chimpanzees consists mostly of fruits, leaves, and insects, it also includes meat from small animals caught and killed with hands and without tools – in contrast with human hunting which relies on tools (Zihlman 1978, 1981).

The gathering hypothesis supposes that the human way of life is based not on a sexual division of labor but on a system where males as well as females collect food and engage in predatory behavior. The emphasis is on the overall behavioral flexibility of both sexes as a major contributing factor to early hominid survival (Zihlman 1981).

A major difficulty with the hunting hypothesis is the absence of evidence for hunting. There is no support for the kind of sexual division of labor envisioned in the hunting hypothesis nor for a pattern of gender hierarchy at this early stage of human evolution. For instance, studies done on associations of animal bones, stone artifacts, and hominid remains cast doubt on the image of early hominids as hunters (Brain 1981).

The presence of "home bases" between 1 and 2 million years ago has also been questioned (Binford 1981; Potts 1988). In fact, the ability of hominids to exploit large animals was probably ineffective prior to the Middle Stone Age (50–100,000 years ago) (Klein 1987). Not until the Later Stone Age (30–40,000 years ago) do bone assemblages suggest "a quantum advance in the human ability to extract animal protein" (Klein 1987:39). It is possible that the later systematic hunting with tools emerged from the technological and social skills established in food gathering.

New information on genetic relationships, on hominid fossils, and on chimpanzees has shifted attention to chimpanzees. Recent findings based on studies of DNA show that of the living apes, chimpanzees are most closely related to humans and that they separated only about 5 million years ago (Sarich and Wilson 1967; Sibley and Ahlquist 1984; Ueda, Matsuda, and Honjo 1988; Caccone and Powell 1989). Although early hominids (2–4 million years ago) exhibited upright posture and bipedal locomotion, their brains and dental development resemble chimpanzees more than those of any other living ape (Falk 1988; Benyon and Dean 1988). These resemblances may reflect common ancestry shared by humans and chimpanzees.

Studies on free-ranging chimpanzees reveal that females and males may differ in ranging patterns, tool using, food sharing, predation and dietary composition (McGrew 1979; Boesch and Boesch 1981, 1984, 1989; Wrangham and Smuts 1980; Nishida, Uehara, and Nyundo 1979; Goodall 1986; Uehara 1986). As a result, some researchers have proposed that a gender division of labor among early humans is an ancient pattern with its roots firmly planted among the ape ancestors (for example, McGrew 1979; Galdikas and Teleki 1981), that greater frequency of termite fishing of females and predation on small animals by males forms a direct evolutionary line to early hominid female gathering and male hunting.

In the absence of direct evidence from the archaeological record of an early sexual division of labor based on male hunting and female gathering, it is tempting to give significant weight to behavioral differences between the sexes among free-ranging chimpanzees. But close examination shows that each behavior does not have simple correlates with chimpanzee anatomy and physiology. Instead, these behaviors form part of a larger picture that takes into account individual energetic requirements and social patterns among community members. Furthermore, the wide variability within and between chimpanzee populations in capturing prey and in tool use and making demonstrates that chimpanzee behavior is more complex than previously thought (Boesch and Boesch 1989, 1990). It is doubtful that early hominid ancestors were any less variable or complex.

Predation

When predation was first observed and reported among chimpanzees (*Pan troglodytes*) at Gombe, Tanzania, male chimpanzees seemed to be the sole actors. Between 1960 and 1967, twenty-eight instances of predation were observed and thirty instances between 1968 and 1969 (Teleki 1973), all carried out by male chimpanzees. However, chimpanzees in the Mahale mountains south of Gombe differed in this activity by sex, in technique, and prey items (Nishida, Uehara, and Nyundo 1979). In this population, predation tends to be more solitary, with females involved in about one-third of the episodes. Furthermore, females more frequently seize small ungulates, whereas the males more often chase monkeys. The prey species is more frequently red colobus among Gombe chimpanzees versus blue duiker at Mahale (Nishida, Uehara, and Nyundo 1979; Nishida and Uehara 1983; Goodall 1986).

Chimpanzees in the Tai Forest, Ivory Coast, also *Pan troglodytes*, differ somewhat from Gombe or Mahale (Boesch and Boesch 1989). They specialize in monkey species as prey items and more often deliberately seek them out as prey than do Gombe chimpanzees; these hunts last longer and are rarely solitary. Adolescents of both sexes actively take part, and 13 percent of adult hunters are females with or without an infant to carry.

Aside from possible ecological variables to account for differences in prey items and method of capture, other factors such as methodology of researchers and ranging patterns of males may also contribute. Compared to those from the Mahale population to the south, Gombe chimp females were rarely observed engaging in predatory activity during the earlier years of the study. A contributing factor to this discrepancy turned out to be methodological because females were rarely focal animals (Takahata, Hasegawa, and Nishida 1984). Female chimps are shyer than males, less gregarious and therefore less easy to follow for full or consecutive days. When this sampling bias was rectified, females were observed to engage in predatory behavior more frequently than previously noted (Goodall 1986).

Differences in frequency of predation may reflect social, travel, and foraging patterns of female and male chimpanzees. Adult females forage with their offspring, siblings, or mother. When in estrus, females move with groups of males and other estrus females. Males, on the other hand, seek each other out, for dominance interactions, grooming, or border patrols (Goodall 1986). In this species of chimpanzee, adult males spend more time with other adult males than adult females do with other females. A number of predatory instances involve more than one individual and in part this may be a social activity. Male chimps are more often together and are more likely to be involved in communal activity and to be observed than are females who are less gregarious. In fact, much of the observed female predatory behavior was "in the context of mixed-party hunts" (Goodall 1986:306).

Termiting

Gombe female chimpanzees engage in termiting more frequently throughout the year and spend a longer time at the mounds than males (McGrew 1979, 1981). In some groups Mahale females feed on insects more frequently than males (Uehara 1986). Several factors probably account for these observed sex differences. One factor may be the greater patience and persistence of females who spend several hours fishing at a termite mound even with little return, and who check driver ant nests more frequently than do males (Goodall 1986). Males, on the other hand, prefer social interaction with other males, which reduces their frequency of fishing behavior (Uehara 1986).

The acquisition of protein by females with minimum expenditure of energy may further contribute to the difference. Females spend much of their adult life pregnant and lactating, and their energetic demands are more pronounced than those of males. Socialization and carrying of the young may contribute to further demands. Young animals accompany their mothers to the termite mounds during the off season, which gives them many opportunities to observe and practice. To master the skill of effective termite fishing young chimpanzees need about five years; presumably learning would take considerably longer if they had fewer opportunities to practice.

Nut-cracking

Forest-living chimpanzees in the Tai Forest, Ivory Coast, use stone and wooden hammers for cracking open hard-shelled species of nuts. Efficiency in opening nuts (measured as hits per nut) is acquired during adolescence. At this time, sex differences appear, and females continue to improve their technique into adulthood. The result is that adult females more frequently perform the two most difficult techniques of nut-cracking and are more efficient than males, both in terms of hits per nut and nuts processed per minute (Boesch and Boesch 1981, 1984).

The Boesches explore several hypotheses to explain the observed differences. Perhaps the most significant variables relate to energetics and social behavior. Adult females may rely more than males on the nutritional value of the nuts. Adult males prefer to maintain visual contact with other group members and often stop hammering in order to follow the movement of other chimpanzees or to engage in social interaction. Panda trees are widely scattered and individual chimps are necessarily out of visual range of each other. As they crack, the males continually look around to check out other animals. Adult females, in contrast, continue cracking nuts even if there is a conflict or the group has moved on. As reported for the Tanzanian chimpanzees, similar themes emerge: female energetics, the nature of social interaction among males, and the persistence of females.

Food sharing

When Goodall first reported food sharing among Gombe chimpanzees it was in the context of meat-eating, with adult males sharing with females and others (Goodall 1968; Teleki 1973). As more data were collected, it became apparent that plants are widely shared, and over half the instances of sharing occur between mother and offspring pairs. In fact most food sharing is between related individuals; 86 percent of instances of plant-food sharing were between related dyads, and items most shared were those difficult to process (McGrew 1975; Silk 1978).

Among pygmy chimpanzees (*Pan paniscus*), food sharing appears to be more frequent and widespread than among common chimpanzees (*Pan troglodytes*) (Savage-Rumbaugh and Wilkerson 1978; Kuroda 1984). For example, in 261 food sharing interactions on eleven species of plants at Wamba, Zaire, over half the instances of sharing were adult females giving to juveniles, infants, and adolescents (Kano 1982). The juvenile category was by far the most frequent (eighty-five instances), then infant (thirty-nine) and adolescent (twenty-four). Adult males gave food to adult females, adolescents, and juveniles. Females gave to other females over twice as often as males gave to females. Food sharing of male to male and female to male was very infrequent.

Overall, adult female pygmy chimpanzees were donors four times more often than adult males (Kano 1982). Food sharing is widespread among group members so that factors other than kinship must be at work. The high frequency of adult female donors, especially to juvenile animals and to each other, suggests that females in this species of chimpanzee may be more social than males and contribute to the well-being of the more vulnerable juvenile animals.

In summary, research reveals that sex differences do occur among both species of free-ranging chimpanzees in behaviors not directly involved in reproduction or mating and in more ways than expected. The differences do not appear to reflect directly overall size or strength or dominance, and no single variable can account for all the observations. Chimp females apparently consume more protein obtained from insects and nuts, though this pattern is not unique to chimps and has been reported for females of other primate species (for example, Gautier-Hion 1980; Wright 1984; Cords 1986). Males engage in predatory behavior more often than females, a pattern which seems to relate to males' ranging and socializing patterns. Females are less distracted from their termiting or nut-cracking activity than are males who are always looking around to interact with other chimps.

These examples demonstrate the absence of a simple correlation between the anatomy and physiology of female and male chimpanzees and the observed frequency of differences in non-sexual behaviors. Furthermore, the sex differences described among chimpanzees and other primates depart markedly from the human sexual division of labor. Chimpanzee behavior is not systematically reciprocal in an economic sense, nor does it imply dominance of males over females. In contrast, the pattern of food sharing among humans, like the sexual division of labor, involves reciprocity, cooperation, agreements, or exploitation, and each instance relies upon symbols and language. Chimpanzee behavior does provide a rich source for speculating about early hominids, but there is no direct behavioral evolution from chimpanzee to human. A human gender division of labor is not simply an expression of the biology of early ancestors.

Given this information on chimpanzees, behavioral variability among the early hominids probably existed. Although among early hominids, hominid females may have had the major responsibility of providing food for their young, some activities no doubt differed in frequency by age and sex. For example, males and females unburdened by young may have ranged more widely around the savanna environment than females with young and may have obtained additional or unusual resources. A male could learn gathering techniques from his mother while she carried and nursed him and collected food. Overall, behavioral flexibility of both sexes, and variability among populations, may have been important for early hominid survival and reproduction in the savanna environment (Zihlman 1981). But behavioral flexibility or sex differences in frequencies of behaviors do not imply a gender hierarchy.

Is aggression sex-linked?

Just as social factors are important in accounting for sex differences in behaviors relating to feeding, we must also consider social factors in other realms of behavior. Again, we must not assume too readily that an anatomical or physiological explanation is sufficient. For example, there is a tendency to view dominance-seeking and aggression as attributes of males associated with their larger body size, better fighting abilities, and aggressive nature. To the contrary, the following examples illustrate the subtlety, complexity, and flexibility of social interaction and demonstrate that dominance, subordination, and aggression are more than expressions of male or female biology.

High-ranking males

A male's rank in the social group may be influenced by, but is less directly determined by, the rank of his mother. Males must spend more time than females in establishing their rank. Contrary to conclusions drawn before long-term data were available, social networks, including kinship, and social "savvy" are central for a male to achieve high status, and individual personality also plays a role in determining the outcome. But among chimpanzees, body size plays little part.

Among chimpanzees, males from high-ranking lineages may become alpha males with the support of mothers and brothers. At Gombe, Figan's rise to alpha status (maintained for about eight years) occurred with the support of his brother Faban and occasionally his mother Flo (Goodall 1986, 1990). Another male took a different route. Goblin, a small-bodied male, perfected his intimidation displays toward the other males over several years. Eventually he enlisted the support of (unrelated) Figan, whom he later dominated. The variation is wide among individual adult males in their route to achieving high rank or in avoiding encounters altogether. High rank relates to intelligence in the ability to assess correctly a social situation, to motivation and willingness to invest energy in displays and fights, and very little to large body size.

Among baboons, males change groups and must establish their place within a troop as a newcomer. A male secures his place and achieves dominance by entering the social network and acquiring allies through social negotiation. Rather than fight his way to the top, a male is more likely to develop friendships with females and their young and use these relationships to gain access to other group members (Smuts 1985; Strum 1987). For baboons as for other primates, social skills, more than brute force, are necessary for animals to achieve their goals, a phenomenon that has been appreciated as a result of observing the same group of animals for many years (Goodall 1986; Strum 1987).

Aggression and injuries

The other side of the friendly behavior coin is unfriendly behavior directed toward members of the social group. There is a tendency among researchers to focus only on aggressive acts that result in injury and then to equate injury with aggression. Aggressive acts usually do not result in direct physical contact or injury, though the potential is present among highly sexually dimorphic species such as baboons and gorillas. When males attack females or other males, their large and dangerous canine teeth and large body size can and do inflict severe wounds.

Aggression is an enormous subject, but I briefly discuss several studies to challenge assumptions that males are always more aggressive than females, and that females are necessarily passive. Several points emerge: in day-to-day situations there may be little difference between females and males in overall frequency of aggressive behavior; females may be more aggressive to each other than previously thought; rates of aggression and infliction of injury do not correlate and must be treated separately; and females may show aggression toward males.

There is a widespread belief that aggression is primarily a male rather than a female characteristic. A review of the primate literature suggests that in frequency of aggressive acts, no consistent differences exist by sex (Smuts 1987). An interesting perspective emerges from a study on three species of social-living mammals: cattle, bison, and rhesus monkeys (Reinhardt, Reinhardt, and Reinhardt 1987). In this study, in the general day-to-day situation the two sexes were equally aggressive in reinforcing their dominance position among familiar social partners. The authors argue that dominant animals have more subordinates than do subordinates, older more than younger, and that age and rank rather than the individual's sex were important determining variables. (The study was not meant to encompass all specific situations where females and males may show temporary differences in aggression, such as territorial defense, defense of progeny, or mating season with hormonal changes.)

Aggression and injury may differ markedly as Smuts (1985) has shown for free-ranging olive baboons. Females attacked other females five times more frequently than males attacked females, but rarely inflicted serious injuries. In contrast, when males attacked females, though much less frequently, they inflicted serious injuries: adult females received on average one serious bite wound per year from males (Smuts 1985). Females lack the "anatomy of aggression" to inflict such wounds, though females do act aggressively.

However, under some conditions, adult female baboons may seriously injure one another. Over a fifteen-year period in Amboseli National Park, Kenya, some female baboons underwent reversals in rank during two periods of about a month each. In one period fourteen of nineteen females sustained injuries at least once and some of the wounds endangered females' lives (Samuels, Silk, and Altmann 1987). In the other period only four of the nineteen adult females were wounded and none of the wounds was life-threatening.

In a number of primate species, females may be aggressive toward and join forces against males. These female coalitions are most common in three contexts: protecting infants, expelling a strange male from the group, and protecting an adult female attacked by a male (Smuts 1987). Usually the females simply force the males to withdraw or run away, but sometimes they severely injure males.

Gender hierarchies among early hominids and contemporary people may seem to have their origins in larger body size and in the aggressive nature of males. However, the above examples based on long-term studies of free-ranging monkeys and apes point to kinship, and individual variation in social skills and in social networks as important influences on the outcome of social interaction. That gender hierarchies are an inherent part of the human condition is not supported by these data.

Sexual dimorphism

Among adult mammals and primates, sex differences in morphology (labeled sexual dimorphism) are expressed in several features involving soft tissue anatomy as well as bones and teeth. The primary sexual characters, the genitals and reproductive organs, are defining features. But females and males also may vary in external features, such as body weight, overall size of head, body and tail dimensions (and the underlying bones). Among non-human primates, sex differences may be pronounced in the dentition, particularly in length and breadth of canine teeth. Coat and hair length and markings may differ between the sexes, as well as seasonal or periodic changes in sexual skin (Crook 1972). In a number of primate species the pelvis is sexually dimorphic and this is most pronounced in humans (Schultz 1949; Leutenegger 1974). Most frequently, morphological features appear during growth and development to become fully expressed in mature adults.

Problems of interpretation

Two problems have plagued the study of primate sexual dimorphism. First, sexual dimorphism has been treated as one-dimensional. In fact, it consists of a mosaic of features involving soft anatomy as well as bones and teeth, and the overall pattern may differ even in closely related species (Cramer and Zihlman 1978; Zihlman 1981). Second, sexual dimorphism most frequently has been correlated with mating systems. As a result, interpretations have not gone on to explore other factors which influence morphological differences between females and males (these problems, discussed below, are reflected in studies of sexual dimorphism of fossil hominids, in attempts first to discover the extent of sexual dimorphism – based on size and weight estimates of fragmentary bones and teeth – then to assign behavioral correlates to this inadequate data base, see Zihlman 1985).

Among primates and other mammals sex differences in body size and weight have received the most attention because they are the easiest to measure. Body weight does differ between males and females in many primate species including humans. However, overemphasis on weight differences obscures the fact that other anatomical features differ between the sexes. In some instances this focus on body weight has provided an easy, if incorrect, basis for assuming male dominance. Furthermore, body weight – especially for humans – is not a uniform attribute. It is not associated with different body and tissue compositions among age, sex, and species categories, as Grand (1977a, 1978) has demonstrated for a variety of primates and other mammals, as well as for new-born versus adult macaques (1977b). For instance, tissue composition and body proportions differ significantly between a ten-pound monkey and a ten-pound dog. Like body weight, sexual dimorphism is not a uniform attribute.

Among Old World monkeys and apes, canine size and shape are reasonably reliable for establishing sexual differences, presumably because canine teeth seem to be less influenced by environmental factors than is body weight (Leutenegger and Kelly 1977; Leutenegger 1982). Canine-size dimorphism and body-weight dimorphism correlate to some degree ($r = 0.76$) within a species, but this correlation does not reflect the variability in canine-tooth size among females (Harvey, Kavanaugh, and Clutton-Brock 1978; Harvey and Kavanaugh 1978; Leutenegger and Kelly 1977). For example, female patas (and other *Cercopithecus*) monkeys have larger canines (though smaller body weight) than female baboons (Lucas 1981; Smith 1981), suggesting that female canine size is influenced by factors other than simply correlating with body weight.

But in contrast, molar-tooth size may differ much less between the sexes than do canine teeth. For instance, male gorilla canine teeth are 60 percent larger than those of females, but molar teeth are only 6 percent larger (McCown 1982). Among orang-utans where males weigh more than twice as much as females, average canine length and breadth are 135 percent of females' whereas molars are less than 10 percent larger (Morbeck and Zihlman 1988). From an allometric point of view, compared to males, female rhesus macaque molar teeth do not scale to body weight, but are relatively larger (Cochard 1985). These patterns suggest differing selective pressures on several body systems and on patterns of growth for males and females, and they illustrate the mosaic nature of sex differences in morphology even within the dentition.

Sexual dimorphism in body size and weight and canine-tooth size has been correlated most frequently with mating systems among mammals and primates (Leutenegger and Kelly 1977; Alexander *et al.* 1979; Willner and Martin 1985; Silk, this volume). Morphological differences in these features have been attributed to male–male competition and sexual selection (Darwin 1871) including parental investment (Trivers 1972), ground living, predator defense, and dominance (DeVore 1963; Crook and Gartlan 1966). Sexual selection has been the most frequently invoked mechanism to explain sexual dimorphism.

Given the observed range of variation in body size and other morphological features in females, Ralls (1976, 1977), Fedigan (1982), and others have challenged sexual selection as an adequate mechanism to account for sexual dimorphism. Ralls, for example, suggests that attention be directed to bioenergetics and factors affecting female size. Now, data from several field studies document sex differences in foraging and feeding behavior – in dietary composition, feeding time, or priority – in indriids (Pollock 1979), titi monkeys (Wright 1984), gelada baboons (Dunbar 1977), mangabeys (Waser 1977), guenons (Gautier-Hion 1980), patas monkeys (Olson and Chism 1984), and orang-utans (Rodman 1977). In particular, lactating female primates show a specific activity pattern of travel and feeding (Altmann 1980). The demands on females during a relatively long period of lactation impose bioenergetic constraints on female body size (Coehlo 1974, 1986).

These and other studies (such as Harvey 1986; Lewin 1982a, 1982b) begin to move beyond sexual selection and mating behavior as primary explanations for sexual dimorphism and toward a broader framework that emphasizes female survival, choice in mating, and energetics during reproduction. Dimorphic features usually attributed to sexual selection alternatively may be more clearly explained by focusing on the demands made on each sex during its lifetime: in survival, effective mating, gestation and lactation (for females), care of offspring, and self-provisioning.

Sexual dimorphism in modern human populations

Women and men differ in their external appearance: in body size and shape, which reflects the underlying skeleton, and in proportions and distribution of soft tissue. These differences become obvious during adolescence and are most marked in adults, and they have been studied from several perspectives (see, for example, Harrison *et al.* 1977; Hall 1982; Dyer 1982; Ghesquiere, Martin, and Newcombe 1985). In living populations, all aspects of morphology can be studied, but in archaeological or fossil populations, only bones and teeth are available.

In body size, women and men within a population differ in average height (reflected in the length of the femur) and body weight. Body shape of men includes broader shoulders (reflected in clavicle size) whereas women have broader hips (related to shape of the pelvis). In contrast to other primates, there is little size difference in canine teeth of women and men and no documented functional difference.

Body shape is also related to the proportions and distribution of soft tissue, in particular muscle and fat. In contemporary populations, women and men differ dramatically: women have almost twice the body fat of men but only about three-quarters the amount of muscle (Holliday 1978; Bailey 1982; Dyer 1982). In women adipose (fat) tissue is stored in the breasts and buttocks and is an important component in reproduction (Lancaster 1985; Frisch 1988). Although other primates and mammals have a similar distribution of adipose (fat) tissue, women have an unusual abundance (Pond 1987). This feature may be the most different between women and men, but it leaves no trace at all in skeletal remains.

Growth and development

Sex differences become pronounced during adolescence. Adult differences in height, for example, are mainly due to the timing and magnitude of the growth spurt (Watts 1986). In women, under the influence of increasing levels of hormones, the epiphyses of the long bones become fused and growth ceases. Men, in contrast, have their growth spurt later, allowing a longer period of pre-pubertal growth. The spurt itself is greater than for women and growth continues for several years after puberty.

In women the pubic bone grows at puberty and contributes to the adult female pelvic shape and to an adequate birth canal. Accompanying the skeletal changes and under hormonal influence, women acquire fat deposits in the breasts and buttocks and so gain weight (Short 1976; Bailey 1982; Frisch 1988). In contrast, testosterone promotes growth of the upper body and the development of muscle tissue. The cranium is dimorphic at birth and has a pubertal growth spurt only in boys (Baughan and Demirjian 1978).

Because of sex differences in the pattern of human growth, women and men do not respond similarly to the same environmental conditions (Hamilton 1982; Lieberman 1982; Stini 1969, 1971, 1982; see also Cohen and Bennett, this volume). For example, an absolute increase in stature due to improved nutrition occurred among the northern and central Bushmen in Southern Africa, and was twice as great in males as in females (Tobias 1962).

Therefore, a trait like stature estimated from adult femur length is influenced by nutrition and other environmental factors as well as by genetics. It is not always possible to distinguish the contribution of each variable, especially in archaeological skeletal series, and any single trait is not a reliable indicator of sex (Borgognini Tarli and Repetto 1986a). Among modern human skeletal populations, the pelvis is the only bone which directly reflects the primary differences between the sexes and is reliable in assigning sex in archaeological populations. Furthermore, there is little correlation among traits which differ by sex, such as cranial capacity, facial features, and limb-bone size, nor between any of these traits and body weight, so that these cannot be used for non-living individuals.

In the fossil record

The assessment of sexual dimorphism in fossil hominids is central to several issues: in accounting for observed variation, particularly in the postcranial skeleton, of *Australopithecus* "afarensis" (see below); in establishing the direction of change in sex differences from the prehominid ape ancestor to the earliest hominids; in assessing trends in sexual dimorphism during the past 3 million years of hominid evolution; and in interpreting past human behavior. When we attempt to assign biological sex to individual skeletons or single bones in the archaeological or hominid fossil record, the data are more problematic than when dealing with living populations. Even when the entire skeleton is preserved, skeletal and dental remains represent only 15 percent of an individual's body weight, and few of these features vary in a predictable way by sex. However, complete skeletons uncovered from archaeological series present fewer difficulties in assigning sex, in estimating the degree and pattern of sex differences in a population, and in interpreting behavior, than do the ancient hominid fossils from more than 500,000 years ago.

The hominid fossil record between 2 and 3.5 million years ago in Africa is fragmentary and lacks associated archaeological remains. It is fragmentary in that it does not sample a population or species – very few individuals are represented at any one fossil locality. Second, complete individual skeletons are very rare. Third, a bone is rarely preserved in its entirety. Most individual fossils are scrappy bits of one bone, without the preservation of joint surfaces or other informative parts. From this incomplete (at best!) sample, numerous attempts are made to reconstruct body weight and assign sex. The reality is that there are no reliable methods for accurately assigning sex to a fragmentary or isolated fossil or to one bone among several.

In many cases the problem of reconstructing body weight, assigning sex, or inferring range of variation is compounded by relying only on teeth (usually canine teeth) and ignoring other anatomical parts such as the limb bones or cranium (for example Frayer and Wolpoff 1985; Leutenegger and Shell 1987). Whether dentition or other anatomical parts are used, they are inadequate for drawing inferences about mating patterns and sexual division of labor among Plio-Pleistocene hominids (contra Lovejoy 1981; Leibowitz 1983).

Australopithecus *"afarensis": one species or two?*

A major difficulty in the study of early hominid fossils is distinguishing among the sources of variation, that is, whether the variation observed in bones and teeth is due to species differences or to sex differences within a single population. Fossils from Ethiopia and Tanzania and dated between 3.6 and 2.8 mya (Curtis 1981) have been grouped and named as the species "afarensis" of the genus *Australopithecus* (Johanson and White 1979). The authors argue that these hominid fossils which span several hundred thousand years and about 1000 miles consist of one extremely dimorphic species. This conclusion, however, must be questioned.

Although one extremely dimorphic species may be a possible explanation, its existence has not been well documented. Instead, there is evidence to the contrary: limb size and morphology, cranial features, and newly discovered fossils all suggest the distinct possibility that at least two species are included in what has been called *A*. "afarensis" (Falk and Conroy 1983; Falk 1986, 1988; Susman, Stern, and Jungers 1984; Olson 1981, 1985; Walker *et al.* 1986; Zihlman 1985). In spite of the difficulties in assessing sexual dimorphism in fossil hominids and the questions surrounding taxonomic status, the existence of one extremely sexually dimorphic species (e.g., *A*. "afarensis") has become accepted dogma in much of the writing on human evolution.

Are there trends?

When *A*. "afarensis" is accepted as one highly dimorphic species, then two corollaries have followed: that the prehominid ancestor was highly dimorphic in body size, and that the trend during human evolution was toward decreasing sexual dimorphism (Frayer and Wolpoff 1985; Brace 1973). These assumptions are not supported by any direct evidence.

A number of species of Miocene apes vary widely in size and morphology, from small gibbon-size to large gorilla-size. Presumably they also vary in their patterns of sexual dimorphism. And among Miocene ape species, there is no established phylogenetic line between any of them and the earliest hominids, *Australopithecus*. Furthermore, the recent genetic evidence places humans and chimpanzees as most closely related, strongly implying that their common ancestor (yet to be identified in the fossil record) was more like a chimpanzee than any other ape (Lowenstein and Zihlman 1988). Among both species of chimpanzee, as well as humans, sexual dimorphism in body size and weight is not marked; for example, females are between 80 and 85 percent of male body weight in all three species (Zihlman 1976, 1981). Therefore, it is not possible to assume, as some have done, that the common ancestor was highly sexually dimorphic.

The acceptance of *A*. "afarensis" as one highly dimorphic species also has led to the presumed corollary that during the last 3 million years sexual dimorphism in hominid body size and weight has decreased. Such a presumption overlooks a number of points made in this chapter: the difficulty of assigning sex to individual crania, mandibles, long bones, and pelves; the significant difference between women and men in soft tissue; the influence of nutrition on body size and stature; and the similarity in female-to-male body weight among chimpanzees and modern humans, with marked variation among them in social behavior. One can then appreciate the further difficulty of drawing conclusions about mating patterns, sexual division of labor, or gender hierarchies for these ancient hominids.

Interpretations about the increase or decrease in sexual dimorphism over the past 3 million years must depend upon the overall pattern of several traits including the pelvis, long bones, and cranial and dental features. In assessing sexual dimorphism in ancient fossil hominid populations, it is more accurate to study the pattern of potentially dimorphic characteristics than focus on only one or two of them. In fact, the pattern of traits more probably approximates a changing mosaic, and we cannot correctly speak of one trend. It is more likely that each trait fluctuated through this time period, and no one factor can explain the entire shift in pattern.

Toward a more complex view

This chapter scrutinizes the issues surrounding sexual dimorphism for two reasons. First, it is one way to characterize fossil hominids, that is, to attempt to establish biological sex based on morphological differences. Second, morphology provides a basis for interpreting behavior in extinct species.

Because the pattern of sex differences in morphology in modern human populations differs from that of other primates, one challenge in interpreting the hominid fossil record is to document this change. But although canine teeth are a reliable indicator of sex in species of monkeys and apes, this feature is not useful to determine sex in hominids. The most significant difference between modern women and men lies in the differing proportions of soft tissue. But this difference does not leave clues in the bones, so it is not possible to determine from the fossil record when, during the past 3 million years, this distinctly human pattern emerged. It is reasonable to propose, however, that the hominids which lived between 1 and 4 million years ago probably differed from modern human and other primate groups in their pattern of dimorphism.

The problem of determining biological sex from fragmentary fossil bones and teeth representing extinct species of hominids – on which all subsequent interpretations about social behavior depend – underscores the difficulty of drawing conclusions about possible gender-based behavior, such as a sexual division of labor, or dominance and aggression. Even among living human populations, where behavior can be observed and soft tissue can be studied along with bones and teeth, it is not easy to establish correlations between morphology and social behavior.

Compared to the study of hominids prior to the last several thousand years, some more recent archaeological series are more revealing because they contain groups of individuals, there is more material culture present, and more complete information on environmental context is available. This is the case when the archaeological record has preserved a skeletal series with complete bones, reasonably complete skeletons, and samples of several individuals of one population. Along with associated lithic, faunal, and floral information, these data allow us to establish biological sex, to evaluate health status, to correlate such features with climatic, dietary, or technological change, and to speculate about gender hierarchies (see, for example, Borgognini Tarli and Repetto 1986b; Finkel 1982; Cohen and Bennett, this volume).

One trend during the past 3 million years is clear: hominids have come to rely more and more on technological and symbolic means for survival and reproduction. As human populations moved into new ecological zones, especially into temperate regions and tropical rain forests, and later shifted from gathering and hunting to reliance on domesticated species, these changes in obtaining food and dealing with the environment had an impact on their state of health and work patterns. In contexts of human settlements and food production a sexual division of labor became firmly established and thus provided a possible basis for gender hierarchies.

This chapter explores complex areas of behavior – sexual division of labor, dominance, and aggression – and their possible origins in ancient behavior patterns in the ape ancestors or among early hominids. Given the hominid fossil and archaeological records, it is likely that the nomadic gathering–hunting way of life as preserved today in a few human populations probably emerged relatively recently, in the last 100,000 years or less. That way of life may not be correlated with or an outcome of human sex differences in morphology. We do not yet understand when these differences appeared during human evolution nor under what conditions. Rather than looking to the distant past for clues about gender hierarchies, we should look to complex and stratified societies where gender, as well as other divisions of labor become integral to the system.

NOTES

For discussion and comments I thank Mary Ellen Morbeck, Melissa Remis, Catherine Borchert, and Robin McFarland. Research support from Division of Social Sciences and Faculty Research Committee, University of California at Santa Cruz, is gratefully acknowledged.
1 I do not believe the term "gender" applies to non-human primates, and I therefore reserve its use for human behavior and its implicit symbolic base and social construction. When discussing non-human primates I talk about "sex differences" in behavior, and for early hominids of 2 to 4 million years ago which are still very much like the apes, I also use "sex" rather than "gender."

REFERENCES

Alexander, R. D., J. L. Hoogland, R. D. Howard, K. M. Noonan, and P. W. Sherman 1979 Sexual Dimorphism and Breeding Systems in Pinnipeds,

Ungulates, Primates and Humans. In *Evolutionary Biology and Human Social Behavior: An Anthropological Perspective.* Napoleon A. Chagnon and William Irons, eds., pp. 402–35. North Scituate, MA: Duxbury Press.

Altmann, Jeanne 1980 *Baboon Mothers and Infants.* Cambridge, MA: Harvard University Press.

Bailey, S. M. 1982 Absolute and Relative Sex Differences in Body Composition. In *Sexual Dimorphism in* Homo sapiens. Roberta L. Hall, ed., pp. 363–90. New York: Praeger.

Baughan, B. and A. Demirjian 1978 Sexual Dimorphism in the Growth of the Cranium. *American Journal of Physical Anthropology* 49:383–90.

Benyon, A. D. and M. C. Dean 1988 Distinct Dental Development Patterns among Early Hominids. *Nature* 335:509–14.

Binford, Lewis R. 1981 *Bones: Ancient Men and Modern Myths.* New York: Academic Press.

Boesch, Christophe and Helwige Boesch 1981 Sex Differences in the Use of Natural Hammers by Wild Chimpanzees: A Preliminary Report. *Journal of Human Evolution* 10:585–93.

1984 Possible Causes of Sex Differences in the Use of Natural Hammers by Wild Chimpanzees. *Journal of Human Evolution* 13:415–40.

1989 Hunting Behavior of Wild Chimpanzees in the Tai National Park. *American Journal of Physical Anthropology* 78:549–73.

1990 Tool Use and Tool Making in Wild Chimpanzees. *Folia Primatologica* 54:86–99.

Borgognini Tarli, Silvana M., and E. Repetto 1986a Methodological Considerations on the Study of Sexual Dimorphism in Past Human Populations. *Human Evolution* 1(1):51–66.

1986b Skeletal Indicators of Subsistence Patterns and Activity Regime in the Mesolithic Sample from Grotta dell'Uzzo (Trapani, Sicily): A Case Study. *Human Evolution* 1(4):331–52.

Brace, C. Loring 1973 Sexual Dimorphism in Human Evolution. *Yearbook of Physical Anthropology* 16:31–49.

Brain, C. K. 1981 *The Hunters or the Hunted? An Introduction to African Cave Taphonomy.* Chicago: University of Chicago Press.

Caccone, A. and J. R. Powell 1989 DNA Divergence among Hominoids. *Evolution* 43:925–42.

Cochard, Lawrence 1985 Ontogenetic Allometry of the Skull and Dentition of the Rhesus Monkey. In *Size and Scaling in Primate Biology.* W. L. Jungers, ed., pp. 231–55. New York: Plenum.

Coehlo, Anthony 1974 Socio-bioenergetics and Sexual Dimorphism in Primates. *Primates* 15:263–369.

1986 Time and Energy Budgets. In *Comparative Primate Biology. Vol. 2, Behavior, Conservation and Ecology.* Gary Mitchell and Joe Erwin, eds., pp. 141–68. New York: Alan R. Liss.

Cords, Marina 1986 Interspecific and Intraspecific Variation in Diet of Two Forest Guenons, *Cercopithecus ascanius* and *C. mitis. Journal of Animal Ecology* 55:811–27.

Cramer, Douglas L. and Adrienne L. Zihlman 1978 Sexual Dimorphism in the Pygmy Chimpanzee, *Pan paniscus.* In *Recent Advances in Primatology. Vol. 3,*

Evolution. D. J. Chivers and K. A. Joysey, eds., pp. 487–90. London: Academic Press.

Crook, John H. 1972 Sexual Selection, Dimorphism and Social Organization in the Primates. In *Sexual Selection and the Descent of Man 1871–1971.* Bernard Campbell, ed., pp. 231–81. Chicago: Aldine.

Crook, John H. and J. S. Gartlan 1966 The Evolution of Primate Societies. *Nature* 210:1200–3.

Curtis, Garnis 1981 Man's Immediate Forerunners: Establishing a Relevant Time Scale in Anthropology and Archaeological Research. *Philosophical Transactions of the Royal Society, London [Biology]* 292:7–20.

Darwin, Charles 1871 *The Descent of Man, and Selection in Relation to Sex.* New York: D. Appleton and Company.

DeVore, Irven 1963 A Comparison of the Ecology and Behavior of Monkeys and Apes. In *Classification and Human Evolution.* Sherwood L. Washburn, ed., pp. 301–19. Chicago: Aldine.

Dunbar, Robin 1977 Feeding Ecology of Gelada Baboons: A Preliminary Report. In *Primate Ecology: Studies of Feeding and Ranging Behaviour in Lemurs, Monkeys and Apes.* Tim H. Clutton-Brock, ed., pp. 251–73. London: Academic Press.

Dyer, Kenneth F. 1982 *Catching Up the Men. Women in Sport.* London: Junction Books.

Estioko-Griffin, Agnes 1986 Daughters of the Forest. *Natural History* 95:37–43.

Estioko-Griffin, Agnes and P. Bion Griffin 1981 Woman the Hunter: The Agta. In *Woman the Gatherer.* Frances Dahlberg, ed., pp. 121–51. New Haven, CT: Yale University Press.

Falk, Dean 1986 Evolution of Cranial Blood Drainage in Hominids: Enlarged Occipital/Marginal Sinuses and Emissary Foramina. *American Journal of Physical Anthropology* 70(3):311–24.

1988 Enlarged Occipital/Marginal Sinuses and Emissary Foramina: Their Significance in Hominid Evolution. In *Evolutionary History of the "Robust" Australopithecines.* Frederick Grine, ed., pp. 85–96. New York: Aldine.

Falk, Dean and Glen C. Conroy 1983 The Cranial Venous Sinus System of *Australopithecus afarensis. Nature* 306:779–81.

Fedigan, Linda 1982 *Primate Paradigms: Sex Roles and Social Bonds.* Montreal: Eden Press.

Finkel, D. J. 1982 Sexual Dimorphism and Settlement Pattern in Middle Eastern Skeletal Populations. In *Sexual Dimorphism in* Homo sapiens. Roberta L. Hall, ed., pp. 165–85. New York: Praeger.

Frayer, David W. and Milford H. Wolpoff 1985 Sexual Dimorphism. *Annual Review of Anthropology* 14:429–73.

Frisch, Rose E. 1988 Fatness and Fertility. *Scientific American* March: 88–95.

Galdikas, Birute and Geza Teleki 1981 Variations in Subsistence Activities of Female and Male Pongids: New Perspectives on the Origins of Hominid Labor Division. *Current Anthropology* 22:241–55.

Gautier-Hion, A. 1980 Seasonal Variations of Diet Related to Species and Sex in a Community of *Cercopithecus* Monkeys. *Journal of Animal Ecology* 49:237–69.

Ghesquiere, J., Robert D. Martin, and F. Newcombe 1985 *Human Sexual Dimorphism*. Philadelphia, PA: Taylor and Francis.

Goodall, Jane 1968 The Behaviour of Free-Living Chimpanzees in the Gombe Stream Reserve. *Animal Behaviour Monographs* 1:165–311.

1986 *The Chimpanzees of Gombe: Patterns of Behavior*. Cambridge, MA: Harvard University Press.

1990 *Through a Mirror: My Thirty Years with the Chimpanzees of Gombe*. New York: Houghton-Mifflin.

Gouzoules, Sarah and Harold Gouzoules 1986 Kinship. In *Primate Societies*. Barbara Smuts *et al.*, eds., pp. 299–305. Chicago: University of Chicago Press.

Grand, Theodore I. 1977a Body Weight: Its Relation to Tissue Composition, Segment Distribution and Motor Function. I. Interspecific Comparisons. *American Journal of Physical Anthropology* 47:211–39.

1977b Body Weight: Its Relation to Tissue Composition, Segment Distribution and Motor Function. II. Development of *Macaca mulatta*. *American Journal of Physical Anthropology* 47:241–8.

1978 Adaptations of Tissue and Limb Segments to Facilitate Moving and Feeding in Arboreal Folivores. In *The Ecology of Arboreal Folivores*. G. G. Montgomery, ed., pp. 231–4. Washington, DC: Smithsonian Institution Press.

Hall, Roberta, L., ed. 1982 *Sexual Dimorphism in* Homo sapiens: *A Question of Size*. New York: Praeger.

Hamilton, Margaret E. 1982 Sexual Dimorphism in Skeletal Samples. In *Sexual Dimorphism in* Homo sapiens. Roberta L. Hall, ed., pp. 107–63. New York: Praeger.

Harding, Robert S. O. and Geza P. Teleki, eds. 1981 *Omnivorous Primates: Gathering and Hunting in Human Evolution*. New York: Columbia University Press.

Harrison, Geoffrey A. *et al.*, eds. 1977 *Human Biology: An Introduction to Human Evolution, Variation, Growth and Ecology*. Oxford: Oxford University Press. 2nd edition.

Harvey, Paul H. 1986 Energetic Costs of Reproduction. *Nature* 321:648–9.

Harvey, Paul H. and Michael Kavanaugh 1978 Sexual Dimorphism in Primate Teeth. *Journal of Zoology* 186: 475–85.

Harvey, Paul, H., Michael Kavanaugh, and T. H. Clutton-Brock 1978 Canine Tooth Size in Female Primates. *Nature* 276:817–18.

Holliday, M. A. 1978 Body Composition and Energy Needs During Growth. In *Human Growth. Vol. 2, Postnatal Growth*. Frank Falkner and J. M. Tanner, eds., pp. 117–39. New York: Plenum Press.

Johanson, Donald C. and Timothy D. White 1979 A Systematic Assessment of Early African Hominids. *Science* 203:321–30.

Kano, T. 1982 The Social Group of Pygmy Chimpanzees (*Pan paniscus*) of Wamba. *Primates* 23:171–88.

Klein, Richard 1987 Reconstructing How Early People Exploited Animals: Problems and Prospects. In *The Evolution of Human Hunting*. Matthew H. Nitecki and Doris V. Nitecki, eds., pp. 11–45. New York: Plenum Press.

Kuroda, S. 1984 Interaction Over Food Among Pygmy Chimpanzees. In *The*

Pygmy Chimpanzee: Evolutionary Biology and Behavior. Randall L. Susman, ed., pp. 301–24. New York: Plenum Press.

Lancaster, Jane 1985 Evolutionary Perspectives on Sex Differences in the Higher Primates. In *Gender and the Life Course.* Alice A. Rossi, ed., pp. 3–26. New York: Aldine.

Laughlin, William S. 1968 Hunting: An Integrating Biobehavior System and Its Evolutionary Implications. In *Man the Hunter.* Richard B. Lee and Irven DeVore, eds., pp. 304–20. Chicago: Aldine.

Lee, Richard B. 1979 *The !Kung San: Men, Women and Work in a Foraging Society.* New York: Cambridge University Press.

Leibowitz, Lila 1983 Origins of the Sexual Division of Labor. In *Women's Nature: Rationalizations of Inequality.* Marian Lowe and Ruth Hubbard, eds., pp. 123–47. New York: Pergamon Press.

Leutenegger, Walter 1974 Functional Aspects of Pelvic Morphology in Simian Primates. *Journal of Human Evolution* 3:207–22.
1982 Sexual Dimorphism in Nonhuman Primates. In *Sexual Dimorphism in Homo sapiens.* Roberta L. Hall, ed., pp. 11–36. New York: Praeger.

Leutenegger, Walter and J. T. Kelly 1977 Relationship of Sexual Dimorphism in Canine Size and Body Size to Social, Behavioral and Ecological Correlates in Anthropoid Primates. *Primates* 18:117–36.

Leutenegger, Walter and Bettina Shell 1987 Variability and Sexual Dimorphism in Canine Size of *Australopithecus* and Extant Hominoids. *Journal of Human Evolution* 16:359–67.

Lewin, R. 1982a. How Did Humans Evolve Big Brains? *Science* 216:840–1.
1982b Food Fuels Reproductive Success. *Science* 217:238–9.

Lieberman, L. S. 1982 Normal and Abnormal Sexual Dimorphic Patterns of Growth and Development. In *Sexual Dimorphism in* Homo sapiens. Roberta L. Hall, ed., pp. 263–316. New York: Praeger.

Lovejoy, C. Owen 1981 The Origin of Man. *Science* 211:341–50.

Lowenstein, Jerold M. and Adrienne L. Zihlman 1988 The Invisible Ape. *New Scientist* 120:56–9.

Lucas, P. W. 1981 An Analysis of Canine Size and Jaw Shape in Some Old and New World Nonhuman Primates. *Journal of Zoology* 195:437–8.

McCown, Elizabeth R. 1982 Sex Differences: The Female as Baseline for Species Description. In *Sexual Dimorphism in* Homo sapiens. Roberta L. Hall, ed., pp. 37–83. New York: Praeger.

McGrew, W. C. 1975 Patterns of Plant Food Sharing by Wild Chimpanzees. In *Contemporary Primatology: Proceedings.* S. Kondo, M. Kawai, and A. Ehara, eds., pp. 304–9. New York: S. Karger.
1979 Evolutionary Implications of Sex Differences in Chimpanzee Predation and Tool Use. In *The Great Apes.* D. A. Hamburg and E. R. McCown, eds., pp. 440–63. Menlo Park, CA: Benjamin/Cummings.
1981 The Female Chimpanzee as a Human Evolutionary Prototype. In *Woman the Gatherer.* Frances Dahlberg, ed., pp. 35–73. New Haven, CT: Yale University Press.

Morbeck, Mary Ellen and Adrienne L. Zihlman 1988 Body Composition and Limb Proportions in Orangutans. In *Orangutan Biology.* J. Schwartz, ed., pp. 285–97. New York: Oxford University Press.

Nishida, T. and S. Uehara 1983 Natural Diet of Chimpanzees (*Pan troglodytes schweinfurtheii*): Long Term Record for the Mahale Mountains, Tanzania. *African Studies Monograph* 3:109–30. Kyoto: Kyoto University.

Nishida, T., S. Uehara, and R. Nyundo 1979 Predatory Behavior among Wild Chimpanzees of the Mahale Mountains. *Primates* 20:1–20.

Olson, Dana K. and Janice Chism 1984 Mating Season and Diet among Wild Patas Monkeys. *American Journal of Physical Anthropology* 63(2):199–200.

Olson, Todd R. 1981 Basicranial Morphology of the Extant Hominoids and Pliocene Hominids: The New Material from the Hadar Formation, Ethiopia, and Its Significance in Early Human Evolution and Taxonomy. In *Aspects of Human Evolution.* C. B. Stringer, ed., pp. 99–128. London: Taylor and Francis.

1985 Cranial Morphology and Systematics of the Hadar Formation Hominids and "Australopithecus" Africanus. In *Ancestors, the Hard Evidence: Proceedings of the Symposium Held at the American Museum of Natural History April 6–10, 1984.* pp. 102–19. New York: Alan R. Liss.

Peacock, Nadine 1985 Time Allocation, Work and Fertility among Efe Pygmy Women of Northeast Zaire. Ph.D. Dissertation, Harvard University.

Pollock, J. 1979 Female Dominance in *Indri indri. Folia Primatologica* 31:143–64.

Pond, Caroline M. and Christine A. Mattacks 1987 The Anatomy of Adipose Tissue in Captive *Macaca* Monkeys and Its Implications for Human Biology. *Folia Primatologica* 48:164–85.

Potts, R. 1988 *Early Hominid Activities at Olduvai.* New York: Aldine de Gruyter.

Ralls, Katherine 1976 Mammals in Which Females are Larger than Males. *Quarterly Review of Biology* 51:245–76.

1977 Sexual Dimorphism in Mammals: Avian Models and Unanswered Questions. *American Naturalist* 11:917–38.

Reinhardt, Viktor, Annie Reinhardt, and Catherine Reinhardt 1987 Evaluating Sex Differences in Aggressiveness in Cattle, Bison and Rhesus Monkeys. *Behaviour* 102:58–66.

Rodman, Peter 1977 Feeding Behavior of Orangutans of the Kutai Nature Reserve, East Kalimantun. In *Primate Ecology: Studies of Feeding and Ranging Behaviour in Lemurs, Monkeys, and Apes.* T. H. Clutton-Brock, ed., pp. 384–413. London: Academic Press.

Rosaldo, Michelle Zimbalist 1974 Woman, Culture and Society: A Theoretical Overview. In *Woman, Culture, and Society.* Michelle Z. Rosaldo and Louise Lamphere, eds., pp. 17–42. Stanford: Stanford University Press.

1980 The Use and Abuse of Anthropology: Reflections on Feminism and Cross-Cultural Understanding. *Signs* 5(3):389–417.

Samuels, Amy, Joan Silk, and Jeanne Altmann 1987 Continuity and Change in Dominance Relations among Female Baboons. *Animal Behavior* 35:785–93.

Sarich, Vincent M. and Allan Wilson 1967 Immunological Time Scale for Hominid Evolution. *Science* 158:1200–3.

Savage-Rumbaugh, E. S. and B. J. Wilkerson 1978 Socio-sexual Behavior in *Pan paniscus* and *Pan troglodytes*: A Comparative Study. *Journal of Human Evolution* 7:327–44.

Schultz, A. H. 1949 Sex Differences in the Pelves of Primates. *American Journal of Physical Anthropology* 7:401–23.

Short, R. V. 1976 The Evolution of Human Reproduction. *Proceedings of the Royal Society* B 195:3–24.

Sibley, Charles G. and Jon E. Ahlquist 1984 The Phylogeny of the Hominoid Primates, as Indicated by DNA–DNA Hybridization. *Journal of Molecular Evolution* 20:2–15.

Silk, Joan B. 1978 Patterns of Food-Sharing among Mother and Infant Chimpanzees at Gombe National Park, Tanzania. *Folia Primatologica* 29(2):129–41.

Smith, R. J. 1981 Interspecific Scaling of Maxillary Canine Size and Shape in Female Primates: Relationships to Social Structure and Diet. *Journal of Human Evolution* 10:165–73.

Smuts, Barbara B. 1985 *Sex and Friendship in Baboons*. New York: Aldine.
    1987 Gender, Aggression and Influence. In *Primate Societies*. Barbara B. Smuts et al., eds., pp. 400–12. Chicago: University of Chicago Press.

Stini, William A. 1969 Nutritional Stress and Growth: Sex Differences in Adaptive Response. *American Journal of Physical Anthropology* 31:417–26.
    1971 Evolutionary Implications of Changing Nutritional Patterns in Human Populations. *American Anthropologist* 73:1019–30.
    1982 Sexual Dimorphism and Nutrient Reserves. In *Sexual Dimorphism in Homo sapiens: A Question of Size*. Roberta L. Hall, ed., pp. 391–419. New York: Praeger.

Strum, Shirley 1987 *Almost Human: A Journey into the World of Baboons*. New York: Random House.

Susman, Randall L., Jack T. Stern, and William L. Jungers 1984 Arboreality and Bipedality in the Hanar Hominids. *Folia Primatologica* 43:113–56.

Takahata, Y., T. Hasegawa, and T. Nishida 1984 Chimpanzee Predation in the Mahale Mountains from August 1979 to May 1982. *International Journal of Primatology* 5:213–34.

Teleki, Geza 1973 *The Predatory Behavior of Wild Chimpanzees*. Lewisburg, PA: Bucknell University Press.
    1975 Primate Subsistence Patterns: Collector-Predators and Gatherer-Hunters. *Journal of Human Evolution* 4:125–84.

Tobias, Phillip V. 1962 On the Increasing Stature of the Bushman. *Anthropos* 57:801–10.

Trivers, Robert L. 1972 Parental Investment and Sexual Selection. In *Sexual Selection and the Descent of Man, 1871–1971*. Bernard Campbell, ed., pp. 136–79. Chicago: Aldine.

Ueda, Shintaroh, Fuymihiko Matsuda, and Tasuku Honjo 1988 Multiple Recombinational Events in Primate Immunoglobin Epsilon and Alpha Genes Suggest Closer Relationship of Humans to Chimpanzees than to Gorillas. *Journal of Molecular Evolution* 27:77–83.

Uehara, S. 1986 Sex and Group Differences in Feeding on Animals by Wild Chimpanzees in the Mahale Mountains National Park, Tanzania. *Primates* 27:1–13.

Walker, A., R. E. F. Leakey, J. M. Harris, and F. H. Brown 1986 2.4 Myr *Australopithecus boisei* from West Lake Turkana, Kenya. *Nature* 322:517–22.

Wallace, John A. 1975 Dietary Adaptations of *Australopithecus* and Early *Homo*. In *Paleoanthropology, Morphology and Paleoecology*. Russell H. Tuttle, ed., pp. 203–23. The Hague: Mouton.

Waser, Peter 1977 Feeding, Ranging and Group Size in the Mangabey (*Cerocebus albigena*). In *Primate Ecology: Studies of Feeding and Ranging Behaviour in Lemurs, Monkeys, and Apes*. T. H. Clutton-Brock, ed., pp. 183–222. London: Academic Press.

Washburn, Sharwood L. and C. S. Lancaster 1968 The Evolution of Hunting. In *Man the Hunter*. Richard B. Lee and Irven DeVore, eds., pp. 293–303. Chicago: Aldine.

Watts, Elizabeth 1986 Evolution of the Human Growth Curve. In *Human Growth*. Vol. I. Frank Falkner and J. M. Tanner, eds., pp. 153–66. New York: Plenum Press.

Willner, L. A. and Robert D. Martin 1985 Some Basic Principles of Mammalian Sexual Dimorphism. In *Human Sexual Dimorphism*. J. Ghesquiere, R. D. Martin, and F. Newcombe, eds., pp. 1–42. Philadelphia, PA: Taylor and Francis.

Wrangham, Richard W. and Barbara B. Smuts 1980 Sex Differences in the Behavioural Ecology of Chimpanzees in the Gombe National Park, Tanzania. *Journal of Reproductive Fertility Supplement* 28:13–31.

Wright, Patricia 1984 Biparental Care in *Autus trivirgatus* and *Callicebus moloch*. In *Female Primates: Studies by Women Primatologists*. Meredith E. Small, ed., pp. 59–75. New York: Alan R. Liss.

Zihlman, Adrienne L. 1976 Sexual Dimorphism and Its Behavioral Implications in Early Hominids. In *IX Congrès, Union Internationale des Sciences Préhistoriques et Protohistoriques Colloque VI "Les plus ancient hominides."* P. V. Tobias and Y. Coppens, eds., pp. 268–93. Paris: Centre Nationale de la Recherche Scientifique.

1978 Women in Evolution: Part II: Subsistence and Social Organization among Early Hominids. *Signs* 4(1):4–20.

1981 Women as Shapers of the Human Adaptation. In *Woman the Gatherer*. Frances Dahlberg, ed., pp. 75–120. New Haven, CT: Yale University Press.

1985 *Australopithecus afarensis*: Two Species or Two Sexes? In *Hominid Evolution: Past, Present and Future*. P. V. Tobias, ed., pp. 213–20. New York: Alan R. Liss.

1987 American Association of Physical Anthropologists Annual Luncheon Address, April 1985: Sex, Sexes and Sexism in Human Origins. *Yearbook of Physical Anthropology* 30:11–19.

3 The evolution of human gender hierarchies: a trial formulation

Marvin Harris

Cultural selection is a process that operates in the main without short-term or even long-term feedbacks to naturally selected genetic changes. But cultural determinism (i.e. "constructionism") does not commit us to ignore the existence of species-specific anatomical and bio-psychological features, needs, and drives. Indeed, in order to calculate the costs and benefits of alternative modes of behavior and thought, without which nomothetic (i.e. "processual") understandings of sociocultural differences and similarities cannot be achieved, one must accept a minimum set of species-specific attributes. This stricture applies to attempts to explain the evolution of gender hierarchies.[1]

Cultural determinist strategies (e.g., cultural materialism [Harris 1979]) do not require us to reject all considerations of genetically imposed sexual differences in dealing with the origin and evolution of gender hierarchies. What is required is that we reject vague, subjective, facile, and hypothetical sex differences such as innate aggressiveness, brain hemisphere dominance, genes for female or male reproductive strategies, and innate intelligence differences. But human males remain unquestionably different from human females in stature, weight, and musculature, and in reproductive physiology, especially with respect to pregnancy and lactation. I contend that this obvious and minimal set of bio-sexual differences is an appropriate starting point for the construction of a general theory of gender hierarchies, as long as one bears in mind that the influences of these dimorphisms are not uniform across all varieties of sociocultural systems and evolutionary periods. In no sense therefore is my position to be compared with sociobiological reductionist (i.e. "essentialist") explanations of gender hierarchies or the position that "anatomy is destiny."

In every human population men are consistently taller than women – the difference on average is about 7 percent (Gray and Wolfe 1980:442). Women have lighter bones and more fat (which weighs less than muscle) than men, and therefore weigh less for their height. Women are about two-thirds to four-fifths as strong as men, depending on the group of muscles tested. The biggest strength differences are concentrated in the arms, chest, and shoulders (Percival and Quinkert 1987:136). Men therefore out-perform women in archery and javelin hurling athletic contests. In archery the women's hand bow record for distance is 15 percent less than the male record. In compound bow competition the gap is 30 percent. In javelin hurling it is 20 percent. Add to these a 9 percent difference in the marathon and 100 meter dash, and about 12 percent for intermediate distances (Boehm *et al.* 1987). While athletic training programs and psychological incentives have greatly improved women's track and field performance, there is little prospect that differences that now exist between male and female athletes in sports based on muscular strength and body build will ever be significantly narrowed (except perhaps through genetic engineering).

These differences are clearly related to the most consistent cross-cultural feature of the division of labor by sex, namely assignment of big game hunting without firearms to males. With a few exceptions such as the Agta of Luzon whose women hunt deer and wild pigs[2] with knives and bows and arrows (Estioko-Griffin and Griffin 1981, 1985), women hunt and collect only those animal species which do not require the use of spears, spear throwers, heavy clubs, or bows and arrows (Murdock 1937). While extrapolations from modern to paleolithic foragers are often methodologically unsound, the great variety of ecological settings and levels of political organization under which males specialize in the capture of large game strongly suggest that prehistoric foragers followed the same practice. It seems likely, therefore, that men were recurrently selected to prey on large animals because their height, weight, and brawn advantages made them on average more efficient at this task than women. Moreover, the male advantage in the use of muscle-powered hunting weapons increases considerably for the many months during which women are less mobile because they are pregnant or lactating.

Sex-linked anatomical and physiological differences do not preclude women from participating in hunting to some degree. But the systemically rational option is to train men rather than women to be responsible for big game hunting, especially since women are never at a disadvantage in hunting smaller game or collecting wild fruits, berries, or tubers which are just as important in foragers' diets as meat from big game. The selection of males to do the hunting of large game means that at least since upper paleolithic times men have been the specialists in the manufacture and use of weapons such as spears, bows and arrows, harpoons, clubs, and boomerangs – weapons that have the capacity to wound and kill human beings as well as animals.

I am not saying that male control over these weapons automatically leads to male dominance and the sexual double standard. On the contrary, many foraging societies with a sexual division of labor between male hunters and female gatherers have nearly egalitarian relations between the sexes. For example, writing of her fieldwork among the Montagnais-Naskapi foragers of Labrador, Leacock (1983:116) notes that "they gave me insight into a level of respect and consideration for the individuality of others, regardless of sex, that I had never before experienced." In his study of the forest dwelling Mbuti of Zaire, Turnbull (1982) found a high level of co-operation and mutual understanding between the sexes and considerable authority and power vested in women. Despite his skills with bow and arrow, the Mbuti male does not see himself as superior to his wife. He "sees himself as the hunter, but then he could not hunt without a wife, and although hunting is more exciting than being a beater or a gatherer, he knows that the bulk of his diet comes from the goods prepared by the women" (1982:153).

Shostak's biography (1981) of Nisa shows the !Kung to be another foraging society in which nearly egalitarian relationships between the sexes prevail. Shostak states that the !Kung do not show any preference for male children over female children. In matters relating to child-rearing, both parents guide their offspring, and a mother's word carries about the same weight as the father's. Mothers play a major role in deciding whom their children will marry and after marriage !Kung couples live near the wife's family as often as they live near the husband's. Women dispose of whatever food they find and bring back to camp as they see fit. "All in all !Kung women have a striking degree of autonomy over their own and their children's lives. Brought up to respect their own importance in community life, !Kung women become multifaceted adults and are likely to be competent and assertive as well as nurturant and cooperative" (1981:246).

Nonetheless, I cannot agree with Leacock and other feminist anthropologists who claim that gender roles in foraging societies are completely complementary and egalitarian. My reading of the etic behavioral evidence (see Harris 1990) indicates that in the realm of public decision-making and conflict resolution, men generally have a slight but nonetheless significant edge over women in virtually all foraging societies (Begler 1978). As Shostak points out for the !Kung, men "more often hold positions of influence – as spokespeople for the group and as healers – and their somewhat greater authority over many areas of !Kung life is acknowledged by men and women alike" (1981:237). Men's initiation rites are held in secret, women's are held in public. If a menstruating woman touches a hunter's arrows, his quarry will escape, but men never pollute what they touch. The !Kung, therefore, are somewhat short of having a perfectly balanced set of separate but equal gender roles.

The same is true of the Mbuti. Turnbull writes "that the hunters [i.e., the men] may be considered the political leaders of the camp" and that "In this the women are almost, if not fully, the equals of the men" (1965:127). But "a certain amount of wife beating is considered good" even if "the wife is expected to fight back" (p. 287). And for children "mother is associated with love" while "father is associated with authority" (p. 271).

Lee (1979:453) recorded thirty-four cases of non-lethal bare-handed fighting among the !Kung. Fourteen of these involved a man attacking a woman; only one involved a woman attacking a man. Lee remarks that despite the higher frequency of male-initiated attacks, "women fought fiercely and often gave as good or better than they got" (1979:377). But the men in these encounters were restrained by the presence of a newly installed government constable and did not use their weapons. Delving deeper into the past, Lee learned about twenty-two killings that had taken place prior to his fieldwork. None of the killers but two of the victims were women. Lee interpreted this finding to mean that men were unable to victimize women as freely as they do in really oppressive male sexist societies. Another interpretation seems more apt. !Kung women may have been more timid in the past when there were no constables nearby and refrained from getting into brawls with men, knowing that they would be in mortal danger if the men began to use their spears and poisoned arrows.

The monopoly men maintain over the manufacture and use of hunting weapons combined with their advantages in weight, height, and brawn explains why women are almost but not fully the equals of men in public authority and conflict resolution among band-organized foragers. Trained to kill large animals with deadly weapons from boyhood on, men can be more dangerous and hence more coercive than women when conflicts between men and women break out. "I'm a man. I've got my arrows. I'm not afraid to die" (Shostak 1981:307), say the !Kung hunters when disputes start to get out of hand. Yet the !Kung are not trained to kill humans. While homicides are not rare, they seldom occur as part of an organized premeditated effort to hunt and kill one's enemies. Many of the victims of homicides are bystanders, killed by spears or arrows intended for others. Lee (1979:392) notes that the "!Kung are excellent shots when hunting game, but are poor shots when aiming at each other."

Although the !Kung seldom resort to organized armed conflict, they fall short of being the peaceful paragons depicted in Elizabeth Marshall Thomas' book, *The Harmless People* (1965). Richard Lee's estimate of twenty-two homicides over a period of fifty years mentioned above works out to a homicide rate of 29.3 per 100,000 persons per year, considerably less than Detroit's 58.2 but considerably more than the FBI's overall US average of 10.7 (Knauft 1987:454). But as Lee points out, the rate of homicide in modern industrial nations is much higher than official criminal-justice figures show because of a peculiar semantic deception: killings carried out during wartime by modern states against the "enemy" are not counted as murders. Deaths caused by military action against combatants and civilians boost the homicide rate of modern state societies far above that of the !Kung with their virtual absence of warfare.

Hayden et al. (1986) provide evidence that wherever conditions favored the development of warfare among bands and villages, the political and domestic subordination of women increased. Using a sample of thirty-three hunter-gatherer societies they found that the correlation between low status for females and deaths due to armed combat was "unexpectedly high."

The reasons for overwhelming male dominance in societies where warfare is pronounced seem relatively straight-forward. The lives of group members depend to a greater degree on males and male assessment of social and political conditions. Male tasks during times of warfare are simply more critical to the survival of everyone than is female work. Moreover, male aggressiveness and the use of force engendered by warfare and fighting renders female opposition to male decisions not only futile but dangerous (p. 458).

Men rather than women were trained to be warriors and therefore to be more aggressive, more fearless, and more capable of hunting and killing other human beings without pity or remorse. Males were selected for the role of warriors because the anatomical and physiological sex-linked differences that favored the selection of men as hunters of animals favored the selection of men as hunters of people. In combat with hand-held weapons dependent on muscle power, the slight 10 or 15 percent edge that men hold over women in track and field performances becomes a life and death issue, while the restrictions imposed on women by pregnancy loom as an even greater handicap in war than in hunting, especially among pre-industrial societies that lack effective contraceptive technology.

The fact that thousands of women served as combat troops in the Russian Revolution and in World War II on the Russian front as well as in the Viet Cong and other nineteenth and twentieth century guerrilla movements, and that they serve today as terrorists, police officers, and prison guards (Goldman 1982) does not alter the importance of warfare in shaping gender hierarchies among band and village peoples. The weapons used in all of these instances are firearms, not muscle-powered weapons. The same holds true for the famous corps of female warriors who fought for the West African kingdom of Dahomey during the nineteenth century.

Of a force of about 20,000 in the Dahomey army, 15,000 were males and 5,000 women. But many of the women were unarmed and performed duties as scouts, porters, drummers, and litter-bearers rather than as direct combatants. The elite of the female fighting force – numbering between 1,000 and 2,000 – lived inside the royal compound and acted as the king's personal bodyguard. During several recorded battles, the women seem to have fought as fiercely and as effectively as the men. But their principal arms were muskets and blunderbusses, not spears or bows and arrows, thereby minimizing the physical differences between them and their male adversaries. In addition, the Dahomey king viewed pregnancy among his female soldiers as a serious threat to his security. Although they were technically married to him, he did not have sex with them. And those who became pregnant were accused of adultery and executed (Herskovits 1938). Clearly the circumstances which made it possible for the Dahomey to rely on female warriors even to a limited extent did not exist in war-making bands and villages. The populations of bands and villages were too small to maintain a professional standing army; they lacked centralized leadership and the economic resources needed to train, feed, house, and discipline a standing army, male or female; and above all they were militarily dependent on bows and arrows, spears, and clubs rather than firearms. As a consequence, among band and village societies, the more warfare, the more women suffered from male oppression.

To have war one must have teams of armed combatants. None of the killings reported by Lee (1979) was carried out during raids by combat teams and therefore they were not acts of war. Two of Lee's informants indicated that raiding by armed teams did take place long ago before the Bechuanaland Protectorate Police appeared in the area. If so, it could not have been very common or intense or more people would have remembered. The virtual absence of raiding or other warlike manifestation among the !Kung therefore goes hand in hand with their primarily egalitarian gender roles.

Unlike the !Kung, many band-level societies engage in moderate amounts of warfare and have correspondingly more pronounced forms of male sexism. This was true of the native peoples of Australia when they were first encountered and studied by European scientists. The Aborigines of Queensland and northeast Australia, for example, who were organized into bands of forty to fifty people and made their living exclusively from foraging for plants and animals, regularly dispatched teams of warriors to avenge the wrongdoings of enemy bands. Eyewitness accounts testify not only to a high level of organized inter-group killing but to the cooking and eating of captives, a reward reserved exclusively . for male warriors, but a fate which mainly befell women and children

(Harris 1987). Along with these warlike interests, the Aborigines possessed a well-developed male-dominated gender hierarchy. One index of this hierarchy was the prevalence of polygyny especially among older Aboriginal males, some of whom had as many as four wives. In contrast, only 5 percent of !Kung marriages were polygynous and none involved more than two wives (Shostak 1981:169).

As White and Burton (1988:884) argue, although polygyny may sometimes produce benefits for senior wives, it has negative effects on junior wives, especially those captured in warfare. Unlike polygynous West African societies (see below), Aboriginal women did not enter into polygynous marriages because it was economically advantageous for them to do so, but because it was forced upon them either through capture or male-dominated marital exchange and alliances. A classic sexual double standard prevailed. Men beat or killed their wives for adultery but wives did not have similar recourse. In addition, men discriminated against women in the distribution of food. Lumholtz observed that a man "often keeps the animal food for himself, while the woman ·has to depend principally upon vegetables for herself and her child" (quoted in Harris 1987:375). And the division of labor between the sexes was anything but equal:

[The woman] must do all the hard work, go out with her basket and her stick to gather fruits, dig roots, or chop larvae out of the tree-stems ... [She] is often obliged to carry her little child on her shoulders during the whole day, only setting it down when she has to dig in the ground or climb trees ... when she comes home again, she usually has to make great preparations for beating, roasting, and soaking the fruits, which are very often poisonous. It is also the woman's duty to make a hut and gather the materials for the purpose ... She also provides water and fuel ... When they travel from place to place the woman has to carry all the baggage. The husband is therefore always seen in advance with no burden save a few light weapons, such as spears, clubs, or boomerangs, while his wives follow laden like pack-horses with even as many as five baskets containing provisions. There is frequently a little child in one of the baskets, and a larger child may also be carried on the shoulders. (Lumholtz quoted in Harris 1987:377)

Yet there was no pattern of ruthless subordination of women. What Warner reported about gender roles among the Murngin, another group of bellicose foragers who lived in northern Australia, probably applied to the Aborigines of Queensland as well:

A wife has considerable independence. She is not the badly treated woman of the older Australian ethnologists' theories. She usually asserts her rights. Women are more vocal than men in Murngin society. Frequently they discipline their husbands by refusing to give them food when the men have been away too long and the wives fear they have had a secret affair. (Warner 1958:91)

While it is clear that foraging societies were often violent and warlike (Knauft 1987; Ember and Ember 1988), village-organized societies which derive their subsistence in part from rudimentary forms of agriculture generally carry warfare (and male dominance) to greater extremes. This contrast can be seen in the case of the much-studied Yanomami of Venezuela.[3] Yanomami boys start to train for warfare at an early age. According to Lizot (1985), when little boys strike each other, their mothers urge them to return blow for blow. Even if a child gets knocked down by accident, the mother shouts from afar: "Avenge yourself, go on avenge yourself!" Lizot saw one boy bite another. The victim's mother came running, told him to stop crying, grabbed the other boy's hand and put it into her son's mouth and said, "You bite him now!" (Lizot 1985:74). Should another child hit her son with a stick, the mother "places the stick into her son's hand and, if necessary, she herself will move his arm." Yanomami boys learn cruelty by practicing on animals. Lizot watched as several male juveniles gathered around a wounded monkey. They poked their fingers into the wounds and pushed sharp sticks into its eyes. As the monkey dies, little by little, "its every contortion stimulates them and makes them laugh" (1985:153). Later in life, men on the warpath treat their enemies the same way. In one engagement, a raiding party wounded a man who had tried to escape by jumping into the water. Lizot says that the pursuers dove into the water after him, dragged him onto the bank, lacerated him with the tips of their arrows, shoved sticks through his cheeks and gouged his eyes by pushing the end of a bow into them (1985:155).

The Yanomami's preferred form of armed engagement is the surprise raid at dawn. Under cover of darkness the members of the raiding party pick a trail outside the enemy village and wait for the first man or woman to come along at daybreak. They kill as many men as they can, take the women as captives, and try to leave the scene before the whole village can be roused. On other occasions they get close enough to the village to shower it with arrows before retreating. A deadly form of attack occurs when one village visits another ostensibly for a peaceful purpose. Once the guests settle down and put aside their arms, their hosts attack them. Or it can be the other way round: unsuspecting hosts can find themselves the victims of their supposedly friendly guests. These raids, counter-raids, and ambushes take a heavy toll of Yanomami life – about 33 percent of adult male deaths in certain villages result from armed combat (Chagnon 1988). Knauft (1987:464) lists their overall homicide rate as 166 per hundred thousand or five times greater than among the !Kung.

In keeping with this intense pattern of warfare, relations between Yanomami men and women are markedly hierarchical and androcentric.

To begin with, the Yanomami are polygynous – more so than the Queensland aborigines. Successful men usually have more than one wife; some have as many as six at a time. Occasionally a second husband may be forced on a wife as a favor to the husband's brother. Husbands beat their wives for disobedience, but especially for adultery. Chagnon (1968:83) reports that during domestic squabbles, husbands yank on the sticks of cane that women wear through their pierced earlobes. One husband chopped a big piece out of his wife's arm. Others beat their wives with clubs (p. 9), swung at them with machetes and axes (p. 95), or burned them with firebrands (p. 82). Some shot barbed arrows into their wives' legs; one aimed wrong and shot his wife in the stomach (p. 124).

Yanomami fathers choose a husband for their daughters while they are still children. But betrothals may be altered and contested by rival suitors. Lizot (1985:69) and Shapiro (1971) independently describe scenes in which rival husbands-to-be grabbed a girl's arms and pulled in opposite directions while she shrieked in pain.

The Yanomami are far from being the world's most ardent male chauvinists. That dubious distinction may belong to certain village societies found throughout highland Papua New Guinea whose central institution is the Nama, a male initiation cult that trains men to be fierce warriors and to dominate women. Inside the cult house, which no woman may enter, the Nama men store their sacred flutes whose sounds terrorize the women and children. Only male initiates learn that it is their fathers and brothers who make the sounds and not carnivorous supernatural birds. They swear to kill any woman or child who learns the secret even by accident. Periodically, the initiates make their noses bleed and induce vomiting to rid themselves of the polluting effects of contact with women. After being secluded in the cult house the initiates emerge into adulthood. They are given a bride whom they promptly shoot in the right thigh with an arrow to "demonstrate ... unyielding power over her" (Feil 1987:201). Women work in the gardens, raise pigs, and do all the dirty work while men stand around gossiping, making speeches, and decorating themselves with paint, feathers, and shells. Abusive treatment of women by men is described by Feil:

Women were severely punished for adultery by having burning sticks thrust into their vaginas, or they were killed by their husbands; they were whipped with cane if they spoke out of turn or presumed to offer their opinions at public gatherings; and were physically abused in marital arguments. Men could never be seen to be weak or soft in dealings with women. Men do not require specific incidents or reasons to abuse or mistreat women; it is part of the normal course of events; indeed, in ritual and myth, it is portrayed as the essential order of things. (Feil 1987:203)

Extreme among extremists are the Sambia, a highland Papuan group whose males are obsessed with acquiring semen through fellatio practiced between junior and senior men (Herdt 1987 and this volume). Here not only do men exclude women from their sacred clubhouse but they so fear women's breath and vaginal odors that they partition the whole village into men's and women's areas complete with separate paths for each sex. Sambia men assault their wives both verbally and physically and equate them with enemies and treachery, and treat them as worthless inferiors. For many women, suicide was the only way out. Sambia men faced a multiplicity of physical dangers. A man could be ambushed, cut down in battle, or axed to death in his gardens; his only defense was lifelong training for physical strength, stamina, and phallic mastery. Women were his primary victims.

In keeping with the predicted relationship between male superordination and band and village warfare, war was "general, pervasive, and perpetual" (Feil 1987:69) among highland groups. People lived in villages protected by palisades, yet so endemic was the raiding and counter-raiding that a man could not eat without looking over his shoulder or leave his house in the morning to urinate without fear of being shot. Among the Bene Bene raiding was so common that the men, armed to the teeth, would cautiously escort the women out of the stockade in the morning and stand guard over them while the women worked in the fields until it was time to go back in (Langness 1967:261). It seems likely that the homicide rate among the Bene Bene and Sambia resembled the rates known for other highland New Guinea groups such as the Tuade among whom as many as 533 per 100,000 people were victims of homicides – more than twelve times greater than among the !Kung (Knauft 1987:464).

Let me emphasize that the formula, the-more-warfare-the-more-sexism, holds for band and village societies that practice internal warfare but not for chiefdoms which typically engage in warfare with distant enemies or for states (see below) in which the majority of men do not receive training for combat (Harris 1977:60; compare Whyte 1978:130). External warfare enhances rather than worsens the status of women since it results in avunculocal or matrilocal domestic organizations (Divale 1974; Divale and Harris 1976; Keegan and Maclachlan 1989).

One of the circumstances that make life so difficult for women in highland Papua New Guinea and among the Yanomami is that the societies they live in practice patrilocality. This residence system isolates women from their closest kin who might otherwise intervene if they were being mistreated. Women in patrilocal village societies are doubly disadvantaged since they usually come from different villages and are comparative strangers to each other as well as to their husband's relatives, while all the men have lived together since infancy and know each other intimately. The practice of patrilocality in these villages clearly reflects the influence of internal warfare since success in war depends on the formation of combat teams, of men who have trained together, trust each other, and have reason to hate and kill the same enemy. Combat teams that meet these criteria consist of co-resident fathers, sons, brothers, uncles, and paternal nephews. To remain together after they get married, these paternally related males must bring their wives to live with them rather than go off to live with their wives' families. There is one drawback. Success in raiding depends not only on well-coordinated teamwork but on the size of the combat force. For groups living in small villages, the only possibility of enlarging the combat force lies through forming alliances with neighboring villages.

In evolutionary perspective, military alliances can be seen as part cause and part effect of the process by which single-village political units become transformed into bigger and more complex multi-village chiefdoms. As this transformation progresses, unallied villages recede into the distance, to be encountered only after several days on the trail. Multi-village combat forces consisting of several hundred men now take to the field for months at a time, motivated by the opportunity to hunt in distant no-man's lands, to trade with far away villages, or to raid their granaries and storehouses.

But these long sojourns away from a man's fields, crops, and storehouses create a dilemma. Who can care for them in his absence? His wife is not to be trusted since she comes from another village and is loyal to her own father, brother, and other paternal kin rather than to her husband and his kin. The woman a man can trust most is his sister, for she shares with him a common interest in their paternal lands and property. A man who must be away from the village for weeks and months therefore would benefit from refusing to let his sister follow the patrilocal rule by denying her in marriage unless her husband agrees to live with her rather than she with him. Needless to say, women would be eager to make this change. As increasing numbers of brothers and sisters adopt this strategy, patrilocal residence would gradually give way to matrilocal residence. Followed consistently across several generations, matrilocality results in the co-residence of a continuous line of mothers, sisters, and daughters. Husbands become the outsiders; it is they who feel isolated and who must cope with a united front of members of the opposite sex who have been living together all their lives. Where matrilocality prevails, therefore, women tend to take control of the entire domestic sphere of life. Husbands become more like visitors than permanent residents and divorce is frequent and as easy for women as for men. If a man mistreats his wife, or if she grows tired of him, she and her sister, mother, and maternal aunts send him packing to his own maternal family. The fact that he is frequently away makes divorce that much easier to carry out. The effects of matrilocality on women's status extend beyond the domestic sphere. As men transfer responsibility for managing the cultivation of their lands to female kin, women come to possess the means for influencing political, military, and religious policies.

The classic example of the effect of external warfare on gender hierarchies were the matrilocal, matrilineal Iroquois who dispatched armies composed of as many as 500 men to raid targets as far away as Quebec and Illinois. Upon returning to his native land, the Iroquois warrior joined his wife and children at their hearth in a village long-house. The affairs of this communal dwelling were directed by a senior woman who was a close maternal relative of his wife. It was this matron who organized the work that the women of the longhouse performed at home and in the fields. She took charge of storing harvested crops and drawing on them as needed. When a husband was not off on an expedition – absences of a year or more were common – he slept and ate in the female-headed longhouse but had virtually no control over how his wife lived and worked. If a husband was bossy or uncooperative, the matron might at any time order him to pick up the blanket and get out, leaving his children to be taken care of by his wife and the other women of the longhouse.

Turning to public life, the formal apex of political power among the Iroquois was the Council of Elders consisting of elected male chiefs from different villages. The longhouse matrons nominated the members of this council and could prevent the seating of the men they opposed. But they did not serve on the council itself. Instead they influenced the council's decisions by exercising control over the domestic economy. The longhouse matrons could withhold the stored foods, wampum belts, feather work, moccasins, skins, and furs under their control if a proposed action was not to their liking. Warriors could not embark on foreign adventures unless the women filled their bearskin pouches with the mixture of dried corn and honey men ate while on the trail. Religious festivals could not take place either unless the women agreed to release the necessary stores. Even the Council of Elders did not convene if the women decided to withhold food for the occasion (Brown 1975). But in the final reckoning, matrilocal societies such as the Iroquois fall far short of subordinating men in the way that the fiercely male chauvinist villages of highland Papua subordinate women. Despite their control over the longhouses and the agricultural and craft components of production, Iroquois women did not humiliate, degrade, and exploit their men. In the public domain women possessed almost as much influence as men, but only by indirect means.

Why does matrilocality not result in the reversal of village level patrilocal gender hierarchies? Why are there patriarchies but no matriarchies? One answer is that women's feminine nature prevents them from doing unto men what men have done unto women. This idea, which serves, incidentally, as a common bed for sociobiologists and some radical feminists (di Leonardo 1985; Salter 1980; Pierson 1987), is refuted by the extensive record of women's involvement in the combat units of numerous industrial-age armed forces and their participation in various terrorist organizations and guerrilla movements. Also with specific reference to warlike matrilocal chiefdoms, women have been observed as enthusiastic participants in the torture, dismemberment, and consumption of war captives (Staden 1929).

The absence of matriarchies does not reflect the innate reluctance of women to be brutal and vindictive. Rather it reflects the fact that even in matrilocal and matrilineal societies, men, not women, monopolize the weapons and skills of war. Women in matrilocal societies therefore lacked the material means to boss, degrade, and exploit men in a mirror image of patriarchy. It was lack of power and not lack of masculinity that prevented women in pre-industrial societies from turning the tables. For just as warfare created the conditions that led to matrilocality, so did it set the limits on how far women could subordinate men without supplanting them on the battlefield.

In evolutionary perspective, egalitarian chiefdoms recurrently evolved into stratified chiefdoms and states characterized by ruling classes and centralized governments (Carneiro 1981, 1988). Stratified societies have bigger armies and wage war on a much grander scale than classless societies, but the effect of warfare on women in state-level societies is less direct and generally less invidious than in patrilocal bands and villages – but not as favorable as in matrilocal societies. What makes the difference is that in state societies soldiering becomes a specialty reserved for professionals. Most males no longer train from infancy to be killers of men, nor even to be killers of animals (since there are few large animals left to hunt, except in royal preserves). Instead they find themselves reduced to being unarmed peasants who are no less terrified of professional warriors than their wives and children. Warfare did not cease to create a demand for suitably macho men to be trained as warriors. But most women no longer had to deal with husbands whose capacity for violence was honed in battle. Nor did their survival depend on training their sons to be cruel and aggressive. Female status therefore depended less on the intensity, frequency, and scale of warfare than on the roles played by men and women in production.

Pre-industrial chiefdoms and states in the forested areas of West Africa are well known for their relatively female-favorable gender relations (Hart 1985:263; Sudarkasa 1973). Among the Yoruba, Ibo, Igbo, and Dahomey, women had their own fields and grew their own crops. They dominated the local markets and could acquire considerable wealth from trade. To get married, West African men had to pay brideprice – iron hoes, goats, cloth and, in more recent times, cash – a transaction which in itself indicated that the groom and his family and the bride and her family agreed that the bride was a valuable person and that her parents and relatives would not give her away without being compensated for her economic and reproductive capabilities. In fact, West Africans believed that to have many daughters was to be rich. Although men practiced polygyny, they could do so only if they consulted their senior wife and obtained her permission. Women, for their part, had considerable freedom of movement to travel to market-towns where they often had extra-marital affairs. Furthermore in many West African chiefdoms and states, women themselves could pay brideprice and "marry" other women. Among the Dahomey a female husband built a house for her "wife," and arranged for a male escort to get her pregnant. By paying brideprice for several such "wives" an ambitious woman could establish control over a busy compound and become rich and powerful (Herskovits 1938).

West African women also achieved high status outside the domestic sphere. They belonged to female clubs and secret societies, participated in village councils, and mobilized *en masse* to seek redress against mistreatment by men. Among the Igbo of Nigeria women met in council to discuss matters that affected their interests as traders, farmers, or wives. A man who violated the woman's market rules, let his goats eat a woman's crops, or persistently mistreated his wife ran the risk of mass retaliation. The miscreant would be awakened in the middle of the night by a crowd of women banging on his hut. They danced lewd dances, sang songs mocking his manhood, and used his back yard as a latrine until he promised to mend his ways. They called it "sitting-on-a-man" (Van Allen 1972).

The supreme rulers of these West African chiefdoms and states were almost always males. But their mothers, sisters, and other female relatives occupied offices which gave women considerable power over both men and women. In certain Yoruba kingdoms, the king's female relatives directed the principal religious cults and managed the royal compounds. Anyone wanting to arrange rituals, hold festivals, or call up communal labor brigades had to deal with these powerful women first before they could gain access to the king. Among the Yoruba, women occupied an office known as "mother of all women," a kind of queen over females, who coordinated the voice of women in government, held court, settled quarrels, and decided what position women should take on the opening and maintenance of markets, levying of taxes and tolls, declarations of war, and other important public issues. And in at least two Yoruba kingdoms, Ijesa and Ondo, the office of queen over women may have been as powerful as the office of king over women (Awe 1977). Each met separately with his or her council of chiefs to discuss matters of state, reported what their respective followers had advised, relayed this information to the councils, and awaited further approval or disapproval before taking action. Unfortunately, Awe does not state what happened when the two sides disagreed. It seems likely that since the male half controlled the army, it probably got its way in any final showdown. But the degree of gender equality in West Africa as compared with other agricultural chiefdoms and states remains impressive.

Unlike West Africa, the Gangetic plains area of northern India has long been characterized by a high rate of female infanticide and a marked preference for sons (Miller 1981). Another striking contrast is that a North Indian man who has many daughters regards them as an economic calamity rather than an economic blessing. Instead of receiving bride-price, the North Indian father commonly transfers to each daughter's husband a dowry consisting of jewelry, cloth, and cash. In the 1980s, it has been documented that disgruntled or merely avaricious husbands and in-laws have taken to demanding supplementary dowries. The trend has been accompanied by a spate of "bride burnings" in which wives who fail to supply additional compensation are doused with kerosene and set on fire by husbands and other in-laws who pretend that the women killed themselves in cooking accidents (Sharma 1983; Miller 1992). North Indian culture has also always been extremely unfriendly to widows. In the past a widow was given the opportunity of joining her dead husband on his funeral pyre. Facing a life of seclusion with no hope of remarrying, subject to food taboos that brought them close to starvation, and urged on by the family priest and their husband's relatives, many women chose fiery death rather than widowhood. The contrast with how widows were treated in West Africa is striking. West African widows often remarried their deceased husband's brother – the levirate – or were welcome to continue their normal activities as single women within their sons' households. While some West African widows fared better than others, their prospects were seldom as ominous as in northern India (Potash 1986).

In West Africa, the main agricultural implement was not an ox-drawn plow as in the plains of North India, but a short-handled hoe (Goody 1976). The West Africans did not use plows because in their humid shady habitat the tsetse fly made it difficult to rear plow animals. Besides, West African soils do not dry out and become hard-packed as in the arid plains of North India so that women using nothing but hoes were able to be as competent as men in preparing fields and had no need for men to grow, harvest, or market their crops. In North India men maintained a monopoly over the use of ox-drawn plows. These implements were indispensable for breaking the hard-packed soils of the long dry season. Men achieved this monopoly for essentially the same reasons that they achieved a monopoly over the weapons of hunting and warfare: their greater bodily strength enabled them to be 15 to 20 percent more efficient than women. This advantage often meant the difference between a family's survival and starvation, especially during prolonged dry spells when every centimeter to which a plowshare penetrates beneath the surface and every minute less it takes a pair of oxen to complete a furrow was crucial for retaining moisture. As Maclachlan (1983) found in his study of the sexual division of labor in Karnataka, southern India, the question is not whether peasant women could be trained to manage a plow and a pair of oxen but whether in most families training men to do it leads to larger and more secure harvests. Maclachlan estimates that a plow typically weighs about 40 pounds and that a pair of small oxen exerts a pull of about 180 pounds. To get to the end of the day, the plowman has to guide his bulky ensemble back and forth for a distance of almost 20 miles keeping the furrows straight and at a maximum uniform depth. As Machlachan notes, anyone can control a plow for short periods. But plowing takes place under ecologically imposed time constraints and a pace of about an acre a day must be maintained. Adolescent boys (and by extrapolation, women) cannot maintain this pace; after a few hours the instrument begins to wobble, the share bucks up and out of the soil, and the furrows become wavy (*ibid.*:98ff).

The basic difference between West African and Eurasian gender hierarchies clearly relates to differences in modes of production and reproduction (the demo-techno-econo-environmental infrastructure). In West Africa, the presence of the tsetse fly prevented the raising of cattle or other draft animals. Agriculture remained dependent on the hoe, population density remained relatively low; that is, land was abundant, and labor in short supply. Women's productive and reproductive contributions therefore were in great demand. Hence, brideprice, the levirate, and women's relatively independent economic, social, and political status. In northern India (and Eurasia in general), plow agriculture led to higher population densities, shortages of land, and a lower value on women's productive and reproductive contribution. Hence, dowry, female infanticide, the desperate plight of widows, and women's subordinate social, economic, and political status. As noted by Schlegel and Barry (1986:147) "where men control women's subsistence, men also control their sexuality." More specifically with respect to brideprice versus dowry:

Bridewealth is seen to occur where women's economic value is high, either because they do a good deal of the subsistence labor, as in tropical horticulture, or because they are the producers of children who are needed for the economic expansion of the household. Dowry occurs primarily within the classes that own private property in agricultural societies: the elite castes and classes of the Old High Culture regions of the Middle and Far East and the Mediterranean world, and the elites, artisans, and landowning peasants of preindustrial Europe. (Schlegel and Eloul 1988:301)

This model corresponds in part to formulations first presented by Goody (1973, 1976). However, Goody's approach does not provide answers to certain crucial questions. First, why was it women's status rather than men's which suffered with the rise of intensive plow agriculture? If land becomes scarce and labor abundant, why should not sons rather than daughters be regarded as relatively more burdensome? The shortcomings in Goody's paradigmatic framework also come to the fore in his treatment of the dowry which he regards as egalitarian "premortem" inheritance even though the female portion of the estate consists of jewelry, cloth, furniture, and other movable assets while the male portion consists of land. Goody's explanation of why daughters need to be dowered is that their sexuality must be closely controlled lest they get pregnant and ruin their family's social standing. But why does the sexuality of sons not need to be controlled for the same reason? And why not give sons the movable pre-mortem "inheritance" which, as I have argued elsewhere (Harris 1979:306), is actually pre-mortem disinheritance, and give the land to daughters?

These questions cannot be answered without considering the different implications of hoes and plows for the sexual division of labor as related to male and female anatomy and physiology in cultural evolutionary perspective. Where hoe agriculture prevails, women tend to be as productive as men in agricultural operations. This is what keeps their labor force in high demand and makes them independent of men. In contrast, where plow agriculture prevails, plowing constitutes a critical task (an "energy gate") which men perform (or operate) more efficiently than women. And this is what underlies the Eurasian pattern of female dependency and subordination.

Is a factor as simple as male control over plowing sufficient to explain female infanticide, dowry, and a widow throwing herself onto her husband's funeral pyre? Not if one thinks only of the direct effects of animal-drawn implements on agriculture itself. But in evolutionary perspective this male specialty was linked to a chain of additional specializations which cumulatively do point to a plausible explanation of many features of the depressed status of women in northern India as well as in other agrarian state societies with similar forms of agriculture in Europe, southwest Asia, and northern China. Wherever men gained control over the plow, they became the masters of large traction animals. Whenever they yoked these animals to the plow, they also yoked them to all sorts of carts and vehicles. Therefore with the invention of the wheel and its diffusion across Eurasia, men yoked animals to the principal means of land transport. This gave them control over the bulk transportation of crops to market and from there it was a short step to their domination of local and long-distance trade and commerce. With the invention of money, men became the first merchants. As trade and commerce increased in importance, records had to be kept, and it was to men active in trade and commerce that the task of keeping these records fell. Therefore, with the invention of writing and arithmetic, men came to the fore as the first scribes and accountants. By extension, men became the literate sex; they read and wrote, and did arithmetic. Therefore men, not women, were the first historically known philosophers, theologians, and mathematicians in the early agrarian states of Europe, southwest Asia, India, and China.

All of these indirect effects of male control over traction animals acted in concert with the continuing androcentric effects of warfare. By dominating the armed forces, men gained control over the highest administrative branches of government including state religions. And the continuing need to recruit male warriors made the social construction of aggressive manhood a focus of national policy in every known state and empire. No wonder that at the dawn of industrial times men dominated politics, religion, art, science, law, industry, and commerce, as well as the armed forces, wherever animal-drawn plows had been the basic means of agricultural production.

The theory presented above requires that more-nearly equal gender hierarchies be found in agrarian state societies in which plowing with traction animals does not constitute a crucial energy gate. Gender hierarchies in wet rice areas of South India (Miller 1981), southeast Asia (Bacdayan 1977; Potter 1977; Peletz 1987, 1989; Spiro, this volume), and Indonesia (Tanner 1974) appear to conform to the predicted pattern. In these regions, noted for their strong matrifocal and complementary gender relationships, rice rather than wheat is the principal crop and the principal function of traction animals in agriculture is puddling (softening and mixing the mud of rice paddies in preparation for planting) rather than plowing. This operation can be performed as efficiently by women and children as by men. Moreover, the operation of transplanting which is as crucial as that of plowing or puddling can also be carried out by women at least as efficiently as by men.

During the smokestack phase of industrialism women had little opportunity to overthrow the heritage of the classic Eurasian gender hierarchy. After an initial period of intense exploitation in factory employment, married women were excluded from industrial work and confined to domestic tasks in order to assure the reproduction of the working class. Male factory breadwinners collaborated in this effort in order to preserve their androcentric privileges while fending off the threat that women posed to the male wage rate. The decisive break came after World War II with the shift in the mode of production to information and service production which led to the call-up of a reserve army of literate women into low paid, non-unionized information and service jobs, the feminization of the labor force, the fall in fertility rates to historic lows, and the destruction of the male breadwinner family (Harris 1981).

An obvious point, but one likely to be missed in the absence of an evolutionary perspective is that today's hyperindustrialism is almost totally indifferent to the anatomical and physiological differences between men and women (except to the extent that women still may wish to have children). It is no accident that women's rights are rising as the strategic value of masculine brawn declines. Who needs 10 or 15 percent more muscle power when the decisive processes of production take place in automated factories or while people sit at desks in computerized offices? Men continue to fight for the retention of their old androcentric privileges, but they have been routed from one bastion after another as women fill the need for service and information workers by offering competent performance at lower wage rates than males. Even more than the market women of West Africa, women in today's advanced industrial societies have moved toward gender parity based on an ability to earn a living without being dependent on husbands or other males. But there is one last barrier to complete equality between the sexes. Despite the waning importance of brute strength in warfare, women continue to be excluded from combat roles in the armed forces. Clearly women can be as competent as men with intercontinental ballistic missiles, smart bombs, and computerized firing systems. But men and women must jointly decide whether to push for equality of opportunity in the killing fields or to push for the end of war and an end to the social need to raise macho warriors, whether they be males or females.

NOTES

1 For the purposes of this chapter, gender hierarchy means etic behavioral and etic mental inequalities (Harris 1990) in sex-linked power relationships as evidenced by physical abuse (homicide, assault and battery, rape, etc.); differential access to food and sex; ability to give orders to individual adults and have them obeyed; access to political office; access to wealth; and relative degree of freedom of movement and association (no claustration, foot-binding, chaperonage, infibulation, etc.). Anthropologists who do not distinguish between emic and etic superordination and subordination or who opt for emic over etic criteria, or who indiscriminately mix the two (Bourgignon 1980:325; Deaver 1980), may be charged with being oblivious to the fact that superordinate social groups always have a vested interest in getting subordinates to believe that their subordination is deserved.

2 The Agta are a frail reed on which to lean for upending the commonly accepted generalization that men hunt large game. Women hunting without male companions capture only 22.2 percent of Agta game by weight, not including animals taken by traps which only men use (Estioko-Griffin and Griffin 1985:70).

3 The amount of violence and sexism in Yanomami life varies according to the groups of villages studied by various ethnographers. But there is no reason to question the accuracy of the ethnographic data presented independently by Lizot (1985) and Chagnon (1968, 1988) with respect to the degree of violence and sexism in the particular villages they have lived and worked in (compare Carneiro da Cunha 1989 and Chagnon 1989).

REFERENCES

Aquino, Belinda 1985 Feminism Across Cultures. In *Women in Asia and the Pacific*. Madeleine J. Goodman, ed., pp. 317–51. Honolulu: University of Hawaii Press.

Awe, Bolanle 1977 The Iyalode in the Traditional Yoruba Political System. In *Sexual Stratification: A Cross-Cultural View*. Alice Schlegel, ed., pp. 144–60. New York: Columbia University Press.

Bacdayan, Albert S. 1977 Mechanistic Cooperation and Sexual Equality among the Western Bontoc. In *Sexual Stratification: A Cross-Cultural View*. Alice Schlegel, ed., pp. 270–91. New York: Columbia University Press.

Baker, Mary 1987 Sensory Functioning. In *Sex Differences in Human Performance*. Mary Baker, ed., pp. 5–36. New York: John Wiley and Sons.

Begler, Elsie 1978 Sex, Status and Authority in Egalitarian Society. *American Anthropologist* 80:389–405.

Boehm, David *et al.*, eds. 1987 *Guinness Sports Record Book 1987–1988*. New York: Sterling Publishing Co.

Bossen, Laurel 1988 Toward a Theory of Marriage: The Economic Anthropology of Marriage Transactions. *Ethnology* 27:127–44.

Bourgignon, Erika 1980 Comparisons and Implications: What have We Learned? In *A World of Women: Anthropological Studies of Women in the Societies of the World*. Erika Bourgignon, ed., pp. 19–42. New York: Praeger.

Brown, Judith K. 1975 Iroquois Women: An Ethnohistoric Note. In *Toward an Anthropology of Women*. Rayna Reiter, ed., pp. 235–51. New York: Monthly Review Press.

Carneiro, Robert 1981 Chiefdom: Precursor of the State. In *The Transition of Statehood in the New World*. Grant Jones and Robert Kautz, eds., pp. 37–75. New York: Cambridge University Press.

1988 The Circumscription Theory: Challenge and Response. *American Behavioral Scientist* 31:497–511.

Carneiro da Cunha, Maria 1989 Letter to the Editor. *Anthropology Newsletter* 30(1):3.

Chagnon, Napoleon 1968 *The Fierce People*. New York: Holt, Rinehart and Winston.

1988 Life Histories, Blood Revenge, and Warfare in a Tribal Population. *Science* 239:985–92.

1989 Letter to the Editor. *Anthropology Newsletter* 30(1):24.

Deaver, Sherri 1980 The Contemporary Saudi Women. In *A World of Women: Anthropological Studies of Women in the Societies of the World*. Erika Bourgignon, ed., pp. 19–42. New York: Praeger.

di Leonardo, Micaela 1985 Morals, Mothers and Militarism: Anti-militarism and Feminist Theory. *Feminist Studies* 11(3):599–617.

Divale, William T. 1974 Migration, External Warfare, and Matrilocal Residence. *Behavior Science Research* 9:75–133.

Divale, William T. and Marvin Harris 1976 Population, Warfare and the Male Supremacist Complex. *American Anthropologist* 78:521–38.

Ember, Melvin and Carol Ember 1988 Fear of Disasters as an Engine of History: Resource Crises, Warfare and Interpersonal Aggression. Paper presented at the Conference on What Is the Engine of History? Texas A&M University.

Estioko-Griffin, Agnes and P. B. Griffin 1981 Woman the Hunter: The Agta. In *Woman the Gatherer*. Frances Dahlberg, ed., pp. 121–51. New Haven: Yale University Press.

1985 Women Hunters: The Implications for Pleistocene Prehistory and Contemporary Ethnography. In *Women in Asia and the Pacific*. Madeleine J. Goodman, ed., pp. 61–80. Honolulu: University of Hawaii Press.

Feil, Daryl 1987 *The Evolution of Highland Papua New Guinea Societies*. New York: Cambridge University Press.

Goldman, Nancy L., ed. 1982 *Female Soldiers – Combatants or Noncombatants? Historical and Contemporary Perspectives*. Westport, CT: Greenwood Press.

Goody, Jack 1973 Bridewealth and Dowry in Africa and Eurasia. In *Bridewealth and Dowry*. Jack Goody and S. J. Tambiah, eds., pp. 1–58. New York: Cambridge University Press.

1976 *Production and Reproduction: A Comparative Study of the Domestic Domain*. New York: Cambridge University Press.

Gray, Patrick and Linda Wolfe 1980 Height and Sexual Dimorphism of Stature among Human Societies. *American Journal of Physical Anthropology* 53:441–56.

Harris, David 1987 Aboriginal Subsistence in a Tropical Rain Forest Environment: Food Procurement, Cannibalism and Population Regulation in Northeastern Australia. In *Food and Evolution: Toward a Theory of Human*

78   *Marvin Harris*

Food Habits. Marvin Harris and Eric Ross, eds., pp. 357–85. Philadelphia, PA: Temple University Press.

Harris, Marvin 1977 *Cannibals and Kings: The Origins of Cultures.* New York: Random House.

1979 *Cultural Materialism: The Struggle for a Science of Culture.* New York: Random House.

1981 *America Now: The Anthropology of a Changing Culture.* New York: Simon and Schuster.

1990 Emics and Etics Revisited. In *Emics and Etics: The Insider/Outsider Debate.* Thomas Headland, Kenneth Pike, and Marvin Harris, eds., pp. 48–61. Newbury Park, CA: Sage Publications.

Hart, Keith 1985 The Social Anthropology of West Africa. *Annual Review of Anthropology* 14:243–72.

Hayden, Brian, *et al.* 1986 Ecological Determinants of Women's Status among Hunter-Gatherers. *Human Evolution* 1:449–74.

Herdt, Gilbert 1987 *The Sambia: Ritual and Gender in New Guinea.* New York: Holt, Rinehart and Winston.

Herskovits, Melville J. 1938 *Dahomey: An Ancient West African Kingdom.* New York: J. J. Augustin.

Keegan, William and Morgan Maclachlan 1989 The Evolution of Avunculocal Chiefdoms. *American Anthropologist* 91:613–30.

Knauft, Bruce 1987 Reconsidering Violence in Simple Societies: Homicide among the Gebusi of New Guinea. *Current Anthropology* 28:457–500.

Langness, L. L. 1967 Sexual Antagonism in the New Guinea Highlands: A Bene Bene Example. *Oceania* 37:161–77.

Leacock, Eleanor 1983 Ideologies of Male Dominance as Divide and Rule Politics: An Anthropologist's View. In *Woman's Nature.* Marian Lowe and Ruth Hubbard, eds., pp. 111–21. New York: Pergamon Press.

Lee, Richard 1979 *The !Kung San: Men, Women and Work in a Foraging Society.* New York: Cambridge University Press.

Lizot, Jacques 1985 *Tales of the Yanomami: Daily Life in the Venezuelan Forest.* New York: Cambridge University Press.

Maclachlan, Morgan 1983 *Why They Did Not Starve: Biocultural Adaptation in a South Indian Village.* Philadelphia, PA: Institute for the Study of Human Issues.

Miller, Barbara D. 1981 *The Endangered Sex: Neglect of Female Children in Rural North India.* Ithaca, NY: Cornell University Press.

1992 Wife-beating in India: Variations on a Theme. In *Sanctions and Sanctuary: Cultural Perspectives on the Beating of Wives.* Dorothy Ayers Counts, Judith K. Brown, and Jacquelyn C. Campbell, eds., pp. 173–84. Boulder, CO: Westview Press.

Murdock, George 1937 Comparative Data on the Division of Labor by Sex. *Social Forces* 15:551–3.

Peletz, Michael G. 1987 Female Heirship and the Autonomy of Women in Negeri Sembilan, West Malaysia. In *Research in Economic Anthropology: A Research Annual,* Vol. 8. Barry L. Isaac, ed., pp. 61–101. Greenwich, CT: JAI Press.

1989 *A Share of the Harvest: Kinship, Property, and Social History among the Malays of Rembau.* Berkeley: University of California Press.

Percival, L. and K. Quinkert 1987 Anthropometric Factors. In *Sex Differences in Human Performance*. Mary Baker, ed., pp. 121–39. New York: John Wiley and Sons.

Peirson, Ruth R. 1987 Did Your Mother Wear Army Boots? Feminist Theory and Women's Relation to War, Peace and Revolution. In *Images of Women in Peace and War: Cross-Cultural and Historical Perspectives*. Sharon Macdonald, P. Holden, and S. Ardener, eds., pp. 205–27. Madison: University of Wisconsin Press.

Potash, Betty 1986 Widows in Africa: An Introduction. In *Widows in African Societies: Choices and Constraints*. Betty Potash, ed., pp. 1–43. Stanford: Stanford University Press.

Potter, Sulamith Heins 1977 *Family Life in a Northern Thai Village: A Study in the Structural Significance of Women*. Berkeley: University of California Press.

Salter, Mary Jo 1980 Annie, Don't Get Your Gun. *Atlantic* 245(6):83–6.

Schlegel, Alice and Herbert Barry III 1986 The Cultural Consequences of Female Contributions to Subsistence. *American Anthropologist* 88:142–50.

Schlegel, Alice and R. Eloul 1988 Marriage Transactions: Labor, Property and Status. *American Anthropologist* 90:291–309.

Shapiro, Judith 1971 Sex Roles and Social Structure among the Yanomamo Indians. Ph.D. dissertation, Columbia University.

Sharma, Ursula 1983 Dowry in North India: Its Consequences for Women. In *Women and Property, Women as Property*. Renée Hirschon, ed., pp. 62–74. London: Croom Helm.

Shostak, Marjorie 1981 *Nisa: The Life and Words of a !Kung Woman*. Cambridge, MA: Harvard University Press.

Staden, Hans 1929 *The True History of His Captivity*. New York: Robert McBride. (Original 1557.)

Sudarkasa, Niara 1973 *Where Women Work: A Study of Yoruba Women in the Market Place and in the Home*. Museum of Anthropology, Anthropological Papers No. 53. Ann Arbor: University of Michigan.

Tanner, Nancy M. 1974 Matrifocality in Indonesia and Africa and among Black Americans. In *Woman, Culture and Society*. Michelle Z. Rosaldo and Louise Lamphere, eds., pp. 129–56. Stanford: Stanford University Press.

Thomas, Elizabeth Marshall 1965 *The Harmless People*. New York: Random House.

Turnbull, Colin 1965 *Wayward Servants: The Two Worlds of the African Pygmies*. Garden City, NY: Natural History Press.

   1982 The Ritualization of Potential Conflict between the Sexes among the Mbuti. In *Politics and History in Band Societies*. Eleanor Leacock and Richard Lee, eds., pp. 133–55. New York: Cambridge University Press.

Van Allen, J. 1972 Sitting on a Man: Colonialism and the Lost Political Institutions of Igbo Women. *Canadian Journal of African Studies* 6(2):165–82.

Warner, W. L. 1958 *A Black Civilization*. New York: Harper and Row.

White, Douglas and M. Burton 1988 Causes of Polygyny: Ecology, Kinship, and Warfare. *American Anthropologist* 90:871–87.

Whyte, Martin King 1978 *The Status of Women in Preindustrial Societies*. Princeton: Princeton University Press.

Part 2

Sex and gender hierarchies from conception to death

4 Blood: cultural effectiveness of biological conditions

Brigitta Hauser-Schäublin

Members of all cultures personally or indirectly know about the fundamental conditions of living and dying to which animals and humans are subject. In this chapter I discuss how different cultures in New Guinea "react" to these basic facts which express themselves most clearly in blood and its properties, what these cultures make out of them, and how they interpret them and employ them as a means of creating gender hierarchies primarily between the genders but, consequently, also between different social groups. I provide a brief comparison at the end with ritual blood-brotherhood among the Zande and Kaguru of Africa where blood is used to create intra-gender (male) equality.

In contrast to current anthropological approaches which maintain that the meaning of these biological facts is determined by social organization or social structure only (Biersack 1983; Collier and Rosaldo 1981:311; Yeatman 1984:5; Strathern 1987:289),[1] I assert that biological facts remain unaltered no matter what cultural interpretations try to make out of them. Because each generation and each individual is able to observe and to experience them alike, the cultural interpretation of them has to readapt to them. The culturally constructed knowledge and interpretations of these basic experiences have to some extent to be congruent with the facts themselves. Because they are omnipresent at any time and can be reexperienced ("verified"), their interpretation cannot become disguised or projected back into a mythical past and there become mystified.

Unalterable conditions of blood

The following facts about blood are fundamental in all societies:
> Blood is a fluid that leaves the body wherever the skin is injured. If blood flows excessively the animal or human being (of either sex) may lose consciousness and finally die.
> Blood changes its color and its consistency when exposed for some time to air; it subsequently turns black and thickens.

If somebody survives a severe bleeding he/she may feel weak for some time but the body will gradually replace the blood loss.

Bleeding out of one of the body orifices without any external, intentionally induced influences may announce illness and, subsequently, death.

A young girl starts menstruating when her breasts have grown and maturation thus has become visible.

Menstruation occurs regularly. It is a determined cycle (Harrell 1981). Its phases are similar to those of the moon (see also Buckley 1982).

Menstruation ceases temporarily when a pregnancy has started. When a pregnancy is over it reappears. Menstruation ceases forever at a certain age (Skultans 1970).

After conception an embryo not only grows in its mother's womb but is also closely linked to it by the umbilical cord through which mother and child maintain a continuous exchange of blood. This fact becomes evident after delivery when the umbilical cord has to be severed. The bodily bond between mother and child continues afterwards in a different and looser form: in breastfeeding (which of course can be interpersonally exchanged, that is, a mother can nurse a child other than her own).

A flow of blood accompanies the delivery of the baby which is covered with its mother's fluids. It is followed by the afterbirth which is lifeless. In Western culture blood group factors give the impression that a child inherits its blood from either its father or its mother. But these factors blur the fact that a baby's blood as a fluid originates exclusively from its mother.

The navel is a lifelong mark every human being has. It demonstrates that once an individual was tied to his/her mother's body.

There is no culture which denies that the red fluid which runs in the veins of animals and humans can be completely spilled without death occurring. There is no culture which denies the fact that women menstruate and, at least to my knowledge, none which does not bring the stop of the monthly flow in a direct relationship with a pregnancy. One of the main facts which in many cultures has a great influence on creating gender hierarchies is that women somehow have a closer and obviously more direct relationship to blood than men do. Often they are therefore perceived to manage blood *per se*. To put it another way: blood performs itself more clearly in women than in men. In this sense, blood reinforces the genital differences between males and females. It demonstrates not only a complementarity between the genders, as the sexual organs of men and women correspondingly do, but also a physiological asymmetry which no society has surpassed completely, although they emphasize these differences in their perception and interpretation in varying degrees.

A further characteristic of blood is that when removed from the body it came from, it cannot be identified either in color or in consistency to originate from animals or humans or from either males or females. Nevertheless in almost all cultures people distinguish in their attitudes toward it, for example when using blood in rituals, between human and animal blood as well as between women's and men's blood.

Procreation theories

In all cultures women's contribution to procreation is acknowledged, though in varying degrees, ranging from an exclusive and intimate ever-lasting blood-bond between a child and its mother, to a woman's womb being said to fulfil only the necessity of an "incubator."[2] Conception theories do not simply mirror social facts but are important factors or agents which show joints of biological (physiological) observations and social structure each of which influences the other but neither having primacy over the other. If social organization had primacy, there would certainly be, analogous to "virgin birth,"[3] publicly shared ideologies which maintain physiological (and not social or ritual) birth from males only. Thus, I consider procreation theories to be an illuminating concurrence between basic facts of life and death and what a culture tries to make out of them on different levels of its organization.

Since 1975 much has been written on "procreation theories" in Papua New Guinea.[4] Most authors conclude that these theories are basically those of body substances and fluids which men and/or women are said to possess. Concerning procreation, most New Guinea cultures consider male and female fluids, often semen and blood, to be of equal importance. But the fundamentality of blood beyond procreation ideas is expressed in many ways. The Baruya maintain: "Le sang est la force et la vie ... " (Godelier 1982a:101). The Sambia state (Herdt 1981:192): "Menstrual blood is for giving babies ... Menstrual blood is for giving blood to women. The blood is the mother [i.e., provider] of women. That blood keeps women healthy; they hold the arse [base] of blood. Women can produce new blood for themselves ... Women give us [as a fetus] half their blood, while half stays inside them."

Blood, therefore, among the Sambia as well as among many other New Guinea cultures, such as the Hua (Meigs 1984:61), is said to be generated in women who then transmit it to their babies of both sex but who are said to possess more of it than men. As among the Mae Enga, it is a widespread belief not only in the Highlands of New Guinea but also in the Lowlands, that maternal blood and paternal semen mingle in the womb and a fetus is created, whereby several acts of intercourse are necessary to "build" a child. Each of the two different contributions forms different parts of the body. Most common is the belief that out of the blood the soft parts of a body arise, of semen the strong, hard parts. Often the flesh and the blood of the baby are said to come from its mother, the bones from its father. Sometimes the different parental contributions to the child are also classified as forming different layers of the body. From the mother originate often less-specified intestines whereas from the father – besides the bones, teeth, and nails – come the most prominent organs like heart, liver, and kidney. Although blood is believed in many cultures to be responsible for forming some parts of the body of boys and girls, it is considered additionally as an agent which later causes menstruation in a girl's body. If different parts of the body are formed by the different contributions of the parents to their child, the ways the two substances act in the womb are not identical. Blood is often believed to be an amorphous substance, therefore fit only to form soft parts, whereas semen is considered to be the structuring principle, therefore responsible for the bones, the solid structuring part of the body, the skeleton.

The Bimin-Kuskusmin claim that in the womb first a whitish mass forms which consists of different fertile fluids. This substance is covered by a reddish "skin" of menstrual blood. Conception takes place when semen forms a white cover around it (Poole 1981a:124). Among the Paiela a man's semen wraps around a woman's menstrual blood many times, sufficiently to bind it and keep it from coming outside (Biersack 1983:85): semen transforms unbound blood into bound blood. Semen dries up blood and gives it a solid shape. Sometimes it is said, as among the Baruya (Godelier 1982b:14), that although a fetus is the result of interactions between a man and his wife, it is the man and the sun who actually structure the baby. A man builds his child by contributing semen which also "feeds" it. But the sun is said to be responsible for making its eyes, nose, mouth, hands, and legs. Among the Mae Enga, blood and semen create a child but its personality is derived from the patriclan's ghosts (Joérgensen 1983a:5).

Matrifiliation versus patrilineal descent, or finiteness versus perpetuity

The Bimin-Kuskusmin distinguish two different types of blood: female menstrual blood (which is, besides other sexual fluids, woman's contribution to procreation) and agnatic blood which can be transmitted only by men. The actual transmission of agnatic blood is responsible for classifying an individual into kindred categories. The two different types of blood are distinguished also in terms of colors: the former is black, the latter is red. Closely linked to the agnatic blood are *finiik* spirits which are transmitted through semen. They manifest patrilineal continuity and link past, present, and future generations through males exclusively. Patriclans, ritual moieties, and initiation age groups are reckoned in terms of shared *finiik* spirits (Poole 1981a:132). Thus, the idiom of blood becomes translated into a category of kinship while the idiom of menstrual blood which a mother passes to all her children is one of matrifiliation.

In all cultures mentioned here, a man's contribution to his child is one of duration, not only from the point of view of material solidity (bones) but also from that of social continuity. In contrast to it, the female contribution is regarded as "soft," perishable, and has no recognized continuity in social organization. Bones, of paternal origin, not only survive flesh over years and even generations but also serve as one of the important items, mainly as skulls, in male cults. They are therefore a material expression of social continuity and its patrilineal transmission.[5]

Bones in Papua New Guinea are an expression not only of continuity of social groups but also of territoriality. The fact that a clan holds the skull (or another bone which is considered to be important) of a renowned ancestor is also proof of one's claims to land. The Paiela say "that every ancestor is associated with a bounded territory whose 'bone' his descendants 'own'" (Biersack 1983:87). In this context also (and not only in terms of descent) blood and flesh are of no use in claiming territory.

It is interesting to note that after death the *finiik* spirits of the Bimin-Kuskusmin go to the ancestral underworld. There is a second category of spirits, beside the *finiik*, which are called *khaapkhabuurien*. In contrast to the *finiik* spirits who (representing also the idea of social order) are clearly linked to agnatic blood and semen and are said to reside in the heart, the *khaapkhabuurien* are conceived to be the polar opposite. They cannot easily be located in the human body. A *khaapkhabuurien* can be detected as a congealed mass of black (!) blood near the diaphragm[6] at the time of death. These spirits are associated with disordered, compulsive, wild aspects of personality. In men, through their possession of semen, they are dominated by *finiik* spirits. In women they become strengthened not only by the absence of semen but mainly by their possession of menstrual blood. At death these spirits leave the corpse and wander around, frighten people, and sometimes attack them. These spirits which are associated rather with female aspects of anatomy obviously fit into all other categories like a mother's contribution to a child, the soft parts of the body which are said to be the first to decay after death, and the lack of continuity over generations.

The Abelam make a similar distinction between two spiritual substances all men and women possess. One is located in the bones (which are a man's contribution to procreation). After death it turns into a white sparkling star and stays in the sky forever. The second spirit is located in the blood which is considered to be a woman's contribution to procreation. After death it changes into the shape of a wild pig and finally disappears in a water hole. Thus, the different spiritual components who have their origin in the child's parents are manifested in material, bodily substances. Their fate is either eternity or mortality, continuity or dissolution.

Two further examples illustrate other facets of the same topic. So far I have mainly dealt with patrilineally organized social groups to show that, in contrast to social organization and rules of descent, there exist some ideas on matrifiliation – which in fact is filiation by blood. But the opposite exists, too. In East New Britain the Maenge are known to be a society with matrilineal descent. But there people have the notion that semen is the vital substance out of which blood develops. Blood is considered to be of paternal origin and is also the locus where the human inner soul resides which, following the rules of descent, is linked to the matriclan. This contradiction remains without any solution given by the Maenge themselves. Panoff (1976) discusses this problem as "patrifiliation in a matrilineal society." To some extent it is apparently the opposite of matrifiliation in a patrilineal society (although I do not take the rules of descent as a condition for beliefs of blood-filiation), but there remains an important difference between the two examples. In the case of the Maenge, men of matrilineal clans and men of patrifiliated groups compete with each other over dominance. In the early examples of matrifiliation, the fact of a woman as *genitrix* competes with the rule of the *pater*.

I have not yet stressed one important point: most authors do not mention who their informants were. I suppose most of them were male. Joérgensen (1983b) has collected among the Telefolmin two remarkably different versions of procreation, one from men and the other from women. Men said that after intercourse "vaginal fluids" and "penis water" together formed a fetus; they did not specify what part of the body each contribution created. Women gave a completely different version. They said out of menstrual blood, which men did not mention to be responsible for procreation, all bones came into being. Thus, one of the most important elements in male cults, bones, has originated in blood

(Joẻrgensen 1983b:61).[7] This example shows one of the potential deficiencies of many ethnographic reports on blood. Most of them implicitly mirror men's version of procreation and the functions of vital fluids. The two different versions which exist among the Telefolmin show how the idiom of blood creates hierarchies between the genders from two opposite points of view.

Reinterpretation of matrifiliation into patrilineal descent

In this section I explore further how some New Guinea cultures attempt to make congruent matrifiliation (by means of blood) and descent in relation to continuity over generations. In the Mount Hagen area the Melpa have ideas about procreation that are similar to those in other New Guinea cultures. There, it is "blood" and "grease" which mother and father contribute to their future child. Although one could call this principle of parental contributions to a child "bilateral filiation," there exists only one possibility of becoming a clan member: through one's father. Among the Melpa, as well as among many other New Guinea cultures, this membership is always transmitted not only in a more or less abstract sense but in a very material one – through the father's contribution to procreation, "grease" or semen. Thus, "descent dogmas posit that clansmen share their 'grease', or semen, of an original male ancestor" (Strathern 1972:221). Therefore only men are able to transmit, by contributing semen to the fetus, lineage or clan membership. In contrast to this construction is matrifiliation, by sharing the same blood, between a mother and her offspring, yet marked by discontinuity through time. But the Melpa have the concept of an extended matrifiliation. They say that the blood of a woman is passed down first to her children, both male and female, and then on to their children. These are all people of "one blood." But this cognatic principle does not go further; the blood is "finished." Sometimes Melpa men use the idiom "of one blood" when they refer to agnatic kin. The concept of discontinuous blood-filiation thus gets fused with that of the continuous agnatic lineage membership: one father, one blood! To put it another way: blood-filiation then becomes a medium which supports in certain contexts the lineality of the agnatic group; the opposite case is not reported, that is the agnatic principle is never used as an idiom to strengthen the relevance of blood-filiation.

Among the Bimin-Kuskusmin (Poole 1981a:137) the tension between matrifiliation by blood and the transmission of agnatic lineage membership becomes clearly visible. Although some of women's fertile fluids are said to have their origin in men, menstrual blood plays an important role in procreation, not only as one element among others out of which the fetus is formed. The placenta, to which the baby is linked by the umbilical cord, is thought to be built by menstrual blood only (Poole 1981a:129). When a child is born its umbilical cord, the material uterine link, is cut by its father's sister and in a chant then sung it becomes evident that at this moment the child is no longer part of its mother but hence only an agnate of its father. Later, at the naming ceremony, when an old woman, a senior female ritual leader, bestows a name on the child, she fetches the child's umbilical cord which she has kept until this moment. If the child is male, she plants it in her taro-garden. (Taro is classified as a male crop, sweet potatoes as female. This ritual leader is not considered any longer as an ordinary woman and thus she is allowed to have a taro-garden on her own.) If the child is female she gives the umbilical cord to the child's father's sister who plants it in her sweet potato garden. She is considered to be the owner of the garden in which the child's mother only holds the rights of usufruct. Thus, the uterine link between mother and daughter becomes literally implanted into the territory and therefore continuity of the child's agnatic group; the umbilical cord becomes transferred to the father's "clan womb." The naming ceremony is accompanied by many gifts, but the child's mother does not get any, "because the 'natural' bond of the umbilical cord between her and the child has been severed at birth. It is said that the mother possesses no vestige of the umbilical cord connection, but that the child possesses an abdominal ('female') navel" (Poole 1981a:140).

The navel as a persistent sign that there once was a uterine bond is perceived as female in many cultures. The Bimin-Kuskusmin consider the navel to be female. But there exists also a male bony "navel" which they locate on the head (frontal cranial sutures). In men's rituals the female navel through which bad female influence or knowledge may enter the body has to be closed and the male navel has to be opened, by shaving and cleaning, to let in male influence and knowledge which should strengthen the body. The Bimin-Kuskusmin's creation of a male navel is remarkable because it shows on the one hand the attempt to create an equivalent to a prenatal reminder of the uterine bond. On the other hand it shows an illuminating opposition between (female) abdomen and head[8] which in other cultures and contexts is made, too, in relation to headhunting practices which are considered men's way to promote fertility of plants, animals, and humans.

Blood is said, as among the Melpa but also among the Bimin-Kuskusmin, to descend only through three generations and then to "die," whereas only agnatic lineage membership transmitted by men is considered to be continuous through time. But, in addition to this acknowledged asymmetry, in many New Guinea cultures attempts are made to weaken the female blood which runs also in a male body and to strengthen the continuous elements between agnatic males within lineages and clans as well as between men in general. So far I have tried to demonstrate how the flows of blood and its absence, a woman's fertility and her biological ability to generate life, and the bond between a mother and her child are experienced and interpreted. Filiation by blood obviously belongs to one of the basic human experiences in New Guinea cultures which is very rarely translated into terms of descent. It is rather negated or transformed into cultural categories which are marked by attributed weakness and discontinuity. Nevertheless, in many New Guinea cultures the principle of blood-filiation is acknowledged as an element which is socially recognized in several contexts, as after a fight, in which blood has been shed, the victim's mother's brother (and not his father) has to be recompensed. The principle of patrilineal descent is in most cases stronger although it is somehow competing and continuously struggling with that of matrifiliation. But if on the level of social organization the strength and continuity of patrilineal descent is established, there is still another level to mention: that of "manhood" and "clanhood,"[9] into which every young man has to become incorporated. On this level, where men as individuals are looking for continuity among themselves, the effects of blood and the way it is perceived are clearly recognizable.

Women's legacy, men's burden

A girl's admission to "womanhood" has in all female rituals to do with first menstruation, even if they take place months or even years before or after menarche, an event which can to some extent be foreseen but which finally happens nevertheless unexpectedly. The onset of the regular monthly flow of blood is mostly considered a sign of fertility "car c'est seulement quand il [the blood] coule et parce qu'il coule que les petites filles, hier encore steriles, seront demain des femmes fecondables" (Godelier 1982a:109). Herdt noticed among the Sambia (1981:190): "A woman's periods are so steady and visible that they serve constant notice of a powerful force alive and operating within her. Nothing else, except the waxing and waning of the moon, so dramatizes cyclical periodicity in the Sambia world."[10]

In contrast to the transformation of girls into women, which happens mainly through blood which starts to flow, boys are not perceived to change so quickly, without human interference, into men. Thus many anthropologists have remarked that "men, as total men, are not born in New Guinea; they are ritually constructed" (Whitehead 1986:88). To make men implies that the female influence in a man's body has to be reduced or even removed because the female component is thought to be still active and endangers him to become feminized instead of masculinized. The harmful effects are perceived to be a consequence of the fact that he had once been in his mother's womb and thus in intimate contact with her blood. During his early years he had been suckled by her and thus still spent most of his early life with and dependent on women.

The rituals in New Guinea which are held to free a boy from female substances and to strengthen his male components are well known. They can be divided into those in which the boys are bled and those in which they are fed with male components.[11] There exist regions where blood-purging rites occur and those where the transmission of male substances is practiced (Whitehead 1986, I:note 2). Concerning the purging rites, which are linked to conceptions of pollution, the range of variations in context and form is large and includes different organs. But the aim is always the same: purging. These purging rituals include induced vomiting, rubbing the eyes until they are bloodshot, sweating, induced bleeding from the penis, the nose, the tongue, and other parts of the body. In some regions like the Sepik where initiation includes scarification, the element of blood-letting is locally seen as quite important although the idea of cutting distinguishing marks on the back, breast, upper arms, and thighs seems to prevail. In many New Guinea cultures bleeding is initiated during the rituals of manhood but thereafter it is individually carried out during large parts of the active life, mostly after direct (sexual) contact with women, or indirect contacts which are considered as polluting, too, before rituals, hunts, and warfare.

But all male bleeding rituals are related in one way or another to menstruation, to get rid of "female" blood. Regularly induced bleeding is often equated to menstruation (Bettelheim 1954) which in many cultures is considered to be a self-occurring purging. Whereas everybody knows that women are menstruating, men try to keep their ritual bleeding as a male secret hidden from women's perception.

In male initiation rituals only men (or more precisely persons of male gender) are acting, whereas in female puberty rites often both men and women perform and in some sequences men are the leaders. This is the case among the Hua (Hays and Hays 1982) where men induce nose bleeding on girls. Whenever men participate in first-menstruation rites they claim control over women's fertility and menstruation, that is, they assert domination by pretending to control women's blood in general. The most important thing is that men literally control the flow of blood be it on themselves or on women because they induce it. Among the Bimin-Kuskusmin, at marriage male agnates are said to control ritually a woman's menstrual capacity by giving her sanctified water and sow blood which has been stored near male and female skulls in the clan cult house (Poole 1984:125).

Inter-male filiation by consumption

In many New Guinea cultures blood letting or sweating/vomiting practices – forced expulsion of body substances which may be harmful to a male body by feminizing or weakening his maleness – are only one aspect of a more complex issue. More dominant, at least to anthropologists, are the so-called homosexual relations[12] between men mostly of different age (for an overview of Melanesia see Herdt 1984). The transmission of semen from senior men to juniors should promote their growth, their masculinization, and, as among the Etoro, implant semen because boys "completely lack the most critical and essential attribute of manhood, i.e., semen" (Kelly 1976:45). Therefore, a youth is continuously inseminated over years until he has become fully masculinized and is ready to inseminate boys himself. This practice occurs in many other New Guinea cultures, such as the Sambia and Baruya where semen is transmitted orally. The Sambia even say that the semen organ can only store, not manufacture, sperm (Herdt 1982a:195). This view is in contrast to woman's self-activating, and self-functional menstrual blood organ which a girl acquires through her blood from her mother.

Semen transmission has to be seen also as an attempt to perpetuate a material bond between males of different generations similar to that created by blood-filiation between a woman and her children, mainly her daughters, who again pass it on. There clearly exist rules concerning age and kinship relations of who gives and who receives semen. Generalizing, it can be said that semen is always transferred from seniors to juniors, thus creating continuity of sperm-transmission through time. If we think again of conceptions of procreation we can speak of an induced sperm-filiation among men, which is never one between a real father and his son. It is important to note that in Western society the mouth is viewed as a possible substitute for a female sexual organ. In contrast, Godelier notes (1982a:93): "Pour les Baruya, ce serait la pire des humiliations, la pire des aggressions que de donner à boire à un jeune qu'on vient de disjoindre brutalement du monde des femmes la semence d'un sexe qui a pénétré une femme. Ce serait traiter la bouche du garçon comme un vagin ... " It is a crucial point he mentions: although men perform a transmission of male sexual fluids, it is not considered as a sexual act as such.[13] The transmission of semen is men's way of transmitting life ("la circulation de la vie" – Godelier 1982a:94).

Although to Western eyes the giving and orally receiving of semen is spectacular, it should be considered in broad terms. The structural opposition between mouth and vagina which certainly exists in most New Guinea cultures should not be overlooked. Giving semen is an act of nurturing which, among the Baruya and Sambia as well as others, is paralleled to a baby being suckled by its mother. In fact, semen and breast milk have in their notions many similarities, and a man gives his semen orally to his wife[14] in order to give her strength after illness. Although this practice seems to be an exception rather than a rule in the ethnographic continuum, it is obviously not seen as a variant of sexual play. Giving and receiving semen should be viewed as a form of creating communion among men by ritual consumption. This consumption may include special food such as, among the Bimin-Kuskusmin, ritual taro infused with semen (Poole 1981a:131) which older men give to juniors. Among the Arapesh and the Hua (Meigs 1976:400) some drops of their father's blood are given to boys who have to consume it. This transfer should promote their growth and strengthen their masculinity. Among the Iatmul a boy is given some scrapings of the skull of the founding ancestor of his clan. Among the Abelam, famous for cultivating extremely long yam tubers, boys are given specially grown yam during initiation. But it is not just ordinary food because these tubers are conceived to be "children" created only by men without women's contribution; they are said to possess their "father's" blood.[15] Thus, the ritual consumption of yam is in this context the same as in other cultures the consumption of special portions of pork, of bone scrapings, blood, and semen.

These examples all present oral incorporations of elements which represent in one way or another the principle of continuity. And by consumption the continuity of the past generations (symbolized by ritual food) gets extended to a further, new link. Hence, among men, inter-male continuity is created by consumption. That, at least in some cases, this inter-generational transmission which men act out is equated to the transmission of blood by women is supported by several facts. The Sambia say that in procreation a mother gives half of her blood to her child, while half stays inside her (Herdt 1981:192). The same is true for the procreation of an adult man: only half of the semen goes into the young man while half stays inside the semen-giver (p. 248). In contrast to this inter-male transmission – which is never mutual but always asymmetric, from the older to the younger – in sexual intercourse between a man and his wife a complete semen depletion is said to occur.

Thus, inter-male and inter-generational transmission of semen is far more than just the transmission of a material body substance which is believed to have bodily effects upon the receiver. It is also a transmission of spiritual substance, which does not follow the agnatic principle as in procreation of a child. But it is also a transmission, as among the Etoro, of a general male life-force which can be augmented only by ingestion. And, analogous to the ideology of only half depletion at inter-male semen transmission but complete depletion during intercourse, the giver only loses substantially of his life-force during coitus with a woman (Kelly 1976:46). In Etoro male ideology, inter-male semen transmission means continuation of life-force, fertility, and bountiful yields of crops. Inter-sexual semen transmission means depletion, diminishing yields of gardens, and also death. Male inter-generational transmissions thus create continuous bonds between men in general. They link every young individual to them, almost independently from (or parallel to) lineage and clanship.[16] Moreover these transmissions are an attempt to create bonds similar to those believed to exist by means of blood between women and their children. It is important to note that in New Guinea and many other cultures there exist almost no rituals in which women try to get rid of or to diminish a bodily or spiritual male component in their body. On the contrary, women perform most menarche rituals without men, and they celebrate this event extensively because first menstruation is in itself a proof of abundant female fertility.

From these two different forms of creating continuity and mainly unisex-bonding, it is evident that the one men elaborate is exclusive, whereas blood-filiation also includes boys who later, as young men, have to free themselves of it. The two modes are considered, probably mainly from the point of view of men, as antithetical. The many taboos to which women are subjected during menstruation or after giving birth result in varying degrees of spatial and social separation of men and women. They make intimate contact and sexual relations risky. Men's fear of women polluting them by using menstrual blood to harm them voluntarily or involuntarily, or depleting them of semen and thus of life-force, exists in most New Guinea cultures. Women's fear of becoming polluted by men is far less common, and even when it exists it is much weaker. Thus, menstrual blood is often abhorred by men and contact with it is said to provoke illness, premature aging, and even death. It is certainly this flow of blood, the occurrence of which remains uncontrollable – in spite of all efforts to control it – and beyond direct male influence, to which most of the danger is attributed. But also it is the part of the body from where this red fluid flows that augments its danger.

The blessings of intentionally spilled blood

In many New Guinea cultures people's attitudes toward blood, even their own, are thus full of ambivalence. It would be unthinkable for a New Guinean to suck his finger when he has cut himself as Westerners tend to do. And blood of anybody is always, if possible, avoided even if it only comes from a killed mosquito which had been full of blood. But, on the contrary, blood which is shed voluntarily is considered to be beneficial, prolific. It is only then, when under controlled conditions and when intentionally induced, that all fears are shaken off and its effects become the very opposite. Among the Baruya (Godelier 1982a:101), when men had killed an enemy, they dipped their weapons in the victim's blood and shouted their victory cry. When they had a captured enemy, they pierced his body and bathed in his blood. Then they took out his liver, cooked and consumed it.

For many rituals, such as for the opening ceremony of men's houses, an enemy had to be killed and his blood spilled to "cool down" the cere- monial house, as among the Kiwai (Landtman 1927:17–18): only then was it fit for men to use it. Otherwise the house could kill its inhabitants. The idea that blood has to be spilled seems to be as important as the act of killing itself. In many cases only by spilling blood can prosperity of a village and its inhabitants, animals, and crops be attained. Among the Marind a man has to kill an enemy before he is capable of begetting a child. In these contexts blood is considered to be the life-force *par excellence*, but here without the polluting effects attributed to it.

Among the most secret objects used in men's cults are sacred flutes which are a material manifestation of men's dominance over women and unity among themselves. In some rituals the flutes are rubbed with pig blood; the same is done with stones, symbols of eternal continuity, which are also used to promote fertility. Among the Telefolmin (Joérgensen 1983b:62) it is said that blood has to be kept out of taro gardens because the growing taro would immediately be destroyed by contact with blood: blood is inimical to these male tubers. But during the final phase of the taro rite a pig is slaughtered in the taro garden prior to the harvest and it is essential that the pig's blood flow into the ground. Joérgensen adds: "Exegetial commentary makes it clear that this harvest is in some way seen as a 'birth' of the taro from the garden." Among the Bimin- Kuskusmin, boys are ritually rubbed with pig blood which clearly has in some contexts the connotation of menstrual blood. This blood rubbed on the boys' bodies should help to transform the boys into men because it is not polluting, not feminizing them – unlike womb's blood during birth – but masculinizing when applied by men. Subsequently blood of a sow and then of a boar is used, the blood of the female animal mainly to close the boy's female navel, that of the boar to open the male navel (Poole 1982).

In men's cults pig blood is in many cases the reverse of what women's blood in everyday life is said to be. But there also exist examples where menstrual blood is used in rituals. I have mentioned earlier that, among the Telefolmin, women's version of procreation claims that out of their blood the sacra of men's cults, bones, are formed. During initiation red ochre, not pig blood, is applied to the skin of initiates. This ochre is called by the same secret name as menstrual blood. In some sequences of initiation blood of a woman who is menstruating at that time is used (Joérgensen 1983b:61). Among the Abelam, menstrual blood plays an important role when red ochre is manufactured, a paint which is used also in initiations and which then is identified with menstrual blood itself.

In all cases where menstrual blood is used during rituals of men, it is in controllable quantities, exempted from direct contact with female bodies and especially from female sexuality. The use of menstrual blood in men's rituals reveals the outstanding potency which is culturally attached to it and also manifests successful domination of what in everyday life is uncontrollable. It is a similar domination which the Bimin-Kuskusmin have attained. But they employ post-menstrual women, who no longer lead a sexually active life, as female ritual leaders who, among other things, handle menstrual blood in men's rituals. Such a woman has led a sexually active life during her earlier years and has preferably given birth to many sons. As a ritual leader she acts as a sister, that is as a member of the agnatic lineage, on behalf of the patrilineage to which she remains restricted (Weiner 1982:63). During her initiation into her new function as a senior female ritual leader she receives, like men, taro infused with semen which is thought to strengthen the agnatic ("male") blood. She also has to undergo a ritual bleeding near her male navel at the head, which is shaved and cleaned, in order to remove the remaining residues of menstrual blood. Her female navel is covered with yellow mud and thus closed. She receives a male name and male regalia and is allowed to have a taro garden. She is called "male mother." The initiates pass beneath her genitalia during a ritual whereby she "drip[s] 'menstrual blood' (actually pig blood) on their head" (Poole 1981a:note 19). Actual menstrual blood is smeared on the ridgepoles of the initiation house. When a senior ritual leader dies a male ritual is performed for her. Her female uterine kin have to bear away parts of her female substances (uterus and interior part of the vagina) and to consume them partially. Her skull is carried to the clan's cult house where "a gaping hole is broken in the male navel to admit the sacred male knowledge that she was denied in life" (Poole 1981a:154). This senior ritual leader, who actually is of female sex but has been transformed into male gender identity, thus does not act as a fertile woman and mother but as a being who has stopped producing menstrual blood and no longer has sexual relations. Men exempt her ritually from female sexuality which manifests itself in blood. It is the most complete success of domination because they have succeeded in transforming a woman into a man who then, although still controlled by full male ritual leaders, is able to handle menstrual blood and is responsible for the rebirth of boys as men.

Terrorism of the uncontrollable: witchcraft

The antithesis to the controlled use of blood in men's rituals, where it is the expression of utmost fertility, is the active use of blood, uncontrolled ritually by men. When used intentionally or arbitrarily against somebody illness and death will result. The Lusi in West New Britain speak of a lethal poison if used by Lusi women: "It is not 'sorcery' ... It is not classed with other forms of sorcery in the Lusi language. It differs from sorcery in that it is an inherent quality shared by all women of child-bearing age rather than being an acquired skill; it requires no spells, secret knowledge ... " (Counts and Counts 1983:51). Without using the appropriate expression the authors have made the famous distinction between sorcery and witchcraft which the Zande of Central Africa make (Evans-Pritchard 1929). Obviously it is witchcraft Lusi women are said to possess.[17] There is much evidence of witchcraft in New Guinea. In most of the cases it is closely linked to notions of menstrual blood[18] and therefore of women's capacity to produce something that oscillates between utmost fertility and death; moreover it is also men's suspicion of women employing it against them. Among the Bimin-Kuskusmin it is explicitly said the "menstrual blood carries the capacity for *tamam* witchcraft" (Poole 1984:201). The *tamam* capacity is transmitted through the peculiar flow of menstrual blood in the umbilical cord; it preferably passes from a mother to her daughter. When passed to a son it becomes weaker and after three descending generations it is no longer effective. If compared to the capacities of agnatic blood *tamam* is just the reverse, but the principles of how it works are the same. In fact it is said that *tamam* attacks can be launched only through the links of agnatic blood that connects witch and victim. *Tamam*, then, is a continuous threat to dissolve agnatic ties.[19] It is said that the same threat comes also from menstrual blood alone, without the additional notion of witchcraft, which is antithetical to agnatic blood. Further, it is said that although men can become witches too, and hence bring illness to their victims, it is only a female witch who is able to launch a lethal attack (Poole 1981a:135).

The witch who is the polluting woman *par excellence* is in diametric contrast with the image of a senior female ritual leader. The victims killed by witches are all men; witches are said to consume male foods to enhance the female procreative aspect of their anatomy, especially menstrual blood (Poole 1981b:59 and note 16). Witches are in constant search of male substance which they turn into polluting female substances. Witches are constantly menstruating even during pregnancy; a witch nurses her young with menstrual blood. Witches are said to perform cannibalistic acts; they consume male parts of the anatomy, especially the genitalia. They also eagerly swallow the victim's agnatic blood. Most of the attacks are carried out during the night. The spirit of a witch does not join those of other people in an ancestral world but completely disintegrates. Witches in the Bimin-Kuskusmin area are feared so much because they live in a community as an apparent friend though, in fact, they are enemies. Their necrophagous, homosexual behavior is the inversion of normal human activity (Zelenietz 1981:8) as well as the inversion of a senior female ritual leader.

The innate qualities of women and how they are perceived, perhaps mostly by men, have probably given rise to witchcraft beliefs.[20] These qualities are beyond control because they have turned savage and ferocious. Instead of menstruating periodically (as "normal" women do), instead of being under any ritual control of men, the witch is constantly producing menstrual blood, free of any influence. Instead of cessation of this flow during pregnancy, it goes on and on. Instead of forming normal children in her womb she often produces abnormalities and turns male substances, notably semen, into further female (witch) substance. Instead of producing members of the community, she kills and consumes them, she induces death not life. Instead of her sexuality being kept within boundaries by rules of conduct and behavior it is constantly overflowing, polluting or depleting men.

The relations between witchcraft and attributed inherent qualities in women exist in varying degrees, if not transculturally then at least in New Guinea cultures where the notion of witchcraft exists. Among the Etoro, Kelly (1976) has tried to establish an equation between witchcraft, witch, and victim and sexual relations, whereby the cultural meaning of witchcraft is informed by the idiom of sexual relations and vice versa. A woman who encourages, entices, or demands her husband to engage in needless copulation, which gradually depletes his life-force, approaches the purely negative role of a witch. The identification of woman and witch is "applicable to the potential characteristics of aggressive and demanding feminity and unregulated feminine sexuality" (Kelly 1976:49). As a matter of fact not only women are accused of being witches although in New Guinea most of them indeed seem to be women. Iatmul men told me that a man who acts as a witch has somehow to transform himself into a woman (Hauser-Schäublin 1977:139). Among the Abelam, witches are always women who become so only after reaching puberty.

Zelenietz (1981:5) has remarked that witchcraft, as well as sorcery, is always enmeshed in the exercise of power. Witchcraft is a threat to the very existence of those New Guinea cultures where it is known because it challenges all foundations and principles of social organization. Zelenietz quotes Lindenbaum who has said that those who are "powerless" in a society are often feared most, for they have the "power" to threaten established social existence. From this point of view blood – its first occurrence during puberty, its regular flow, its absence during pregnancy (when it is said to contribute at least partially to the future child), and its reoccurrence until it ceases completely – is clearly a power context. It is the power of the uncontrollable, although I am not quite sure whether beliefs in witchcraft are created by men as a further means of suppressing women or if women can cause witchcraft as an instrument in power contexts for their own ends. In any case, in relation to witchcraft, blood becomes a category which creates hierarchies and is also a social explosive.[21]

Equality by blood: blood-brotherhood

To clarify the acuteness of blood concepts and their use in creating gender hierarchies in many New Guinea cultures, I turn now to contrasting material from Africa for which no counterpart exists in New Guinea. In some African cultures, blood is used not only in creating hierarchies but also in creating equality among men. Anthropologists term these phenomena blood-covenants, blood-brotherhood, or blood-pacts. To enter such a bond two men ritually exchange some drops of blood which are then eaten. The Zande take the blood from the arm or the chest, drip it on a piece of special wood or on some groundnuts which then are consumed by the covenant partner. Evans-Pritchard (1933:369) has called blood-brotherhood "a pact or alliance formed between two persons by a ritual act in which each swallows the blood of the other. The pact is one of mutual assistance and is backed by powerful sanctions. It may bind only the two participants to certain obligations, or it may also involve the social groups of which they are members." Blood-brotherhood among the strongly patrilineal Zande contains also many obligations, for example that a man must assist in digging the grave of a member of his blood-brother's family and kin. The Zande word for blood-brother has linguistically to do with "to cut" and "blood."

Among the Zande blood-brotherhood was ritually established between men when bonds of comradeship already existed. Sometimes it took place solely for commercial purposes. For example, if a man traveled in foreign countries he made blood-brotherhood with a man who thereby became responsible for his safety. Evans-Pritchard called the exchange of blood a "typical magical rite," because blood used in this context had "a different sociological meaning from ordinary blood" (*ibid.*:383). The main points of discussion between scholars (which lasted for decades) concern whether the exchange of blood means establishing a psycho-physical kinship with the clansmen of his blood-brother or whether the blood creates merely a magical bond between them, whether it is a bond of true kinship or simply a contract established by exchange of blood. Evans-Pritchard argued that Zande do "not regard kinship as a community of blood, and hence there is no idea of artificially creating bonds of kinship by transfusion of blood ... Azande speak of members of the same clan as having sprung from the same seed, but the filiation is not spoken of as one of blood." He concluded: "If kinship and common blood were synonymous in Zande thought their mode of reckoning descent would be matrilineal, since a child is formed out of his mother's blood" (*ibid.*:397). It has to be mentioned, too, that blood is never exchanged between kinsmen, because "they were already bound to one another by the sociological ties of kinship."

In contrast to kin-brothers the relationship between blood-brothers is intimate and egalitarian. Moreover, it is "a legal contract entered into by two men of their own accord" (*ibid.*:400). Evans-Pritchard demonstrated convincingly that the blood itself is the "medicine," the material element of the magical complex, and it becomes such through association with the spell and rite performed at the exchange of blood.

Having considered the perception and interpretation of blood in New Guinean cultures we must ask: why this use of blood in these African societies? Evans-Pritchard has mentioned that kinship and common blood are not synonymous in Zande society, and the same is true in New Guinea. But what blood means among the Zande is difficult to reconstruct because evidence concerning conceptions of blood, menstruation, procreation, and spilled blood in rituals, hunts, and warfare is incomplete. A child is formed out of the contributions of both his parents, vaginal fluids and semen. The information available (Evans-Pritchard 1974:20–1) indicates that somehow the idea seems to exist, too, that when a woman has become pregnant her menstrual blood instead of leaving her body accumulates in her womb. Women's contribution to a child is seen mostly as one of providing large quantities of blood. In other contexts, concerning witchcraft, Evans-Pritchard (1937:56–7) hints at "other unlucky agencies, such as menstruating women ... "; I therefore assume that menstruating women are avoided because their effects on men are considered to be either polluting, depleting, or just unfortunate. Whether this avoidance is linked in a narrower sense than in New Guinea to blood on women's genitalia,[22] or whether it also includes menstrual blood as such, remains uncertain. At least in some respect blood is considered to be an innate female rather than male substance, not gender-neutral.

Among the Kaguru, blood-pacts are also made (Beidelman 1963). In contrast to the Zande, the Kaguru are matrilineal and they express matrilineal kinship in terms of common blood which also symbolizes life and continuity, perpetuity of the descent group. It represents to some extent also a spiritual life-force. In contrast to the aspect of fertility, blood is associated, too, with death and anger, life passion and the uncontrollable. The ambivalence of blood is expressed clearly when a woman is menstruating because she has to be segregated from the community. The Kaguru refer to kinship relations when speaking about blood-covenant. But although both matrikin and blood-brothers are said to share common blood – a bond which cannot be dissolved – the Kaguru insist that both are not the same. Relations between siblings even of the same sex are never equal because they always involve ranking according to age. On the contrary, blood-brotherhood establishes relationships characterized by equality and mutuality.

Nevertheless, blood-brothers are considered to belong to another category than mere friends. The blood used to establish this special relationship is drawn from the breast near the heart, which is conceived to be the center of thought and feeling. It is applied to meat which is then eaten by the partner. The Kaguru believe that it enters the veins and organs of that person and that it mixes indissolubly with his own blood.

It is very rare among the Zande as well as among the Kaguru that a blood-covenant is established between a man and a woman, and it is almost never established between women. The Kaguru say that such persons were always in danger of having sexual relations with one another, which would ruin the covenant relationship's proper character. In contrast to the Zande and Evans-Pritchard's conclusions, Beidelman considers that for the Kaguru the element of blood itself, rather than any magical associations with the covenant ritual, is the crucial factor in making a covenant tie, because they conceive of blood as the physiological basis of their most important social groups.

The importance of blood is also reflected in Kaguru procreation ideas. Out of blood and semen a fetus is formed; the blood is responsible for flesh and blood while semen forms the bony structure around which these insubstantial parts coagulate (Beidelman 1971:41). Children share their blood with their mother but not with their father. Blood links them to the land and to other traditions associated with their clan. There are other beliefs of the Kaguru concerning blood which could be compared with New Guinea cultures, but I can add only one more: at the circumcision ceremony for boys the moisture-producing, feminine part of men is removed in order to transform boys into men.

Blood is seen in these African cultures as a genuine feminine contribution to the body on which the navel remains forever a mark of its parental bond to the womb. In both Zande and Kaguru culture, blood is a bodily substance associated with women, but to different degrees.

Conclusions

The New Guinea perspective offers the following points. In contrast to the principles of establishing direct relations of kinship, either by creating affines by marrying or by creating new agnates by begetting children, no women as such are needed in establishing blood-brotherhood. Instead a means that is classified as female is used. The female medium/substance *par excellence* in both African cultures (and probably in all cultures where blood-covenants are practiced) is blood. Among the Kaguru it is said that milk may be used, another female substance. In contrast to sexual relations (between men and women) which are needed to create new kin, blood-brotherhood is made by eating, by mutual consumption of a body substance. This substance is definitely not linked to maleness, as is semen, and hence does not compete with that of one's own body or reinforce it.

The difference between kinship and blood-brotherhood is that in the first case a man gets his blood from his mother, in a hierarchical context in terms of generations, gender, and situation (giving and receiving by bonds to the womb). In the second he gets it from another man who in turn receives it from his partner, and both consume it. This equal exchange has nothing to do with procreation, as in New Guinea where asymmetrical insemination takes place in order to transform boys into men. Semen received from another man finally becomes part of one's own body fluids, one's own semen included. Therefore, through procreation it would contribute to forming a child. I think one of the main reasons why in Zande as well as in Kaguru culture blood is used in creating this pact between men is that blood does not leave a man's body, that is, it is not passed on to his offspring. Because blood "ends" within a man, it can be used not as a means of domination and competition but rather of creating equality.

If one views African "blood pacts" from a New Guinea perspective one can conclude that in both Africa and New Guinea, and probably also in other parts of the world, blood is classified as a female or maternal body fluid, associated with procreation, life, and flesh, but also with finiteness, death, and mortality (Hauser-Schäublin 1989). The values attached to it in a broader sense, however, differ remarkably: whereas one cannot imagine New Guinea men mutually exchanging blood, blood expelling rituals are almost unknown in the African cultures discussed here. Apart from different cultural traditions, which have evolved independently, and different modes of subsistence which are crucially related to the value complex attached to blood, there are corresponding fundamental notions of blood which are due to the culturally unalterable conditions of this red vital fluid.

NOTES

1 Biersack (1983:86), for example, maintains that conception theory is "an expression of certain social structural (rather than natural) facts. I implicitly challenge the assumption that so-called indigenous conception theories reflect local procreative views at all ... "

2 The Lusi of West New Britain are a striking example. There people maintain that the fetus originates only from "father's water" and also the umbilical cord is composed of coagulated seminal fluid (Counts and Counts 1983:49–51).

3 I shall not repeat the main issues of the famous anthropological discussion on "virgin birth" (Leach 1967) but add to it indirectly.

4 For a helpful survey on this topic see *Mankind* 14(1), 1983, 1–83.

5 There are many related aspects of bones, continuity of the agnatic patrilineal group, and male cults which I am unable to discuss here.

6 One could suppose that the spot where this black clot of blood is located is near a "female" organ.

7 Space does not allow me to discuss conceptions of transformation from one color into another, as here red blood into white bones (see also Joérgensen 1983b:61–2 on bones and blood, white and red). It is superfluous, but nevertheless stimulating, to speculate how much less important blood would be conceived if it had the same color as water or if semen were as red as blood.

8 In many cultures beyond New Guinea the skulls of important men are kept.

9 Whitehead (1986:85) has used these two expressions in discussing fertility cults in New Guinea. Her argument is that in the Lowlands the fertility cults are dominated mainly by the theme of "making men," whereas in the Highlands it is rather the "making of clansmen."

10 The length of the phases of the moon and of women's menstruation cycle are identical though not synchronical. Most New Guinea cultures relate the moon to women in one way or the other. Thus, it is often said that the moon has "killed" her when she is menstruating.

11 I consider Kulick's division (1985) into blood-purging rites and transmission-of-semen rites too limited to the current body fluids discussion on New Guinea.

12 For a critical discussion of the adequacy of the expression homosexuality see Kulick (1985).

13 The current literature on gender in New Guinea lacks illumination of how these cultures conceive "sexuality." My fieldwork among the Iatmul and the

Abelam reveals that for the men there exists no sexuality in which women are not included, but only genitality. Sexuality is conceived primarily to be a female potency or ability in which men engage. Moreover, sexuality is limited to a woman's genitals.

14 Among the Sambia (Herdt 1981:178) occasionally a man gives semen to his bride, then still a premenstrual girl. It should strengthen her, promote her growth, and eventually initiate the flow of breast milk. I would consider this as a demonstration of man's power to control female fertility.

15 The phenomenon that a product grown by a man contains his blood is not exceptional. It is a well-known fact that among hunting people in New Guinea it is said that the hunter's blood goes into his prey. For this reason he is not allowed to consume the meat but has to give it to somebody else. One could speak of blood-filiation by killing.

16 I have mentioned earlier the anthropological concept of manhood versus clanhood (Whitehead 1986). I cannot follow this distinction because clanhood in New Guinea always includes manhood.

17 It is interesting to note that the Lusi do not have the notion of menstrual pollution as such (Counts and Counts 1983:51).

18 Spiro (this volume) also sees, from a different point of view, a link between "the dangerous female" and witchcraft in Burma.

19 Witchcraft is said to have entered the Bimin-Kuskusmin area through intermarriage with women from the Oksapmin.

20 That members of other groups often are the preferred targets of witchcraft accusations is well known but I consider it as a consequence not as a cause of witchcraft.

21 It is beyond the scope of this chapter to discuss witchcraft at a sociological, ideological, and psychological level, or in what cases and under what conditions witchcraft accusations, trials, or even killings (Steadman 1975) take place.

22 The part of the body from where blood is drawn is also important. Among the Kaguru I presume, from what Beidelman (1971) said about the heart as the center of thoughts and feelings, that it is perhaps rather a part which is classified as being male rather than female. But here I can only speculate because the data required are lacking.

REFERENCES

Beidelman, Thomas O. 1963 The Blood Covenant and the Concept of Blood in Ukaguru. *Africa* 33:321–42.
    1971 *The Kaguru: A Matrilineal People of East Africa.* New York: Holt, Rinehart and Winston.
Bettelheim, Bruno 1954 *Symbolic Wounds: Puberty Rites and the Envious Male.* New York: Collier Books.
Biersack, Aletta 1983 Bound Blood: Palela "Conception" Theory Interpreted. *Mankind* 14(2):85–100.
Buckley, Tim 1982 Menstruation and the Power of Yurok Women: Methods in Cultural Reconstruction. *American Ethnologist* 9:47–60.
Collier, Jane F. and Michelle Z. Rosaldo 1981 Politics and Gender in Simple

Societies. In *Sexual Meanings: The Cultural Construction of Gender and Sexuality*. Sherry B. Ortner and Harriet Whitehead, eds., pp. 275–329. New York: Cambridge University Press.

Counts, Dorothy Ayers and David R. Counts 1983 Father's Water Equals Mother's Milk: The Conception of Parentage in Kaliai, West New Britain. *Mankind* 14(1):46–56.

Evans-Pritchard, E. E. 1929 Witchcraft (*Mangu*) amongst the Azande. *Sudan Notes and Records* 12:163–249.

1933 Zande Blood-Brotherhood. *Africa* 6:369–401.

1937 *Witchcraft, Oracles and Magic among the Azande*. Oxford: Clarendon Press.

1971 *The Azande: History and Political Institutions*. Oxford: Clarendon Press.

Evans-Pritchard, E. E., ed. 1974 *Man and Woman among the Azande*. New York: Free Press.

Godelier, Maurice 1982a *La Production des grands hommes: pouvoir et domination masculine chez les Baruya de Nouvelle-Guinée*. Paris: Arthème Fayard.

1982b Social Hierarchies among the Baruya of New Guinea. In *Inequality in New Guinea Highlands Societies*. Andrew Strathern, ed., pp. 3–34. New York: Cambridge University Press.

Harrell, B. B. 1981 Lactation and Menstruation in Cultural Perspective. *American Anthropologist* 83:796–823.

Hauser-Schäublin, Brigitta 1977 *Frauen in Kararau: Zur Rolle der Frau bel den Iatmul am Mittelsepik, Papua New Guinea*. Basler Beiträge zur Ethnologie, Vol. 18. Basle.

1977/78 *Vom Terror und Segen des Blutes. Oder: Die Emanzipation des Mannes von der Frau*. Wiener Volkerkundliche Mitteilungen, Vol. 24/5. Vienna.

1989 The fallacy of "Real" and "Pseudo" Procreation. *Zeitschrift für Ethnologie* 114:179–94.

Hays, Terence E. and Patricia H. Hays 1982 Oppositions and Complementarity of the Sexes in Ndumba Initiation. In *Rituals of Manhood: Male Initiation in Papua New Guinea*. Gilbert H. Herdt, ed., pp. 201–38. Berkeley: University of California Press.

Herdt, Gilbert H. 1981 *Guardians of the Flutes: Idioms of Masculinity*. New York: McGraw-Hill.

1982a Sambia Nosebleeding Rites and Male Proximity to Women. *Ethos* 10:189–231.

1984 Ritualized Homosexual Behavior in the Male Cults of Melanesia: 1862–1983. In *Ritualized Homosexuality in Melanesia*. Gilbert H. Herdt, ed., pp. 1–81. Berkeley: University of California Press.

Herdt, Gilbert H., ed. 1982b *Rituals of Manhood: Male Initiation in Papua New Guinea*. Berkeley: University of California Press.

Joérgensen, Dan 1983a Introduction: The Facts of Life, Papua New Guinea Style. *Mankind* 14(1):1–12.

1983b Mirroring Nature? Men's and Women's Models of Conception in Telefolmin. *Mankind* 14(1):57–65.

Kelly, Raymond C. 1976 Witchcraft and Sexual Relations: An Exploration in the Social and Semantic Implications of the Structure of Belief. In *Men and Women in the New Guinea Highlands*. Paula Brown and Georgeda Buchbinder, eds., pp. 36–53. Special Publication of the American Anthropological Association No. 8.

Kulick, Don 1985 Homosexual Behavior, Culture and Gender in Papua New Guinea. *Ethnos* 1–2:15–39.

Landtman, Gunnar 1927 *The Kiwai Papuans of British New Guinea: A Nature-Born Instance of Rousseau's Ideal Community*. London: Macmillan.

Leach, Edmund R. 1967 Virgin Birth. *Proceedings of the Royal Anthropological Institute of Great Britain and Ireland for 1966*:39–49.

Lindenbaum, Shirley 1979 *Kuru Sorcery: Disease and Danger in the New Guinea Highlands*. Palo Alto, CA: Mayfield Publishing Company.

Meigs, Anna S. 1976 Male Pregnancy and the Reduction of Sexual Opposition in a New Guinea Highlands Society. *Ethnology* 14(4):393–408.

1984 *Food, Sex, and Pollution: A New Guinea Religion*. New Brunswick, NJ: Rutgers University Press.

Mosko, Mark 1984 Conception, De-conception and Social Structure in Bush Mekeo Culture. *Mankind* 14(1):24–32.

Newman, Philip L. and David J. Boyd 1982 The Making of Men. In *Rituals of Manhood: Male Initiation in Papua New Guinea*. Gilbert H. Herdt, ed., pp. 239–85. Berkeley: University of California Press.

Ortner, Sherry B. and Harriet Whitehead, eds. 1981 *Sexual Meanings: The Cultural Construction of Gender and Sexuality*. New York: Cambridge University Press.

Panoff, Michel 1976 Patrifiliation as Ideology and Practice in a Matrilineal Society. *Ethnology* 15(2):175–88.

Poole, Fitz John Porter 1981a Transforming "Natural" Woman: Female Ritual Leaders and Gender Ideology among Bimin-Kuskusmin. In *Sexual Meanings: The Cultural Construction of Gender and Sexuality*. Sherry B. Ortner and Harriet Whitehead, eds., pp. 116–65. New York: Cambridge University Press.

1981b Taman: Ideological and Sociological Configurations of "Witchcraft" among Bimin-Kuskusmin. *Social Analysis* 8:58–76.

1982 The Ritual Forging of Identity. In *Rituals of Manhood: Male Initiation in Papua New Guinea*. Gilbert H. Herdt, ed., pp. 99–154. Berkeley: University of California Press.

1984 Symbols of Substance: Bimin-Kuskusmin Models of Procreation, Death, and Personhood. *Mankind* 14(3):191–215.

Skultans, Vieda 1970 The Symbolic Significance of Menstruation and the Menopause. *Man* 5(4):639–51.

Steadman, Lyle 1975 Cannibal Witches in the Hewa. *Oceania* 46(2):114–21.

Strathern, Andrew 1972 *One Father, One Blood: Descent and Group Structure among the Melpa People*. New York: Barnes and Noble.

Strathern, Marilyn, ed. 1987 *Dealing with Inequality: Analysing Gender Relations in Melanesia and Beyond*. New York: Cambridge University Press.

Weiner, Annette B. 1982 Sexuality among the Anthropologists: Reproduction among the Informants. *Social Analysis* 12:52–65.

Whitehead, Harriet 1986 The Varieties of Fertility Cultism in New Guinea, Parts I and II. *American Ethnologist* 13(1–2):80–99, 271–89.

Yeatman, Anna S. 1984 Introduction: Gender and Social Life. *Social Analysis* 15:3–10.

Zelenietz, Marty 1981 Sorcery and Social Change: An Introduction. *Social Analysis* 8:3–14.

5 Reproduction and gender hierarchy: amniocentesis in America

Rayna Rapp

The connection between reproduction and gender hierarchy is central to anthropological theory. Multiple anthropological discourses, both feminist and anti-feminist, have placed reproduction at the heart of their explanations of female subordination. Such theories of male dominance focus on a need to control women's fecundity, to secure rights in the next generation and its labor, to construct a domestic domain which is formed around childbearing and rearing, or symbolically to elevate the cultural over the natural. Some other theories, both evolutionary and feminist, have argued the opposite: that in tribal cultures, awe and respect (rather than the fear and loathing so often expressed in Western societies) surround women's ability to menstruate and to give birth; that mothers, especially in their role as "matrons," control many resources; and that even/especially in traditional patrilineal, patrilocal groups, women's highest status is gained through the production of children, particularly sons, for their husbands' kin groups. Readings of female subordination through reproduction are thus ethnocentric, reflecting the colonial and patriarchal bias of the societies from which many early (and not so early) anthropologists drew their own gender values.

In some senses, these doubled discourses – of female reproductive power and subordination, of feminism and a- or anti-feminism – mirror one another closely in assigning such totalizing power to the connection between reproduction and gender hierarchy. My goal in this chapter is to untangle that connection, using two strategies. The first is a critical review of some of the anthropological literature on reproduction, interrogating our sources for what they have to say about the construction of gender hierarchy. The second is a case study of amniocentesis in contemporary American culture, where the "male take-over" and technological transformation of pregnancy can be viewed as contributing to either liberation or social control. Through both these strategies, I demonstrate that neither "reproduction" nor "gender hierarchy" are unified phenomena, nor is their connection inevitably constructed in one pattern. Rather, their connections and contradictions must be located and analyzed in concrete, historic terms.

108

Anthropology and reproduction

"Reproduction" is a complex term. In a classic article on women's subordination, Edholm, Harris, and Young (1977) point out three different meanings which are often conflated in its use: the common-sense notion of human biological reproduction; and two Marxist notions, one focusing on the reproduction of the labor force, the other on total social reproduction. Anthropologists have made contributions to all three uses, and each has implications for the understanding of gender hierarchies. The following review considers work in each of the three areas in turn.

Human biological reproduction

Anthropological analyses of human reproduction often intersect and take issue with received notions in the field of demography (Michaelson 1981; Nag 1980; Mamdani 1972). Anthropologists tend to disaggregate such general models as the "demographic transition," insisting on the specific rationalities of diverse subcultures. Population dynamics, according to the anthropological view, cannot be understood apart from sociocultural phenomena: ecology, food sources, migration, warfare, famine, and the like which condition the development of cultural patterns of childbearing. Low-technology societies often code population practices directly in their cultural prescriptions: age of marriage and conjugal patterns, ritual control of heterosexuality, beliefs and practices surrounding contraception, abortion, infanticide, acceptable pregnancies, and child spacing all help to shape a group's population (Polgar 1971, 1975).

Despite the rhetoric of Western development interests, the desire for large numbers of children in non-industrial societies is not irrational (see Mamdani on rural India, 1972). High infant and juvenile mortality dictates a focus on "redundant" childbearing. Child labor is often crucial to family and community survival, and grown children may be the only "social security" aging parents have in many societies (Michaelson 1981; Nag 1980; Nag, White, and Peet 1978). Moreover, factors which appear distant from "family planning," such as changes in world agribusiness, land and labor taxes, international warfare, Euroamerican experiments with medical technologies in Third World countries, and the development of consumer demand for Western products may all affect population dynamics. World hierarchies of power are thus central to the anthropological understanding of demographic processes.

The anthropological analysis of demography has a major contribution to make: it reminds us that local-level dynamics of reproduction are systemic, and linked to world power relations. But it also has a drawback:

it rarely looks at gender relations, assuming that men and women, the old and the young, hold unified interests in cultural practices. Thus "family relations" rather than gender hierarchies are a subject of its attention. There is little sense that gender relations – both cooperative and antagonistic, collective and individual – help to construct demographic patterns, rather than simply reflect them.

In part as a response to the lack of gender-sensitivity in anthropological demography, in part as a playing out of the popular interest in "women's culture," the 1980s witnessed the growth of a remarkable "cottage industry": the birth of the "anthropology of birth." Harkening back to Mead and Newton's classic article on perinatal behavior (1967), the new anthropology of birth focuses on pregnancy, birth, and mother–newborn relations (Newman 1970, 1972; Jordan 1980; MacCormack 1982; Kay 1982; Browner 1982; Ginsburg and Rapp 1991). While a range of methodologies – ecological, political-economic, symbolic, culture, and personality – are deployed, this new literature most commonly focuses on three things: birth as a *rite de passage* which has been woefully neglected in mainstream anthropology, birth in the total context of life-cycle and community culture rather than as a medical event, and the importance of mother–infant relations in the reproduction of culture itself as well as of individual persons. Implicitly, and sometimes explicitly, these works are critical, for they start from the symptomatic silences of Western culture where none of the three is granted much scholarly or popular recognition.

But exactly what it is that these scholars are critical *of* requires some discussion. Many of the new studies of birth take the mother–newborn dyad, and indeed, the process of "matrescence" (Raphael 1975) as central to the cultural construction of femininity. Likewise, the value of home-birthing, removed from the rigidities of Western biomedicine, is virtually assumed. Husbands, fathers, and other male community members enter most such analyses only marginally, as supporters or witnesses of women's reproductive accomplishments. While it is easy to feel sympathy for these perspectives, authors who use them may romanticize conditions that not only empower but oppress women in diverse cultures. Like the home-birth movement in contemporary North America from which some of its cultural consciousness comes, this stance runs the risk of systematically overlooking gender hierarchy.[1] This is an odd elision, given the necessarily multiple and often competing interests expressed in any serious ritual, and, indeed, in any culture's stakes in recruitment of the next generation of its members. As Browner points out (1982), struggles over contraception, abortion, infanticide, and child custody may express male–female antagonism as often as cooperation.

These are cases where anthropologists do link the interpretation of cultural practices surrounding birth to analyses of social hierarchies. Some take direct aim at male-dominant beliefs and practices central within the "women's world" of birth itself. For example, Morsy (1982) discusses the meaning of semen and pregnancy rituals which cast men as the active parties in women's gestation in an Egyptian village (see also Hauser-Schäublin's analysis, this volume, of male ritual cooptation of women's reproductive powers in New Guinea). Callaway (1978) reinterprets birth practices among the Gisu and Zulu, where a seemingly female-centered, supportive birthing environment is highly unstable and can be transformed into a terrifying interrogation of the laboring woman, whose alleged acts of disloyalty to husband and patriline are used to explain her difficult, indeed, life-threatening situation.

Other works have the virtue of linking the analysis of birth to cross-cutting relations of social dominance. In Cosminsky's analysis (1980) of the struggles between indigenous and government-trained midwives in Guatemalan villages, power differences are palpable. Indigenous Mayan *iyom* are disdained by public health officials who are not only male, but Ladino, Spanish-speaking, and nationally oriented as well. At issue in the struggle over such micro-practices as birth position, appropriate tasks and payments to midwives, and connection to religious specialists, are all the dominant relations of the non-Indian, Spanish-speaking, professionalized and male-identified state. Indeed, the power hierarchies at work in labor may represent the struggle for international hegemony, as Jordan (1987) points out in her analysis of the mystification of modern birth technologies. The lure of biomedicine's arcane secrets is considerable when compared to traditional, generally shared forms of birth knowledge.

Like the wider field of anthropological demography, the anthropology of birth opens up both problems and possibilities for the understanding of gender hierarchies. At its most insightful, it uses birth as a *rite de passage* to reveal the embeddedness of material practices and systems of meaning: dietary taboos in pregnancy, resistance to biomedical technologies which might promote infant-maternal survival at the price of lessening cultural autonomy, attitudes toward reproductive loss, infertility, and contraception "make sense" when viewed in context. Sometimes, anthropologists focusing on birth are able not only to reveal female strength and subordination enacted in the same practices, but to link gender relations to other seemingly distant hegemonic forms (Cosminsky 1980; Sargent 1982). But the anthropology of birth literature exhibits problematic aspects, as well. Too often there is a romanticization of "women's worlds" at the expense of developing a critical understanding of the power relations implicit in this, as in any other, non-trivial aspect of culture (Browner 1982).

Reproduction of the labor force

The second meaning of reproduction concerns the reproduction of the labor force. Beyond birthing babies, there is a set of social relations which extend over time to insure that children will be cared for and socialized to appropriate cultural futures. At the heart of that process lies the sexual division of labor and the construction of the domestic domain. For it is female efforts, often mystified by their invisibility (usually to Western anthropologists, and sometimes to indigenous observers as well, see Ochs this volume), which turn children into appropriate adults and sustain adult males so they can continue their productive roles. Hidden in the household, women's work is often assumed by most social analysts to be tiresomely static and unworthy of interest. But as Harris (1981, 1982; see also Sanjek 1982) points out, there is more to domestic work than an ahistoric, universal pattern of "breeding and feeding." The construction of households involves social, not natural processes. The tasks organized within the domestic domain are part of global and local history, not natural history.[2]

The gender hierachy involved in the sexual division of labor may involve female exploitation. In capitalized economies where the majority of the population has been separated from its means of production, women's work may be exploited directly in at least two ways. The first is characterized by the injustices of the "double day," where women, not men, work a second, unpaid shift in caring for households and children in addition to their participation in the paid labor force.[3] Exploitation may also be present when women have a vulnerable relation to underemployment and underpaid work in the most unstable sectors of the economy, in comparison to the men of their class. The vulnerability of marketing women in India to divorce and domestic violence as well as to economic disaster has been analyzed in these terms (Lessinger 1986; Naponen 1985). Female economic vulnerability may then be seen as both cause and consequence of women's domestic subordination to men.

In kin-based societies where people are only partially separated from their means of production, women may be exploited through the sexual division of labor as well. In Meillassoux's (1981) analysis of the exploitation of the "domestic community," male migratory labor is reproduced by the female farmers left behind. Thus, South African tribal peoples are forced into a "traditional" and "modern" sector, one predominantly female, the other predominantly male. Women's work raises up children for migration, sends resources to the men in the mines, and tends the exhausted and dying male workers when they are expelled back to the native reserves. Somewhat less dramatically, in Deere's (1976, 1977) analysis of the reproductive labors of Peruvian hacienda wives, women's work may be automatically assumed in their husband's labor contracts and used to take up the slack when relations of production require additional unpaid labor.

There are, however, problems with examining gender hierarchies through the analysis of the reproduction of the labor force. The "reproduction of the labor force" is a contingent operation, as Marx pointed out (1947). It is not inevitable that any given sector of the population be reproduced, despite its own struggles for survival and continuity. We cannot assume that women's domestic labor is essential to the reproduction of the capitalist, and capitalizing, modes of production. To do so lands us in a lurking functionalism: women are subordinate because capital requires their unpaid labors to reproduce labor power. It is the precise connection between domestic labors and larger social relations of production that must be analyzed, not assumed, in specific, historical cases. When this analysis is properly performed, it can reveal the stresses and contradictions of gender hierarchies, rather than an automatic model of female subservience. Examples of this more nuanced type of analysis of gender contradictions are mentioned in the following discussion of the third and last meaning of reproduction.

Total social reproduction

The third meaning resides in the analysis of "total social reproduction," a vexsome phrase in contemporary Marxist theoretical debates. This focus comes from Marx's initial insight that for the capitalist mode of production to continue, it must not only produce commodities but also establish production cycles which are capable of reproducing themselves. Recent discussions of social reproduction interrogate the connections between the social relations of production and all the social conditions which appear to lie "outside" productive processes, but which serve to reproduce the conditions under which production can take place. Such writing builds on the insights of Althusser and his colleagues, who hoped to move the "science of Marxism" beyond an uncritical analysis of base–superstructure relations.

In a series of acrimonious articles and books appearing through the 1970s and into the early 1980s, the notion of "total social reproduction" has exploded in two directions.[4] The first focuses on the mystification of productive relations in other social institutions. Donham's analysis of fertility fetishism among the Maale of the Sudan, for example, reveals how women's fertility is culturally produced and controlled by marital and labor arrangements among fathers and husbands (1985a, 1985b).

Thus men appear to give one another the "gift" of female fecundity. Not only is women's baby-making obscured and devalued, but the immense amount of productive labor women contribute to the economy is also thereby mystified. Sometimes the mystification involved in reproducing gender hierarchy is so weighted as to provide ballast toward a more systemic transformation. Witness, for example, the "apolitical" nature of the Mothers' Movement in Argentina, where women whose children had disappeared were, for a time, the only moral agents whose protest the state could not and did not actively repress (DuBois, n.d.).

The second development in the concept of "total social reproduction" examines productive relations in light of the boundaries of the units within which production takes place. It assumes that modes of production are abstractions, and concrete productive processes depend in some profound sense on a worldwide, often distant set of political and economic relations. Thus it becomes possible, for example, to examine the relation of the multinational corporations and free-trade zones to the use of third-world, recently proletarianized women on "the global assembly line." Does the constant decomposition and recomposition of different sectors of the working class in a worldwide and fragmentary process of proletarianization actively require the reproduction of the sexual division of labor? Is exploitation by age and sex, as well as nationality and class, essential to the reproduction of the current global economy (Elson and Pearson 1981; Ehrenreich, Fuentes, and Sklar 1983)? Such analyses of social reproduction, which place any local division of labor by sex in the context of regional, national, and international contradictory pressures, have a great advantage. They are sensitive to the layers of tension and contradiction which overlay any particular cultural practice or gender hierarchy.

Thus, the "defense of traditional women's work" may mobilize peasant women in India to resist multinational deforestation in the name of protecting the firewood they need to feed their families (Sharma 1984; see also Berreman this volume). It may also call forth the famous "march of the pots and pans" in which privileged women marched (or sent their domestic servants as their representatives!) against food and consumer shortages, caused in part by the United States blockade of Chile, and contributed to the downfall of Allende. Gender ideologies, themselves based on hierarchical cultural practices which grow out of and reproduce the division of labor by sex, may be deployed by both the left and the right. As Molyneux (1985) points out, women are often mobilized for social change using quite traditional "feminine" concerns and networks. Whether women's mobilization represents a practical gender interest, capable of restoring the traditional divisions of labor and power, or a strategic gender interest, capable of challenging and transforming those traditions, is a highly political question.

This excursion through the literature on the conflated concept of reproduction provides several lessons toward the analysis of gender hierarchies. The first is that local population dynamics of human reproduction are systemic and part of world political economic hierarchies. They are both produced by and help to reproduce uneven distributions of power, not only between women and men, but regionally, nationally, and internationally. The second is that birth may be richly analyzed as a *rite de passage*, a microcosm in which power hierarchies are continuously enacted. Gender hierarchy is central to such ritual performances but it is not the only hegemonic form thus implicated. Third, a focus on the reproduction of labor power alerts us to the importance of the division of labor by sex, especially in its non-commoditized, domestic forms. But even as we place issues like the "double day" squarely within the frame of our analysis, we must be careful not to assume that the domestic exploitation of women is inevitable, or "required" by a given mode of production. Fourth, sensitivity to the tensions and contradictions of total social reproduction allows us to see that conditions of gender hierarchy which appear to be "about" reproduction often mystify productive relations as well. Moreover, hierarchical gender arrangements that seem at one moment to be central to a given social system may at another be so ideologically weighted as to mobilize people toward its transformation. It is with these lessons in mind that I now turn to my second strategy, the interpretation of amniocentesis in contemporary American culture as an expression and potential source of transformation of gender hierarchies in reproduction.

Amniocentesis and reproductive hierarchies

From 1985 on, I have conducted fieldwork in New York City on the social impact and cultural meaning of amniocentesis. The issue of power hierarchies permeates the research, which focuses on the shifting meanings of pregnancy, motherhood, and parenthood in a multicultural population. Before power relations can be explored, however, a few words on both the social context and the methodological boundaries of the data are in order.

Amniocentesis and diagnostic ultrasound, with which amniocentesis is closely associated, are the most routinized of the new reproductive technologies. This test is quite literally an intervention into human reproduction. After counseling and legal acknowledgment of "informed consent," a woman can have the test between her sixteenth and twentieth week of pregnancy. Test results will be known prior to the legal limit on abortion, should she discover a genetic disability in her fetus and want to end the pregnancy. Initially developed to provide a prenatal screen for Down's Syndrome, one òf the leading causes of mental retardation worldwide, the test can also be used to detect up to 200 conditions, most of them quite rare recessively transmitted diseases. The test and appropriate genetic counseling can provide a couple with the opportunity to know in advance if their fetus will have a disability, and then to decide, if the test is positive, whether to continue or end the pregnancy.

The New York City study

In America, amniocentesis has become a new pregnancy ritual for white, middle-class, professional families in which women have delayed child-bearing till their mid-thirties or later in order to further their education and careers. In New York City, the situation is somewhat different. The Prenatal Diagnosis Laboratory was set up by the city's Health Department explicitly to offer the test to low-income women. Its services are partially subsidized by city and state health budgets; it accepts Medicaid, and all third-party insurance, and uses a sliding-scale fee which begins at zero. In principle, no woman who wants the test should be denied it in New York City. In practice, the Lab collects amniotic fluid samples from a population which is approximately one-third Hispanic, one third African–American, and one-third white. About 50 percent of the women seen by the Lab's genetic counselors are clinic (low-income) patients, and about 50 percent are private (middle-class) patients. From an anthropologist's perspective, the facility is thus a useful "social" laboratory as well as a biological one.

My fieldwork covered seven contexts, or constituencies in pursuit of locating and interpreting conflicting interests in and meanings of the technological transformation of pregnancy, motherhood, and family life.

> I worked in the Laboratory itself, observing the daily, dense interactions of geneticists, labor technicians, genetic counselors, and service personnel who work on this frontier of reproductive medicine.
>
> I interviewed thirty-five genetic counselors, at least one from each facility in New York City where amniocentesis is performed, in order to understand both the formation of a new female profession and its practitioners' perceptions of their polyglot patient population.
>
> I observed over 250 intake interviews in city hospitals, where genetic counselors explain heredity and amniocentesis to preg-

nant women of different ethnic and linguistic backgrounds who must decide to have or refuse the test.

I interviewed a sample of Hispanic, African–American, and white women, and their families who were awaiting results from their tests at home, to discover what they think about the potential benefits and burdens that the new reproductive technology offers.

I retrospectively interviewed thirty-five women who received positive diagnoses and had to make a decision to end or continue a pregnancy after technology revealed a fetus with a disability.

I participated in a support group for families whose children have Down's Syndrome to understand better the social, rather than just the medical, impact of a genetic disability which can now be prenatally diagnosed.

Lastly, I interviewed thirty women who refused to use amniocentesis or, having used it, opted to continue their pregnancies after receiving a positive diagnosis, in order to understand the rejection of the new reproductive technology and its consequences.

Hierarchies of discourse

Deploying the language and technology of genetics and reproductive medicine, genetic counselors, obstetricians, radiologists, and sometimes geneticists express concern for a woman's reproductive choice. But the language in which that concern is communicated is already constructed by prior hierarchies. Most obviously, the language of genetic counseling is English. While perhaps 20 percent of the genetic counselors practicing in city hospitals speak some Spanish (and at least five are native speakers), only one claims any French, and most are monolingual. This is an essential problem: all clinic counselors report 20 to 95 percent Spanish-speaking patients, and in at least one hospital virtually all the African–American patients are recently arrived Haitian migrants who speak little or no English. Budget cuts in the 1980s cost the city its medical translation services, so the information a woman needs to make an ethically and culturally complex choice is often being communicated to her in a foreign language. Sometimes, translation problems are subtle. As one Hispanic counselor put it.

When I see confusion, I go to work, I tell them in language they will understand, language of the streets. This knowledge is more than genetic. They learn about things that were completely hidden, where the eggs are, what sperm does, how children get to look like their parents. They have ideas, but this is female physiology, it is knowledge, not just information, for this, they come back.

English-speaking counselors rarely communicate this way. At other times, translation problems are dramatically literal: no term exists in Haitian Creole for Down's Syndrome, and pregnant women do not recognize the French term. For them, the rationality of prenatal diagnosis via medical discourse is questionable at best.

The discourse of medicine itself is a hierarchical one. It assumes scientific literacy, a focus on the individual body as the locus of health and illness, and a trust in specialists to effect prevention and cure. This is, of course, a world view which belongs to the powerful sectors of the American class structure, and is not shared by members of less powerful sectors. Given the multiple translation problems of language and discourse and the anger and mistrust many clinic patients feel in crowded, busy hospitals, radical breaks in communication often occur. As one Haitian father, firmly rejecting amniocentesis on his pregnant wife's behalf, told me, "The counselor says this baby could be retarded. What is this retarded? They always say Haitian children are retarded in the schools. But when we put them in the Haitian Academy [a community-based school], they do just fine." In his experience, chromosomes do not loom large as an explanation for the problems a Haitian child may face. Reliance on English and medical discourse allows medical personnel to mirror the concerns of many of the white middle-class women and couples who come for amniocentesis, but such linguistic practices often signal a language gap which is also a power gap when addressing patients of other classes and ethnic groups.

Home-based interviews reveal other power hierarchies involved in the use of amniocentesis. Most obviously, there are women who are coerced into the test by their men in their lives who do not want a "defective" child. Several Hispanic women told me they would never consider abortion, but that their mates insisted on the test. The reverse situation also occurs. Some Hispanic women took the test secretly, and were determined to plead miscarriage should they decide to abort, in order to silence the mistrust of a mate. They want the "freedom of choice" it represents but are distressed by the "selfish image" its use summons up. Gender hierarchy is locally fraught with instability: a woman may use the cultural meaning of motherhood to define and defend herself as nurturant, even to disabled fetuses, or she may claim the power of abortion to define herself against the cultural status of a madonna. Or, the test may force her to become conscious of the competing definitions of women through maternity that currently inform her own life.

Amniocentesis is also an emergent *rite de passage* for many of the women who use it. Most obviously, the obligatory sonogram which accompanies the test powerfully shapes the pregnant woman's image of her fetus. Such sonograms and the karyotypes constructed in the lab to examine fetal chromosomes sometimes are used in birth announcements. Sadly, sonograms are also placed in family Bibles and funerary rituals of women who aborted after prenatal diagnoses revealed fetal disabilities. Technology here creates strong images which give medicine the power to separate and define the fetus, apart from its mother. Such decomposition and recompositon of fetal imagery loom large in both the feminist critique of the new reproductive technologies, and the political right, where anti-abortionists have used sonography to gory advantage (Rothman 1986; Corea 1985; Arditti, Klein, and Minden 1984; Petchesky 1987). In complex ways, both movements identify fetal imaging and amniocentesis as "male." Many feminists see it as a patriarchal take-over of women's reproductive capacities, while the political right sees it as the necessary reassertion of paternal authority over women run selfishly amuck.

But the ritual of amniocentesis may hold multiple meanings. Many African-American women I interviewed consider amniocentesis and sonography opportunities to confirm signs, dreams, and pregnancy lore – alternative systems of understanding the meaning of a given pregnancy. For Hispanic women, there was a tendency to discuss amniocentesis and possible abortion in light of maternal/child fusion. Many Latina women, whatever their class, referred implicitly or explicitly to suffering madonnas and Christ-children. Neither group was likely to use the discourse of self-actualization and selfishness which permeated my interviews with white women.

Paradoxically, the group which is best served by advances in modern reproductive medicine, white middle-class women, also seems most vulnerable to its powerful definitions of motherhood and the political struggles that now surround the issue of abortion. White women seem most frightened of becoming "agents of quality control on the reproductive production line." Amniocentesis may indeed be becoming an emergent ritual of pregnancy. But it reflects and refracts the complex fault lines along which gender hierarchy joins with class, ethnicity, and religion in constructing the polyglot culture of contemporary American life.

Hierarchies of work

It is possible to interpret amniocentesis through the lens of "reproduction" in the sense of reproducing the labor force as well. Most obviously, reproductive labors are women's work – not only are pregnant women the clients for this new reproductive service, but virtually all the workers in this "industry" are female. Geneticists working in this field are disproportionately women. Unlike the research frontiers of molecular biology where men predominate, medical genetics is known to be hospitable to women. The field is "female" because it provides 9-to-5 working hours without late-night emergencies. It is thus compatible with the domestic sexual division of labor. More than 98 percent of all genetic counselors are female, and while they are experts in a technical and rapidly changing science, they are situated like social workers in the medical hierarchy. They "interface" with female patients, providing both epidemiological statistics and empathy. They are paid commensurately with social workers. Most lab technicians are women, as well. This work is often cited as appropriately "feminine" because it focuses on pregnancy and it does not disrupt family responsibilities. A new field of employment at the cutting edge of genetics thus emerges with job descriptions, prestige, and pay scales that reproduce current American hierarchies.

Does the use of amniocentesis affect the reproduction of labor power in any obvious ways? Most ideologically, it appears to give new "choices" about the limits of the work imposed by motherhood. The New Woman who has genetic counseling is offered the possibility of defining the boundaries of what constitutes an acceptable child and what kind of child she will mother. She may well decide that a child with a disability is more than she wants to undertake, given a choice. Sometimes, New Men emerge (most often, among white middle-class couples), articulating their desires, fears, and fantasies about disabled and able-bodied children.

But this New Woman is limited in at least two ways. The first is the meaning of acceptable and unacceptable children, when viewed without the universalizing and eugenic lens of the new reproductive technologies. The meaning of each disability that amniocentesis can now diagnose is, of course, particular. Down's Syndrome is not spina bifida, nor is it sickle-cell anemia or Tay-Sachs disease. Mental retardation, physical limitations, pain, suffering, child death all have specific cultural and individual meanings. Down's Syndrome may be much more frightening to a family in which all relatives are college-educated and hold professional aspirations for their children than it is in minority communities. There, childhood disabilities are more common, and the ideals of advancement toward the American dream through education and professional status are filtered through the realities of ghetto life. And some diseases have political meanings, as well: sickle-cell screening was offered with great insensitivity and highly politicized in the early 1970s. African–American women offered the test are less likely to want it, or to abort affected fetuses after a diagnosis, than is the population offered amniocentesis for chromosome defects. It is equally important not to romanticize the suffering and nurturance of minority mothers, not to stigmatize the judgments against mental retardation often made by white middle-class mothers. Both are responding to the shifting meanings of motherhood and health politics in their respective communities.

There is another way in which the choices offered by amniocentesis are limited. Despite the rhetoric of "post-feminist" assertions that women now "have it all" which pervades popular American culture, the realities of the double day are not so dramatically transformed. Being the working mother of any child is hard work, and a disabled child is assumed by many to add to those burdens. "Career women" may not want to cope with a disabled child. But that seemingly private and "selfish choice" must be interpreted in relation to public culture. In American society, little has changed for working mothers. The social services, day care, job opportunities, equity following divorce, and the like, which would make the "choice" of motherhood less problematic still lag behind the discourse of female freedom articulated in mainstream America. For the families of disabled children, even less has changed. Despite a decade's ferment around educational opportunities, the services needed to allow disabled children and their families to flourish barely exist. A disproportionate share of the work of finding resources for disabled children is done by their mothers. More pervasively, the social stigmas – including a family's "courtesy stigma" in Goffman's (1963) provocative term – with which Americans view "dependency" make it difficult to "choose" actively to give birth to a disabled child.

Gender hierarchies define child-raising as "women's work" which takes place in the private domain. American society takes less responsibility for social services affecting parents and children than most other Western societies. And class/race hierarchies powerfully mold the possibilities for maternal employment, maternal/child health, and children's futures. Disability remains a cultural stigma and a fantasized nightmare for many able-bodied Americans. Given these attitudes, the segregation and fear of disabled people remains widespread. As long as these multiple hierarchies of power and powerlessness continue to intersect and reproduce one another, the "liberation" offered to women by amniocentesis will remain limited, at best.

The reproduction of gender hierarchies

When we turn to "total social reproduction," the power of the cross-cutting hierarchies described above is clear. They are implicated in the cultural ideology which amniocentesis both represents and reproduces. The discourse of heredity and genetics has provided metaphors for human perfectibility in American culture for over a hundred years. Mainstream America is enchanted with the potentialities each human being appears to hold within itself, to develop itself. Yet the clamor of heredity often silences the social limitations which also shape what individuals, families, and communities can "make of themselves." Exciting developments on the frontier of genetic engineering advance claims for the perfectibility of individuals that are deeply consonant with American cultural traditions.

But those claims are fraught with tensions and contradictions. It is true that amniocentesis offers some women relief from the privatized, individualized burdens of raising children stigmatized as unacceptable, in a society which gives little social support or cultural respect to the work that all mothers do. But the price many women pay for using prenatal diagnosis is the internalization of its contradictions. They fear their own "selfishness," even as they welcome their own "self-actualization" outside the private domain of motherhood. For minority women, the contradictions are multiple. They are far less likely than white women to have access to adequate prenatal care in the first place, and amniocentesis is articulated in a language they may not understand very well, for reasons of literal mistranslation or lack of scientific literacy. For some, it has eugenic overtones, as well. Their suspicions about prenatal diagnosis lend themselves to both a reproduction of, and a resistance to, the burdens of mainstream American definitions of motherhood.

The silences surrounding disability also reproduce American cultural hierarchies. There is little mention of disability in social, rather than medical, terms in the training of genetic counselors and most obstetricians and geneticists, and in the discourse of popular culture through which pregnant women of all classes, races, and language groups come to their values about motherhood. While the "tragedy of birth defects should not come as a surprise" (to quote one March of Dimes poster), the cultural suppression of difference in American life is profound. Disability remains an individual, medically defined problem, rather than an issue of social and cultural values and potentials. Under these conditions, refusing amniocentesis seems an unlikely choice for rational women to make. Thus the discourse and the silences surrounding amniocentesis contribute to the reproduction of hierarchies of gender, class, and able-bodiedness in American life.

But amniocentesis may hold the potential to disrupt some of the most deeply held American ideologies, as well. For its routinization points to the cultural instability of pregnancy, motherhood, and family life in contemporary America. As "reproduction" becomes an increasingly contested domain, its social, rather than private, nature is increasingly revealed. Struggles over abortion rights, sterilization abuse, services for children, access to medical care as well as relief from medical abuses have all erupted during the period since World War II. New social groups in formation, like disability rights activists, and older groups in trans-formation, like feminists and minority community activists, are engaged in a complex choreography of cultural self-definition. Their claims must be viewed as part of the political life of advanced capitalist states, where contests over equality and the socially necessary "quality of life" are often phrased in legal-medical language. In this political discourse, quality control of fetuses is not inconsistent with demands for decent prenatal care.

Only in this larger context of a politicized social drama can we begin to see how amniocentesis both reproduces existing hierarchies and might hold out the potential for their disruption. As reproduction is increasingly understood as cultural not natural, and social not private, the technocratic promise of prenatal diagnosis might be redeemed through the radical demedicalization of scientific literacy and the development of humane social services for all. In such a Utopian scenario, the connections between reproduction and gender hierarchy would cease to appear totalizing.

NOTES

I thank the National Science Foundation and the National Endowment for the Humanities for funding the research on which this chapter is based. Scores of health professionals have encouraged this work because they believe it will help them to serve better their patients from varied cultural backgrounds. Hundreds of women have shared their amniocentesis stories with me. I am grateful to them all. For other descriptions of the findings from this study, see Rapp 1987, 1988a, 1988b, 1990.

1 These perspectives work best, and most critically, when anthropologists turn their gaze directly toward the analysis of North American and European reproductive practices. In this literature, male dominance and medical hege-mony hold pride of place, along with the romance of natural maternity (see Romalis 1981; Homans 1985; Stolcke 1986).

2 There is a vast Marxist–feminist literature which has been glossed as "the housework debates" concerning the value and function of domestic labor in the capitalist mode of production. Introductions to it are found in Barrett (1980), Fox (1980), and Luxton and Rosenberg (1980). The applicability of debates on domestic labor to incompletely capitalized, kin-based societies is discussed by Benería and Sen (1981, 1982).

3 Double-day analyses first emerged in Latin America and Eastern Europe where activists called attention to the burdens of housework for women who also participate in the labor market. The relation of waged to wageless work for women is explored in Young, Wolkowitz, and McCullagh (1981) and Benería and Sen (1981, 1982).

4 The initial debate was fueled by Althusser and Balibar (1971) and Althusser (1971). Responses include Hindess and Hirst (1975), but see also Thompson (1978) for a criticism of Althusser, and see Elliott (1986) for a political history and critique of Hirst.

REFERENCES

Althusser, Louis 1971 Ideological Apparatuses of the State. In *Lenin and Philosophy, and Other Essays*. Ben Brewster, trans., pp. 23–70. New York: Monthly Review Press.

Althusser, Louis and Etienne Balibar 1971 *Reading Capital*. Ben Brewster, trans. New York: Pantheon Books.

Arditti, Rita, Renate Duelli Klein, and Shelley Minden, eds. 1984 *Test-Tube Women: What Future for Motherhood?* Boston: Routledge & Kegan Paul.

Barrett, Michele 1980 *Women's Oppression Today: Problems in Marxist Feminist Analysis*. London: NLB.

Benería, Lourdes and Gita Sen 1981 Accumulation, Reproduction, and Women's Role in Economic Development. *Signs* 7(2):279–98.

1982 Class and Gender Inequalities and Women's Role in Economic Development. *Feminist Studies* 8:157–76.

Browner, Carole 1982 The Social Formation of Childbirth: A Review of Recent Research. *Medical Anthropology Newsletter* 14(1):6–13.

Callaway, Helen 1978 The Most Essentially Female Function of All: Giving Birth. In *Defining Females: The Nature of Women in Society*. Shirley Ardener, ed., pp. 163–85. New York: John Wiley and Sons.

Corea, Gena 1985 *The Mother-Machine: Reproductive Technologies from Artificial Insemination to Artificial Wombs*. New York: Harper and Row.

Cosminsky, Sheila 1980 Childbirth and Change: A Guatemalan Study. In *Ethnography of Fertility and Birth*. Carol P. MacCormack, ed., pp. 205–30. New York: Academic Press.

Deere, Carmen Diana 1976 Rural Women's Subsistence Production in the Capitalist Periphery. *Review of Radical Political Economics* 8:9–17.

1977 Changing Social Relations of Production and Peruvian Peasant Women's Work. *Latin American Perspectives* 4:48–69.

Donham, Donald 1985a History at One Point in Time: "Working Together" in Maale, 1975. *American Ethnologist* 12(2):262–84.

1985b *Work and Power in Maale*. Ann Arbor, MI: UMI Research Press.

DuBois, Lindsay n.d. The Museum of the Disappeared: Culture, Politics and Gender in Recent Argentine History. Ph.D. dissertation in progress, Department of Anthropology, New School for Social Research, New York City.

Edholm, Felicity, Olivia Harris, and Kate Young 1977 Conceptualising Women. *Critique of Anthropology* 3(9/10):101–30.

Ehrenreich, Barbara, Annette Fuentes, and Holly Sklar 1983 *Women and the Global Assembly Line*. Institute for Policy Studies pamphlet. Boston: South End Press.

Elliot, George 1986 The Odyssey of Paul Hirst. *New Left Critique* 159:81–105.

Elson, Diane and Ruth Pearson 1981 The Subordination of Women and the Internationalisation of Factory Production. In *Of Marriage and the Market:*

Women's Subordination in International Perspective. Kate Young, Carol Wolkowitz, and Rosalyn McCullagh, eds., pp. 144–66. London: CSE Books.

Fox, Bonnie, ed. 1980 *Hidden in the Household: Women's Domestic Labour under Capitalism.* Toronto: Women's Educational Press.

Ginsburg, Faye and Rayna Rapp 1991 The Politics of Reproduction. *Annual Review of Anthropology* 20:311–43.

Goffman, Erving 1963 *Stigma: Notes on the Management of Spoiled Identity.* Englewood Cliffs, NJ: Prentice-Hall.

Harris, Olivia 1981 Households as Natural Units. In *Of Marriage and the Market: Women's Subordination in International Perspective.* Kate Young, Carol Wolkowitz, and Rosalyn McCullagh, eds., pp. 49–68. London: CSE Books.

1982 Households and Their Boundaries. *History Workshop Journal* 13:143–52.

Hindess, Barry and Paul Q. Hirst 1975 *Pre-Capitalist Modes of Production.* Boston: Routledge and Kegan Paul.

Homans, Hilary, ed. 1985. *The Sexual Politics of Reproduction.* London: Gower.

Jordan, Brigitte 1980 *Birth in Four Cultures: A Crosscultural Investigation of Childbirth in Yucatan, Holland, Sweden and the United States.* 2nd edition. Montreal: Eden Press Women's Publications.

1987 The Hut and the Hospital: Information, Power and Symbolism in the Artifacts of Birth. *Birth* 14(1):36–40.

Kay, Margarita A., ed. 1982 *Anthropology of Human Birth.* Philadelphia, PA: F. A. Davis Co.

Lessinger, Johanna 1986 Work and Modesty: The Dilemma of Women Traders in South India. *Feminist Studies* 12:581–600.

Luxton, Meg and Harriet Rosenberg 1980 *Through the Kitchen Window: The Politics of Home and Family.* Toronto: Garamand Press.

MacCormack, Carol P., ed. 1982 *Ethnography of Fertility and Birth.* New York: Academic Press.

Mamdani, Mahmood 1972 *The Myth of Population Control: Family, Caste, and Class in an Indian Village.* New York: Monthly Review Press.

Marx, Karl 1947 *Capital.* Vol. 1. New York: International Publishers.

Mead, Margaret and Niles Newton 1967 Cultural Patterning of Perinatal Behavior. In *Childbearing: Its Social and Psychological Aspects.* Stephen A. Richardson and Alan Guttmacher, eds., pp. 142–244. Baltimore, MD: Williams and Wilkins Co.

Meillassoux, Claude 1981 *Maidens, Meal, and Money: Capitalism and the Domestic Community.* Felicity Edholm, trans. New York: Cambridge University Press.

Michaelson, Karen L., ed. 1981 *And the Poor Get Children: Radical Perspectives on Population Dynamics.* New York: Monthly Review Press.

Morsy, Soheir 1982 Childbirth in an Egyptian Village. In *Anthropology of Human Birth.* Margarita A. Kay, ed., pp. 147–74. Philadelphia, PA: F. A. Davis Co.

Nag, Moni 1980 How Modernization Can Also Increase Fertility. *Current Anthropology* 21(5):571–88.

Nag, Moni, Benjamin N. F. White, and R. Creighton Peet 1978 An Anthropological Approach to the Study of the Economic Value of Children in Java and Nepal. *Current Anthropology* 19(2):293–306.

Naponen, Helzi 1985 Organizing Women Petty Traders. Paper presented at the Asian Regional Conference on Women and the Household in Asia, New Delhi.

Newman, Lucile 1970 Cultural Factors in Family Planning. *Annals of the New York Academy of Sciences* 175 (30 October):833–46.

1972 *Birth Control: An Anthropological View.* An Addison-Wesley Module in Anthropology, Module 27. Reading, MA: Addison-Wesley Publishing Company.

Petchesky, Rosalind 1987 Fetal Images: Reproductive Politics in the Age of Visual Culture. *Feminist Studies* 13(2):263–92.

Polgar, Stephen, ed. 1972 *Culture and Population.* New York: Schenkman.

1975 *Population, Ecology and Social Evolution.* The Hague: Mouton.

Raphael, Dana 1975 Matrescence, Becoming a Mother, a New/Old *Rite de Passage.* In *Being Female: Reproduction, Power and Change.* Dana Raphael, ed., pp. 65–72. The Hague: Mouton.

Rapp, Rayna 1987 Moral Pioneers: Women, Men and Fetuses on a Frontier of Reproductive Technology. *Women and Health* 13(1/2):101–16.

1988a Chromosomes and Communication: The Discourse of Genetic Counseling. *Medical Anthropology Quarterly* 2(2):143–57.

1988b The Power of "Positive" Diagnosis. In *Childbirth in America: Anthropological Perspectives.* Karen Michaelson, ed., pp. 103–16. South Hadley, MA: Bergin and Garvey Publishers.

1990 Constructing Amniocentesis: Maternal and Medical Voices. In *Negotiating Gender in America.* Faye Ginsburg and Anna Tsing, eds., pp. 28–42. Boston: Beacon Press.

Romalis, Shelly, ed. 1981 *Childbirth: Alternatives to Medical Control.* Austin: University of Texas Press.

Rothman, Barbara Katz 1986 *The Tentative Pregnancy.* New York: Norton.

Sanjek, Roger 1982 The Organization of Households in Adabraka: Toward a Wider Comparative Perspective. *Comparative Studies in Society and History* 24:57–103.

Sargent, Carolyn 1982 Solitary Confinement: Birth Practices among the Sariba of the People's Republic of Benin. In *The Anthropology of Human Birth.* Margarita Kay, ed., pp. 193–210. Philadelphia, PA: F. A. Davis Co.

Sharma, Kumud 1984 Women in Struggle: A Case Study of the Chipko Movement. *Samya Shakti: A Journal of Women's Studies* 1(2):55–62.

Stolcke, Verena 1986 New Reproductive Technologies: Same Old Fatherhood. *Critique of Anthropology* 6:5–32.

Thompson, E. P. 1978 *The Poverty of Theory and Other Essays.* New York: Monthly Review Press.

Young, Kate, Carol Wolkowitz, and Rosalyn McCullagh, eds. 1981 *Of Marriage and the Market.* London: CSE Books.

6   Variations in male–female dominance and offspring care in non-human primates

Patricia Chapple Wright

Many of the early stereotypes of gender hierarchies within non-human primates were based on cursory observations of baboons, vervets, and macaques (Hall and DeVore 1965). In these groups a strict dominance hierarchy between males and females exists, with males dominant over females in most cases (Kawai 1958; Kawamura 1958; Sade 1967). Because of a combination of factors – including a lack of extensive fieldwork on most non-human primates and the prevailing social and political climate – the image or dominant, "corporation-type" males having roots in our primate history intrigued the press and became ingrained in the public's mind (Ardrey 1967; Tiger 1969).

In the 1970s the surge in examining human behavior from a sociobiological perspective led to superficial assumptions about dominance based on studies of insects and birds (Wilson 1975; Barash 1977). Early models derived from these studies suggested that images of the coy, nurturing female, and the protective, dominant male had a biological basis. The doctrine that appeared in the press was deterministic and oversimplified. It was not so much the basic concepts of evolutionary theory that were problematic, but more the limited data base on few species and the interpretations of these data which resulted in these representations. The simple fact that evolutionary pressures act on both males and females was ignored and this oversight resulted in a male bias in interpreting observations (Hrdy 1981; Small 1984). Fortunately, these sociobiologists inspired a wave of behavioral ecologists to do extensive fieldwork to test some of these hypotheses.

Reviewing the data that primatologists have obtained from recent in-depth field observations, we realize how naïve and biased the earlier images were. There are approximately 200 species of primates, and in about 40 percent of them females are dominant or equal to males in status. At the family level, six out of ten families have females equal in rank or dominant over males and one of these families (Cebidae) has genera with females either equal, subordinate or dominant. Only in the great apes (Pongidae), the Old World monkeys (Cercopithecidae), and the bush-babies and lorises (Lorisidae) are females below males in the gender hierarchy. Long-term studies have shown that in one species of great ape, the female has the option of transferring out of her social group into a new one if circumstances, including the male's behavior, do not suit her (Harcourt 1978; Moore 1984; Symington 1987; Thompson-Handler *et al.* 1986).

As more data are accumulated from the wild on both male and female primates, it is increasingly obvious that females play an important role in structuring primate societies. In fact it may be the female's needs and her relationship to ecological factors that have led to the evolution of each type of social system and gender hierarchy (Wrangham 1980; Hrdy and Williams 1983; Wright 1986b; Van Schaik 1989). There is evidence that the central organizing principle of primate social life may be competition between females and between female lineages (Janson 1985; Van Schaik 1983). The basic dynamics of the mating system may depend on the degree to which females tolerate each other. The female of many species is not the coy, submissive, faithful creature that the early rhetoric proclaimed. Examining primate patterns we find that many females in many species are aggressive, competitive, promiscuous, and wander from their natal group (Small 1984). Males in some species are primary caretakers of infants (Wright 1984; Goldizen 1987) and in others are always subordinate to females (Pollock 1979a, 1979b; Jolly 1966, 1984; Hrdy and Whitten 1987; Richard 1978, 1987; Smuts 1987).

Gender hierarchies where females are first, second, or equal are all represented in the order Primates. In this chapter I examine these different gender hierarchies from an evolutionary perspective, placing special emphasis on the variations in female dominance and division of infant care, and the relationship between the two in non-human primates.

Female dominance

Definition and occurrence

One definition of a social system with female dominance is a social hierarchy in which females have feeding priority and can displace males from a location by physical combat or by more subtle signals (Jolly 1966, 1984; Hrdy 1981; De Waal 1986). Females lead groups in all travel, determine ranging behavior, and are first to reach food resources. Often males are excluded from fruit trees until the females have finished eating (Pollock 1979a). In groups with more than one adult female, dominance hierarchies may be determined by matrilineal descent, and the group leader is an older, established female, mother and grandmother to many of her group members (Taylor 1986; Sussman and Taylor 1985). Male group members are found on the periphery of the group. During most of the year they are docile followers, last in progressions, and last to enter food trees. In some species (for example, squirrel monkeys) males are ignored by females most of the year, being excluded from social inter-actions, even "conversations." A study of wild squirrel monkeys in Peru revealed that females gave and answered calls among each other, but males vocalized rarely (Smith 1984). In most lemurs the peripheralized males are amiably tolerated by the females and enter into "grooming groups." In most "spontaneous" situations, signals including grimaces, calls, or tail waving are enough to elicit male deference (De Waal 1986). But in a situation where there is priority, the male defers to the female. If he does not defer, he is cuffed across the face (Jolly 1966; Taylor 1986). This dominance continues into the breeding season, and female choice may be a major factor in mating.

Females are first in the gender hierarchy in all the Malagasy primates that have been studied. These prosimian primates have often been acknowledged as most closely allied to the early primate ancestors of humans (Clark 1959; Cartmill 1972). This fact suggests that perhaps in the earliest primate social hierarchies females had priority. It is an important question why this type of social system evolved so early in the order Primates; and if this social hierarchy evolved so early in the order Primates, we need to know which factors selected for the reverse in three of the ten primate families.

Species in which there is female dominance include squirrel monkeys from South America, talapoin monkeys, the smallest Old World monkey, and all the extant Malagasy primates from the tiny mouse lemur to the largest indri. Both the talapoin monkeys and the squirrel monkeys are small (1 kg), found in large groups (up to fifty to eighty members), have large home ranges, and have larger males than females (20 to 30 percent by body weight). The Malagasy primates range in size from the tiniest primate (50 gr) to the large indri (8 kg).

Breeding seasonality

All of the primates in which female dominance is systematic are strict seasonal breeders. Jolly (1984) suggests that strict seasonality implies food scarcity which may present extreme hardships and a particularly costly reproductive effort for females. This hypothesis is reasonable but not satisfactory as a sole explanation. Galagos are seasonal breeders in some locations, yet males are separate, but dominant. The small callithri-cids and cebids of South America have a costly reproductive effort and undergo seasons of the year when food is scarce, but are not seasonal breeders. For female primates the costs of lactation are heavy (Altmann 1980), yet female feeding priority and female dominance are not exclusive throughout the order Primates. Energetics alone cannot account for this system. As a corollary to this idea, a link has been suggested between female dominance, female higher energetic needs, and low metabolic rate (Richard and Nicoll 1987). All primates with low metabolic rate do not, however, have female dominance (McNab and Wright 1987), and this energetic explanation should be studied further.

If the cost of reproduction in an environment of scarce resources is not a total explanation for female priority, are there other factors that could contribute? In cases where females are seasonal breeders and the annual breeding is concentrated into a two to four-week period, there is male–male competition for mating only within this short period. The remainder of the year males do not harass females for sexual access. This means that females (and offspring) do not need to be "guarded" against other males and the advantage to females of having males close by may be minimal. If there are predators, and the males are big enough to fight them off, then it is always to the female's advantage to have males near to protect her and her infants. But the monkeys with female dominant systems are small in size, and the island of Madagascar, where the remainder of the female dominance occurs, has few predators. If males are not important for protection against predators, protection against harassment by other males, or assistance in infant care, it may be to the female's advantage to keep them peripheralized. The males then become solitary, as among mouse lemurs, or followers, thus missing out on choice food items as in the cases of diurnal lemurs and squirrel monkeys.

The dynamics of the society of seasonal breeding in non-human primates change during the two to four weeks of the breeding season. Squirrel monkey males have gained weight, increased testosterone levels, and are ready to fight continually for access to females (Jolly 1984). Lemur males, which have peanut-sized testicles throughout most of the year, suddenly have large testicles, more than double in size (Jolly 1966). Aggression between males becomes acute and canines are used as effective weapons. The winner in the competition will have the option to mate with the female, but she retains the choice of vetoing the male's advances. The lemur female is in estrus for less than ten hours. Like the squirrel monkey female, she can cycle a second or even third time, but then she stops cycling for another year. Timing is important to the reproductive success of both males and females. Strictly seasonal mating and male–male competition may be a major factor in the evolution of female priority.

Male care of infants

I should raise the possibility of a relationship between male care of infants and primate societies where females have priority. In no instance is extensive male care of infants – where the cost of infant care is energetically expensive – associated with seasonal breeding. Females do not assert their dominance by giving the infants over to males to help raise them. There is no correlation between male infant care and female dominance among the non-human primate species.

Co-dominance

Definition and occurrence

In co-dominant primate societies males and females have an equal opportunity for decision making in travel direction, in spatial location, and in priority to resources. The co-dominant system occurs in various taxonomic groups including the Tarsidae, Callithricidae, Cebidae (*Aotus, Callicebus*, and *Brachyteles*), Lemuridae (*Hapalemur griseus* and *Lemur mongoz*), and Hylobatidae. These species range in diet from the totally carnivorous tarsier to the leaf-eating siamang and gentle lemur to the fruit-eating tamarins, night monkeys, and gibbons. Most of the social systems are monogamous or polyandrous, but the muriquis of southeastern Brazil (*Brachyteles*) are found in multimale, multifemale groups with little sexual dimorphism (Milton 1985a, 1985b; Strier 1986). Many of the species are small or medium-sized, but gibbons, siamangs, and muriquis are among the largest of arboreal primates. Some species have extensive male parental care while in others the female is the primary caretaker.

Paternal certainty and male care of infants

In this section I review the relationships between co-dominance, body size, and male parental care among monogamous primates and then polyandrous primates. In almost all monogamous primates males and females are co-dominant; one exception is the Malagasy indri, with females dominant. By definition, a male is assured of paternal certainty in this mating system. Data from long-term field studies of primates indicate that some monogamous pairs remain together in a territory for many years. These pairs insure the fidelity of their mates by excluding all members of their species of the same sex from the territory. Territorial boundaries are rigid and defended by both sexes. Territories are advertised daily by elaborate duetting in almost all monogamous primates

(Wright, in press). Mating is a relatively rare event in monogamous pairs, but field observations of mating in the dusky titi (*Callicebus moloch*), night monkey (*Aotus trivirgatus*), yellow-handed titi (*Callicebus torquatus*), and the gibbon (*Hylobates lar*) indicate that only the paired adult male mates with the female (Koyama 1971; Robinson, Wright, and Kinzey 1987).

According to sociobiological theory, male parental care should evolve only where paternal certainty exists (Trivers 1972). Monogamy unquestionably exists in seven genera of primates (*Aotus, Callicebus, Hylobates, Symphalangus, Tarsius, Indri,* and *Avahi*), but the amount of paternal care varies widely among these groups. At one extreme there is extensive infant care by fathers in two of the South American genera (*Aotus* and *Callicebus*). Among these primates, fathers carry the offspring on their backs for the first three months, share food, babysit, and protect the infant for the first year. Females feed the infants milk only (Wright 1984). In the siamang (*Symphalangus*), an Asian ape, males carry the juveniles over long tree gaps during the second year, but the mother is the primary caregiver in the first year (Chivers 1974). In the indri (*Indri*), the largest lemur in Madagascar, and the Asian gibbon (*Hylobates*), the only paternal care that the infants and juveniles are given is protection from predators (Pollock 1979a; Raemakers 1979). The Asian tarsier has not been well studied in the wild, but no male parental care has been described and the tarsier male is too small even to offer the infant protection from predators.

This variation in the extent of paternal investment in primates that all have paternal certainty suggests that the evolution of male care involves other selection pressures. In order to understand better the relationship between body size, ecology, and extent of male care, I now review what is known about these topics for three size classes of monogamous primates.

First, I consider the small monogamous primates (150 grams). There are four species of tarsiers located on certain islands of the Philippines, Sumatra, Sulawesi, and Borneo. Only one species has been studied extensively in the wild (MacKinnon and MacKinnon 1981). This spectral tarsier (*Tarsius spectrum*) was found to be monogamous with each family group defending a small territory of 1 ha against other pairs and invading singles. The tarsier is nocturnal and among the smallest of all primates. Because of its size, the male tarsier cannot defend itself or its offspring. Instead, the infant is left alone on a branch where it remains motionless, hidden from predators. When the mother does move it from perch to perch, she carries it in her mouth like a mother cat carries a kitten. Tarsiers eat only large, living prey items such as lizards, orthopterans, snakes, small birds, and small mammals. Mothers deliver food to the infant and fathers have not been observed to bring food to the infant or to carry the infant. Perhaps additional fieldwork will reveal more care by fathers, but current knowledge indicates that tarsier infants are cared for only by their mothers.

There are two genera of South American monkeys (*Aotus* and *Callicebus*) and two species of Malagasy lemur (*Avahi laniger* and *Hapalemur griseus*) which fit into the category of medium-small monogamous primates (1 kg). The two South American monkeys have extensive paternal care, but male care of infants has not been described for the nocturnal lemur (*Avahi*) nor the diurnal lemur (*Hapalemur*). Nocturnal versus diurnal activity pattern can be eliminated as a causal factor for this difference since one of the South American monkeys is diurnal (*Callicebus*), while the other is nocturnal (*Aotus*). What factors can account for this distinct difference in parental care in primates of the same size? Let us examine ecological and behavioral differences between these two groups. The two South American monkeys eat primarily fruit, range about 700 m each day (or night) and have a territory of from 8 to 20 ha (Wright 1986b, 1989). The avahi is a sedentary leaf-eater whose home range is from 1 to 2 ha (Ganzhorn 1985). The diet of the gentle lemur (*Hapalemur griseus*) is primarily bamboo leaves and stems and home-range size is 4 to 10 ha with a daily path length of 425 m (Wright 1986a). The energetic requirements of traveling far along arboreal pathways in search of fruit for a small primate may be much higher than for a sedentary leaf-eater. Therefore the energetic constraints on the mother monkey may be so great that she cannot successfully obtain enough food to be able both to lactate and feed herself. (A lactating mother needs 50 percent more calories than a male of the same size to maintain body weight.) The mother lemur spends most of her time browsing on vegetation in trees or bamboos which are not spaced far apart. Perhaps this leaf-eating diet is less energetically costly to obtain and the mother can afford to lactate, feed herself, and give the infant primary care without assistance. The gentle lemur mother leaves her infant alone unprotected while she forages during the first month (Petter and Peyrieras 1970; Wright 1990), while the more sedentary avahi mother carries her infant during this first month (Ganzhorn 1985). The infants of both species are carried by mothers from the second to fourth month. Infant lemurs travel and feed independently after the fourth month.

Predation pressure may also be a factor affecting parental care. In the South American jungle there are many species of hawks, eagles, cats, snakes, and other monkeys which eat infant monkeys. Therefore fleeing from predators is an important skill. If a lactating mother has to flee from predators with an infant on her back, she might not successfully escape. The male is under less energetic constraints and it would be to the advantage of father, mother, and infant for the male to carry the infant to safety. In Madagascar there are fewer species to prey on lemur infants. There is only one carnivore big enough to be a threat and that is the puma-like fossa (*Cryptoprocta ferox*). Fewer species of large raptors are found in Madagascar than in South America. A possible explanation for the differences in male parental care in these two species could be related to a combination of an increased need for energy expenditure and a high risk from predation pressure in the South American monkeys. Therefore the male must share the burden of infant care in order for the infant to survive.

Large monogamous primates include all the lesser apes from Asia, the siamang weighing 13 kg and seven species of gibbon from 4 to 8 kg, and the largest of the Malagasy lemurs, the indri, weighing about 8 kg. All of these species are diurnal. Because of their size, and life in high treetops, predation pressure is minimal. All three range daily from 700 to 1000 m and have territories of 10 to 60 ha (Ellefson 1974; Chivers 1974; Pollock 1979b). All three eat leaves and fruits, but the gibbon is the most frugivorous of the group. Locomotor behavior is more costly for small animals than for larger-bodied forms (Taylor, Schmidt-Nielson, and Raab 1970). These large monogamous primates are about ten times larger than the small monogamous primates and yet their daily path length and territory size are only slightly longer and larger. The infant/maternal weight ratio is different between small and large-bodied primates, being much higher in the former. It is more costly energetically for a mother to carry an infant 45 percent of her body weight the same distance as for a mother whose infant is 10 percent of her body weight. Energetic constraints on larger females are no doubt much less than on smaller females and therefore carrying and nursing an infant may be possible without aid. If aid is not necessary, as in the large-bodied species, then the male does not help.

A polyandrous breeding system has been documented for one small primate group. Based on observations in captivity, early studies reported that the social system of the small callithricid primates was monogamous (Kleiman 1977). However, in the past decade field studies of these South American monkeys have revealed that the social system is an unusual one for mammals. There is most often one breeding female in each group while there may be two to four breeding males. A study (Terborgh and Goldizen 1985; Goldizen 1987) of saddle-backed tamarins in the Peruvian rain forest suggests that these males are unrelated, copulate with nearly equal frequency with the female, and all males help care for offspring by carrying, food sharing, and playing. Goldizen's long-term data on reproductive success of groups suggest that this cooperative breeding system is necessary for the survival of offspring. Although monogamous pairs were observed, there was not one case of a monogamous pair successfully rearing offspring. After a group recruits an additional adult male to help, one or two offspring a year are reared (Goldizen 1987). Shorter-term observations of other species of tamarins and marmosets in the wild suggest that this pattern of breeding system may be found throughout this family (Sussman and Kinzey 1984).

Although more studies are needed on these small South American callithricids before we can understand the evolutionary mechanisms that resulted in this breeding system, there is some suggestion that the factors that select for extensive male parental care in *Aotus* and *Callicebus* may be even more intense for the callithricids. These species are half the size of the monogamous species, eat fruits and insects, have larger territories (20 to 120 ha) and almost always give birth to twins. Energetically the females are carrying an even greater burden than *Aotus* and *Callicebus* females. Yet because of the distribution of small fruits and insects in the forest, a larger group size means increased territory size and more traveling, which is energetically more expensive. An addition of a female means a female and offspring which may more than double group size (twins are born annually and each offspring remains with the group for at least three years). If all the males mate with the female with equal frequency, there is an equal chance that any of them is the father of the twins. Males seem to be willing to opt for "probable paternity" in these species, and with this paternal "probability" factor, such unrelated males are willing to invest heavily in the raising of these infants.

Male dominance

Definition and occurrence

In social systems with male dominance, males have feeding priority, spatial priority, and often decide on travel routes. In these social systems, in most circumstances, all males can be dominant over all females (as among most cercopithecids, pongids and some Cebidae like *Ateles*) or a dominant male is first in a dominance hierarchy, but a female can be second, third, and fourth (as among some Cebidae like *Cebus*). In the latter system all males are not dominant over all females, but a male is always first in the overall hierarchy. Male priority is found in one-male groups, multi-male groups, or groups where males are separate or solitary much of the year (galagos, lorises, and orang-utans). Except for the lorises and galagos, males are larger in body weight than females and often the canines of males are larger. This sexual dimorphism may be a result of male–male competition, but evidence on the Malagasy primates (Richard 1987), as well as on the galagos and lorises, suggests that male competition is not an all-inclusive explanation.

Patterns of male parental care

Among one-male groups, a lone male remains with a group of two to thirty females, mates with all of them, and has priority over all the females. Theoretically, male parental care might evolve in these harems, since males are assured of paternity (Trivers 1972), but male parental care, except for defense of females, has not been observed in one-male social systems (Hrdy 1977; Fossey 1982). All of these species are large, and the same arguments may hold for them as for the large, monogamous primates. The energetic costs of raising an infant are not as high as for a smaller primate. If male aid is not necessary for the survival of the infant, then the male does not invest in paternal care. In harem systems females can also enlist other females to assist with infant care (Hrdy 1977).

Multi-male, multi-female groups are found among baboons, macaques, capuchins, spider monkeys, and chimpanzees. Group size can range from a dozen animals to hundreds. All of these species are large and many are terrestrial. Male parental care is found in many of these species including capuchins (Janson 1984), baboons (Stein 1984; Strum 1984, 1987; Smuts 1985), and macaques (Busse and Hamilton 1981; Taub 1984). However, the care is incidental, situation-dependent, and appears to be a strategy to gain access to the infant's mother the next time she is in estrus (Smuts 1985), or to avoid male aggression (Busse and Hamilton 1981). Paternal certainty is not a consideration in these cases. The males are not protecting their genetic investment but rather are protecting themselves from male aggression or expending energy toward successful mating in the future.

Reproductive strategies

There is growing evidence that some female primates can mate outside the period in which fertilization is possible, or extend their period of receptivity, depending on mating conditions. Many of the females found in multi-male, male-dominated groups have sexual swellings which may be a long-distance advertisement for males, announcing female receptivity. In some baboon groups receptive females lead groups to the outer limits of the home range where the chance of encounters with males from other groups is increased. Some female long-tailed macaques in Sumatra retain their swellings for many weeks (Van Noordwijk 1985). Female pygmy chimpanzees show sexual swellings for extended periods and mate at all stages of their cycle (Thompson-Handler, Malenky, and Badrian 1984; Thompson-Handler *et al.* 1986; White 1986). In pygmy chimpanzees, some females mate with males and then take their food (Kano 1980), or feed closer to them in food trees (White 1986). All of these cases suggest that in multi-male groups there are many possibilities of manipulations by females to enhance mating success. Perhaps such manipulations serve as counter-strategies to offset a male-dominance gender hierarchy.

In yet another social system, solitary males visit several separate female territories (Charles-Dominique 1977). Species with solitary males include the nocturnal prosimians of Asia and Africa, the galagos and lorises, and one great ape, the orang-utan. Females may or may not show signs of estrus. Females may have consorts with males which last days or weeks (in the case of orang-utans) (Galdikas 1981). It is generally agreed that this separation of the sexes could be caused by the distribution of food resources (fruit and insects). Food is too scarce for both males and females to forage together in one area. In the case of the orang-utan, the large body size necessitates large quantities of food. In the case of the smaller nocturnal species, a solitary individual is more cryptic and thus avoids predators. The great apes have large body size and the infant/ maternal weight ratio is low which would predict that males do not carry offspring. They do not. In fact, male orang-utans avoid contact with mothers with infants. In galagos, where small body size might lead to paternal care, females instead have opted for leaving offspring in nests or parking them alone rather than carrying them while foraging. Females avoid and harass males when infants are vulnerable, and when lactating and needing more nutrition. In this social system, males are dominant but competition for food is high and the reproductive strategy for females is to avoid male interference.

Comparative perspective

Non-human primate patterns of gender hierarchy are rich and complex. Although many Old World monkeys have social systems where males and females have distinct dominance hierarchies, and all males are dominant over all females, females have strategies to protect themselves from males. Females with young avoid most males except fathers, and may use special relationships with other males to aid them in conflicts. Among the great apes, males may take food or supplant a female, but a female always has the option to transfer into another group without male interference, if the social situation does not suit her. Therefore, as seen in chimpanzees, the male is courteous to females (Noe *et al.* 1980; Smuts 1987). In the Malagasy prosimians and several species of monkeys, females are always dominant over males. In many monogamous species including the lesser apes (gibbons and siamangs) and several species of South American monkey, male and female are co-dominant. In many of these species females lead the group in food-finding and often get more and better nutrition by taking first choice of food items. In some of these species males assume the major burden of infant care. Carrying, playing, food-sharing, and protection are all duties of the father or helpers, while the mother's main duty is providing milk. In the larger-bodied monogamous species males do not provide assistance with infants because infant carry-ing is not as energetically costly. In the social system described for the tamarins and marmosets, females and males are co-dominant, but a female copulates with all adult males in the group. These unrelated males have possibilities of being the father of any offspring and invest heavily in infant care. In other species (baboons and macaques) there is some male parental care and general protection, yet this involvement appears to be a strategy to gain favor with certain females rather than to assure the survival of a male's infant (Smuts 1985; Goodall 1986).

An examination of the data obtained since the first explosion of sociobiological theory in the 1970s should convince us that the evolution of primate behavior has no simple explanation. Each species has evolved complex social behavior to adapt to certain environmental conditions. With this new field information in hand, we can make some important generalizations emerging from comparisons of non-human primate gender hierarchies that also are relevant to the study of gender inequality among humans:

1. Division of labor: In non-human primates there is little or no division of labor (that is, tasks specifically done only by males or females) for food procurement, and yet gender hierarchies with both males and females higher in the society or equal have been documented.

2. Sexual dimorphism: Female primates which have priority are not heavier in body weight than males (see also Silk, this volume). Might alone does not assure dominance. In co-dominant species (gibbons, muriquis, night monkeys, tamarins, and marmosets), the body weights of males and females are similar. Canines in female dominant or co-dominant social systems are similar for both sexes. If male–male com-petition is the principal pressure that selects for large male body weight and canine dimensions (Darwin 1871; Trivers 1972; Clutton-Brock and Harvey 1977), we must examine the lemurs more closely. In lemurs male–male competition is intense, but only seasonally. Perhaps female choice in selecting males of equal size is an influence (Richard 1987). Such

hypotheses cannot be tested with the data currently available, but these differences in sexual dimorphism should be kept in mind.

3. Male care of infants: There is no association between extensive male care of infants and gender hierarchies with female priority or even co-dominance. The new data suggest that male care of infants has evolved in small, co-dominant primates with paternal certainty, but is not as extensive in large co-dominant species with paternal certainty. Extensive male care has also evolved in co-dominant species where two to four unrelated males copulate without competition with a polyandrous female. Even with only the possibility of paternity these males are willing to invest heavily in infant care. In both of these cases of male care, field evidence suggests that the female might not be able to rear offspring successfully alone or, in the latter case, with only one male helper. Male care of infants is not found in one-male (male dominance) groups in Old World monkeys or apes, but is occasionally found in multi-male (male dominance) groups. There is evidence that in these multi-male groups, male assistance is a male strategy to gain sexual access to particular females (Smuts 1985; Taub 1984; Strum 1984). In all incidences males help with infants only when it is important to their reproductive success (successful raising of their offspring), or their protection or future mating effort.

4. Mating receptivity: The variations in receptivity of females found in the order Primates range along a continuum, with the Malagasy primates, squirrel monkeys and talapoins as strict seasonal breeders at one end, and the humans and pygmy chimpanzees (bonobos) with continual (situation-dependent) receptivity at the other extreme. The strictly seasonal breeders have female dominance, the one-female groups with the female in estrus during a brief period each year or every other year have co-dominance, and groups with more than one female have male dominance (except for the muriqui). From field studies we know that some of the females without outward signs of estrus can mate out of estrus – sham estrus (Hrdy 1977). Other females with sexual swellings that proclaim estrus can extend their time of receptivity (Van Noordwijk 1985) or mate at any time in the sexual cycle, for example pygmy chimpanzees (White 1986). Our recent knowledge of female promiscuity, wanderings, and deception leads us to re-evaluate the possibility that large male size may be a counter-strategy against female reproductive strategies in certain situations. A male in a multi-male, multi-female breeding system, in which females routinely solicit multiple partners and are sexually assertive, experiences a special challenge. But instead of just dominating females with large body size, they (for example in chimpanzees) may develop large testicles and the contest for reproductive success is partially decided at the level of sperm competition (Short 1977). However, it should be kept in mind that

consortship in common chimpanzees results in a higher frequency of pregnancy (Goodall 1986). This sperm competition may also be the strategy of the muriqui, a species where females and males are co-dominant, but live in multi-female, multi-male groups (Milton 1985b).

5. Predation pressure: It has been suggested that males are dominant over females in dangerous environments where predators are a major hazard (Ardrey 1967). Females may need large males as sentinels and protectors in many African habitats. It is hard to assess whether the South American rain forest is less dangerous than Asian or African rain forests. Predation pressure may account for the large size of males in medium–large primates in rain-forest environments, but it is difficult to explain in the same environment why muriquis, gibbons, and siamangs are co-dominant. The effect of predators on lemurs in Madagascar is being studied now to understand the relationship between predation and female dominance (Wright, work in progress). However, gorillas and orang-utans have less worry about predators and sexual dimorphism is most extreme in these species. Extremes of predation pressure are not the only factor influencing gender hierarchies in primates (Van Schaik and Van Hooff 1983; Van Schaik *et al.* 1983).

This review of gender hierarchies throughout the order Primates enables us to examine patterns seen in various environments and in taxonomic groups. If we examine factors such as division of labor, sexual dimorphism, male care of infants, female mating receptivity, and predation pressures seen in various non-human primates, no simple selective pressure emerges that explains the dominance of one sex over the other in any society. We do not understand fully the evolution of female-dominant or egalitarian societies among non-human primates, but these examples of the complexities of gender hierarchies in our order challenge us to have a broader understanding and perception of variations in human gender hierarchies.

NOTE

This chapter is dedicated to Dana Wheeler, linguist and primatologist, whose perspective, expertise, and inspiration helped to guide this writing. Dana died in a car collision in Spain before she could see this volume. I am grateful also to Adrienne Zihlman, Carel van Schaik, and Tab Rasmussen for additional excellent comments.

REFERENCES

Altmann, Jeanne 1980 *Baboon Mothers and Infants*. Cambridge, MA: Harvard University Press.
Ardrey, Richard 1967 *The Territorial Imperative*. London: Anthony Blond.
Barash, David 1977 *Sociobiology and Behavior*. New York: Elsevier Scientific Publishing Company.

Busse, Curt and William J. Hamilton 1981 Infant Carrying by Male Chacma Baboons. *Science* 212:1281–3.

Cartmill, Matt 1972 Arboreal Adaptations and the Origin of the Order Primates. In *The Functional and Evolutionary Biology of Primates*. Russell H. Tuttle, ed., pp. 97–122. Chicago: Aldine.

Charles-Dominique, Pierre 1977 *Ecology and Behaviour of Nocturnal Prosimians*. London: Duckworth.

Chivers, David J. 1974 *The Siamang in Malaya: A Field Study of a Primate in Tropical Rain Forest*. New York: S. Karger.

Clark, Wilfred E. LeGros 1959 *The Antecedents of Man: An Introduction to the Evolution of the Primates*. Edinburgh: Edinburgh University Press.

Clutton-Brock, Timothy H. and Paul H. Harvey 1977 Primate Ecology and Social Organization. *Journal of the Zoological Society London* 183:1–39.

Darwin, Charles 1871 *The Descent of Man, and Selection in Relation to Sex*. London: J. Murray.

De Waal, Frans 1986 Integration of Dominance and Social Bonding in Primates. *Quarterly Review of Biology* 611(4):459–79.

Ellefson, John O. 1974 A Natural History of White Handed Gibbons in the Malayan Peninsula. In *Gibbon and Siamang*, Vol. 3. Duane M. Rumbaugh, ed., pp. 1–136. Basle: S. Karger.

Fossey, Diane 1982 Reproduction among Free-Living Gorillas. *American Journal of Primatology Supplement* 1:97–104.

Galdikas, Birute 1981 Orangutan Reproduction in the Wild. In *Reproductive Biology of the Great Apes*. C. E. Graham, ed., pp. 281–300. New York: Academic Press.

Ganzhorn, Jorg U. 1985 Some Aspects of the Natural History and Food Selection of *Avahi laniger*. *Primates* 26(4):452–63.

Garber, Paul, Luis Moya, and Carlos Malaga 1984 A Preliminary Field Study of the Moustached Tamarin Monkey (*Saguinus mystax*) in Northeastern Peru: Questions Concerned with the Evolution of a Communal Breeding System. *Folia Primatologica* 42:17–32.

Goldizen, Anne W. 1987 Tamarins and Marmosets: Communal Care of Offspring. In *Primate Societies*. Barbara B. Smuts *et al.*, eds., pp. 34–43. Chicago: University of Chicago Press.

Goodall, Jane 1986 *The Chimpanzees of Gombe: Patterns of Behavior*. Cambridge, MA: Harvard University Press.

Hall, K. R. L. and Irven DeVore 1965 Baboon Social Behavior. In *Primate Behavior: Field Studies of Monkeys and Apes*. Irven DeVore, ed., pp. 53–110. New York: Holt, Rinehart and Winston.

Harcourt, Alexander H. 1978 Strategies of Emigration and Transfer by Primates, with Particular Reference to Gorillas. *Zeit Tierpsychologie* 48:401–20.

Harvey, Paul H. and Alexander H. Harcourt 1984 Sperm Competition, Testes Size and Breeding System in Primates. In *Sperm Competition and the Evolution of Animal Mating Systems*. David Smith, ed., pp. 589–600. New York: Academic Press.

Hrdy, Sarah Blaffer 1977 *The Langurs of Abu*. Cambridge, MA: Harvard University Press.

1979 Infanticide among Animals: A Review, Classification and Examination of the Implications for the Reproductive Strategies of Females. *Ethnology and Sociobiology* 1:13–40.

1981 *The Woman that Never Evolved*. Cambridge, MA: Harvard University Press.

Hrdy, Sarah Blaffer and Patricia Whitten 1987 The Patterning of Sexual Activity. In *Primate Societies*. Barbara B. Smuts *et al.*, eds., pp. 370–84. Chicago: University of Chicago Press.

Hrdy, Sarah Blaffer and G. Williams 1983 Behavioral Biology and the Double Standard. In *The Social Behavior of Female Vertebrates*. S. K. Wasser, ed., pp. 3–38. New York: Academic Press.

Janson, Charles H. 1984 Female Choices and Mating System of the Brown Capuchin Monkey (*Cebus apella*). *Zeit Tierpsychologie* 65:177–200.

1985 Aggressive Competition and Individual Food Consumption in Wild Brown Capuchin Monkeys (*Cebus apella*). *Behavioral Ecology and Sociobiology* 18:125–38.

Jolly, Alison 1966 *Lemur Behavior: A Madagascar Field Study*. Chicago: University of Chicago Press.

1984 The Puzzle of Female Feeding Priority. In *Female Primates: Studies by Women Primatologists*. Meredith E. Small, ed., pp. 197–215. New York: Alan R. Liss.

Kano, Takayoshi 1980 Social Behavior of Wild Pygmy Chimpanzees (*Pan paniscus*) of Wamba: A Preliminary Report. *Journal of Human Evolution* 9:243–60.

Kawai, Masao 1958 On the System of Social Ranks in a Natural Troop of Japanese Monkeys 1: Basic Rank and Dependent Rank. *Primates* 1:111–30.

Kawamura, S. 1958 Matriarchal Social Ranks in the Minoo-B Troop: A Study of the Rank System of Japanese Monkeys. *Primates* 1:148–56.

Kleiman, Devra 1977 Monogamy in Mammals. *Quarterly Review of Biology* 52:29–69.

Koyama, N. 1971 Observations on Mating Behavior of Wild Siamang Gibbons at Fraser's Hill, Malaysia. *Primates* 12:183–9.

Kummer, Hans 1968 *Social Organization of Hamadryas Baboons*. Chicago: University of Chicago Press.

MacKinnon, John 1974 The Behavior and Ecology of Wild Orangutans: *Pongo pygmaeus*. *Animal Behavior* 22:3–74.

MacKinnon, John and Kathleen MacKinnon 1981 The Behavior of Wild Spectral Tarsiers. *International Journal of Primatology* 1:361–79.

McNab, Brian and Patricia Wright 1987 Temperature Regulation and Oxygen Consumption in the Philippine Tarsier (*Tarsius syrichta*). *Physiological Zoology* 60(5):596–600.

Milton, Katharine 1985a Multimale Mating and Absence of Canine Tooth Dimorphism in Woolly Spider Monkeys (*Brachyteles arachnoides*). *American Journal of Physical Anthropology* 68:514–23.

1985b Mating Patterns of Woolly Spider Monkeys: Implications for Female Choice. *Behavioral Ecology and Sociobiology* 17:53–9.

Moore, James 1984 Female Transfer in Primates. *International Journal of Primatology* 5:537–89.

Noe, R., F. de Waal, and J. Van Hooff 1980 Types of Dominance in a Chimpanzee Colony. *Folia Primatologica* 34:90–110.

Petter, J. and André Peyrieras 1970 Observations éco-éthologiques sur les lémuriens malgaches du genre *Hapalemur*. *Terre et Vie* 24:356–82.

Pollock, Jonathan I. 1979a Female Dominance in *Indri indri*. *Folia Primatologica* 31:143–64.

1979b Spatial Distribution and Ranging Behavior in Lemurs. In *The Study of Prosimian Behavior*. Gerald A. Doyle and Robert D. Martin, eds., pp. 359–409. New York: Academic Press.

Raemakers, Jeremy 1979 Ecology of Sympatric Gibbons. *Folia Primatologica* 31:227–45.

Richard, Alison F. 1978 *Behavioral Variation: Case Study of a Malagasy Lemur*. Lewisburg, PA: Bucknell University Press.

1987 Malagasy Prosimians: Female Dominance. In *Primate Societies*. Barbara B. Smuts *et al.*, eds., pp. 25–33. Chicago: University of Chicago Press.

Richard, Alison F. and Martin E. Nicoll 1987 Female Dominance and Low Basal Metabolism in a Malagasy Primate, *Propithecus verreauxi*. *American Journal of Primatology* 12(3):309–14.

Robinson, John G., Patricia C. Wright, and Warren G. Kinzey 1987 Monogamous Cebids and their Relatives: Intergroup Calls and Spacing. In *Primate Societies*. Barbara B. Smuts *et al.*, eds., pp. 44–53. Chicago: University of Chicago Press.

Rodman, Peter 1979 Individual Patterns and the Solitary Nature of Orangutans. In *The Great Apes*. David A. Hamburg and Elizabeth McCown, eds., pp. 234–55. Menlo Park, CA: Benjamin/Cummings Publishing Company.

Sade, Donald S. 1967 Determinants of Dominance in a Group of Free-Ranging Rhesus Monkeys. In *Social Communication among Primates*. Stuart A. Altmann, ed., pp. 94–114. Chicago: University of Chicago Press.

Short, R. V. 1977 Sexual Selection and the Descent of Man. In *Proceedings of the Canberra Symposium on Reproduction and Evolution*. J. H. Calaby and C. H. Tyndale, eds., pp. 3–19. Canberra: Australian Academy of Sciences.

Small, Meredith E., ed. 1984 *Female Primates: Studies by Women Primatologists*. New York: Alan R. Liss.

Smuts, Barbara B. 1985 *Sex and Friendship in Baboons*. New York: Aldine.

1987 Sexual Competition and Mate Choice. In *Primate Societies*. Barbara B. Smuts *et al.*, eds., pp. 385–99. Chicago: University of Chicago Press.

Stein, David M. 1984 Ontogeny of Infant–Adult Male Relationships during the First Year of Life for Yellow Baboons (*Papio cynocephalus*). In *Primate Paternalism*. David M. Taub, ed., pp. 213–45. New York: Van Nostrand Reinhold Company.

Strier, Karen B. 1986 The Behavior and Ecology of Woolly Spider Monkeys or Muriquis (*Brachyteles arachnoides*). Ph.D. dissertation, Harvard University.

Strum, Shirley C. 1984 Why Males Use Infants. In *Primate Paternalism*. David M. Taub, ed., pp. 146–85. New York: Van Nostrand Reinhold Company.

1987 *Almost Human: A Journey into the World of Baboons*. New York: Random House.

Sussman, Robert W. and Warren G. Kinzey 1984 The Ecological Role of the Callitrichadae: A Review. *American Journal of Physical Anthropology* 64:419–49.

Sussman, Robert W. and Linda L. Taylor 1985 A Preliminary Study of Kinship and Social Organization in a Semi-Free Ranging Group of *Lemur catta*. *International Journal of Primatology* 6(6):601–13.

Symington, Margaret M. 1987 Sex Ratio and Maternal Rank in Wild Spider Monkeys: When Daughters Disperse. *Behavioral Ecology and Sociobiology* 20:421–6.

Taub, David M. 1980 Female Choice and Mating Strategies among Wild Barbary Macaques (*Macaca sylvanus L.*). In *The Macaques: Studies in Ecology, Behavior, and Evolution*. Donald G. Lindberg, ed., pp. 287–344. New York: Van Nostrand Reinhold Company.

   1984 Male Caregiving Behavior among Wild Barbary Macaques (*Macaca sylvanus*). In *Primate Paternalism*. David M. Taub, ed., pp. 20–55. New York: Van Nostrand Reinhold Company.

Taylor, C. R., Kurt Schmidt-Nielson, and J. L. Raab 1970 Scaling of Energetic Cost of Running to Body Size in Mammals. *American Journal of Physiology* 219:1104–7.

Taylor, Linda 1986 Kinship, Dominance and Social Organization in a Semi-Free Ranging Group of Ringtailed Lemurs (*Lemur catta*). Ph.D. dissertation, Washington University.

Terborgh, John T. 1983 *Five New World Primates: A Study in Comparative Ecology*. Princeton, NJ: Princeton University Press.

Terborgh, John T. and Anne W. Goldizen 1985 On the Mating System of the Cooperatively Breeding Saddle-Backed Tamarin (*Saguinus fuscicollis*). *Behavioral Ecology and Sociobiology* 16:293–9.

Thompson-Handler, Nancy, Richard K. Malensky, and Noel L. Badrian 1984 Sexual Behavior of *Pan paniscus* under Natural Conditions in the Lomako Forest, Equateur, Zaire. In *The Pygmy Chimpanzee: Evolutionary Biology and Behaviour*. Randall L. Sussman, ed., pp. 347–68. New York: Plenum Press.

Thompson-Handler, Nancy, Richard K. Malenky, Frances J. White, and Annette Lanjouw 1986 Reproductive and Affiliative Behavior and the Social Organization of Pygmy Chimpanzees. Paper presented at Understanding Chimpanzees Symposium, Chicago Academy of Sciences, Chicago.

Tiger, Lionel 1969 *Men in Groups*. New York: Random House.

Trivers, Robert L. 1972 Parental Investment and Sexual Selection. In *Sexual Selection and the Descent of Man, 1871–1971*. Bernard G. Campbell, ed., pp. 136–79. Chicago: Aldine.

Van Noordwijk, Maria A. 1985 Sexual Behavior of Sumatran Long-Tailed Macaques (*Macaca fascicularis*). *Zeit Tierpsychologie* 70:277–96.

Van Schaik, Carel P. 1983 Why Are Diurnal Primates Living in Groups? *Behaviour* 87:120–44.

   1989 The Ecology of Social Relationships amongst Female Primates. In *Comparative Socioecology: The Behavioral Ecology of Humans and Other Mammals*. Valerie Strander and Robert Foley, eds., pp. 195–223. Oxford: Blackwell Scientific Publications.

Van Schaik, Carel P. and Jan F. Van Hooff 1983 On the Ultimate Causes of Primate Social Systems. *Behaviour* 85:91–117.

Van Schaik, Carel P., Maria A. van Noordwijk, Bambang Warsono, and Edy Sutriono 1983 Party Size and Early Detection of Predators in Sumatran Forest. *Primates* 24:211–21.

White, Frances J. 1986 Behavioral Ecology of the Pygmy Chimpanzee. Ph.D. dissertation, State University of New York at Stony Brook.

Wilson, Edmund O. 1975 *Sociobiology: The New Synthesis.* Cambridge, MA: Harvard University Press.

Wrangham, Richard W. 1980 An Ecological Model of Female-Bonded Primate Groups. *Behaviour* 76:262–300.

Wright, Patricia C. 1984 Biparental Care in *Aotus trivirgatus* and *Callicebus moloch.* In *Female Primates: Studies by Women Primatologists.* Meredith E. Smith, ed., pp. 59–75. New York: Alan R. Liss.

1986a Diet Ranging Behavior and Activity Pattern of the Gentle Lemur (*Hapalemur griseus*) in Madagascar. *American Journal of Physical Anthropology* 69(2):283.

1986b Ecological Correlates of Monogamy in *Aotus* and *Collicebus.* In *Primate Ecology and Conservation.* James G. Else and Phyllis C. Lee, eds., pp. 159–67. New York: Cambridge University Press.

1989 The Nocturnal Primate Niche in the New World. *Journal of Human Evolution* 18:635–58.

1990 Paternal Care Patterns in Primates. *International Journal of Primatology* 11(2):89–102.

in press The Evolution of Loud Duets in Primates: A Comparison of the Behavioral Ecology of *Collicebus moloch* in Peru and *Hapalemur grisens* in Madagascar *Behavioral Ecology and Sociobiology.*

7 Indexing gender

Elinor Ochs

The micro-ethnography of gender hierarchy

Gender hierarchies display themselves in all domains of social behavior, not the least of which is talk. Gender ideologies are socialized, sustained, and transformed through talk, particularly through verbal practices that recur innumerable times in the lives of members of social groups. This view embodies Althusser's notion that "ideas of a human subject exist in his actions" and his rephrasing of Pascal's ideas in terms of the imperative "Kneel down, move your lips in prayer, and you will believe" (1971:158). Mundane, prosaic, and altogether unsensational though they may appear to be, conversational practices are primary resources for the realization of gender hierarchy.

In the course of the following discussion, I argue that the relation between language and gender is not a simple straightforward mapping of linguistic form to social meaning of gender. Rather the relation of language to gender is constituted and mediated by the relation of language to stances, social acts, social activities, and other social constructs. As such, novices come to understand gender meanings through coming to understand certain pragmatic functions of language (such as expressing stance) and coming to understand local expectations regarding the distribution of these functions and their variable expression across social identities.

With respect to gender hierarchy, I argue that images of women are linked to images of mothering and that such images are socialized through communicative practices associated with care-giving. Although mothering is a universal kinship role of women and in this role women universally have positions of control and power, their communicative practices as mothers vary considerably across societies, revealing differences in social positions of mothers. Mothers vary in the extent to which their communication with children is child-centered, or accommodating. Differences in caregiver communicative practices socialize infants and small children into different local images of women. These images may change over developmental time in the case that these young novices see

146

women using different communicative practices to realize different social roles (familial, economic, political). On the other hand, continuity in women's verbal practices associated with stance and social action in the enactment of diverse social roles may sustain images of women that emerge in the earliest moments of human life.

In the discussion I compare communicative practices of mothers in white, middle-class American households and in traditional Western Samoan households. Insights concerning mainstream American mothers derive from numerous child language development studies, particularly earlier research carried out by Schieffelin and myself on language socialization (Ochs and Schieffelin 1984; Schieffelin and Ochs 1986a, 1986b). Insights concerning mothering in Western Samoan households are based on a longitudinal language acquisition and language socialization study conducted in Falefaa, Western Samoa, during 1978–9 and in 1981 (Ochs 1982, 1986, 1987, 1988, 1990).[1]

Social meanings and indexicality

This section provides a general consideration of the relationship between language and gender, both how it has been examined, and how it can be more fruitfully examined. These comments on language and gender should be taken as representative of a more general relation between language and social meaning.

Sociological and anthropological studies of language behavior are predicated on the assumptions that language systematically varies across social contexts and that such variation is part of the meaning indexed by linguistic structures. Sociolinguistic studies tend to relate particular structures to particular situational conditions or clusters of structures to such conditions. The meanings so indexed are referred to as social meanings, in contrast to purely referential or logical meanings expressed by linguistic structures. Hence, two or more phonological variants of the same word may share the identical reference but convey different social meanings, for example, differences in social distances between speaker and addressee, differences in affect. In every community, members have available to them linguistic resources for communicating such social meanings at the same time as they are providing other levels of information. This system of multifarious signaling is highly efficient. Competent members of every community have been socialized to interpret these meanings and can without conscious control orchestrate messages to convey social meanings. Sociological and anthropological research is dedicated to understanding these communicative skills, interpretive processes, and systems of meaning indexed through language.

Research on indexicality has been carried out within several major disciplinary frameworks. Current thinking about social meaning of language draws heavily on the theoretical perspectives of the Soviet literary critics and philosophers Bakhtin (1981) and Voloshinov (1973). This approach stresses the inherently social construction of written and spoken language behavior. Part of the meaning of any utterance (spoken or written) is its social history, its social presence, and its social future. With respect to social history, Bakhtin and Voloshinov make the point that utterances may have several "voices" – the speaker's or writer's voice, the voice of someone referred to within the utterance, or the voice of another for whom the message is conveyed. The voices of speaker/writer and others may be blended in the course of the message and become part of the social meanings indexed within the message. This perspective is a potentially critical one for investigating the relation of language to gender, where gender may generate its own set of voices.

A second tradition examining social indexicality of language is sociological and anthropological research on speech events and speech activities. Bateson's (1972) and Goffman's (1974) work on keying and frames for events, discussions by Gumperz (1982) on contextualization cues, Hymes (1974) on speech event keys, and Silverstein (1976) on shifters and indexes are useful in analyzing the social potential of language behavior. Silverstein provides further specification of indexes in terms of whether social context is indexed referentially or non-referentially. That is, social conditions may be communicated through the referential content of a word, phrase, or clause or through some linguistic feature that has no reference. With respect to indexing of gender in English, referential indexes include such items as the third person pronouns "he" and "she," and the titles "Mr" and "Mrs" and "Sir" and "Madam." Referential indexes have been a major source of discussion among those concerned with the linguistic construction of gender ideology (see especially Silverstein 1985).

From a sociolinguistic point of view, however, referential indexes are far fewer than non-referential indexes of social meaning, including gender. Non-referential indexing of gender may be accomplished through a vast range of morphological, syntactic, and phonological devices available across the world's languages. For example, pitch range may be used in a number of speech communities to index gender of speaker. Research on pre-adolescent American male and female children indicates that young girls speak as if their vocal apparatus were smaller than young boys of the same age and same size vocal chords (Sachs 1975). Here it is evident that pitch has social meaning and that young children have come to understand these meanings and employ pitch appropriately to these ends.

Other studies (see especially Andersen 1977) indicate that children as young as four years of age can use pitch to index male and female identities.

A concern with indexicality is also at the heart of linguistic and philosophical approaches to the field of pragmatics, the study of language in context (Levinson 1980). Here a major concern is broadening the notion of presupposition beyond logical presupposition to include pragmatic presupposition, that is context-sensitive presupposition. Thus, an utterance such as "Give me that pen" logically presupposes that there exists a specific pen and pragmatically presupposes that the pen is some distance from the speaker and the speaker is performing the speech act of ordering. From this perspective, we can say that utterances may pragmatically presuppose genders of speakers, addressees, overhearers, and referents. For example, in Japanese, sentences that include such sentence-final morphological particles as *ze* pragmatically presuppose that the speaker is a male whereas sentences that include sentence-final particle *wa* pragmatically presuppose that the speaker is a female.

The indexing of gender

The concept of gender centers on the premise that the notions of men and women/male and female are sociocultural transformations of biological categories and processes (see, for example, Ortner and Whitehead 1981; Rosaldo and Lamphere 1974; McConnell-Ginet, Borker, and Furman 1980; Gilligan 1982). Social groups organize and conceptualize men and women in culturally specific and meaningful ways. Given that language is the major symbolic system of the human species, we would expect that language is a source and moving force of gender ideologies. In other words, we should expect language to be influenced by local organizations of gender roles, rights, and expectations and to perpetuate actively these organizations in spoken and written communication (Bourdieu 1977). In relating sociocultural constructions of gender to the social meaning of language, an issue of importance emerges: few features of language index gender.

In light of this fact we must work toward a different conceptualization of the relation between language and gender. In the discussion to follow, I examine three characteristics of the language–gender relation: the non-exclusive relation, the constitutive relation, and the temporally transcendent relation.

Non-exclusive relation

In looking at different languages and different speech communities, the most striking generalization that emerges is the paucity of linguistic features that alone index local concepts of men and women or even more minimally the sex of a speaker/addressee/referent (Brown and Levinson 1979; Ochs 1987; Seki 1986; Silverstein 1985). Most linguistic features, particularly if we go beyond the lexicon (such as kin terms that index this information), do not share such a strict – presuppositional – relation to the semantic domain of gender.

Rather, overwhelmingly we find that the relation between particular features of language and gender is typically non-exclusive. By non-exclusive, I mean that variable features of language may often be used by/with/for both sexes. Hence, strictly speaking, we cannot say that these features pragmatically presuppose male or female. What we find, rather, is that the features may be employed more by one than the other sex. Thus, for example, in British and American English, women tend to use prestige phonological variants more than men of the same social class and ethnicity. Indeed, women more than men in these communities overuse the prestige variants, producing "hypercorrect" words (Labov 1966; Trudgill 1974). Women in New York City, for example, overuse the postvocalic /r/ to the extent that they sometimes insert an /r/ in a word that has no "r" in its written form; instead of saying "idea," they hypercorrect to "idear" (Labov 1966). In this and other examples, the relation between language and gender is distributional and probabilistic.

In addition, non-exclusivity is demonstrated by the fact that many linguistic forms associated with gender are associated as well with the marking of other social information, such as stance and social action. Thus, for example, tag questions in English are associated not only with female speakers (Andersen 1977), but with stances such as hesitancy and social acts such as confirmation checks. Certain sentence-final particles in Japanese are associated not only with male and female speakers but with stances of coarse versus delicate intensity. This system of linguistic forms conveying multiple social meanings is highly efficient from the point of view of linguistic processing and acquisition (Slobin 1985). Further, the multiplicity of potential meanings allows speakers to exploit such inherent ambiguities for strategic ends, such as avoiding going "on-record" in communicating a particular social meaning (Brown and Levinson 1987).

A question raised is: why is there this distribution? Further, how does the distribution of linguistic resources relate to rights, expectations, and other conceptions of men and women in society? These questions are in line with those asked by social scientists concerned with the position of men and women in terms of access to and control over resources and activities.

Linguistic form	Direct index	Indirect index
ze	coarse intensity	male "voice"
wa	delicate intensity	female "voice"

Fig. 7.1 Indexing gender in Japanese

Constitutive relation

By positing a constitutive relation between language and gender, I mean that one or more linguistic features may index social meanings – such as stances, social acts, social activities – which in turn helps to constitute gender meanings. The pursuit of such constitutive routes is a far more interesting activity than assessing either obligatory or probabilistic relations between language and sex of speaker/addressee/referent, for here we begin to understand pragmatic meanings of features and their complex relation to gender images.

Let me provide a few examples of constitutiveness. Many of the linguistic features that in the literature are associated primarily with either men or women have as their core social meaning a particular affective stance. As noted earlier, certain linguistic features associated with men's speech in Japanese coarsely intensify the force of an utterance, while those associated with women's speech typically convey an affect of gentle intensity (Uyeno 1971; Seki 1986). The former features directly index coarse intensity and the latter a soft or delicate intensity. The affective dispositions so indexed are part of the preferred images of men and women and motivate their differential use by men and women. When someone wishes to speak like a woman in Japanese, they may speak gently, using particles such as the sentence-final *wa* or to speak like a man they may speak coarsely, using the sentence-final particle *ze* (Fig. 7.1).

Similarly, particular linguistic features directly index social acts or social activities, such as the imperative mode indexing the act of ordering in English or respect vocabulary terms in Samoan indexing the activity of oratory. These acts and activities in turn may be associated with speaking like a male or speaking like a female and may display different frequencies of use across the two social categories.

It is in this sense that the relation between language and gender is mediated and constituted through a web of socially organized pragmatic meanings. Knowledge of how language relates to gender is not a catalogue of correlations between particular linguistic forms and sex of speakers, referents, addresses, and the like. Rather, such knowledge entails tacit understanding of how particular linguistic forms can be used to perform particular pragmatic work (such as conveying stance and social action), and norms, preferences, and expectations regarding the distribution of this work regarding particular social identities of speakers, referents, addressees. To discuss the relation of language to gender in these terms is far more revealing than simply identifying features as directly marking men's or women's speech.

A model encompassing these complexities relates linguistic forms to gender either indirectly through other social meanings indexed or directly (Fig. 7.2). This model displays different kinds of language-gender relations and begins to specify the kinds of meanings men and women are likely to index through language, the relation of these patterns to the position, and images of men and women in society. According to this model, linguistic forms are resources for conveying a range of social meanings. Further, particular social meanings may be constituted through other social meanings.[2] The model indicates that constitutive relations obtain between stances, acts, and activities as well as between each of these and gender meanings.

Two kinds of relations between language and gender are indicated by the model. The first and less common is the direct indexical relation, as when a personal pronoun indexes gender of speaker or a kin term indexes gender of speaker and referent. This relation is represented by radiating lines from linguistic resources to social meanings. The second relates gender to language through some other social meaning indexed. In this second relation, certain social meanings are more central than others. These meanings, however, help to constitute other domains of social reality. That is, a domain such as stance helps to constitute the image of gender. This sort of constitutive relation is represented by two-headed arrows.

Gender, according to the model, enters into complex constitutive relations both within the category of social identity and with other categories of social meaning. Gender is not the only category of social meaning that may be affected by a different social domain. For example, speech acts contribute to the establishment of speech activities and the other way around, the expression of stance contributes to the definition of speech acts, and so on.

A more complex representation of language and gender would specify which types of conversational acts, speech activities, affective and episte-

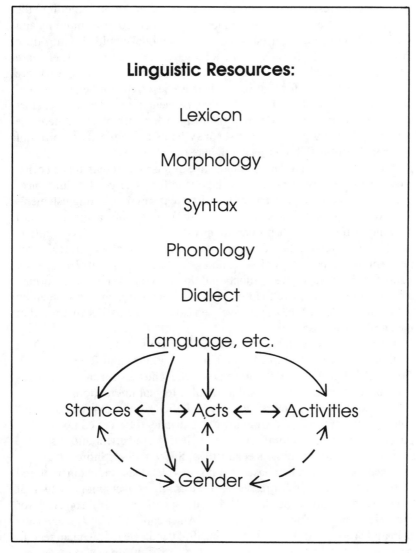

Fig. 7.2 Language and gender

mological stances, participant roles in situations, and more, enter into the constitution or construction of gender within a particular community and across different communities. A more refined model would also introduce the notion of markedness. Certain acts, activities, stances, roles, etc., are frequently enacted by members of a particular sex, that is, they are unmarked behaviors for that sex. Others are less frequent behaviors, and yet others are highly unusual for that particular sex. These behaviors would be interpreted differently than unmarked behaviors. Where the behavior is highly marked, one sex may be as assuming the "voice" of another (Bakhtin 1981), or as acting like the other sex.

One of the major advances in language and gender research has been a move away from relating isolated linguistic forms to gender differences and toward specifying clusters of linguistic features that distinguish men's and women's speech in society. This shift represents a move toward defining men's and women's communicative styles, their access to different conversational acts, activities, and genres, and their strategies for performing similar acts, activities, and genres (Borker 1980). The starting point for this perspective is functional and strategic rather than formal. That is, researchers have focused primarily on what men and women do with words (Austin 1962), and have then isolated linguistic structures that men and women use.[3]

A range of studies are now available that are stylistic and strategic in orientation (see for example Schieffelin 1987; Philips and Reynolds 1987; Brown 1980). Several studies have noted the tendency for men to participate more in speech activities that involve formal interactions with outsiders and women to be restricted to activities within family and village contexts. In these cases, men and women display different competence in particular genres, including, of course, their grammatical and discourse structures (see for example Keenan 1974; Sherzer 1987; Shore 1982).

Other studies have emphasized ways in which men and women attend to the "face" of their addressees in performing conversational acts that may offend the other. Studies of women's speech in several societies, for example, Tenejapa (Brown 1979, 1980), American (Lakoff 1973; Zimmerman and West 1975), Japanese (Uyeno 1971), indicate that women tend to be more polite than men. Brown's study of Tenejapa Mayan society indicates that Tenejapa women talking with other women tend to be more polite than men talking with men. When women and men talk to one another, they are equally polite. Tenejapa women talking with other women tend to use different kinds of politeness features than do men with other men. They use linguistic structures that show support, approval of one another, what Brown and Levinson (1987) have called "positive politeness," whereas men tend to use linguistic forms that indicate a sensitivity to the other's need not to be intruded upon, what Brown and Levinson have called "negative politeness."

The association of women with greater politeness is not universal. Among the Malagasy, men are far more polite than women (Keenan 1974). Women are seen as abrupt and direct, saying exactly what is on their mind, whereas men are seen as speaking with care and indirectness. Hence, women are seen as inappropriate spokespersons in formal speech activities involving other families, where delicacy and indirectness are demanded. Women rather are selected for other activities. They are the ones to confront others directly, hence they are the primary performers of accusations and bargaining with Europeans. Men control oratorical genres as well as a wide range of poetic and metaphoric forms highly prized in this society.

Similarly, in a recent study of men's and women's speech in Western Samoan rural society, I have not found that Samoan women are more polite than men of the same social status, except in one context. As listeners to narrative tellings, women tend to use more positive politeness supportive feedback forms than do men of the same status. In other contexts, however, the expression of politeness differs more in terms of social rank of speaker – titled person or spouse of titled person, untitled person – than in terms of gender. Research on men's and women's attention to face and expression of politeness needs to be pursued more in the future, taking into account a range of situational parameters: the speech activity, the speaker-addressee-author-audience-overhearer-referent relationships, the genre, and more. A wider data base is needed to understand differences in men's and women's communicative strategies and to resolve contradictory findings within the same society (see Connor-Linton 1986 on politeness among American middle-class adolescents).

Temporally transcendent relation

Thus far we have considered how linguistic forms may help constitute local conceptions of male and female at the time a particular utterance is produced or perceived. Language in this sense has the power to constitute the present context. The constitutive power of language, however, transcends the time of utterance production/perception, hence the property of temporal transcendence. Language can also constitute past and future contexts. I call the constitution of past contexts "recontextualization" and the constitution of future contexts "precontextualization" (Ochs 1990). Each of these functions can be carried out through a variety of verbal practices and forms. For example, the practice of speculation can recontextualize past events or precontextualize future events by changing "certain" events into "uncertain" events (Ochs 1982). Similarly, the practice of praising can recontextualize a past act as an accomplishment, and accusations can recontextualize past acts as wrongdoings and personal characters as irreputable. All controversial acts that function as first pair parts of adjacency sequences (Sacks, Schegloff, and Jefferson 1974) – questions, invitations, and compliments – precontextualize the future in that they set up expectations for what the next conversational act is likely to be – answers, acceptances/declines.

The relevance of temporal transcendence to this discussion of language and gender is that societies establish norms, preferences, and expectations concerning the extent to which and the manner in which men and women can verbally recontextualize the past and precontextualize the future. The roles and status of men and women are partly realized through the distribution of recontextualizing and precontextualizing acts, activities, stances, and topics. The potential of language to recontextualize and precontextualize will be of import to our discussion of mothering. The status of women in white, middle-class American society and Western Samoan society is in part constituted through the particular ways women as mothers recast the past and precast the future in their interactions with infants and small children.

Communicative styles of mothers and other caregivers

One of the major concerns in gender research has been the social and cultural construction of gender in society. A logical locus to examine this process is interaction between young children and older members of society. By examining the kinds of activities and acts caregivers of both sexes engage in with children of both sexes and the manner in which these activities and acts are carried out, we can infer local expectations concerning gender and articulate how these expectations are socialized. One important tool of socialization is language. Not only the content of language but the manner in which language is used communicates a vast range of sociocultural knowledge to children and other novices. This use of language we call "language socialization" (Schieffelin and Ochs 1986a, 1986b; Ochs 1986, 1988). Language socialization includes both socialization through language and socialization to use language. Here I propose a relation between the position and image of women in society and language use in caregiver–child interaction.

Although mothering is a universal kinship role of women and in this role women have positions of control and power, their communicative styles as mothers vary considerably across societies. Such variation in the language of mothering reveals differences in the social position of mothers *vis-à-vis* their young charges. I will contrast caregiving communicative styles among white, middle-class (WMC) Americans with Western Samoan caregiving styles. Based on research carried out with Schieffelin (Ochs and Schieffelin 1984; Schieffelin and Ochs 1986a, 1986b), I will argue that images of women in WMC American society are socialized through a communicative strategy of high accommodation to young children. A very different image of women is socialized in traditional Samoan households, where children are expected to be communicatively accommodating to caregivers.

In their ground-breaking volume on sexual meanings, Ortner and Whitehead (1981:12) comment that "women's universal and highly visible kinship function, mothering, is surprisingly underrated, even ignored, in definitions of womanhood in a wide range of societies with differing kinship organizations." I argue that the white middle-class social scientists' lack of attention to the role of mothering is an outcome of the very language socialization practices described here. I focus on cross-cultural differences in strategies associated with three pervasive verbal practices of mothers and other caregivers: verbal strategies for getting messages across to young children (message production strategies); verbal strategies for clarifying messages of young children (interpretive strategies); and verbal strategies for evaluating accomplishments of children and others (praising strategies). Through each of these verbal strategies, WMC American mothers, in contrast to traditional Samoan mothers, construct a low image of themselves. The strategies adopted by WMC American mothers minimize their own importance by lowering their status, giving priority to the child's point of view, and even denying their participation in accomplishing a task (Fig. 7.3).

Strategies	WMC American (child-centered)	Samoan (other-centered)
production	extensive simplification	little simplification
interpretive	express, guess and negotiate meaning	display minimal grasp
praising	unidirectional	bidirectional

Fig. 7.3 Verbal strategies that constitute mothering

Organization of caregiving

Before detailing these strategies, let us consider briefly the organization of caregiving in the two societies under consideration. In traditional Samoan households, caregiving is organized in a somewhat different manner from that characteristic of WMC American households. First, caregiving is shared among a number of family members of both genders. Mothers are primary caregivers in the first few months of the infant's life, but they are always assisted, usually by siblings (both brothers and sisters) of the young infant. Once an infant is somewhat older, these sibling caregivers assume most of the basic caregiving tasks, although they are monitored at a distance by older family members. In the village in which I carried out research, siblings took turns staying home from school during the week to care for a younger child. This type of caregiving arrangement is character-istic of most of the world's societies (Weisner and Gallimore 1977).

Samoan society is hierarchically organized (Mead 1930; Sahlins 1958; Shore 1982). Social stratification is evident in the political distinctions of *ali'i* ("chief"), *tulaafale* ("orator"), and *taule'ale'a* ("untitled person"); in titles within the rank of *ali'i* and within the rank of *tulaafale*, and among untitled persons along the dimensions of relative age and generation. Hierarchical distinctions are evident in domestic as well as public inter-actions. Caregiving is also hierarchically organized. Untitled, older, higher generation caregivers assume a social status superior to younger, untitled caregivers who are co-present in a household setting. Further, caregivers enjoy a higher status than the young charges under their care.

Among the demeanors Samoans associate with social rank, direction of accommodation is most salient. Lower-ranking persons are expected to accommodate to higher-ranking persons, as in other stratified societies. Lower-ranking caregivers show respect by carrying out the tasks set for them by their elders. They provide the more active caregiving, while others stay seated and provide verbal directives. Samoan caregivers say that infants and young children are by nature wild and wilful and that accom-modation in the form of respect is the single most important demeanor that young children must learn. A core feature of respect is attending to others and serving their needs. A great deal of care is taken to orient infants and young children to notice others. Infants, for example, are usually held out-wards and even spoonfed facing the group members present.

Message production strategies

WMC American mothers use a special verbal style or register (Ferguson 1964, 1977), often called "Baby Talk" or "Motherese" (Newport 1976). It is a simplified register and shares many features of other simplified registers, such as Teacher Talk, Foreigner Talk, and talk to the elderly, to lovers, and to pets. Characteristics of this register include restricted lexicon, baby talk words (child's own versions of words), shorter sentence length, phonological simplification (such as avoidance of consonant clusters in favor of consonant-vowel alternation, for example, tummy versus stomach), morpho-syntactic simplification (such as avoidance of complex sentences, copula), topical focus on here-and-now versus past/future, exaggerated intonation, slower pace, repetition, cooperative proposition-making with child (for example, expanding the child's utterance into adult grammatical form, providing sentence frames for the child to complete.)

Baby talk register has been a major area of investigation over the last decade or so in the field of language acquisition. The existence of such a register was argued by many to indicate that language acquisition was facilitated by such input. More recently cross-cultural observations of caregiver–child communication indicate that simplified registers are not characteristic of this communicative context in all societies (Heath 1982; Ochs 1982; Ochs and Schieffelin 1984; Schieffelin and Ochs 1986a, 1986b; Ward 1971). We now know that the process of language acquisition does not depend on this sociolinguistic environment. Western Samoan, Kaluli New Guinea, and working-class African-American children are not surrounded by simplified speech of the sort described above and yet they become perfectly competent speakers in the course of normal development. Given that such simplification is not necessary for the process of language acquisition, we might ask why caregivers in certain societies choose to communicate in this fashion with their children whereas others do not.

Baby talk is part of a pervasive cultural orientation to children among WMC Americans (Ochs and Schieffelin 1984). WMC American society is highly child-centered and there is a very strong expectation that those in the presence of young children will accommodate to children's perceived wants and needs. Such accommodation is both non-verbal and verbal. It manifests itself in a vast range of child-oriented artifacts such as child-proof medicine bottles, safety catches on cabinets and electrical outlets, miniaturization of furniture and clothes, and so on. Adults in the presence of sleeping children will similarly accommodate to them by lowering their voices.

In the domain of verbal communication, accommodation takes many forms. Beyond the use of baby talk register, a widely observed behavior of WMC American mothers is their participation in conversation-like interactions with tiny infants. Mothers have been observed engaging in greeting exchanges with infants as young as 24 hours after birth (Stern 1977); this occurrence obviously requires much communicative accommodation on the part of the mother. Indeed what is characteristic of these proto-conversations (Bates *et al.* 1977) is the mother's willingness to take on the conversational work of the infant as well as her own. Thus, mothers "ventriloquate" through infants (Bakhtin 1981) and in this way sustain "conversations" for some time.

Throughout the course of their infancy, WMC American children are thus participants in exchanges which are strongly scaffolded (Bruner 1975) by their mothers. Mothers are able to enter into and sustain communication with small children not only by speaking for them but also by taking into consideration what the child is holding, what the child is looking at, what event just took place, when the child last slept and ate, and a variety of other child-oriented conditions that may assist in the interpretation of children's gestures and vocalizations. In this way, mothers are able to respond to children in what they perceive to be communicatively appropriate ways. Scaffolding is also manifest in non-verbal interactions between mothers and children, as when mothers assist young children in building play structures or to realize some intention associated with other tasks. In Vygotsky's terms (1978), mothers are providing a "zone of proximal development" for their children, a socially structured environment which enhances the attainment of particular skills.

Such extensive verbal and non-verbal accommodation on the part of mothers and others in caregiving roles is expected as part of the WMC American caregiving role. Being a "good mother" or "good teacher" is to empathize with and respond to the child's mind set. Once a caregiver believes she/he understands this mind set, a good caregiver will either intervene and prevent or assist the child in carrying out her/his desired activity.

In the sociocultural world of traditional Samoan households, where children are socialized to accommodate to others, it is not surprising to learn that mothers and other caregivers do not use a simplified register in speaking to infants and young children. Such a register indexes a stance of accommodation by speaker to addressee. Samoan does have a simplified register, but this register is used toward foreigners, who historically have been missionaries, government representatives, and others in high social positions. In this context, a stance of accommodation is appropriate, just as host accommodates to guest.

Thus, linguistic forms in collocation convey particular stances – here simplified speech conveys accommodation to addressee – and these social meanings in turn help to constitute and index particular social identities.

Of cross-cultural significance is the observation that societies differ in the social identities of speakers and addressees associated with this stance. Here, the same set of linguistic features that directly index one social meaning, such as accommodation, in two speech communities – WMC American and traditional Western Samoan – indirectly index different social identities, that is, caregivers to children, members to foreign dignitaries. Simplified registers display accommodation in that they respond to a perceived communicative desire or need of the addressee, for example, the need or desire to decode a message.

Accommodation is universally associated with demeanor of lower toward higher-ranking parties. That WMC American mothers use a simplified register pervasively has a constitutive impact on the image of women in that this practice socializes young children into an image of women as accommodating or addressee-centered in demeanor. In traditional Western Samoan households, mothers and other caregivers rarely simplify their speech to young children. This practice socializes young children to be accommodating, to attend carefully to the non-simplified speech and actions of others.

Interpretive strategies

A second manifestation of child-centeredness versus other-centeredness or accommodating versus non-accommodating verbal practices is located in cross-cultural differences in mothers' and other caregivers' responses to children's unintelligible utterances. As with simplified registers, Western Samoa and mainstream American speech communities generally display similar verbal practices in responding to unintelligible utterances. However, important differences lie in the social conditions under which particular practices are preferred and appropriate.

In both communities, unintelligible utterances may be ignored, responded to by indicating unintelligibility ("What?" "I don't understand," "Huh?"), or responded to by verbally guessing at the meaning of the utterance (Ochs 1982). The two communities differ in their preferences for using these strategies when speaking to young children. Overwhelmingly, WMC American mothers prefer to respond to young children's unintelligible speech by verbally guessing. Overwhelmingly, Western Samoan mothers and other caregivers prefer to ignore or point out the unintelligibility of the child's utterance.

These differences reinforce different images of mothers and other caregivers in the two societies: more or less child-centered and more or less accommodating. Verbal guesses are more child-centered and accommodating than simply indicating unintelligibility in two senses. First, expressed guesses entail greater perspective-taking – taking the child's point of view. Guessing involves attempting to formulate the child's intended message, which in turn may entail taking into consideration what the child is looking at, holding, what the child just said and other clues. Pointing out that the child's utterance is not clear does not entail this kind of sociocentrism, and if the child wishes to get a message across, he or she must reformulate the message better to meet the recipients' communicative requirements. Otherwise the utterance will be ignored.

Second, expressed guesses are hypotheses or candidate interpretations presented to the child for confirmation, disconfirmation, or modification. Expressed guesses thus allow the child to participate in negotiations over the meanings of utterances produced by the child. Another way of looking at this phenomenon is to say that in verbally expressing a guess, mothers give the child the right to influence mothers' interpretations of the child's utterances. In contrast, displays of non-understanding do not engage the child in such negotiations.

Another way of analyzing message production practices and interpretive practices is to say that Samoan and WMC American mothers define different goals in their interactions with young children and that these goals entail different linguistic practices. WMC American mothers often set the goal of engaging infants and small children as conversational partners, and they do so from within hours of their child's birth for lengthy stretches of time (Ochs and Schieffelin 1984). Once they establish conversation as a goal, mothers are obliged to make enormous linguistic accommodation for that goal to be accomplished. Children who are a few hours old, for example, can hardly be expected to speak for themselves, therefore the WMC American mother who insists on such conversations takes on both conversational roles, speaking for the infant as well as herself. The generalization of importance here is that WMC American mothers systematically set goals that are impossible for a child to achieve without dramatic scaffolding by the mother.

The Samoan way is different, for Samoan mothers and other caregivers do not establish goals for the child that demand such extensive accommodation from others. They do not engage infants in proto-conversations, which demand that the caregiver assume the perspective of the infant and speak for the infant, as characteristic of the WMC American interactions with young babies. Samoan caregivers do not place infants in communicative contexts that demand this kind of verbal scaffolding. The Samoan way is to delay such communicative exchanges until the child displays more verbal and communicative competence.

Praising strategies

The final strategy relevant to the construction of gender meanings in society concerns mothers' and other caregivers' evaluative comments on an activity involving a child. In this discussion, we attend to the property of language introduced earlier as temporal transcendence, that is the capacity of language to recontextualize the past and precontextualize the future in addition to contextualizing the present. Among their many functions, evaluative comments reframe or recontextualize a past act or set of acts. Praising, for example, recontextualizes a past act as an accomplishment. In this sense, praising has a backwards performative function. Through the uttering of a praise, the speaker turns any act or set of acts into an accomplishment. WMC American and Western Samoan mothers and other caregivers recontextualize past acts/activities as different kinds of accomplishments and these different contextualizations help to constitute weak and strong images of the mothers and others.

WMC American mothers, as I have shown, provide extensive assistance in communicating with young children – simplifying, guessing, and even speaking for them. WMC American mothers tend to assist children in carrying out certain activities, such as constructing a toy, drawing a picture, or tying a shoelace. From a Vygotskian perspective, such activities may be seen as "joint activities" (Vygotsky 1978), accomplished by mother and child. However, WMC American mothers typically recontextualize such activities as the child's sole accomplishments (Ochs and Schieffelin 1984). This outcome is accomplished by directing praises at the child such as "Good!" or "Look at the beautiful castle you made!" with no mention of the mother's role nor any expectation that the child should praise the mother for her part in accomplishing the task at hand. In other words, these mothers deny their own participation; through their own praising practices, they make themselves invisible. It is precisely such verbal reframing that socializes infants and small children into images and expectations of mothers.

This kind of behavior defines the child as more competent than she or he may actually be (Ochs and Schieffelin 1984), since the child could not do these activities without the caregiver's scaffolding. This behavior as well lowers the position of the caregiver, usually the mother. These behaviors, along with the widespread use of baby talk and other verbal behaviors, serve to minimize the asymmetry in knowledge and power between caregiver and child. Indeed, caregivers in WMC American society are uncomfortable with such asymmetry and they mask differences in competence by acting as if the other were more competent and they less competent. Hence with respect to other societies, caregiver–child communication in current WMC American society both reflects and creates (socializes) a more egalitarian relationship. This is not to say that these caregivers do not exercise power and control over their charges (compare, for example, Corsaro 1979), but rather that they do so less than in other societies. WMC American caregivers do not claim "ownership" to products of joint activity; they speak like small children (simplified register). They take the perspective of the child and do not expect the child to assume their perspective until rather late in their development.

In contrast to WMC American households, in traditional Samoan communities, activities are often recognized as jointly accomplished. This recognition is realized linguistically through a praising practice distinct from that typical of WMC American praising. Whereas in WMC American interactions, praising is typically unidirectional, in Samoan interactions, praising is typically bidirectional. There is a strong expectation that the first one to be praised will in turn praise the praiser. Typically the praise consists of the expression "*Maaloo!*" ("Well done!"). Once the first *maaloo* is uttered, a second *maaloo* is to be directed to the producer of the original *maaloo*. In these *maaloo* exchanges, each *maaloo* recontextualizes the situation. Like WMC American praising, the first *maaloo* recontextualizes an act/activity of the addressee as an accomplishment. The second *maaloo*, however, recontextualizes the act/activity as jointly accomplished. The second *maaloo* acknowledges the support of the first speaker as contributing to the successful achievement of the task at hand. In other words, the second *maaloo* recontextualizes the congratulator as someone to be congratulated as well. Children in Western Samoan households are socialized through such bidirectional praising practices to articulate the contribution of others, including mothers.

Mothering and gender hierarchies

Mothering cannot be taken for granted in assessing gender identity across societies. While women's position in society has been reckoned in terms of their roles as sisters and wives, little ethnographic work has been devoted to assessing their position as mothers. In the realm of verbal behavior, significant cultural patterns exist in mothering. Transcripts of children's interactions reveal a set of cultural meanings about the position of mothers, hence about women, being conveyed to children hundreds of times in the course of their early lives throughout linguistic forms and the pragmatic practices these forms help to constitute.

I do not pretend to know fully about women's position in either current WMC American society or traditional Samoan society (Mead 1928; Shore 1981, 1982), but from a sociolinguistic standpoint, it is clear that Samoan mothers enjoy a more prestigious position *vis-à-vis* their offspring than do WMC American mothers. On a communicative level, Samoan mothers are accommodated to more often by children and starting at a much earlier age than is characteristic of WMC American households. They socialize young children to recognize the contribution of caregivers and others to achieving a goal, in contrast to WMC American mothers who tend to socialize their children to ignore or minimize the role of the mother in reaching a goal. Samoan mothers have command over human labor in that they are typically the highest-status caregivers present and have the right to delegate the more time-consuming and physically active caregiving tasks to younger, lower-status caregivers at hand. Thus, even among caregivers they are the least accommodating, and the linguistic record indexes this demeanor in numerous ways.

Samoan women enjoy their prestigious position in the hierarchy of caregiving and in caregiver–child relationships. WMC American mothers use certain indexes of power in their communicative demeanor, but not to the extent manifest in Samoan mothers' speech. American mothers enter into negotiations with their children over the meaning of children's unclear utterances; Samoan mothers, and other caregivers, do not. WMC American mothers treat even the tiniest of infants as conversational partners; Samoan mothers do not. And the list of communicative manifestations of the relative statuses of mothers in these two societies goes on.

We are now in a better position to evaluate Ortner and Whitehead's remark that the role of mothering "is surprisingly underrated, even ignored, in definitions of womanhood" (1981:12). This state of affairs is precisely what we would predict from the language socialization practices in WMC American households in the United States and much of middle-class Western Europe as well. "Mother" is underrated in the Western family and society, because she does not socialize children to acknowledge her participation in their accomplishments. "Mother" is ignored by Western social scientists, because through language behaviors of mothers, "mother" is made invisible.

NOTES

This chapter is based on research supported by the National Science Foundation (Grant No. BNS 77–23843, Elinor Ochs, principal investigator, 1978–80; Grant No. BNS 86–08210, Alessandro Duranti and Elinor Ochs, co-principal investigators, 1986–9); the Australian National University Research School of Pacific Studies (1980–1); the Howard Foundation (1982–3), the John Simon Guggenheim Memorial Foundation (1984–5), and the National Institute of Child Health and Human Development (Grant No. HUD–1, 5 RO1 Hd20992–02, Elinor Ochs and Thomas Weisner, co-principal investigators, 1986–9).

1 Data are from two field studies conducted on the island of Upolu, Western Samoa. The first study, carried out in 1978–9 by Alessandro Duranti, Elinor Ochs (principal investigator), and Martha Plat, documented language development in children under the age of four, language use in formal classroom settings, and adult–adult speech behavior across formal and informal settings. Over 134 hours of household interaction were recorded, yielding approximately 18,000 pages of transcription of speech to, by, and about young children. The second study, carried out in 1981 by Alessandro Duranti and Elinor Ochs, documented through film children's social activities at work and play across familial and educational settings.

2 Although our discussion is focused on gender, the model can be taken as exemplary of how language conveys social identities more generally.

3 Studies that start out by isolating particular linguistic forms associated with male or female speakers/addressees/referents tend not to reach this kind of functional or strategy based account of men's and women's speech. Such studies do not initially focus on activities and situations and examine men's and women's speech within those social contexts. These studies, rather, describe a distributional pattern of linguistic forms across the two sexes, and once this pattern is isolated, some *ad hoc* accounting is inferred.

REFERENCES

Althusser, Louis 1971 *Lenin and Philosophy and Other Essays*. Ben Brewster, trans. New York: Monthly Review Press.

Andersen, Elaine 1977 Learning How to Speak with Style. Ph.D. dissertation, Stanford University.

Austin, J. L. 1962 *How to Do Things with Words*. New York: Oxford University Press.

Bakhtin, Mikhail 1981 *The Dialogic Imagination*. M. Holquist, ed. Austin: University of Texas Press.

Bates, Elizabeth, Laura Benigni, Inge Bretherton, Luigia Camaioni, and Virginia Votterra 1977 From Gesture to First Word: On Cognitive and Social Prerequisites. In *Interaction, Conversation, and the Development of Language. The Origins of Behavior*, Vol. 5. Michael Lewis and Leonard A. Rosenblum, eds., pp. 247–307. New York: John Wiley and Sons.

Bateson, Gregory 1972 *Steps to an Ecology of Mind*. New York: Ballantine Books.

Borker, Ruth 1980 Anthropology: Social and Cultural Perspectives. In *Women and Language in Literature and Society*. S. McConnell-Ginet, R. Borker, and N. Furman, eds., pp. 26–44. New York: Praeger.

Bourdieu, Pierre 1977 *Outline of a Theory of Practice*. New York: Cambridge University Press.

Brown, Penelope 1979 Language, Interaction and Sex Roles in a Mayan Community: A Study of Politeness and the Position of Women. Ph.D. dissertation, University of California-Berkeley.

1980 How and Why Women are More Polite: Some Evidence from a Mayan Community. In *Women and Language in Literature and Society*. S. McConnell-Ginet, R. Borker, and N. Furman, eds., pp. 111–36. New York: Praeger.

Brown, Penelope and Stephen Levinson 1979 Social Structure, Groups, and

Interaction. In *Social Markers in Speech*. K. Scherer and H. Giles, eds., pp. 291–341. New York: Cambridge University Press.

1987 *Politeness: Some Universals of Language Usage*. New York: Cambridge University Press.

Bruner, Jerome 1975 The Ontogenesis of Speech Acts. *Journal of Child Language* 2:1–21.

Connor-Linton, Jeff 1986 Gender Differences in Politeness: The Struggle for Power among Adolescents. In *Southern California Occasional Papers in Linguistics*, pp. 64–98. Los Angeles: University of Southern California.

Corsaro, William 1979 Sociolinguistic Patterns in Adult–Child Interaction. In *Developmental Pragmatics*. Elinor Ochs and Bambi Schieffelin, eds., pp. 373–89. New York: Academic Press.

Ferguson, Charles 1964 Baby Talk in Six Languages. *American Anthropologist* 66(6 part 2):103–14.

1977 Baby Talk as a Simplified Register. In *Talking to Children*. C. Snow and C. Ferguson, eds., pp. 219–37. New York: Cambridge University Press.

Gilligan, Carol 1982 *In a Different Voice: Psychological Theory and Women's Development*. Cambridge, MA: Harvard University Press.

Goffman, Erving 1974 *Fame Analysis*. New York: Harper and Row.

Gumperz, John 1982 *Discourse Strategies*. New York: Cambridge University Press.

Heath, Shirley 1982 What No Bedtime Story Means: Narrative Skills at Home and School. *Language in Society* 11:49–77.

Hymes, Dell 1974 *Foundations in Sociolinguistics*. New York: Cambridge University Press.

Keenan (Ochs), Elinor 1974 Conversation and Oratory in Vakinankaratra, Madagascar. Ph.D. dissertation, University of Pennsylvania.

Labov, William 1966 *The Social Stratification of English in New York City*. Washington, DC: Center for Applied Linguistics.

Lakoff, Robin 1973 Language and Woman's Place. *Language in Society* 2:45–79.

Levinson, Stephen 1980 *Pragmatics*. New York: Cambridge University Press.

McConnell-Ginet, Sally, Ruth Borker, and Nelly Furman, eds. 1980 *Women and Language in Literature and Society*. New York: Praeger.

Mead, Margaret 1928 *Coming of Age in Samoa*. New York: Morrow.

1930 *Social Organization of Manua*. Honolulu: B. P. Bishop Museum Bulletin 76.

Newport, Elissa 1976 Motherese: The Speech of Mothers to Young Children. In *Cognitive Theory*, Vol. 2. N. John Castellan, David B. Pisani, and George R. Potts, eds., pp. 177–218. Hillsdale, NJ: Lawrence Erlbaum Associates.

Ochs, Elinor 1982 Talking to Children in Western Samoa. *Language in Society* 11:77–104.

1986 From Feelings to Grammar. In *Language Socialization across Cultures*. Bambi Schieffelin and Elinor Ochs, eds., pp. 251–72. New York: Cambridge University Press.

1987 The Impact of Stratification and Socialization on Men's and Women's Speech in Western Samoa. In *Language, Gender and Sex in Comparative Perspective*. Susan U. Philips, Susan Steele, and Christine Tanz, eds., pp. 50–70. New York: Cambridge University Press.

1988 *Culture and Language Development: Language Acquisition and Language Socialization in a Samoan Village.* New York: Cambridge University Press.

1990 Indexicality and Socialization. In *Cultural Psychology: Essays on Comparative Human Development.* James W. Stigler, Richard A. Schweder, and Gilbert Herdt, eds., pp. 309–27. New York: Cambridge University Press.

Ochs, Elinor and Bambi Schieffelin 1984 Language Acquisition and Socialization: Three Developmental Stories. In *Culture Theory: Essays in Mind, Self and Emotion.* Richard A. Schweder and Robert A. LeVine, eds., pp. 276–322. New York: Cambridge University Press.

Ortner, Sherry B. and Harriet Whitehead 1981 Introduction: Accounting for Sexual Meanings. In *Sexual Meanings: The Cultural Construction of Gender and Sexuality.* Sherry B. Ortner and Harriet Whitehead, eds., pp. 1–27. New York: Cambridge University Press.

Philips, Susan U. and Anne Reynolds 1987 The Interaction of Variable Syntax and Discourse Structure in Women's and Men's Speech. In *Language, Gender and Sex in Comparative Perspective.* Susan U. Philips, Susan Steele, and Christine Tanz, eds., pp. 71–94. New York: Cambridge University Press.

Rosaldo, Michelle Zimbalist and Louis Lamphere, eds. 1974 *Woman, Culture and Society.* Stanford, CA: Stanford University Press.

Sachs, Jacqueline 1975 Cues to the Identification of Sex in Children's Speech. In *Language and Sex: Difference and Dominance.* B. Thorne and N. Henley, eds., pp. 152–71. Rowley, MA: Newbury House.

Sacks, Harvey, Emanuel Schegloff, and Gail Jefferson 1974 A Simplest Systematics for the Organization for Turn-Taking in Conversation. *Language* 50(4):696–735.

Sahlins, Marshall 1958 *Social Stratification in Polynesia.* Seattle: University of Washington Press.

Schieffelin, Bambi 1987 Do Different Worlds Mean Different Words? An Example from Papua New Guinea. In *Language, Gender and Sex in a Comparative Perspective.* Susan U. Philips, Susan Steele, and Christine Tanz, eds., pp. 249–62. New York: Cambridge University Press.

Schieffelin, Bambi and Elinor Ochs 1986a Language Socialization. *Annual Review of Anthropology* 15:163–246.

Schieffelin, Bambi and Elinor Ochs, eds. 1986b *Language Socialization across Cultures.* New York: Cambridge University Press.

Seki, Minako 1986 Gender Particles and Linguistic/Nonlinguistic Context. Unpublished manuscript, Department of Linguistics, University of Southern California.

Sherzer, Joel 1987 A Diversity of Voices: Men's and Women's Speech in Ethnographic Perspective. In *Language, Gender and Sex in Comparative Perspective.* Susan U. Philips, Susan Steele, and Christine Tanz, eds., pp. 95–120. New York: Cambridge University Press.

Shore, Bradd 1981 Sexuality and Gender in Samoa: Conceptions and Missed Conceptions. In *Sexual Meanings: The Cultural Construction of Gender and Sexuality.* Sherry B. Ortner and Harriet Whitehead, eds., pp. 192–215. New York: Cambridge University Press.

1982 *Sala'ilua: A Samoan Mystery.* New York: Columbia University Press.

Silverstein, Michael 1976 Shifters, Linguistic Categories, and Cultural Description. In *Meaning in Anthropology*. K. Basso and H. A. Selby, eds., pp. 11–55. Albuquerque: University of New Mexico Press.

1985 Language and the Culture of Gender: At the Intersection of Structure, Usage and Ideology. In *Semiotic Mediation*. Elizabeth Mertz and Richard Palmentiers, eds., pp. 219–59. New York: Academic Press.

Slobin, Dan I. 1985 Why Study Acquisition Crosslinguistically? In *The Crosslinguistic Study of Language Acquisition*, Vol. 1: *The Data*. Dan Isaac Slobin, ed., pp. 3–24. Hillsdale, NJ: Lawrence Erlbaum Associates.

Stern, Daniel 1977 *The First Relationship: Infant and Mother*. London: Fontana/ Open Books.

Trudgill, Peter 1974 *Sociolinguistics: An Introduction*. Harmondsworth: Penguin Books.

Uyeno, T. 1971 A Study of Japanese Modality: A Performative Analysis of Sentence Particles. Ph.D. dissertation, University of Michigan.

Voloshinov, V. N. 1973 *Philosophy and the Philosophy of Language*. L. Matejka and I. R. Titunik, trans. New York: Seminar Press. (Original in Russian, 1929.)

Vygotsky, Lev 1978 *Mind in Society*. Cambridge, MA: Harvard University Press.

Ward, M. C. 1971 *Them Children*. New York: Holt, Rinehart and Winston.

Weisner, Thomas and Ronald Gallimore 1977 My Brother's Keeper: Child and Sibling Caretaking. *Current Anthropology* 18(2):169–90.

Zimmerman, Donald and Candace West 1975 Sex Roles, Interruptions and Silences in Conversation. In *Language and Sex: Difference and Dominance*. B. Thorne and N. Henley, eds., pp. 130–51. Rowley, MA: Newbury House.

8 The politics of polygyny in Mende education and child fosterage transactions

Caroline Bledsoe

Suicide is rare in Africa. For this reason, a recent article in a Freetown, Sierra Leone, newspaper commanded immediate attention. A despondent 23-year-old primary school teacher took his life with an overdose of codeine tablets. His motive? Although he passed his Ordinary Level exams at the end of secondary school with high distinction,

> he could not find any means of furthering his education at university level ... In his suicide note he maintained: "I'm taking my life because I've been disappointed. My mother is helpless." It is alleged that his father being a [polygamist] is influenced by the boy's stepmother [the father's other wife] not to show any such interest of advancing the boy's education. (*The New Citizen* 1985)

Although the act of suicide is rare, the incident crystallized two themes that preoccupy many contemporary West Africans: fervent ambitions for education and conflicts among polygynous wives over the educational prospects of the children.

Polygynous wives in Sierra Leone are sometimes close and cooperative. Indeed, at times the husband is almost a peripheral member of the household, especially if a senior wife initiated the search for a junior wife and paid all or part of the bridewealth (see Bledsoe 1980 for Liberian marital patterns). However, co-wives eventually compete explicitly or implicitly (see, for example, Wilson 1971:122 on the Nyakyusa and Price 1984 on the Caribbean). A focus of contemporary competition is children – how many a woman has and the likelihood of their future success, in contrast to those of her co-wives. In Sierra Leone, the likelihood of children succeeding increasingly centers on education.

Among those involved in Third World development, recent interest has focused on a woman's own education status and how it affects her upward aspirations, fertility, and quality of life. However, formal schooling remains beyond the reach of most rural African women. Few enrol at all, and most who do must drop out early to marry and bear children. Lacking educational opportunities themselves, women increasingly seek benefits from their children's schooling. Although most women do not wish to curtail their fertility, they recognize increasingly that high fertility is useless unless some of their children eventually acquire patronage and jobs. Their aims, however, frequently conflict with those of co-wives who are simultaneously vying for scarce household resources to help their own children. I examine co-wife ranking among rural Mende families in Sierra Leone, as based primarily on the status of a woman's family background, in determining whose child gains the best opportunities for education and advancement. In conclusion, I discuss the implications of these patterns of intra-household female hierarchies for stratification in the larger society, for rethinking the well-known West African pattern of separate male and female budgets, and for gaining insights into continued high fertility.

Setting

Many Mende practice slash-and-burn rice agriculture, though cash crop-ping and diamond mining have intensified the demand for imported staples. Prestige comes from living in large towns and having access to modern amenities such as imported foods and motorized transportation. The hierarchical system of local chieftaincies has been incorporated into the national Parliamentary and Presidential system. Yet despite its formal nomenclature, the political system consists basically of patron–client ties. Even rural people seek patrons in the modern sector who can offer employment and intervene with the government hierarchy; and while the modern system offers enticing opportunities, court cases that strip people of land, money, and dependants are commonly trumped up against individuals with weakly developed patronage ties. As in the past, children are valued for labor and old-age support as well as for advantageous affinal and patronage links they can forge. Although there has long been a cultural notion of "development" (*tɛɛ-guloma*), in the sense of bigger farms and larger families, people now seek to "develop" the family's social standing and access to resources through formal schooling and powerful urban contacts.

Polygyny

Some scholars view African polygyny as an anomaly in urban settings and in rural populations that orientate increasingly toward the city (Lombard 1954; Goode 1970). It is seen as incompatible with pressures of modern urban life, where plural wives drain rather than add to household resources. However, World Fertility Survey data from Kenya (1980) reveal only slight differences among polygynous women by age cohorts, educational status, and urban versus rural residence (see also Clignet 1970: Van de Walle and Kekovole 1984). Even where urban formalities necessitate having only one wife, institutions such as the "outside wife" (Baker and Bird 1959; Harrell-Bond 1975), "deuxième bureau" (Lacombe 1983), or "serial monogamy" (Comaroff 1977) offer functional substitutes.

For rural Mende men, plural wives provide farming and household labor and hospitality to important visitors. Co-wives may share house-keeping duties, and fill in for each other during sicknesses or absences. Polygyny allows a man whose wife is breastfeeding to maintain a sexual life, yet follow the expectations of post-partum sexual abstinence. Families eligible for chieftaincies view polygyny as essential for maintaining their voting strength and a pool of viable candidates. Even for lesser families, polygyny increases the likelihood of producing children who can help them advance. These forces result in a high incidence of polygyny. In my survey of 154 households, 38.7 percent of all married men (mostly middle aged or older ones) were currently polygynous. For married women, 56.1 percent were in polygynous marriages. Of these, most had one or two co-wives (39 percent and 35 percent respectively). The highest reported was ten. Yet even women who are not currently in a polygynous marriage are likely to be so at some point because divorce and widowhood are common, as are remarriage and widow inheritance (see also Van de Walle and Kekovole 1984).

Sources of co-wife competition

Because husbands should avoid overt signs of favoritism, many provide their wives and children with a few basics, leaving the women to furnish everything else for their own children. Yet despite the ideal of the husband's impartiality, there are some important differences among wives. Temporal precedence in the house is crucial: the senior or "head" wife (*nyaha-waai*, "big woman/wife") has authority over the junior or "small" wives (*nyaha-wului*, "small woman/wife"), each of whom is ranked above the next who came in. The senior wife handles the house-hold's administrative and fiscal tasks and can delegate burdensome chores to junior wives. These rankings are reflected in terminology: a junior wife refers to her senior as her "big wife" and calls her "older sister" or "mother" if the age gap is wide. Two other kinds of wives are important: an "official wife," required by an important urban man who must appear in official contexts with only one wife who is most educated, attractive, and cultured; and the "beloved wife," who may receive better clothes, more money, and a separate house, and may be seen more often in public with the husband. A third category, "outside wife," refers to a woman not officially married to the man, but who may actively compete for his favors and resources. In sum, polygyny appears to benefit women who, as senior wives, can control the productive enterprises of their junior subordinates (see also Steady 1987:212).

Co-wife ranks and labels lend structure to the household, but they also lay the groundwork for rivalries. Small acts of favoritism, whether real or perceived, infuse polygynous life. A husband who buys a shirt for one wife's child should buy an article of clothing of equal value for the other's child. If he shares some of his leftover food with one wife's children, the other wives are watching. If he gives one wife money to take her desperately sick child to the clinic, the others broodingly recall the times they were told to "try for themselves" with their own trading endeavors. This is a no-win situation, as one man complained: "Even if you give one wife some money to take her child to the clinic, the others will be watching, and will soon demand more things of you." Such patterns suggest that as the number of co-wives increases, the stipulation that men should refrain from favoritism intensifies, making the separation between men's and women's incomes, for which Africa is noted (Boserup 1970), strongest in polygynous households.

Not surprisingly, arguments among wives often center on who is the "favorite wife." Typically a senior wife will claim this status, but her junior will counter, "Although you were brought in earlier, I was brought in because our husband loved me." If the husband must have a favorite, he is expected to choose the first one he married, out of respect for her seniority. But youth and beauty influence his sentiments. Many domestic battles are waged by senior wives who resent the impertinence of a pretty, young wife who seeks the husband's intervention to escape drudgery. Family status also influences favoritism. A new wife from a high-status family may become the official wife and gain favor over older wives (see Murphy and Bledsoe 1987 on the Kpelle of Liberia).

In some cases the favoritism accorded one wife and her children is accepted by the rest, especially when it follows temporal precedence in the house. And, as a rule, the greater the age differential between a senior, favored wife and her co-wives, the less the jealousy. However, resentments flare if the senior, favored wife hoards household resources, or if a man favors his pretty, young wife, perhaps because she used mystical means to sway him. Biological anomalies can also create discord: a junior wife's son born before the senior wife's first son may receive a disproportionate share of household resources usually accorded the senior wife's son. But worse problems grow out of inequalities in maternal family statuses. Though a man may profess to treat all his offspring equally, he will try hardest to educate the children of a wife from a high-status family whose good will he is cultivating, regardless of their ages or their mother's temporal precedence.

These status relations among wives and the consequences of favoritism are by no means insignificant. They carry far beyond the immediate household, and impact upon the futures of children of the polygynous union. Ranking among siblings in the next generation rests on their mothers' statuses in their father's home, and the father is likely to choose as his favorite children those of his favorite wife. Thus, seemingly trivial acts of favoritism to wives become bellwether indicators of whose children will receive the best opportunities.

Competition through children

A woman's principal claim to her husband's present resources as well as her expectations of receiving benefits from his estate is through her children. Mothers, more than anyone, must defend their children's interests in polygynous households, and women, more than men, need children for future support. Whereas wide age differences between spouses mean that a man is likely to have at least one wife in his old age, an older woman is likely to be come a marginal "inherited" wife of her dead husband's agnate from whom support is unreliable (Potash 1986). Nor surprisingly, these factors make children the focus of competition in polygynous households. Women realize they need ·to squeeze as many resources as possible out of the marriage for their children.

Because most Mende women will be polygynous at some point, they realize that their children may compete with a wide array of half siblings – present, future, and past – for cash, land, and assistance. As Caldwell and Caldwell have argued: "many women [in Africa], whether monogamously or polygynously married, feel that the central family unit consists of themselves and their children, thus blurring the distinction between monogamy and polygyny" (1981:184–5).

Although everyday relations among wives are often cordial or even warm, women gradually realize that their best long-term security lies in their own children, not those of their co-wives. One of a mother's chief concerns is her children's agnatic rights to property and to positions of leadership. Although all the children of one father technically have equal inheritance rights, the family must choose a head to handle the agnatic property. As the head, this person should allocate family resources to the members for their rents or harvests, house construction, bridewealth, court fines, and so on. Nowadays, because of so many encounters with the national government bureaucracy, the family head is typically an older son with the best education.

The family head inevitably generates controversy. Even a man who tries to allocate resources fairly must meet his own expenses. He is likely, despite his intentions, to be perceived as usurping the father's property and money for himself and his own children. Complained one man, who claimed he brought up most of his fifty-seven younger brothers and sisters after his father died:

> Most of these boys and girls who I brought up are today my bitterest enemies. I brought them up, out of my own labor ... I did *very* well for them. They won't even say good morning to me. If I am sick, nobody will stop at my doors to say, "Brother, what is happening?" They may have the feeling that their father died and left fabulous money, so I may have dealt with it the wrong way [embezzled it]. So I am sure that this is one of their reasons. But it never happened so ... But now we [the sibling group] are falling apart. They are going their own way and I am going mine.

Nonetheless, the danger for women and their respective children lies in the fact that whereas the family head is supposed to consider the interest of the entire agnatic group, it is not unknown for a college-educated son with a job in a government ministry to demand prime family lands for his own cash crops and turn his half-siblings into *de facto* client laborers.

Whose child goes to school?

Even more than children's numbers, their "quality" and promise for success determine how their mothers will benefit from them. Since education can give one wife and her children considerable advantage over another, women have much at stake in whose child gets the best education. My survey of local secondary school students asked, "Who has encouraged you most in your schooling?" Fifty-four percent of 105 students reported their mothers, whereas only 17 percent reported their fathers. Interestingly, slightly more boys than girls said their mothers were most encouraging (56 percent compared to 48 percent). Nor did the mother's own education seem to matter, in contrast to standard views that for the most part only educated women stress education for their children.[1]

Education in contemporary Sierra Leone requires substantial investment. A man may be able to pay the school fees for only one wife's child, or he may be able to send one wife's child to a prestigious school if he sends the other child to a less expensive carpentry apprenticeship. While such economies make sense to men, they can lead to open conflict among women, who worry about their own children's educations as well as the school and career potentials of their co-wives' children. If only one wife's child has advanced to a secondary school with a good reputation and then to a university, jealousies grow acute. The others know that he will soon be remitting money and other urban spoils to his own mother. Moreover, he is likely to seek revenge against the co-wives who slighted or wronged him, or his mother, at home. Even women with no schooling are keenly attuned to whose child is going to what school, and to each child's progress. Because education offers room for ranking based on achievement, it can upset delicate rankings at home. A senior wife is galled if the junior wife's child scores first in the class and hers must repeat a year. Even if co-wives are amiable at first, the scholarly success of one child can divide them, as one insightful man pointed out about the rivalry among a local chief's wives: "Some of these women's children have gone very high in education. They are working. So it is hard to stay on good terms with somebody whose child is high above."

Although relations among wives may begin cordially, over time, disparities in the numbers of their children as well as the children's accomplishments and prospects create rifts between the wives, and small conflicts can grow into irreparable gulfs. Like a subfertile woman, a wife whose children hold little promise begins to realize that she is laboring at best in vain and at worst for the betterment of her rival's children. Even in the best of relationships, these unspoken sentiments create ambivalent feelings.

A naïve man may rationalize that investing disproportionately in one child's education is a good idea, because this sibling will be better positioned to help the younger siblings (full siblings as well as half). But successful children do not always support their siblings to the latter's satisfaction. As a woman explained, the older wife will "relay the message of hatred to her own children," who will then grow up to hate the junior wife and her children. She will ask her children: "Why are you doing kindness to those children? Their mother was abusing [insulting] me and doing bad to me because your father was favoring her."

A local chief had sent the children of his early wives to prestigious urban schools. But as he acquired more wives and children, his resources and his desires to send them all to expensive schools dwindled, especially since he already had several highly successful adult children whom he expected to support the rest. However, some of the younger wives feared that because of their own poor relationships with the important senior wives, their children would receive little support from the senior wives' children. Explained a relative of the chief:

They [men] really can't send their children to the children of the wives with whom they are not on good terms. If my brother and I come from one mother and one father, my father can easily send me to my elder brother to be educated. But it is not likely that you would be sent to the son of a woman that your own mother hated. Sometimes, a son will help the other women's children and try to encourage them, but usually it is hard.

Curiously, the blame for co-wife feuds frequently falls on a husband who is weak enough to display favoritism, especially by discriminating in educational opportunities. The consequences could be serious, as an actual case portended:

The father is so partial [to one wife's children] that he gets the uniforms, fees – everything for them fully ... But for these other children, he doesn't do as much. This is a bad mistake. You cannot tell which of these children is going to be somebody tomorrow. And when that happens, then the child who becomes somebody will be ready to victimize these from the other woman ...

When a father divorces one wife but keeps her children with him, the remaining wife resents his expenditures for the children of a woman no longer contributing to the household and who may, indeed, have been her bitter enemy. A dramatic result of such perceptions underlay the suicide described earlier, and is interpreted culturally as a consequence of the child's lack of an intermediary with the father. The child of a divorced woman is even more vulnerable than before to the father's other wife, as a recent secondary graduate wrote despairingly to me:

I am from a polygynous family wherein my mother had separated long since from my father and I have nobody to advocate for me to my father to put serious attention in my education ... [Even] if I go to university who will help to finance my education? Of course my father will say [he will do it], but [he] will not do it because of my step-mother's influence ... My [own] mother who I was thinking could help me when I attain university level is seriously sick that only God knows whether she will survive, so my plan at home has ruin.

Given the depth of such feelings, it is not surprising that some children of divorced mothers who manage to succeed in fact do ignore their step-mothers and even their fathers. If nothing else, the ill treatment they may have received from the stepmothers (who, of course, expect no future gains from the children of their former rivals) will make them turn their backs.

Co-wives' responses to educational favoritism

With so much at stake in the opportunities of co-wives' children, educational favoritism can cause wives to leave in divorce, insult each other (a major legal offense), or "block the progress" of their rivals' children who, they discern, will be "somebody" in the future. They may give these children laborious work assignments, tell the fathers they are lazy and disrespectful (that is, unworthy of investment), and discredit their legitimacy. In extreme cases, co-wives are said to kill their rivals' children through witchcraft (for other treatments of witchcraft, see Spiro and Hauser-Schäublin, this volume). In the past, subfertile co-wives were among the first to be suspected of witchcraft aimed at the children of a highly fertile woman. In contrast, modern witches allegedly worry most about the children of their co-wives with promising school and career potentials. This notion of future threat is important. To the Mende, witches have qualities opposite from normal human beings: whereas ordinary humans can know only the past, witches can see only the future. This makes them exceedingly indifferent to those who have helped them. It also allows them to foresee which children will be successful, and to move quickly to "block their progress." Explained one person:

They try to witch you, because they can see in advance what you will become in the future ... Because they know these schoolgoing children, they know their standard [status] or maturity in the future, where the advancement will stop. They know their wealth in the future. So they will try to destroy it. If the child were allowed to live, he would be very powerful [those who are witched would have succeeded]. That's how the family's progress is debarred.

Because witches must act quickly to quash children of great potential, they may poison the children's food or the mothers' breasts. Witches can also make children go crazy or disfigure their bodies – anything to "thwart their progress" toward becoming powerful adults. To prevent this, fathers and mothers try to disguise their eager hopes for particular children by dressing them shabbily and suppressing signs of favoritism. And parents sometimes foster out promising children to protect them from their mothers' co-wives, especially if glaring imbalances exist in the wives' fertility or in the children's perceived "cleverness."

As children get older, it becomes harder to hide their potentials from witches. Whereas witchcraft is still feared at the end of secret initiation society sessions when young women are ripe for marriage and young men for productive lives, witchcraft is now most feared during exams at the end of primary and secondary school when certain children are beginning to forge ahead. Witches hear about scores and learn which children are likely to get scholarships to go to college and begin successful careers. Such children need not be killed to thwart their progress: a common witchcraft practice nowadays is to make promising students fail their exams. A man described how a witch might do this:

[Let's say] my own child is not doing properly in school or in the vocation he is trying to get and yours is going ahead: every day he is bringing in excellent reports [report cards], topping my own children – just outstanding marks, posts [jobs];

everything is going well. So if I have witch [powers], I will make that charm against him [your child]. I will make that woman's child fail or to block his mind, so he won't pass any examination.

Witches also nullify the effects of education, leaving the victims unable to fulfil their potentials. One man received a doctorate in mathematics in England, enormously outdistancing the achievements of his half siblings. But he languishes in Freetown with no prospects, his unemployment attributed to witchcraft by his mother's jealous co-wives. Alternatively, witches may "convert the hearts" of children who do become successful, making them forget their mothers' needs later in life, arguably the worst fate that could befall a mother. A young man explained: "They [witches] will convert the children's hearts, not to ever love or help the mother, so she will always remain like that [in stagnant living conditions]. They will make the children to hate the mother. They will never visit her." He cited a boy in his family who was favored by his mother and father. They sent him to school and gave him anything he wanted: money, school fees, fine clothes. Seeing how the father – professing poverty – would not pay their own children's school fees, the mother's co-wives made him fail his exams and "converted his heart" through witchcraft. He has since ignored his mother and father and has brought them no "benefit," despite their considerable investments in him.

Fosterage as a response to co-wives' competition

One of the most important ways in which a child's quality can be enhanced to bring the mother security is through fosterage, a common West African institution (Schildkrout 1973; Etienne 1983; Goody 1982; Oppong and Bleek 1982; Isiugo-Abanihe 1985; Bledsoe and Isiugo-Abanihe 1989). In fosterage, a child is sent to, not adopted by, a relative, friend, or patron of the parents (compare Etienne 1983). Often a small child is sent out for weaning to the mother's sister or to the child's real or classificatory "granny." But fosterage also connotes "training" for future life: "household training" (for girls), trade apprenticeship, Arabic training (for Muslims), and formal schooling. Either parents or guardians may pay a child's school fees, but most of the upkeep is left to the guardian.

Thirty-four percent of the children under 18 who were born to women in the households which I surveyed were currently away from their mothers – one definition of fosterage (see also Page 1989) – while 39 percent of the children present in the households were without mothers. Of the children under five, 23 percent were fostered out, as were 28 percent from 6 to 10 years old, and 46 percent from 11 to 15 years old. (These figures, however, are low compared to some other Mende areas of

Sierra Leone, where over 50 percent of the children over 2 years of age are away, see Isiugo-Abanihe 1985:62.)

Co-wives' interests in fostering in children

A guardian's interest is expressed by a Mende proverb: "A child is not for one person." That is, many people have interests in a child. Since foster children usually work harder than children born into the household, even people with children of their own rely on foster children for farming labor, marketing, household chores, and child care. People also foster in children in hopes of future reciprocity. This strategy is expressed in another proverb: "Children are like a young bamboo tree: you don't know which of the shoots will be cut away, and which will remain." That is, a young bamboo tree has many shoots which people gradually cut away as needed, leaving only a few to grow thick and tall. Just as only a few bamboo shoots will remain from a large initial group, one never knows which child will emerge as a "big person." Thus, those children who do succeed have a multitude of claimants. People who made any contribution at all to a young wage earner – school fees, food, even a bowl of rice one day when he was hungry – will demand assistance because they "helped" him.

A subfertile woman often attempts to foster in children to obtain labor as well as future support. She may also foster children to try to dissuade her husband from acquiring another wife to fill his own child gap (see also Harrell-Bond 1975:143). But even for a woman with children of her own, fostering in others provides labor. Foster children become future allies for support against rival co-wives and their children who try to usurp the household's resources. Finally, in case a woman's own children do not advance, or, worse, if they prove "ungrateful" to her, these former foster children broaden her base of potential supporters. Indeed, a woman may invest more in her foster children than in her own, if they are serious students and demonstrate unquestioning loyalty.

Some women attempt to block the progress of their co-wives' foster children – much like "born" children. Especially if a woman's rival brought a child in to educate, she may keep the child busy with chores, feed the child poorly, and complain about the child's laziness and insolence to her husband, hoping he will send the child home. But for the most part, in-fostered children are perceived as less threatening than co-wives' own children. Witchcraft against foster children is rare.

The chief worry about foster children is insuring their loyalty, whether they be her own or those of her husband's family members, non-relatives, or the children of a junior wife. Especially if the senior wife and the biological mother later become enemies, the latter may plant seeds of unrest in the child she gave her co-wife. No matter how much a foster mother invests in other women's children, doubts concerning loyalty always lurk in the background. A woman explained: "You never know whether the children will love you more than their own mothers and thus bring you sufficient benefit."

Out-fosterage

Increasingly, sending older children away to better schools in more urban areas is an avenue of social mobility for them. Parents hope that the education and contacts gained from fosterage will allow their children to rise in the national government or business bureaucracy or to make advantageous marriages. Such children can forestall trouble for parents with government authorities or tax collectors, deflect damaging lawsuits by village rivals, or help their parents lodge their own court suits as plaintiffs.

Because of its potential for upward mobility for children and families, fosterage manifests clear geographical patterns. No one wants all his or her children to grow up in a small town, unless it has a highly reputed school. Small children may be fostered out to live with rural elderly female "grannies," but by the time they reach the "age of sense" (6 to 8 years), most are brought back to the parents or sent on to more urban areas to receive training in "civilized" ways and attend good schools. In turn, guardians' children may be fostered out simultaneously to a yet larger town where they attend more prestigious schools. This situation produces a geographical and stratification gradient of fosterage with fascinating implications for social mobility, fertility, and mortality (see Bledsoe and Isiugo-Abanihe 1989; Bledsoe, Ewbank, and Isiugo-Abanihe 1988). Whereas Western thought posits that a child should grow up with one stable set of caregivers, the Mende hold almost the opposite tenet: a rural child who has not been fostered out to a guardian of higher status or to a more urban area is either unworthy or dull.

Women invest enormous competitive energy in fostering out their own children to the best situations. Many co-wife jealousies erupt over foster-age opportunities for children to live with teachers, who can ensure that the children will study, or with well-placed government and business officials. One man had an opportunity to send one of his sons to an important government official in Freetown. Instead of the senior wife's son, he chose a more junior co-wife's son about the same age as hers. Reported a relative, "She [the senior wife] was vexed because her own son wasn't getting such a great opportunity, because the guardian is such a big man and Freetown is a great opportunity for a child." Whether a child is sent to live with a wealthy urban relative to attend school or to a rural farmer has a decisive impact on his mother's old age. Although a child who has seen the city lights and enjoys the easy urban life may forget his mother's troubles, the possible returns from a child with a steady urban income are well worth the risks, and fosterage opportunities like this are singular prizes.

It is difficult to determine explicit motives for sending children for fosterage. Although a child can be sent for weaning, training, or help for incapacitated or subfertile relatives, these are often surface rationales for underlying battles of advancement in the household. Although a woman may say she sent away a child because she feared harm by jealous co-wives, she may have done this more to promote his interests in a high-status urban household.[2]

Men's problems in appearing fair in fostering out children

When a woman cannot pay her own children's school fees, she must rely on her husband for this money. His own security, however, rests on diversifying his children's training. He may plan to send one child to college, one to typing school, and one to learn carpentry, and keep one on the farm. Yet co-wife rivalries put him in an awkward position. Whose child will he send to school? Whose will he keep on the farm? Even if he has a favorite wife he must at least appear fair, as one polygynist explained: "If you send a certain number of one wife's children to school, you have to send the same number of kids from the other wife to school."

Men talk about which of their children is "clever" and can benefit most from living with a wealthy urban guardian for schooling. But the rationale of academic ability does not alleviate the ill feelings of wives whose children are *not* perceived as clever. Investing only in one child is an act of favoritism, and can result in domestic altercation or even in harm to the child. In the light of limited resources, many men resort to secrecy, as a husband confided:

Usually the husband tries to educate only one child: that of the beloved wife ... And he will do this secretly, often. If he tries to educate a few more, all the wives will come to him, demanding that their children be educated – as many as possible.

Men go to elaborate ends to hide the fact that they are educating such children. According to one man:

... they give their child the money to go back to school – secretly ... When you ask them about their child, they will say, "Oh, that man! I have labored for him, done everything, but he is doing nothing good for me. In fact, I have heard that he has left school. He is just walking in the streets, going up and down. The last time he came, I gave him 150 pounds [US$255 in 1982]. He has embezzled everything! Now he is no longer my child! In fact, if the mother steps in [on his behalf], I will drive her [away]!" All this is to make people forget that he is doing something for the child ...

The mothers of children who are being educated secretly in distant areas may also collude. In fact, continued the same man:

the mother of such a child is really the main one propagating the story that the father is not helping her child to get educated. She will go grumbling, "I am here laboring for the man, but he does not care for my child. Even the last time when my child came for holidays, he would not pay his school fees. I had to go to my brother and he helped me. Also, I borrowed some money." All this deception is ... especially meant to deceive the mates [co-wives], so they won't know the husband is doing more progress for her own child.

Women who arrange advantageous fosterage situations for their children may use tricks to avoid arousing their co-wives' suspicions. One person related that a woman will feign worry at her child's absence, though she herself encouraged him to "wander" over to a house where she wants him to live. After she "finds" him, she will say to the person who took him in, "You have been very kind to my child, so to avoid worries at home, if you don't mind, he can stay here." The issue of education may not come up immediately. Eventually, it will be the child, again, who will be prompted to bring up this subject with the guardian:

Each time the mother meets the child, she will say, "Have you started school? Have you decided to go to school?" Then the child will say, "Well, I want to go to school," and the mother will tell the guardian, "Each time your niece [or nephew] leaves the home for school, he/she is very displeased or very uneasy. Supposing she is sent to school?" [Then] the guardian will say, "This boy or girl is wasting time here. Each time his playmates go to school, he will be very uneasy, very lonely. Supposing he or she is sent to school? Would that suit you?" Then the parents will agree, saying "Okay, that is a nice idea. We will agree." So then they [all] come to the conclusion and the child is sent to school ... [This is how] the woman may try to get advantage for her children.

Polygynous men privately approve of these strategies because they can appear to acquiesce to a *fait accompli*, rather than actively have to arrange an advantageous opportunity for one wife's child. One husband cited such a case: what he called women's "reasonable tricks." His ex-wife, seeking to get her daughter away from him, told her sister in Freetown to ask for the girl. But although the man suspected what his wife was up to, he gave his permission since the benefits he might realize from a child raised and educated in Freetown would probably outweigh the difficulties posed by his attenuated ties to her.

The role of maternal relatives in fosterage

Particularly when co-wife relations are not cordial, a woman looks to her own relatives to support her children's education and their rights to property and office, a pattern that parallels traditional ties to maternal kin for support in the competitive agnatic household (see Fortes 1945; Comaroff and Roberts 1981). Maternal "grannies" can offer such support, raising young children until school age. And when a wealthy urban "granny" offers to send the child to school, it may stay with her until maturity because she will promote its best interests, as a man explained:

You know, sometimes we the fathers are stubborn or may tend to have a lot of children. If I had, say, three wives, and had children from each, and the granny [the mother of one of the wives] was also a well-to-do woman ... she should definitely go with the opinion that if they stay with me, because I have many other children, I wouldn't pay much attention to the sons or grandchildren of hers [her own daughter]. So she would want to take the grandchildren to bring them up to the status she would want.

Besides grandmothers, a mother's sisters frequently take in children, and older children by the same mother take in their younger siblings. But people draw most attention to women's brothers as supporters of their nephews' and nieces' educations.[3] In my secondary school survey, I asked students, "Who paid most of your school fees this year?" Besides those who reported mothers and fathers, eight reported their mothers' brothers compared with four who said their fathers' brothers, despite an ideology of agnates helping each others' children.[4] One young man described why his uncle sent for him:

I am staying with my uncle, my mother's brother, because he felt that if I came to him, my process of education would be easier. When I was with my father, we were farming ... My father had many wives and some of the children they had were [already] going to school, but when I was young, my father didn't pay much attention to my education ... My mother, having a jealous mind for some of her mates [co-wives], thought I should not stay in the home, but should go to school.

To allay co-wife jealousies, the mother secretly asked her brother to ask for her son so that she did not appear actively to be promoting his interests.

Maternal family status and ranking in the agnatic household

Although one Mende ideal holds that fathers should give equal educational opportunities to all their wives' children, fathers actually invest more in "clever" children or in high birth-order children. However, cleverness and seniority usually take second place to the social and economic status of a child's maternal family. Wealthy maternal relatives have little interest in paying the school fees for children of their sisters' or daughters' co-wives. And a husband cannot offend a high-status wife's family by sending her child to a rural school and the child of a low-status wife to an important urban patron to attend school. Children of high-status wives receive the benefit of the doubt when educational choices must be made.

Occasionally, family background coincides unproblematically with temporal seniority; a young man from an important family may receive his first wife by a high-status family wishing to make its daughter the senior wife of a potential leader. But too often, the criteria conflict. An upwardly mobile young man from a poor background begins to receive women from progressively higher-status families (besides those he receives from clients). In such cases, matrilateral ties create advantages in the household for junior wives who should otherwise be ranked lower (Clignet 1970:51) and unequal advantages for their children. Over time a woman's precedence itself may be reconstructed, rather than comprising an immutable empirical fact. A junior wife from a high-status family may become defined as the senior wife, while a senior wife from a low-status family will be divorced or tucked quietly into the background (Bledsoe and Murphy 1980). These forces bestow advantages on children of high-status mothers.

Even paternal recognition itself may rest on maternal family status, if a successful man's position demands monogamous appearances. As Clignet (1987:204) shows, polygyny is not necessarily at odds with urbanization and modernization. Rather, the wife of the "courtyard" is the wife of the country, while the wife of the "heart" lives with the husband in the city. In one case, a rural secondary-school graduate married a woman who bore him a child. Leaving them in the village, he took a job in Freetown at the Ministry of Works, and eventually married a woman from an elite Creole family. At first he regularly visited his first wife and child. But after bearing a child by the Creole woman, he broke all ties with his village wife and withheld his address from her. Now although he has not divorced her formally, he recognizes only the Creole wife and her children.

Another case even better illustrates mobility strategies of marrying up the educational and stratification hierarchy, as well as sloughing off low-status wives. A young rural man with some primary education married an illiterate wife. Within a few years, his small trading business grew, and a local family removed one of their daughters from school to become his second wife. Both women bore children. In time he moved to Freetown and bought several large cargo trucks and a supermarket. At this point he acquired a Freetown wife much more educated than he, and little more was heard about the first two wives or their children.[5] Indeed, the new wife insisted that she was the only wife. Her children were educated in Freetown, while the others managed to attend school up-country by drawing on meager resources of their own maternal families.

Who ends up as the "official" or "favored" wife, then, is crucial to the life chances of children, particularly when their father is upwardly mobile.[6] Although an occasional "outside" child will be welcomed by the father's legal wife, particularly if she is barren, into the father's household, most wives refuse to acknowledge their husbands' "outside" children. A man may still support children by low-status women if he wants to maintain ties with their families, yet these children generally receive fewer advantages, and they and their maternal families become increasingly marginalized, geographically as well as socially.

Discussion

The material presented in this chapter has several important implications for the study of gender hierarchy. While legal and economic necessities produce a show of co-wife congeniality and equality, co-wife relations are often fraught with inequality and with suppressed tension particularly over children that can erupt in pitched battles or in witchcraft accusations. Female relations, in this case those between co-wives, can be just as unequal as those of males (Tiger 1978).

The ramifications of this competition for larger issues in African social organization are wide indeed. Before discussing them, however, I point out that the number of people involved and the ways in which they figure in the competition are considerably larger than they might appear. This chapter has focused on present co-wives. However, women in polygynous societies implicitly compete with their husbands' children by previous wives. They also compete with their husbands' future wives and children, all quite real threats because of high rates of divorce and remarriage. By rules of lineage extension, moreover, women must worry about their husbands' brothers' wives (past, present, and future – whom they also call "co-wives") and children. Finally, the polygynous model extends to competitors a wife only suspects: "outside" wives and children, whom she may meet only at her husband's funeral when they suddenly appear to lodge inheritance claims. Because of these myriad permutations, women and their children implicitly compete for family resources with a wide range of potential rivals.

Using a competitive polygynous model, we can now attempt to draw fresh interpretations of some key conjugal patterns that heretofore have been explained in other ways. Two such patterns initially seem remote.

Africa is particularly noted for one of these: the separation of husband's and wife's incomes (see, for example, Boserup 1970). This pattern is attributed most often to inherent tension between husbands and wives, and to wives' efforts to build independent economic enterprises. I do not dispute this interpretation. But the separation of incomes – and, indeed, the husband/wife tension itself – may stem as much from competition among women (whether from present co-wives or other potential female competitors) as from competition between the male/female pair. Women attempting to ward off other women's efforts to appropriate their resources can most easily do so by retaining their earnings separately from the resources administered by the husband. Given this framework, it becomes more obvious why men seldom dispute with wives' rights to accumulate their own private resources: men can avoid the appearance of favoritism by invoking the profit motive both to their individual wives, inciting them to support themselves and their children, and to explain to other wives why these resources cannot be shared among the group. Economic separation between the sexes paradoxically benefits husbands as well as wives.

Second, we can ask about the effects of polygynous competition on attitudes toward fertility. The material presented here suggests that it is not simply power struggles with men or affinal relatives that make women anxious to bolster their positions by having many children.[7] The Mende readily point out that polygynous competition makes women anxious to keep having children to gain as many resources from the agnatic house-hold as their co-wives (past, present, and future). Infertility or subfertility, an anguishing problem in general for African women, is particularly severe in the context of polygyny, since a subfertile wife must watch whatever productive efforts she exerts for the household going to benefit her co-wives' children. Women jealously observe the children their co-wives bear and the number that survive. Even when a man marries a woman with children by a previous man, she wants to "catch up" and have as many children by the man as her new co-wives, to derive as many benefits from the marriage as they do.[8] Fearing to shortchange some of their wives, men are reluctant advocates of birth control.

Recasting issues in these ways forces us to ask whether patterns of female competition influence status relations between husbands and wives in ways that are usually examined more narrowly simply as issues of male/ female relations. This more balanced approach plays on different sets of female as well as male rankings within households and on individuals' relationships to the wider society.

Turning now to issues of education and ranking, co-wife competition certainly bears important implications for discussions of education in countries such as Sierra Leone. It is true that fathers tend to be more educated than mothers. But by spelling out the factors that create and intensify intra-household inequalities among wives, this chapter questions the assumption particularly common in development studies that the most educated people, by definition, will most value education and promote it for their children. Even women who have never set foot in a school have become aggressive promoters of the education of their children, who draw on the status they derive in the outside world to compete for paternal resources with their half-siblings. Because women are reticent to reveal to the other wives that they are trying to push their own children ahead, their surface indifference to education can mask covert strategies to educate their children. Here fosterage is significant, for someone else can appear to send the child to school.

Another issue on which the competitive co-wife model can shed light is social stratification in the wider society. Polygyny is often seen as an equalizer in Africa, spreading resources among a man's children regardless of maternal family status (Goody 1971, 1976). This institution, among others, lends an overall quality of classlessness to African social organization. In contrast to the Eurasian model, microlevel African inequalities typically cross-cut kin groups rather than differentiate them. However, this chapter shows that acute social differences can flourish within a single polygynous household.

Although this phenomenon was undoubtedly true in the past with "favorite" or "official" wives, recent legal and religious pressures may have sharpened these differences. Men who must appear monogamous redefine low-status wives as non-wives by divorcing them, labeling them "outside" or "country" wives, or eventually choosing one legal wife from among several partners. The woman in whom a man eventually invests the most resources is almost invariably the most educated and has the best family connections (see also Comaroff and Roberts 1977). As Baker and Bird (1959:115; see also Harrell-Bond 1975:141) point out for urban Africa, "if a woman cannot fulfil the stringent qualifications normally required for a statutory marriage, namely a high degree of education and social status, she may herself be an 'outside' wife, that is, a partner to an unregularised conjugal union ... she stands, as it were, in a 'second class' position."

Women's status and education in turn lay the basis for their children's own educations in successive generations. Children of higher-status mothers generally receive more resources than those of lower-status mothers, not to say "outside" children. Moreover, women who were born as "outside" children are themselves likely to become "outside" wives (Harrell-Bond 1975:134). Thus, co-wife competition, by intensifying inequalities among women in the polygynous household, can create differential opportunities in the modern world for children of the same man. Education becomes a basis of inequality across the generations, but through the use of fosterage which obscures the increasing inequality among the wives.

Aside from the effects of co-wife competition on inequality at the familial level, the material examined here suggests that inequality is widening inter-generationally and probably sharpening hierarchy – in the sense of systematic gaps between groups – in the wider society. As polygyny moves into the modern world, co-wife tensions become institutionalized early in marriage, since decisions requiring household resources must be made for very young children; even 3-year-olds can now enter primary school. Present structures of inequality thus move toward more rigidly defined hierarchy through the opportunistic use of education. Ever-increasing competition at the household level over children's chances for education may actively drive the wider system itself toward more stratification. What is significant about the present case is that because maternal ties are so crucial to women and their children, the same man's children can be born with drastically different life chances by virtue of their mothers' statuses. Hence, the demise or continuation of polygyny may have little impact on the development of hierarchically ranked groups, if not classes.

Although mobility strategies may induce husbands and their "official" or favorite wives toward more "nuclear" family structure and class division, since norms of equal agnatic treatment cannot realistically be followed, Mann (1985:70) demonstrates on the basis of her study in Lagos, Nigeria, that change is not linear. Monogamous men can take on additional or "outside" wives as easily as polygynous men can become monogamous, in certain economic and social circumstances. In addition, the material presented here suggests that educated people do not simply abandon polygyny because of their modern acculturated beliefs. Rather, educated men and their educated wives can define their marriages as legitimate monogamy, while reclassifying other women either as low-status "country" wives or "outside" wives. Therefore, polygyny itself can become more "monogamous" through failure to recognize lower-status co-wives and their children, or through marginalizing them. That is, polygyny can become monogamy through an active process of reducing wives, rather than a man deciding at the outset of his marital career to marry only one woman at a time.

NOTES

This chapter is based on material from 1981–2 fieldwork in a rural Mende town of about 4,500 in eastern Sierra Leone and from a 1985 trip to a larger town in the

Southern Province. The project was financed by support from the Ford and Rockefeller Foundation, the Population Council, and the National Science Foundation. I am grateful to the following people for comments, insights, and other assistance rendered for this chapter: Bruce Bellingham, John Comaroff, Uche Isiugo-Abanihe, Kathy Mason, William Murphy, Anne Pebley, and Etienne van de Walle.

1 Substantiation comes from attendance records at a local primary school. Contrary to my expectations, students who attended school most regularly were not those living with both parents, or with fathers (and fathers' wives). The best attenders were living with mothers alone, suggesting that single mothers, despite their illiteracy and needs for household labor, most sought to ensure their children's school progress.

2 It is also true that people use fears of co-wife witchcraft as excuses. I even found myself doing this with a long-time friend, a young woman whose family had forced her to drop out of secondary school and marry a chief. I suggested she allude to witchcraft to get her husband's approval to take her toddler and go to urban relatives who might help her return to school.

3 Demographic facts may play a role in this phenomenon. Since most women are younger than their husbands, their brothers by the same mothers are also likely to be younger and more educated than the women's husbands, and less likely to be married or have school-age children. Brothers can help their sisters before they face demands from their own conjugal families.

4 Maternal relations can also suffer by efforts to push children ahead. Even full sisters compete for their brothers' assistance, much as co-wives compete for their husband's resources. One woman grew angry when her brother took the son of her twin sister and sent him to school, but did not ask for one of her own children. Her resentment only increased when this child became a school teacher, while her own children showed little ambition.

5 However, men play off definitions of marriage in different contexts. When an elite man deals with important urbanites, he ignores his rural wives or refers to them as "outside wives." But if he returns to strengthen rural ties, he treats them as legitimate customary wives.

6 This phenomenon cannot be explained entirely by the onset of urbanization and a cash economy. While differing codes of marriage highlight the contemporary contrast between "official" and "outside" wives, children were also differentiated in the past by maternal family status (Murphy and Bledsoe 1986). See also La Fontaine (1962) for an analysis of emerging class differences in Gisu marriages.

7 See Mason (1984) for a review of the relationship of fertility to the status of women in developing countries.

8 Michele Garenne's figures for Senegal (pers. comm. in 1985), however, suggest that this does not happen in reality. A wife who comes in with previous children soon faces a biological limit.

REFERENCES

Baker, Tanya and Mary Bird 1959 Urbanisation and the Position of Women. *The Sociological Review* 7:99–122.

Bledsoe, Caroline H. 1980 *Women and Marriage in Kpelle Society*. Stanford: Stanford University Press.

Bledsoe, Caroline, Douglas Ewbank, and Uche C. Isiugo-Abanihe 1988 The Effect of Child Fostering on Feeding Practices and Access to Health Services in Sierra Leone. *Social Science and Medicine* 27(6):627–36.

Bledsoe, Caroline and Uche C. Isiugo-Abanihe 1989 Strategies of Child Fosterage among Mende "Grannies" in Sierra Leone. In *African Reproduction and Social Organization in Sub-Saharan Africa*. Ron Lesthaeghe, ed., pp. 442–74. Berkeley: University of California Press.

Bledsoe, Caroline and William P. Murphy 1980 The Kpelle Negotiation of Marriage and Matrilateral Ties. In *The Versatility of Kinship*. L. S. Cordell and S. Beckerman, eds., pp. 145–63. San Francisco: Academic Press.

Boserup, Ester 1970 *Woman's Role in Economic Development*. New York: St Martin's Press.

Caldwell, John and Pat Caldwell 1981 Cause and Consequence in the Reduction of Postnatal Abstinence in Ibadan City, Nigeria. In *Child-Spacing in Tropical Africa: Traditions and Change*. Hilary J. Page and Ron Lesthaeghe, eds., pp. 73–92. New York: Academic Press.

Clignet, Remi 1970 *Many Wives, Many Powers: Authority and Power in Polygynous Families*. Evanston, IL: Northwestern University Press.

1987 On dit que la polygamie est morte: vive la polygamie. In *Transformations of African Marriage*. David Parkin and David Nyamawaya, eds., pp. 199–209. Manchester: Manchester University Press.

Comaroff, John and S. Roberts 1977 Marriage and Extra-Marital Sexuality: The Dialectics of Legal Change among the Kgatla. *Journal of African Law* 21:97–123.

1981 *Rules and Processes: The Cultural Logic of Dispute in an African Context*. Chicago: University of Chicago Press.

Etienne, Mona 1983 Gender Relations and Conjugality among the Baule. In *Female and Male in West Africa*. Christine Oppong, ed., pp. 303–19. London: George Allen and Unwin.

Fortes, Meyer 1945 *The Dynamics of Clanship among the Tallensi*. London: Oxford University Press.

Goode, William I. 1970 *World Revolution and Family Patterns*. New York: The Free Press.

Goody, Esther 1982 *Parenthood and Social Reproduction: Fostering and Occupational Roles in West Africa*. New York: Cambridge University Press.

Goody, Jack 1971 Class and Marriage in Africa and Eurasia. *American Journal of Sociology* 76:585–603.

1976 *Production and Reproduction: A Comparative Study of the Domestic Domain*. New York: Cambridge University Press.

Harrell-Bond, Barbara 1975 *Modern Marriage in Sierra Leone: A Study of the Professional Group*. The Hague: Mouton.

Isiugo-Abanihe, Uche 1985 Child Fosterage in West Africa. *Population and Development Review* 11:53–73.

Kenya, Central Bureau of Statistics 1980 *Kenya Fertility Survey 1977–78*. First *Report*, Vol. 1. Nairobi.

Lacombe, Bernard 1983 *Le Deuxième bureau: secteur informel de la nuptialité en milieu urbain congolais*. Paris: Stateco, No. 35.

La Fontaine, Jean 1962 Gisu Marriage and Affinal Relations. In *Marriage in Tribal Societies.* Meyer Fortes, ed., pp. 88–120. New York: Cambridge University Press.

Lombard, J. 1954 Cotonou, ville africaine. Tendances évolutive et reaction des coutumes traditionelles. *Bulletin de l'Institut Français d'Afrique Noire* 16(3–4):341–77.

Mann, Kristin 1985 *Marrying Well: Marriage, Status and Social Change among the Educated Elite in Colonial Lagos.* New York: Cambridge University Press.

Mason, Karen Oppenheim 1984 *The Status of Women: A Review of its Relationship to Fertility and Mortality.* New York: The Rockefeller Foundation.

Murphy, William and Caroline Bledsoe 1987 Territory and Matrilateral Kinship in the History of a Kpelle Chiefdom. In *The Internal African Frontier: The Reproduction of Traditional African Societies.* Igor Kopytoff, ed., pp. 121–47. Bloomington: Indiana University Press.

The New Citizen 1985 Teacher Commits Suicide. 13 July.

Oppong, Christine and Wolf Bleek 1982 Economic Models and Having Children: Some Evidence from Kwahu, Ghana. *Africa* 52:15–33.

Page, Hilary J. 1989 Child-Bearing Versus Child-Rearing: Co-Residence of Mothers and Children in Sub-Saharan Africa. In *Reproduction and Social Organization in Sub-Saharan Africa.* Ron Lesthaeghe, ed., pp. 401–41. Berkeley: University of California Press.

Potash, Betty, ed. 1986 *Widows in African Societies: Choices and Constraints.* Stanford: Stanford University Press.

Price, Sally 1984 *Co-Wives and Calabashes.* Ann Arbor: University of Michigan Press.

Schildkrout, Enid 1973 The Fostering of Children in Urban Ghana: Problems of Ethnographic Analysis in a Multi-cultural Context. *Urban Anthropology* 2:48–73.

Steady, Filomena Chioma 1987 Polygamy and the Household Economy in a Fishing Village in Sierra Leone. In *Transformations of African Marriage.* David Parkin and David Nyamawaya, eds., pp. 211–30. Manchester: Manchester University Press.

Tiger, Lionel 1978 Introduction. In *Female Hierarchies.* Lionel Tiger and Heather T. Fowler, eds., pp. 1–20. Chicago: Beresford Book Service.

Van de Walle, Etienne and John Kekovole 1984 The Recent Evolution of African Marriage and Polygyny. Paper presented at the annual meeting of the Population Association of America, Minneapolis.

Wilson, Monica 1971 *For Men and Elders: Change in the Relations of Generations and of Men and Women among the Nyakyusa-Ngonde People 1875–1971.* New York: Africana Publishing Company.

9 Sexual repression, social control, and gender hierarchy in Sambia culture

Gilbert Herdt

The problem of this essay is to consider the nature of gender hierarchy and its maintenance through sexual repression and social controls in a New Guinea society. The Oxford English Dictionary traces the meanings of "hierarchy" back to religious origins: in the system of Dionysius the Areopagite, hierarchy referred to three orders of angels; Middle English defined it as a rule or dominion in holy things; by 1619 it meant a body of priests in successive orders; but after the advent of *Natural Science and Logic* (1643), hierarchy was disengaged from its sacred roots and referred to persons or things ranked in grades or orders. This history of the word is germane to my argument, for, in New Guinea societies in general and Sambia in particular, gender roles and norms are surrounded – legitimized, rationalized, mystified – by notions of religiosity, ritual, and tradition at every turn (Allen 1967; Herdt 1981; Keesing 1982; Langness 1974; Strathern 1988). The gods, ghosts, priests, or shamans, and the sanctity of ritual itself, traditionalists say, make gender what it is, and out of this fabric of gender is woven the design of hierarchy. For New Guinea peoples these sacred things seem to answer Foucault's (1980:159) question[1] about "what makes us love sex," except for the fact that many of the same cultural practices lead people to shun and even despise sex in the name of tradition (Herdt and Poole 1982).

Foucault (1980) argues that, contrary to popular thought, it is because sex is treated in Western culture as forbidden and repressed that its discourse embodies great power for the structuring of sociality. By sociality I mean the concepts of person and gender and the norms and expected social roles of persons in a historically bounded social field. The so-called "repressive hypothesis," Foucault suggests, is a screen or mystification of the socially constructed historical reality of sex in Western culture. Its existence as a fact is to be doubted; its workings of power stem not as much from the unconscious as Freud (1963) outlined it as from social control devices; and the discourse which it addresses belongs as much to the same "historical network" as the thing it denounces (Foucault 1980:10). As Foucault hints and as others have documented (Brundage

1987; Greenberg and Bystryn 1982), it was not the Christian Church alone that forged Western sexual life-designs. Foucault views the so-called "Age of Repression" as a phenomenon of bourgeois societies from the seventeenth century onwards, the outcome of capitalism, state formation, and industrialization which motivated contemporary concepts of the individual, gender, the family, and related elements of sociality (see also Foucault 1985:3–6).

Foucault's treatment of repression has been influential in many quarters – including anthropology. In this chapter I ask how well his question applies to tribal societies, using the Sambia as an illustrative case. How is it that pre-industrialized, pre-literate, stateless, pagan, tribal peoples show, in the design of their gender hierarchies, many if not all of the elements Foucault sketched for repressive bourgeois society? I agree with Foucault's concern to place sexual desires and erotic objects back into an historical field, but I argue against Foucault that the repressive hypothesis is an historical fact in Sambia and that its power stems from a psychosocial process of social control mechanisms and individual repression in people's lives. In my view, these two levels of meaning are complementary, not opposed. As regards Foucault's third critique, however, on "historical networks," I agree with him that gender ideas are created from historical circumstances which shape discourse and in turn "subjectify" people's "ethical substances" and symbolic worlds (Foucault 1985:26ff.). On all three fronts (individual desires, collective symbols, discourse) we must recognize mechanisms in individual experience and cultural structure that are not fully conscious to the agents in question, either as antecedents or consequences. Repression and social control operate outside of awareness and are social structurally "invisible," but "invisible" does not mean "absent," either on the individual or collective levels (Obeyesekere 1981).

While many anthropologists, social historians, and sociologists have argued for the causative influence of non-conscious cultural mechanisms in the determination of gender hierarchies, they tend to dismiss psychological/subjective factors which may structure the same processes (reviewed in Herdt and Stoller 1990). This dismissal is unfortunate and unnecessary; and a purely constructionist or neo-Marxist interpretation in this regard looks increasingly inflated and disingenuous in gender studies (Greenberg 1988; Gregor 1985; Herdt 1981, 1984a, 1987a; Keesing 1982; Murphy 1959; Poole 1985; Rossi 1985; Spiro 1982, 1984; Strathern 1988).[2] To suggest that subjective factors are crucial determinants in the structure of gender relations among Sambia is to open the door to a different perspective on the meaning of desire and necessity in their sexual lives (Herdt 1987c).

An account of Sambia gender stratification which omits an understanding of repression in their lives simply makes no sense. Examples of
repression in this chapter are drawn from a range of domains of
Sambia subjectivity to support this thesis. These domains, as in the
case of ritual secrecy, are culturally constituted and intersubjectively
shared, but their consequences effect individual repression. Cultural
mechanisms, in this view, are proximate causes of gender formations.
They include internalized beliefs and ideas and related mood states and
behaviors. And once these cultural devices are instilled in the person,
not only are the agent's subsequent developmental changes based on
such self-regulated internal states, but they become foundations for the
process of cultural transmission to future generations (LeVine 1982;
Levy 1984).

Neither the cultural nor the subjective factors are ultimate causes of
gender hierarchy, however. For these we must look to the behavioral
environment of ecology and warfare, their exact historical circumstances
and effects upon Sambia society (Herdt 1987c). Langness (1967) implied
as much for the New Guinea Highlands as a whole, in his argument that
warfare and nucleated social grouping precipitated the social sentiments
of "sexual antagonism," which motivated men to deny inherent "dependency needs" upon women. Allen's (1967) classic thesis on male cults in
Melanesia made the parallel point that small patrilineal groups utilize
male cults and rites for social reproduction *vis-à-vis* wives and enemies.
Psychological repression and social control devices thus work in tandem
to stratify and regulate relationships between cohorts of males and
between males and females (Herdt 1982b, 1987a). The fact that this dual
process is shrouded in ideologies and personal idioms of the sacred
represents a crystallization (or perhaps ossification) of long-working systematic interactions between collective and subjective elements set within
a distal environment of warfare as the historical ultimate cause of the
prevailing gender system.

To argue convincingly for the presence of repression in Sambia requires
the use not only of cultural accounts but of personal narratives, which
poses textual problems because of space limitations imposed upon a short
chapter such as this. The greater the range of cultural domains selected
for analysis, furthermore, the more exaggerated the problem becomes, for
more subjective material is indicated. Fortunately, there are published
materials available elsewhere on the subjectivity of Sambia. In this
chapter, my approach to the narrative problem will be to review and
summarize findings on gender-related cultural domains, and to work
forward from this material to understanding the role that repression and
power play in Sambia gender stratification.

The setting

Sambia are a hunting and horticultural people who number some 2,400 and are sparsely dispersed over broken rain forest mountain valleys of the extreme Southeastern Highlands Province of Papua New Guinea. Hamlets are small, nucleated, palisaded enclosures built atop steep mountain ridges. Hamlet populations range from 50 to 150 persons throughout the region. Sweet potatoes are the staple crop, but taro, yams, and greens also supplement the diet. Hunting provides the main meat protein; pigs are few, and pig herding is of secondary economic importance to hunting. A strict division of labor underlies economic routines, with only males hunting, and only females doing routine cultivating. Both sexes are involved in clearing garden plots, and males harvest ceremonial crops, such as taro and yams. Descent is patrilineal and residence is patrivirilocal. Married couples reside together with their children in "women's houses." Co-wives may either reside together or maintain separate huts. All initiated, unmarried males live in the men's clubhouse, situated at the top of a village. Here ritual, military, and hunting activities are organized. The clubhouse is forbidden to women and children. During their periods, women retire to the menstrual hut below the village, a place which is forbidden to men and children.

Historically, Sambia were migrants of coastal and hinterland Anga-speaking peoples. Ethnohistorical evidence indicates that they settled in the Sambia Valley some 200 years ago. Warfare is claimed mythologically as the main cause of their original migration (Herdt 1981). Throughout the region of Sambia and their neighboring tribes, warfare was constant and violent, involving regular war-raiding parties and shifting alliances and enmities between groups (Herdt 1987c). First Western contact occurred in the late 1950s. Pacification and domination by the Australian colonial administration began in 1964–5; the last instance of warfare was in the late 1960s, followed by the advent of missionary and government-related activities, such as regular reconnaissance and census patrols. Although violence resulting from local disputes still occurs, the Sambia have been at peace for nearly twenty years, and unlike certain Highland groups, they have not as yet known neotraditional warfare (Herdt 1987c).

Regional and intra-societal organization occurs mainly through the men's secret society, which is an age-graded initiation cult focused on secret male clubhouse activities. The cult is localized in each hamlet, constituted as a clan-based warriorhood. War leaders, shamans, and elders direct younger males in normative daily routine work and in performing ceremonies. All males at ages 7–10 years are initiated. They are detached from their parents and natal households and forbidden to interact thereafter with women and children. Initiation lasts months and is traumatic. Second-stage initiation is held for this cohort at ages 11–13 years. Third-stage initiation, a puberty rite, is performed for bachelors aged 14–17 years. Thereafter, individualized initiations are held for youths at marriage (fourth-stage rites), their wives' menarche (fifth-stage rites), and the birth of their first child (sixth-stage rites), occurring over some years' time and culminating in the attainment of full ritual personhood for males usually in their mid-twenties. Male ceremonies are secret and forbidden to women and children. Institutionalized homosexual relations occur throughout the entire ritual cycle (Herdt 1984a). Elsewhere I have written of the relationship between this ritual homosexuality and the men's secret flutes, the paramount symbol of their cult and ritual orthodoxy (Herdt 1982a). Because of intra-societal warfare, age-mates were always involved in somewhat contradictory commitments. Though initiated together, and while they engaged in age-structured homoerotic relations (Herdt 1987b), they were potential enemies to those in neighboring villages. Inter- and intra-hamlet marriage tended to constrain this warfare, however, because affines should not directly engage each other in combat. Thus, warfare, initiation, and marriage were interlocking structural institutions that directed the main patterns of daily sociality (see also Godelier 1986).

Warfare, in this model, is the directive force, or "control variable" which has influenced a whole system of factors historically related to gender hierarchy. War has and still does provide a radical pragmatic in rationalizing sex role norms and routines (Herdt 1987c). The imperative to be and to remain an aggressive warrior-hunter makes practical reason (Sahlins 1976) out of the socioeconomic standards that men fight and hunt, whereas women garden; that men should avoid the birth-giving and new-born, as well as daily caretaking and babysitting, for fear that men will grow ill or weak. War rationalizes productive and consumptive roles between the sexes. It has instilled an ethos of *jerungdu* or masculine prowess (Herdt 1981, 1987c). This ethos conditions a discourse and culturally valued stereotypes of men as higher and women as lower, communicated in temporal, spatial, and spiritual representations regarding the place of man and woman in the world. Thus, men should always stand or sit above women to avoid contamination; men are associated with the "clean" and spatially spiritually higher forest territory, whereas women are identified with the dirtier and lower gardens; and the men's clubhouse is highest in the village environs that encompass the menstrual hut as its lowest point. The structure of insemination objectifies these representations (Herdt 1984b). These cosmological and institutional signs of hierarchy serve as cultural baselines within which ideology, social organization, person concepts, and sex-typing occur.

Given these broad historical parameters, however, two central problems arise. First, that in secret ritual discourse women are seen as having powers that men seek or need, which in certain ways contradicts the normative male gender hierarchy. Second, that males are not all equal but are graded into the cult in hierarchical fashion, which in another sense complicates a unified male ideology of domination. These "internal contradictions" (Paul 1980) in the Sambia symbolic system are necessary but unforeseen consequences of their history and cultural organization. They are mediated as such by symbolic and psychological mechanisms ultimately legitimized by male cult religiosity.

The ideology of growth

Sambia believe that all living things and some inanimate entities, such as the sun, have an essence or life-force that is either male or female. They furthermore believe that femaleness is an innate condition, more primordial and more efficient than maleness. In idioms of natural species, such as those concerning birds and trees, for instance, the initial birth or developmental "sex" state is female; if maleness is marked, it comes later and usually grows out of the femaleness. While femaleness is thus more generic, is steady and intrinsically activated and perpetuating, maleness emerges later, is more uneven and explosive in nature – more radiant and vibrant – and requires supports to both activate and sustain itself.

Thus it is in humans: females grow faster, achieve puberty quicker, and attain adult reproductive competence without cultural treatment, whereas males are slower, enter into puberty later, and need ritual aids to attain manhood and reproductive potential. Male infants are perceived to be more "at risk" of illness and death. Punishment or discipline of any kind is therefore avoided, because it would further "block growth." Because males are born from females but must become the cultural things called "men," not "women," male infants exposed to female contaminants must be purified through initiation ceremonies in order for them to "grow up."[3]

This ideology has many psychosocial consequences, but the one I wish to emphasize here concerns its negative sanction on childhood sexual play. From birth until age five or so, boys and girls are allowed to mix in village play groups. Boys are usually naked, while girls are always clothed. After this time parents segregate children into different male and female play groups. All sexual experimentation is at first discouraged, and then condemned and punished, usually with shaming. Parents convey two attitudes about childhood eroticism. One is that children are sexually naïve and should remain so to avoid premarital sex and the development of morally disapproved promiscuity in adulthood. The other is that boys would be polluted and their growth blocked by sexual play with girls and, after puberty, with women. Following initiation, boys should conserve, not "spend" their semen; at least it should not be spent on females until marriage (Herdt 1984b).

Association with persons of the same sex, including holding hands and intimate bodily contact, becomes "normal and natural," whereas inter- action with persons of the opposite sex becomes special, halting, and tinged with feelings of power and eroticism. This extraordinary intimacy is eventually transposed onto an erotic context, which, through reversal of the normative, becomes filled with danger and power. This is why "sexual looking" is always dangerous for Sambia (Stoller and Herdt 1985). For instance, Sambia males and females never kiss, hold hands, or hug each other in public or private; and the barest bodily contact hints of sexual intercourse. These are strong social controls: those who transgress them are sanctioned with penalties of several kinds – public abuse and moral outrage, parental condemnation, peer shaming, and even physical punishment (Herdt 1987c:91–4). Equally as powerful are beliefs that ancestral spirits and ghosts "strike" spontaneously offenders, bringing them illness and death. There is no escape from such invisible forces, because they can be seen everywhere and are revealed in the dreams of shamans, who may report them in contexts of healing, adjudication, and revenge (Herdt 1977).

These sanctions on early childhood sex play thereby establish sexual repression and routinize the Sambia gender hierarchy by late childhood. The latency period of Sambia childhood development – after age 5 and until first initiation – is one of sexual inactivity, which no doubt has to do with Oedipal strivings and conflict (Spiro 1982), feelings eventually reacti- vated but laid to rest after fatherhood, in the context of final initiation and the internalization of the secret myth of parthenogenesis (Herdt 1981).

What is the shape and degree of repression for young Sambia at this point? Retrospective accounts by adults and narratives by adolescents suggest that the vast majority of Sambia males and females had erotic thoughts as children.[4] The cassowary hunter Nilutwo, for example, dis- cussed such childhood sex play, felt titillated and shamed by it, and related it to his adulterous feelings toward women (Herdt 1981:142–4, 342ff; 1987d). My key woman informant, Penjukwi, reports illicit child- hood sex play as well (Herdt and Stoller 1990). Sex play with other children, usually between boys and girls, is reported by a few people, though most adults deny it or have repressed it. Virtually all of my close informants report adolescent thoughts about sex, however. The fact that only rarely are these thoughts acted out – that social controls do check impulses – establishes the strong nexus between external and internalized repressive measures (Gregor 1985; LeVine 1982:85–98, 237–8). Repression makes childhood a *terra incognita* for adult retrospections in this regard. And this fact in turn empowers discourse on sex and love with negativity, especially for males, whose "protest masculinity" signifies the self's refusal to look back at the repressed (Herdt 1987c). No wonder that adults guard the value that Sambia children are sexually ignorant and should remain so until later.

Initiation and cult hierarchy

Initiation into the men's secret society in late childhood constitutes a dramatic change in boys' lives in many ways. The initiation process includes detachment of the boy from his mother and other children; painful ordeals such as blood-letting and burdensome ritual taboos; the revelation of the central – but not all – ritual cult secrets (Barth 1975); hazing and coercion by older males, especially bachelors; the beginning of ritual homoerotic practices; avoidance for years of all women and children; training in warrior skills and preparation for battle; and obedience to elders as absolute moral authorities (Tuzin 1980). This process of psychosocial transformation has been described elsewhere (Herdt 1981, 1987a), and here I concentrate on boys' incorporation into the cult hierarchy and its consequences for their further social control and attendant sexual repression (compare Whitehead 1986).

The Sambia ritual cult must be seen as a dominance hierarchy: boys are second to bachelors, who directly monitor and control them; newly weds are superordinate to bachelors; adult men control and advise newly weds; and elders and war leaders are superior to all others, with shamans predominant in spiritual affairs and war leaders directors in fighting (in fact many war leaders are also shamans; Herdt 1977). Elders are supreme in matters of ritual and mystical knowledge and in details of sorcery, however, and they retain this power until senility or death (see also Tuzin 1980). As a coordinating institution of Sambia society, moreover, the men's secret society is the dominant force in human life – the key instrument of male religious and political control over women and children as well. This does not mean that women agree with everything involved in this institutional network, nor that they themselves do not contradict or oppose its power (Herdt 1987c). Rather, it means that women cannot effectively overrule the cult's regulative effects with regard to such matters as the imperative to initiate boys, the requirement that women contribute resources, and the result that the cult-warriorhood defends the hamlet and simultaneously directs and reinforces dominant roles and norms – even some which exploit women.

The men's cult is thus an age-graded club which doubles as a military society. A pecking order of status and deferment rules, while not entirely inclusive and rationalized, prevails in nearly all male/male interactions. Because of its constitution as a hierarchical system, gender roles, norms, and gender typing are viewed as inflexible moral conventions embodied in and perpetuated by the person, who is bound by ritual strictures to obey these conventions. Gender formation is a function of first and subsequent initiations: initiation is the premier identity context for male gender development (Herdt 1982b). All sexual behavior follows from this development structure, with the norms of morally appropriate sexual conduct dictated by ritual convention. The ideology of growth outlined above internally supports such regulations for the person.

An outstanding developmental consequence of the cult hierarchy is that the kind of sex Sambia are permitted and engage in radically changes through initiation. From late childhood onwards until marriage, all heterosexual behavior of any kind is prohibited, and sex play in childhood is discouraged. Ritual further structures male heterosexuality through the effect of three cultural mechanisms. First, strict female avoidance taboos, reinforced by severe punishments of infractions (ultimately including death inflicted by elders), suppress heterosexual acts. Second, beliefs about women as polluting and depleting are taught in initiation and reinforced through the values, discourse, and homosocial atmosphere of the men's clubhouse and its all-male peer group activities (see also Read 1984). Third is prescribed sexual contact between older and younger males, which channels sexual energy and impulses to only male objects, a form of age-structured homosexuality found in similar tribal systems the world over (Herdt 1987b). These cultural mechanisms have been described elsewhere (Herdt 1981; Stoller and Herdt 1982), but I will consider here the problem of their consequences for sexual repression, a subject which has been ignored. Restated baldly, Foucault's question is: how[5] do Sambia males come to love sex with males and allegedly to hate sex with females?

Task assignment and the rigidity of labor in simple societies like the Sambia surely contribute to repression. Murphy (1959) argued in a paper on Lowland Amazonia that tribal peoples, with limited technology and portable wealth, experience invidious comparisons and envy between the sexes, because cooperation in task assignment is required, and yet few status distinctions exist to create legitimate hierarchy. Thus, males "naturally" envy female fertility and reproductivity, which gives them a "status" potential beyond that of men – a theme reflected in gender systems across New Guinea, as Forge (1966), Mead (1949), and others have remarked (reviewed in Herdt 1981, 1982a). The degree to which such envy is conscious or unconscious has long been debated (Bettelheim 1955; Dundes 1976; Gregor 1985; Langness 1974). There is no simple answer to this question (Herdt 1987e), yet I am persuaded that some of Sambia men's envious behavior is non-conscious or unconscious and results from institutionally imposed repression, which peaks in initiation.[6] The following examples illustrate why I suggest that repression – and not just cultural and historical formations – is operative in this process.

Ritual structure

We can begin with the ritual structure of negations (Freud 1963b). In the key domains of male performance – warfare, ritual, and sex involving females – each performative activity entails a negation of something female followed by the affirmation of something male (Herdt 1981, 1987a). Removal of female pollution is the key form of negation. Some cleansing or purificatory technique, such as nose-bleeding, vomiting, or rubbing of the skin with nettles, must be done before warfare, ritual, or sexual activity. Egestion of something from the body surfaces or insides hints of a deep premise: "I am *not* female or female-substance identified; I am male." This practice points to the kind of process Foucault (1985:26) had in mind when he wrote of "the determination of ethical substances."

Nose-bleeding rites illustrate these signs and this process. Nose-bleeding is the most painful and violent of Sambia ceremonies. The practice is always done in secret. The bleedings are systematically performed at critical junctures in male development: at first initiation, the time of detachment from women; at puberty, as a reminder that the self must avoid adultery with women and suppress heterosexuality; at fifth-stage initiation, as a reinforcer of pollution cleansing associated with heterosexual genital intercourse; and after the first child is born when sixth-stage initiation is held, to remind young men that they must avoid the contaminants of birth and uphold post-partum taboos. Thereafter, adult men communicate, to themselves and to other men, that they are responsible and auto-regulated by the performance of self-induced private nose-bleeding whenever their wives have regular periods.

Sambia themselves compare the egested blood to female menstrual blood in an envious way (compare Lidz and Lidz 1977). Just as importantly they say that men, even old men, must continue to let blood when wives menstruate, or else they will fail to keep "growing" and stay healthy. Their narrative accounts of this "growth" suggest the meaning that unless they simulate this process in themselves, they will not be able to match their wives' fertility and independence. Their sentiment harks back to an earlier developmental period of maternal closeness, a period in the life-course that is repressed. The structure of negations involved in blood-letting maintains a tenuous balance between repression of deep-felt strivings (for example, closeness to mother and females) and cultural beliefs which attribute danger and death to intimate heterosexual contact.

Semen beliefs

The structure of semen beliefs and practices provides another example of repressive consequences (Herdt 1984b). Semen should be conserved and metered out, not wasted, since it is the essence of maleness. Cultural rules dictate to whom and in what circumstances semen exchange may occur. Ritual fellatio for boys, engaged in for some years, builds up their supply of semen. Homosexual activities deplete adult men's semen, but this belief is of scant concern to men. It is heterosexual, not homosexual, activity that is feared, in spite of the fact that males learn of artificial semen-replenishment techniques (such as ingesting white tree sap) for the support of heterosexual coitus. The essence of semen is limited in both cases, yet is most depleted by females. There are several causes of this bifurcated response to depletion, but two are most important: cultural beliefs that women are contaminating and more depleting than boys; and the subjective sense that heterosexual intercourse is more exciting (more dangerous) and involves pair-bonding over a long period of time. Of course, all forms of semen belief and regulation constitute sociosexual controls, but the latter factor entails repression, too.

   The greater banter and excitement attributed to heterosexuality stems ultimately from the feeling that what is hidden or "repressed" may emerge or become more conscious. This includes the dependency needs which Langness (1967) notes; the fear of merging with wife – indexed in nose-bleeding to the notion of having to "match" (keep separate from) her periods; and to fetishism in men, which makes excitement out of their anxieties and misogyny regarding women (Stoller 1985). A major shift occurs in subjective male sexual excitement from puberty to late adolescence, in this regard: the initial wet dreams reported by boys usually involve their dominant homosexual play with a younger boy, whereas their later wet dreams have manifest content pinpointed on coitus with women (Herdt, in press). This shift is mirrored by changes in their sexual fantasies, from those related to boys' mouths to those related to women's vaginas (Stoller and Herdt 1985). Such shifts entail psychodynamic consolidations and compromise formations, including the negations already mentioned, which successively repress fantasies and experiences felt in childhood and at puberty (see also Bateson 1946).

Sexual antagonism

It follows from this line of psychocultural reasoning that "sexual antagonism" toward females is not just a historical antecedent of gender hierarchy, but a developmental outcome of repression itself that keeps such hierarchy in place. As implied in the previous point, men's sexual excitement is constructed, and their heterosexuality is thereby built up from the negation. Sexual drive plays a part in the development of forms and levels of sexual excitation, leading to orgasm, mechanisms of learning sexual stimuli, of inhibiting and acting out impulses, but these do not determine the mode of eroticism.[7] The views of this problem in the Melanesian literature are contradictory. For Read (1954), sex antagonism, including sexual behavior *vis-à-vis* the opposite sex, was derivative of social structure; and for Meggitt (1964), sexual "prudery" and "lechery" were also results of institutional social grouping factors. Both scholars might have agreed with Foucault (1980) that the structural historicity of sex emerged from the collective, not the individual, domains of power and gender pragmatics. Heider (1976), however, presents a radical image, in which he supposes, with the Dugum Dani, that their low-level sexual behavior is the result of "low sexual energy," a notion comprised of elements of folk biology, folk psychology, and cultural salience. Social regulation but not repression is thus hinted at by Heider. Kelly's (1976) presentation of the Etoro is similar to Heider's, though his work suggests strong cultural rules limiting eroticism. In contrast, I would separate the historical-behavioral circumstances of these social systems from the psychosocial consequences of sex antagonism for individual men. The former determinants shape the latter, but they do so via repression. It is only because of sexual antagonism – social regulation – that Sambia males are normatively able to perform as competent heterosexual adults, within the rigid parameters of their gender hierarchy (as hinted in Herdt 1981; Herdt and Poole 1982).

To control and yet express heteroeroticism, in line with the norms of Sambia society, are difficult tasks for the masculine person. Impulse control is not easy, given the impulsive socialization regime under which males, in particular, are reared as children (Herdt 1987c). Added to this fact are the restrictions on sex play in childhood and the traumas of initiation, which are repressive in nearly every way, though homosexual activity provides a spontaneous sexual outlet for years. Here, too, however, homoeroticism leads away from females to males, only later to bridge both forms of contact through late adolescent heterosexual oral intercourse. But by this time, heterosexual contact is power-filled and dangerous, for both sexes. When fears of depletion and pollution are added to the devaluation of women and the praise of men, based on years of opposite-sex avoidance, the conflicts of sexual performance and the potential for dysfunction are great. For example, men are highly fearful of first heterosexual genital contact with women; premature ejaculation is, apparently, fairly common. Sexual antagonism is therefore a mode of relationship. This heteroeroticism is expressed differentially in two ideal types of males: the phallic war leader and the quiet or gentle man. The one relates to women as sexual objects and little more. The other's gentleness may create a marvelously mutualistic marriage – or none at all, as reported in the case study of Kalutuo (Herdt 1980) who, as a middle-aged man, prefers boys and fears women. Mead (1935) and Herdt and Stoller (1990) describe such a range of individual expressions in more depth. My point is that sexual antagonism is not merely a cultural discourse mode, it is a psychological reality for Sambia which arises in part from successive repressions across the lifespan.

Identity

A final and complex domain is that of identity. Identity is a most ambiguous concept, but normative statements regarding male identity abound in the literature. For instance, there is the profound stereotype implied in Mead's (1949) classic work on men as "womb-envying," and Layard's (1942) characterization of Melanesian societies as "male admiring" groups who value the penis above all and hold the glans penis in "extreme reverence." These cultural ideals about gender identity make erotics and reproduction their ultimate index. Yet they are cloaked in local meaning systems. It is likewise for the Sambia, who see the emergence of maleness out of femaleness as tenuous, even miraculous. Male identity is not so fragile as they think, at least in the abstract. But here the abstract does not matter: it is the particular and conflict-laden circumstances of the construction of the kind of aggressive warrior that they fret about.

This is why the core elements of post-childhood, ritual-based gender identity development among Sambia males always occur in a context of ritual cult secrecy. Indeed, secrecy in identity construction and maintenance is tantamount to a mechanism of repression. The nose-bleedings are highly secret. Ceremonial purifications and ingestion of ritual foods are as well. The presentation of the ritual flutes is most secret of all, and this secret surrounds at every turn the secret of homoeroticism, so that the two revelations are forever intertwined. The secret of the flutes is a problem in another sense, because it requires the maintenance of duplicity, an imaginary Other: that female hamlet spirits protect the cult, animate its musical instruments, and provide a comforter for boys. The flutes' spirit is an obvious symbol of mother (Herdt 1982a), and while some colleagues have wondered about this too-Freudian-seeming image – like a just-so story – they have the Sambia to argue with, not me. For nothing is so powerful and compelling to Sambia males as this remarkable female phantasm, who is aggressive and powerful and seductive and yet so very frail, hidden most of the time, mustered out on occasion to service the men's ritual excitement at a time unlike any other when a true crowd psychology moves individual men to the most remarkable and liminal – I mean the return of the repressed – acts (Herdt 1987c). This image of the flute spirit is a bridge, a transitional object, from the childhood to masculine worlds (Herdt 1987e). She represents the giving up of the most profound bond of life – to mother – in favor of a homosocial world that denigrates women. The loss, grief, and yearnings of childhood are, through this collective symbol, converted in time from trauma to triumph. Along the way, comfortableness with women, which earlier obviated sexual arousal, is transformed into sexual antagonism.

The secret of the flutes is that they shield the secret of sexual inequality within homoerotic intercourse. Men were once "on top" of boys; the men as boys were once on "the bottom," too. Feelings of identification with womanly attributes are hidden in ritual, as the equivalence of nose-bleeding with menstruation reveals. Ultimately, the adult form of male identity is inextricably woven from this fabric of secret discourse, which owes its manly vitality to insemination. The power that men attribute to women and heterosexual intimacy arises in part out of fear that such manly secrets will leak out to women. That gender hierarchy is based on a maleness that men give to boys makes masculinity tentative and not unlike femininity enough in its sociality to warrant the male domination of females. This is the institutionalization of repression most profound.

Conclusion

The power surrounding Sambia discourse on sexuality derives as much from personal meanings of repression as from the historical network of factors which control and still sustain their gender hierarchy. These two components of their understanding are inseparable. Theoretical analysis may split them apart, refigure them through jargon, and splice them again; discourse has this plastic nature. But the resulting interpretation is not seamless. When men say that they must nose-bleed boys in order to "grow them," and thus remove them from women's contamination, they are, of course, invoking the sacred in the reproduction of the male hierarchy. Eventually this most masculine act is performed upon the self, as a response to a wife's menstruation, the most feminine of acts. The erotic bond between husband and wife in private mediates these two acts, which, for husband and wife, reassert hierarchy in the public domain. The same holds in another sense for the homoerotic relations between older and younger males. The power contained in both acts is great. It creates contradictions in life, and these contradictions generate many of the key idioms of Sambia sexuality and life. The meanings of nose-bleeding arise in a context of deep trauma, the results of which repress early childhood experience, instill male/male dominance, and later are repeated to control new adolescent feelings incongruent with moral norms. Likewise, homoeroticism redirects and controls men. Control is thus simultaneously repression. And Sambia fear the return of the repressed, I believe, as much as men desire the gender hierarchy it supports, when they refer to these things in their own private discourse.

Perhaps because of these contradictions they use cultural screens, such as the men's myth of parthenogenesis, to do their "speaking" for them. The myth, as mentioned above, reveals to adult men that their maleness came from indeterminant sexual origins. The culture hero, Numboolyu, had to handle the sexual needs of a teenage son. He contemplated allowing his son sexual access to his own wife, the boy's mother, only to rule this out for fear of eventual patricide. The older boy was instructed to use his younger brother as a sexual partner, which was the beginning of ritual homosexuality. Hidden in this story are quiet scripts and blatant Oedipal themes. Yet the narrative context reveals perhaps even more of primordial themes, questions about the essence – absence – of maleness itself hidden inside the story-tellers and audience of this secret all-male group. This myth cannot be revealed earlier than adulthood because the social controls of the male cult have not yet been internalized enough to ward off the doubt that some individuals might resist the myth's message, undermining the cult (Herdt 1981). Social controls are therefore rigidly applied, implying the very theme argued throughout this chapter: repression. Would not Sambia elders fear the expression of repressed desires and impulses in younger males who have not yet fully accommodated themselves to the socially constituted forms of repression which sustain hierarchy? The answer seems to be yes, and I would guess that even Foucault would not dismiss the psychological content of the myth for these men's lives, for this is what empowers their discourse on heteroeroticism and homoeroticism.

This chapter is aimed at making the simple point that control and repression are dual forces in Sambia gender stratification. I would be surprised to find that it is not so in just about every other corner of the world.

NOTES

1 The question is: "Are prohibition, censorship, and denial truly the forms through which power is exercised in a general way, if not in every society, most certainly in our own?" (Foucault 1980:10).
2 Of course, the opposite trend – to psychologize gender, as Freud (1925) usually did, and as exists in the developmental tradition of psychology (Maccoby and Jacklin 1974) – is equally falsifying. But there are signs that the psychological approach is changing, as Gilligan's (1982) controversial work shows (see also Rossi 1985). Besides, this danger is not one that cultural anthropology has to worry about in the still-prevailing neostructuralistic climate.
3 Similar ideologies are common throughout Melanesia; see Herdt 1982b, 1984a; Whitehead 1986.
4 These accounts are reviewed in Herdt and Stoller (1990). Such retrospective narratives are of course "screened or edited"; I do not take them to represent true historical narratives (see Herdt 1982a; Schafer 1976).
5 How, not why: for the questions of the origins of Sambia male eroticism and misogyny require a different kind of analysis from the one adopted here.
6 In another paper I will pursue this line of argument.
7 Even the concept of sex drive – so lineal and egocentric – biases the interpretation from the start, because it implies meanings not shared by many non-Western groups.

REFERENCES

Allen, M. R. 1967 *Male Cults and Secret Initiations in Melanesia*. New York: Cambridge University Press.
Barth, Fredrik 1975 *Ritual and Knowledge among the Baktaman of New Guinea*. New Haven, CT: Yale University Press.
Bateson, Gregory 1946 Arts of the South Seas. *Art Bulletin* 28:119–23.
Bettelheim, Bruno 1955 *Symbolic Wounds: Puberty Rites and the Envious Male*. New York: Collier Books.
Brundage, James A. 1987 *Law, Sex, and Christian Society in Medieval Europe*. Chicago: University of Chicago Press.
Dundes, Alan 1976 A Psychoanalytic Study of the Bullroarer. *Man* 11:220–38.
Forge, Anthony 1966 Art and Environment in the Sepik. *Proceedings of the Royal Anthropological Institute* 1965:23–31.
Foucault, Michel 1980 *The History of Sexuality*, Vol. 1, *An Introduction*. Robert Hurley, trans. New York: Vintage Books.
   1985 The Use of Pleasure. In *The History of Sexuality*, Vol. 2. Robert Hurley, trans. New York: Pantheon.
Freud, Sigmund 1925 Some Psychical Consequences of the Anatomical Distinction

between the Sexes. In The Standard Edition of the Complete Psychological Works of Sigmund Freud. James Strachey, trans. Vol. 19, pp. 243–58. London: Hogarth Press.

1963a Repression. In General Psychological Theory, Papers on Metapsychology by Sigmund Freud. P. Reiff, ed., pp. 104–15. New York: Collier Books.

1963b Negation. In General Psychological Theory, Papers on Metapsychology by Sigmund Freud. P. Rieff, ed., pp. 213–17. New York: Collier Books.

Gilligan, Carol 1982 In a Different Voice: Psychological Theory and Women's Development. Cambridge, MA: Harvard University Press.

Godelier, Maurice 1986 The Making of Great Men: Male Domination and Power among the New Guinea Baruya. Rupert Swyer, trans. New York: Cambridge University Press.

Greenberg, David 1988 The History of Homosexuality. Chicago: University of Chicago Press.

Greenberg, D. and M. Bystryn 1982 Christian Intolerance of Homosexuality. American Journal of Sociology 88:515–48.

Gregor, Thomas 1985 Anxious Pleasures: The Sexual Lives of an Amazonian People. Chicago: University of Chicago Press.

Heider, Karl 1976 Dani Sexuality: A Low Energy System. Man 11:188–201.

Herdt, Gilbert 1977 The Shaman's "Calling" among the Sambia of New Guinea. Journal de la Société des Océanistes 56–7:153–67.

1980 Semen Depletion and the Sense of Maleness. Ethnopsychiatrica 3:79–116.

1981 Guardians of the Flutes: Idioms of Masculinity. New York: McGraw-Hill.

1982a Fetish and Fantasy in Sambia Initiation. In Rituals of Manhood: Male Initiation in Papua New Guinea. Gilbert H. Herdt, ed., pp. 44–98. Berkeley: University of California Press.

1982b Sambia Nose-Bleeding Rites and Male Proximity to Women. Ethos 10(2):189–231.

1984a Ritualized Homosexual Behavior in the Male Cults of Melanesia, 1862–1983: An Introduction. In Ritualized Homosexuality in Melanesia. Gilbert H. Herdt, ed., pp. 1–82. Berkeley: University of California Press.

1984b Semen Transactions in Sambia Culture. In Ritualized Homosexuality in Melanesia. Gilbert H. Herdt, ed., pp. 167–210. Berkeley: University of California Press.

1987a The Accountability of Sambia Initiates. In Anthropology in the High Valleys: Essays in Honor of K. E. Read. L. L. Langness and T. E. Hayes, eds., pp. 237–82. Novato, CA: Chandler and Sharp.

1987b Homosexuality. The Encyclopedia of Religion, Vol. 6, pp. 445–52.

1987c Sambia: Ritual and Gender in New Guinea. New York: Holt, Rinehart and Winston.

1987d Selfhood and Discourse in Sambia Dream Sharing. In Dreaming: The Anthropology and Psychology of the Imaginal. Barbara Tedlock, ed., pp. 55–85. New York: Cambridge University Press.

1987e Transitional Objects in Sambia Initiation Rites. Ethos 15:40–57.

in press Adolescent Transitions among the Sambia of Papua New Guinea. In Transitions through Adolescence. A. Greene and A. Boxer, eds. New York: L. Earlbaum Associates.

Herdt, Gilbert and Fitz John Porter Poole 1982 Sexual Antagonism: The Intellectual History of a Concept in the Anthropology of New Guinea. *Social Analysis* 12:3–28.

Herdt, Gilbert and Robert J. Stoller 1990 *Intimate Communications: Erotics and the Study of Culture*. New York: Columbia University Press.

Keesing, Roger M. 1982 Introduction. In *Rituals of Manhood: Male Initiation in Papua New Guinea*. Gilbert H. Herdt, ed., pp. 1–43. Berkeley: University of California Press.

Kelly, Raymond 1976 Witchcraft and Sexual Relations: An Exploration in the Social and Semantic Implications of a Structure of Belief. In *Man and Woman in the New Guinea Highlands*. P. Brown and G. Buchbinder, eds., pp. 36–53. Washington, DC: American Anthropological Association.

    1977 *Etoro Social Structure: A Study in Structural Contradiction*. Ann Arbor: University of Michigan Press.

Langness, Lewis L. 1967 Sexual Antagonism in the New Guinea Highlands: A Bena Bena Example. *Oceania* 37:161–77.

    1974 Ritual Power and Male Domination in the New Guinea Highlands. *Ethos* 2:189–212.

Layard, John 1942 *Stone Men of Malekula*. London: Chatto and Windus.

LeVine, Robert A. 1982 The Self in Culture. In *Culture, Behavior and Personality*, Robert A. LeVine, ed., pp. 291–304. Chicago: Aldine Publishing Company.

Levy, Robert I. 1984 Emotion, Knowing and Culture. In *Culture Theory: Essays on Mind, Self, and Emotion*. Richard A. Shweder and Robert A. LeVine, eds., pp. 214–37. New York: Cambridge University Press.

Lidz, Theodore and Ruth Wilmanns Lidz 1977 Male Menstruation: A Ritual Alternative to the Oedipal Transition. *International Journal of Psychoanalysis* 58:17–31.

Maccoby, Eleanor E. and Carol N. Jacklin 1974 *The Psychology of Sex Differences*. Stanford: Stanford University Press.

Mead, Margaret 1935 *Sex and Temperament in Three Primitive Societies*. New York: William Morrow and Company.

    1949 *Male and Female: A Study of the Sexes in a Changing World*. New York: William Morrow and Company.

Meggitt, Mervyn J. 1964 Male–Female Relationships in the Highlands of Australian New Guinea. *American Anthropologist* 66(2):204–24.

Murphy, Robert F. 1959 Social Structure and Sex Antagonism. *Southwestern Journal of Anthropology* 15:89–98.

Obeyesekere, Gananath 1981 *Medusa's Hair: An Essay on Personal Symbols and Religious Experience*. Chicago: University of Chicago Press.

Paul, Robert A. 1980 Symbolic Interpretation in Psychoanalysis and Anthropology. *Ethos* 8:286–95.

Poole, Fitz John Porter 1985 Coming into Social Being: Cultural Images of Infants in Bimin-Kuskusmin Folk Psychology. In *Person, Self, and Experience: Exploring Pacific Ethnopsychologies*. Geoffrey M. White and John Kirkpatrick, eds., pp. 183–242. Berkeley: University of California Press.

Read, Kenneth E. 1954 Cultures of the Central Highlands. *Southwestern Journal of Anthropology* 10:1–43.

1984 The Nama Cult Recalled. In *Ritualized Homosexuality in Melanesia.* Gilbert Herdt, ed., pp. 248–91. Berkeley: University of California Press.

Rosaldo, Michelle Zimbalist 1980 The Use and Abuse of Anthropology: Reflections on Feminism and Cross-Cultural Understanding. *Signs* 5:389–417.

Rossi, Alice, ed. 1985 *Gender and the Life Course.* New York: Academic Press.

Sahlins, Marshall 1976 *Culture and Practical Reason.* Chicago: University of Chicago Press.

Schafer, Roy 1976 *An New Language for Psychoanalysis.* New Haven, CT: Yale University Press.

Spiro, Melford E. 1982 *Oedipus in the Trobriands.* Chicago: University of Chicago Press.

1984 Some Reflections on Cultural Determinism and Relativism with Special Reference to Reason and Emotion. In *Culture Theory: Essays on Mind, Self, and Emotion.* Richard A. Shweder and Robert A. LeVine, eds., pp. 246–323. New York: Cambridge University Press.

Stoller, Robert J. 1985 *Presentations of Gender.* New Haven, CT: Yale University Press.

Stoller, Robert J. and Gilbert Herdt 1982 The Development of Masculinity: A Cross-Cultural Contribution. *Journal of the American Psychoanalytic Association* 30:29–59.

1985 Theories of Origins of Homosexuality: A Cross-Cultural Look. *Archives of General Psychiatry* 42:399–404.

Strathern, Marilyn 1988 *The Gender of the Gift: Problems with Women and Problems with Society in Melanesia.* Berkeley: University of California Press.

Tuzin, Donald F. 1980 *The Voice of the Tambaran: Truth and Illusion in Ilahita Arapesh Religion.* Berkeley: University of California Press.

Whitehead, Harriet 1986 The Varieties of Fertility Cultism in New Guinea. *American Ethnologist* 13(1–2):80–99, 271–89.

10   Primatological perspectives on gender hierarchies

Joan B. Silk

In this chapter, I consider gender hierarchies from a wide taxonomic and temporal perspective. Humans share a long evolutionary history with other primates, having diverged from the common ancestor of hominids and chimpanzees less than 10 million years ago (Sarich and Cronin 1976). Humans retain a wide range of physiological, morphological, and life history characteristics that are similar to those of other primates. Since human and non-human primates are such similar organisms, we might also expect to find similarities (analogies and homologies) in the behavior of contemporary primates and humans. Thus, it is useful to outline the range of variability in male–female relationships within the primate order, delineate the proximate factors that influence the pattern of male–female dominance relationships in other species, and consider the evolutionary processes that have shaped social relationships among males and females.

Comparative studies of non-human primates have shown that the extent of sexual dimorphism in body weight and canine size are indices of social organization (Clutton-Brock, Harvey, and Rudder 1977; Harvey, Kavanagh, and Clutton-Brock 1978; Harvey and Bennett 1985) and good predictors of the nature of male–female hierarchical relationships (Smuts 1987). It is reasonable to consider whether we can apply principles derived from comparative analyses of contemporary non-human primates to reconstruct the behavior of our early hominid ancestors. Finally, we might ask what insights we can draw from this body of data about the behavior of contemporary humans. This comparative approach is useful because it can help to identify both consistencies and contradictions between our evolutionary history and contemporary cultural realities.

Social organization of non-human primates

In many mammalian species, social groups are composed of females and their young. Adult males remain apart from these maternal units, and may join females only during brief periods in which females are sexually receptive (Eisenberg 1981). Although males sometimes remain with females until their young are partially independent, males and females are solitary during most of their adult lives. The same pattern is characteristic of many of the prosimian primates (Bearder 1987) who first appeared some 70 million years ago (Sarich and Cronin 1976). Among anthropoid primate species, who diverged from their prosimian ancestors nearly 35 million years ago (Sarich and Cronin 1976), a different form of social organization has emerged. In most species of monkeys and apes, adult males attach themselves for extended periods of time to groups of females and their young (reviewed in Jolly 1985).

Forty years of fieldwork on free-ranging primates by hundreds of researchers have revealed considerable complexity in the social organization of anthropoid primates. Among these species, there are monogamous pairs, single males attached to groups of females, multiple males in association with groups of females, and a few species in which single females are attached to several males (Jolly 1985; Terborgh and Goldizen 1985). There are species in which males disperse from their natal groups at the time of puberty and join established groups of related females, species in which females disperse to join established groups of related males, and species in which young of both sexes disperse to form new groups (Pusey and Packer 1987). In some species, territories are defended vigorously against intruders, but in others the home ranges of neighboring groups overlap extensively (Cheney 1983). While we have established that both ecological pressures and taxonomic affinities may shape social structure (Clutton-Brock and Harvey 1977), the precise determinants of social organization have proven elusive.

Although the size and structure of social groups varies considerably among species, in all of these groups adult males and females establish social relationships with each other. Sometimes females cooperate with one another, and sometimes they compete against each other (Hrdy 1981; Silk and Boyd 1983). Similarly, relationships among adult males and females are characterized by both cooperation and competition (Smuts 1987). Individuals who groom each other, give alarm calls to protect each other from predators, and form alliances with one another, may also harass each other, kill each other's infants, and drive each other out of social groups. Such contradictions are inherent features of sociality. We humans share propensities for aggression and altruism with other primates; we did not invent them.

Dominance relationships in non-human primate groups

Primatologists who analyze the pattern of aggressive interactions among individuals often find that the outcomes of such encounters among pairs of individuals are remarkably uniform over time. That is, individual A consistently defeats individual B in aggressive encounters. Moreover, aggressive interactions among triads are often transitive. This means that if A defeats B, and B defeats C, A can also defeat C. When dyadic dominance relationships are stable over time, and all triadic relationships are transitive, individuals can be ordered in a linear hierarchy (Chase 1980).

Most primatologists now reserve the word "dominance" to refer to the outcome of dyadic aggressive encounters which do not involve direct contests over resources (Bernstein 1981). In practice, however, many workers have found that the outcomes of aggressive and competitive interactions are often highly correlated (Richards 1974). If A can defeat B in an aggressive encounter, A can also displace B from most resources. This finding is not surprising because the threat of escalated aggression from an opponent whose success in aggressive encounters is well established is likely to influence the outcome of contests over resources. Several workers have found strong associations between agonistic dominance rank and access to valuable resources such as food (Fairbanks 1984; Whitten 1983), water (Wrangham 1981), receptive females (Fedigan 1983; Gray 1984; Silk 1987), and grooming partners (Seyfarth 1977, 1980).

At the same time, however, differences in aggressive dominance rank do not always provide a perfect predictor of the distribution of resources. Even if A is apt to be able to displace B handily, it does not necessarily mean that A will challenge B over access to any given resource at any given time. For example, while female baboons in Amboseli National Park in Kenya are normally able to displace lower-ranking individuals from food resources, the composition of the diets of high and low-ranking females apparently does not vary (Post, Hausfater, and McCuskey 1980). Similarly, Smuts (1985) found that male dominance rank does not provide an adequate predictor of access to receptive female baboons, and Wrangham (1975) found that access to meat is not correlated with aggressive dominance rank among male chimpanzees. Such outcomes are usually attributed to the fact that the resources do not have the same value to all competitors, or to the fact that the costs of competitive interactions may differ for them (Clutton-Brock and Harvey 1976).

There is also considerable variation in the prevalence of dominance relationships among species. In some species, dominance interactions are frequent, the outcome of interactions are stable over time, and triadic relationships are consistently transitive. In such cases, linear dominance hierarchies can be constructed with little ambiguity. Such patterns are particularly common among terrestrial Cercopithecine species, such as macaques, baboons, and vervet monkeys. Early criticism that dominance hierarchies are artificial products of observations under unnatural captive conditions (for example, Rowell 1974) has now been effectively countered by thousands of hours of observation which confirm the importance of dominance relationships in these species. At the same time, however, we have learned that in some taxa, dominance relationships are considerably less prominent than in the Cercopithecines. Hundreds of hours of observation of female gorillas, for example, yield so few encounters that females cannot be reliably ordered in a linear hierarchy (Watts 1985).

Dominance relationships between males and females among non-human primates

The diversity of behavior patterns among non-human primate species makes it advisable to proceed with considerable caution when we describe the nature of dominance relationships between males and females (Smuts 1987; see also Wright, this volume). In many species, individual males dominate individual females. However, even in these species, not every male dominates every female, and groups of females are consistently able to dominate males in some contexts. Moreover, in other species, males and females maintain equal status, and in some species, most females dominate most males.

The pattern of dominance relationships between males and females has been associated with morphological differentiation among males and females (Smuts 1987 and references therein). In a few non-human primate species, females are slightly larger than males, and they are able to dominate male members of their groups. Such patterns are characteristic of only one group of prosimians, the Lemuriformes (Richard 1987). It is somewhat more common for males and females to be very similar in size. In such cases, there is no consistent pattern of dominance among males and females, and overt aggression is often uncommon. This pattern is characteristic of several families of New World monkeys and the Hylobatids. Most commonly, however, males are considerably larger and heavier than females, and have larger canine teeth. In these species, males consistently dominate females in dyadic encounters. Male dominance over females is characteristic of baboons, vervets, macaques, squirrel monkeys, talapoins, Hanuman langurs, mantled howler monkeys, gorillas, orang-utans, chimpanzees, and baboons. The degree of sexual dimorphism in body size among males and females also influences the effectiveness of female coalitions against males. Where differences among males and females are relatively small, such coalitions occur and appear to be effective. But when males are considerably larger and have much longer canines than females, as in gorillas and baboons, females rarely form alliances against adult males (Pusey and Packer 1979).

Even among highly dimorphic species dominance relationships represent only one dimension of male–female relationships. In all non-human primate species, females maintain considerable autonomy over their own lives. For example, even when males are twice the size of females, females exercise effective mate choice; forced copulations in non-human primate species are rarely observed (Smuts 1987). Affiliative relationships among highly dimorphic male and female baboons play an important role in the reproductive strategies of both males and females (Smuts 1984a, 1984b, 1985).

Why are males larger than females?

Asymmetric dominance relationships arise when differences in the body weight and canine size of adult males and females occur. Since morphological differences are apparently related to the nature of hierarchical relationships among non-human primate males and females, it is important to ask why differences in body size arise among them.

Traits that distinguish males from females across taxa, and that are not directly related to sexual function, can evolve through two very different processes. Differences in body weight and canine size can reflect ecological niche separation among males and females. In many species of birds, males and females feed upon different foods, and thereby avoid competing with one another over resources (Selander 1972). Here, sexual dimorphism develops in response to these distinct dietary specializations. There is little evidence that the diets of non-human primate males and females differ, although in a few species males appear to obtain more vertebrate prey than females (Jolly 1985). Because sexual dimorphism is considerably more widespread than are dietary differences among males and females, we must look elsewhere for an explanation of morphological differences between non-human primate males and females.

In primates, sexual dimorphism is likely to have evolved through sexual selection, a process that was first described by Charles Darwin (1871). Darwin recognized that natural selection would generally favor the evolution of traits that enabled individuals to survive and reproduce more successfully than other members of their populations. Fitness is formally defined as an individual's *relative* contribution to the gene pool of the next generation. However, Darwin was also puzzled by the existence of characters that seemed to confer no obvious advantage upon individuals' ability to survive and reproduce. The brilliant coloring and extravagant plumage of some birds, the elaborate courtship rituals of some insects, and the massive tusks, horns, and antlers of some mammals seemed to have no clear adaptive function. Moreover, these exaggerated characters were generally limited to members of one sex, often males. There was no reason to expect that such morphological differences would evolve through natural selection.

Darwin believed that in sexually reproducing species, certain traits might evolve because they increased the attractiveness of an individual to members of the opposite sex, or because they provided an advantage in competition over mates among members of the same sex. Traits that influenced mate choice and the outcome of intra-sexual competition might be very different from traits that evolved through normal natural selection, so he coined the term "sexual selection" to distinguish this process. Darwin speculated that individuals of one sex might for some reason be attracted to individuals of the opposite sex who exhibited distinctive traits, such as conspicuous coloration, exaggerated morphological characters, or elaborate courtship behaviors. Even if such characters do not increase male fitness directly, they may be favored if females are able to discriminate among males, and consistently select males who bear a particular trait. Moreover, mate choice may lead to a runaway process (Fisher 1958; Lande 1981) in which such traits become so exaggerated that they impair the individual's ability to survive. If this possibility seems far-fetched, think of peacock tails and the courtship performance of sage grouse.

Darwin suggested that sexual selection might also favor individuals who are able to exclude other members of the same sex from mating, because such competition augments their own relative fitness. A variety of behavioral traits are believed to have evolved in response to intra-sexual competition; these include aggressive exclusion of competitors, guarding access to receptive mates, and infanticide (Hrdy 1979; Hrdy and Hausfater 1984). The large and sexually dimorphic horns, tusks, antlers, and teeth characteristic of many mammals provide effective weapons in intra-sexual combat.

In most cases, sexually selected characters are more pronounced among males than among females. Trivers (1972) argues that this phenomenon arises in mammalian species because mammalian females are predisposed to make greater investments in the production and rearing of offspring than are males. The mammalian reproductive system dictates that females carry their young internally and suckle them after birth. Mammalian males normally play a limited role after fertilization occurs. Although males might be able to provision their mates during pregnancy and lactation, and protect their young from predators, mammalian females are usually able to raise their young without such help. As a result, selection favors males who concentrate their reproductive effort upon obtaining access to receptive females, and inseminating them. Such efforts may lead to competition among males because a single male can potentially inseminate all of the available females. When reproductive competition among males arises, sexually dimorphic characters may evolve.

Thus, sexual dimorphism in primate groups appears to be the product of sexual selection which has favored the evolution of larger bodies, longer canine teeth, and other secondary sexual characteristics among males. This argument receives further support from the work of Clutton-Brock and Harvey (1977). They reason that if sexual dimorphism is the product of sexual selection, we should find that the degree of sexual dimorphism in a given species is correlated with the intensity of com-

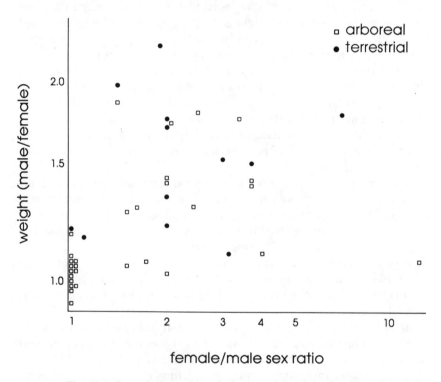

Fig. 10.1 Sexual dimorphism in body weight plotted against the adult sex ratio among non-human primates (from Clutton-Brock, Harvey, and Rudder 1977). For species in which sexual dimorphism exceeds 1.0, males are heavier than females. Monomorphic species tend to live in pair-bonded groups while dimorphic species tend to live in groups in which females outnumber males (with permission of Tim Clutton-Brock 1991)

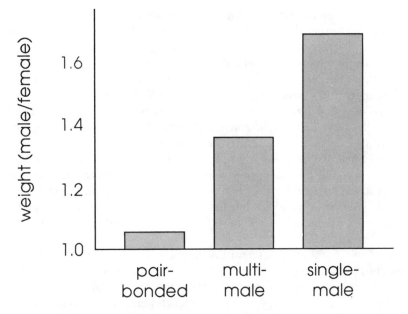

Fig. 10.2 Comparison of sexual dimorphism in body weight for primates that normally live in pair-bonded, multi-male, or single-male groups (from Clutton-Brock and Harvey 1984; with permission of Tim Clutton-Brock 1991)

petition that males in that species typically encounter. They measured the extent of competition among males by calculating the number of adult females per male and determined the extent of sexual dimorphism by comparing the body weights of free-ranging, unprovisioned males and females. The results of their extensive survey of the primate order are presented in Fig. 10.1 (Clutton-Brock, Harvey, and Rudder 1977).

Several conclusions can be drawn from this scatterplot. First, it is clear that sex ratios (females per males) vary widely in non-human primate groups. In pair-bonded or monogamous species, there is usually one male for every female, while in species that form single-male groups there may be as many as a dozen females per male. The extent of sexual dimorphism is consistently associated with the sex ratio. While there is no dimorphism among the monogamous gibbons, siamangs, titi monkeys, marmosets, and tamarins, there is considerable sexual dimorphism among the polygynous species, which include most of the Cercopithecine species and all of the great apes, the primates to whom we are most closely related. Primates that live in one-male groups generally show more pronounced sexual dimorphism than those that form multi-male groups (Clutton-Brock and Harvey 1984) (Fig. 10.2).

The extent of competition among males does not explain all of the variation in sexual dimorphism. Subsequent analysis has revealed that folivores are generally less dimorphic than frugivores, aboreal species are less dimorphic than terrestrial species, and small-bodied species are less dimorphic than larger-bodied species (Clutton-Brock and Harvey 1984; Leutenegger and Cheverud 1982; Gaulin and Sailer 1984). Comparative analysis of sexual dimorphism in the size of canine teeth yield very similar results (Harvey, Kavanagh, and Clutton-Brock 1978); species that are dimorphic in body size also tend to be dimorphic in canine size (Leutenegger and Shell 1987). The significance of this correlation between social organization and the extent of sexual dimorphism is underscored by the fact that similar relationships between the extent of sexual dimorphism and the number of males per females have been found among pinnipeds, ungulates, reptiles, and amphibians (Clutton-Brock and Harvey 1984 and references therein).

Thus, in a number of different taxonomic groups, the extent of sexual dimorphism is associated with the form of social organization and the intensity of intra-sexual competition among males. Sexual dimorphism is most pronounced in polygynous groups when females outnumber males, and males consequently compete over access to females. It is in such dimorphic species that males most consistently dominate females. For non-human primate species we can develop cogent hypotheses about the nature of social relationships between males and females given information about the extent of sexual dimorphism among them.

Inferences about early hominids and contemporary humans

The comparative data suggest that there is a reasonably consistent relationship between morphology, social organization, and social behavior among non-human primates. This body of work may be relevant to understanding gender hierarchies in contemporary human societies in two different ways. First, this body of work can provide well-founded insights about the social organization and behavior of hominid species that preceded the appearance of modern humans. Second, this approach may illuminate our understanding of the relationships between males and females in contemporary societies by identifying both consistencies and contradictions between our evolutionary history and current cultural realities.

Attempts to understand the evolution of human behavior are inevitably frustrated by the fact that behavior is not preserved in the fossil record. Although we can describe some of the morphological characteristics and material remains of extinct hominids, these data do not tell us everything that we would like to know about them. For example, we know that *Australopithecus africanus* was an efficient biped (McHenry 1982), but we do not know if it lived in stable social groups. We think that early hominids manufactured stone tools which were used to butcher game (Potts 1984), but we do not know how they communicated with one another. We know that *Homo erectus* learned to contain fire and buried their dead (Campbell 1985), but we do not know whether males recognized or cared for their own children. Since morphology fossilizes better than behavior, principles derived from comparative studies of non-human primates may provide particularly valuable clues about the social organization and behavior of early hominids.

The validity of such reconstructions clearly depends upon whether it is reasonable to apply evolutionary principles which are derived from comparative studies of non-human primates and other animals to early hominids. For the first few million years after the hominid line diverged from the common ancestor of humans and chimpanzees, there were major changes in postcranial anatomy associated with the transition from quadrupedal to bipedal locomotion, and changes in dentition that were probably associated with changes in dietary specializations. However, these changes occurred well before the brain began to expand, tools were manufactured, or symbolic language was developed (McHenry 1982). At least up to this point, it seems likely that the behavioral repertoire of early hominids was much like that of contemporary anthropoid apes. It seems sensible to accept the working hypothesis that evolutionary rules that apply to other primates also apply to early hominids.

The logical power of such inferences may be diminished with the rapid development of cultural complexity among members of the genus *Homo*. We know that in the last 100,000 years, language, sexual division of labor, warfare, elaborate forms of social learning, food cultivation, and other cultural attributes have become important elements of human adaptation (Campbell 1982). There is now an active debate regarding the nature of the forces that have shaped the evolution of human behavior. On the one hand, some argue that culture is simply an efficient form of phenotypic plasticity, and that humans are only subject to the same selective forces that affect the members of other species (Alexander 1979; Lumsden and Wilson 1981). Others argue that culture must be treated as a system of inheritance which introduces a novel set of evolutionary forces that might shape the behavior of humans in ways that are quite different from what ordinary natural selection would predict (Boyd and Richerson 1985).

I do not intend to dwell on this controversy here. However, we may gain insights about the processes that shape the pattern of male–female relationships in contemporary species if we apply predictions that have been derived from comparative studies of non-human primates to data on contemporary humans. If the patterns of the relationships between sexual dimorphism, social organization, and male–female relationships in contemporary societies are the same as those that have been documented across the primate order, we may have reason to believe that evolutionary principles which explain these relationships in other species are also relevant to understanding them among contemporary humans. If the patterns of these relationships are not consistent with those in other species, we may have reason to suspect that we should look elsewhere to unravel the reasons for gender hierarchies in contemporary societies.

Sexual dimorphism and behavior of the Australopithecines

Comparative analyses of the relationship between social organization and sexual dimorphism suggest that we can make tentative inferences about social behavior and male–female relationships among early hominids if we can assess the amount of sexual dimorphism among them. To do so, paleontologists must be able to interpret the significance of variation in fossil material, but this task is difficult mainly because only very small samples of postcranial material are available for early hominids. This problem often leads to disagreement over the taxonomic affinities of individual specimens. It is generally even more difficult to determine whether individual specimens represent males or females since the diagnostic traits that distinguish one sex from the other are often missing from fossil remains (Wood 1985). Thus, estimates of the extent of sexual dimorphism cited below must be treated with caution, because the sex of fossil material often cannot be assessed directly, and the samples are often small and variable.

Among the oldest known hominids, the Australopithecines, males were considerably heavier than females (McHenry 1988). Current estimates suggest that Australopithecines were even more dimorphic in body weight than contemporary gorillas or orang-utans. While the extent of dimorphism in body size and canine size is strongly correlated in non-human primates, these traits were decoupled early in the hominid lineage. There was relatively little sexual dimorphism in the canine teeth of the Australopithecines (Leutenegger and Shell 1987). It is not clear what selective pressures reduced the size and extent of sexual dimorphism in tooth morphology and simultaneously maintained strong sexual dimorphism in body size. One hypothesis is that there was selection for increased surface area of the premolars, which consequently reduced the amount of room available for the canine teeth (Leutenegger and Shell 1987). At the same time, however, intra-sexual competition among males maintained strong dimorphism in body size.

The evidence suggests that the earliest hominids were dimorphic creatures, although the pattern of morphological differentiation among males and females is unique. The Australopithecines were as dimorphic in body size as primates that now live in multi-male and one-male groups, such as patas monkeys, gorillas, orang-utans, and hamadryas baboons. From this information, we might infer that early hominids lived in one-male groups in which several females were associated with a single male. The extent of sexual dimorphism also suggests that there may have been intense reproductive competition among males over mating opportunities, and little paternal investment in offspring. In non-human primates, such pronounced sexual dimorphism is often associated with male dominance over females and the infrequent formation of effective female coalitions against males.

Sexual dimorphism and behavior in the genus *Homo*

Sexual dimorphism was less pronounced in *Homo habilis* and *Homo erectus* than in the Australopithecines, but remained more pronounced than in modern humans (McHenry 1987). Sexual dimorphism was well within the range of contemporary human populations by the time Neanderthals appeared (Trinkaus 1980). Unfortunately, postcranial material for these species is presently too limited (Walker, Zimmerman, and Leakey 1982; Brown *et al.* 1985) to date this transition precisely.

Some workers have linked the reduction of sexual dimorphism to increased altriciality in infants, which is in turn associated with rapid brain expansion in the genus *Homo* (Potts 1985; Trevathan 1985). The growth of the hominid cranium to accommodate brain expansion is likely to have induced serious obstetric complications for pregnant females (Trevathan 1985; Brown *et al.* 1985). It may have been such complications that eventually led to intensification of parental investment in offspring, modification of social organization, and radical transformations of male–female relationships within the genus *Homo*.

It is plausible that the primary catalyst of this transformation was the increase in hominid cranial capacity. The configuration of the female pelvis limits the head size of an infant that can be safely delivered (Trevathan 1985). Any modifications of the pelvis that would alleviate obstetric problems would impair locomotor efficiency, a costly solution for a terrestrial primate with small canines. Instead, infants were probably born at an earlier stage of gestation than were earlier hominids or contemporary anthropoid primates (Trevathan 1985; Brown *et al.* 1985). These infants would have required extensive sustenance, support, and protection, and their dependence may have limited the range of maternal activities. For example, it might have become more difficult or dangerous for mothers of young infants to participate in hunting or scavenging activities. This restriction of female subsistence activities may have imposed significant hardships upon hominid females living in temperate environments, because vegetable foods may have been difficult to obtain during the cold winter months.

Even if females' hunting activities were not significantly curtailed by childbearing, it may have been difficult to obtain enough food to feed themselves and their growing offspring. Thus, it may have been increasingly important for males to supplement the diet of females and their offspring. In most primate species, animals do not provision each other with food, and even mothers do not often share food with their offspring (Jolly 1985). Foods that are shared are normally those that are difficult to obtain, nutritionally valuable, and/or readily distributed. As hunting became an important element of the hominid subsistence strategy, a valuable, portable, and divisible source of nutrients became available. It may have been access to such resources that initially favored the evolution of food sharing among males, females, and their offspring. The reciprocal exchange of meat and vegetable foods among males and females may have increased the benefits both males and females obtained from such economic bonds. The appearance of home bases at this stage of human evolution further emphasizes the increasing importance of economic cooperation among individuals (Potts 1985).

With these economic bonds, new social traditions might have emerged among members of the genus *Homo*. Evolutionary theory suggests that reciprocity is most likely to occur among individuals who have the opportunity to interact repeatedly (Axelrod and Hamilton 1981), and that kinship facilitates altruism (Hamilton 1964). Thus, we might expect long-term reciprocal relationships to be established between individual males and females, and for males to provision selectively their kin, particularly their own offspring. From here it is only a logical, albeit long, step to monogamy, extensive paternal investment, and reduction of male–male competition over access to females. With such changes in social organization, selection pressures maintaining sexual dimorphism may have been relaxed. These changes may also have led to radical transformations of social relationships among males and females. Like other monogamous primates, human adults are likely to have maintained equal dominance status and close affiliative ties with their partners. Hominid males and females are likely to have fulfilled complementary economic roles and cooperated extensively with one another.

The expansion of the brain may have significantly altered the human life cycle, and fundamentally altered the reproductive strategies of

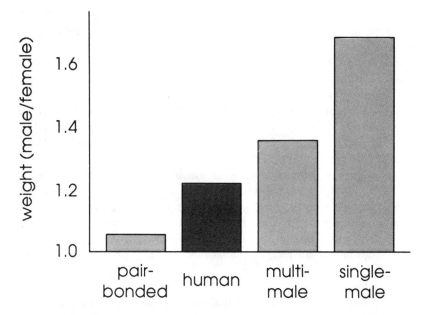

Fig. 10.3 Extent of sexual dimorphism among contemporary humans compared with extent of sexual dimorphism in pair-bonded, multi-male, and single-male groups of non-human primates (from Clutton-Brock and Harvey 1984; with permission of Tim Clutton-Brock 1991)

hominid males and females. Reduction of sexual dimorphism may reflect changes in social organization that occurred as cooperation among males and females became economically profitable, reproductively beneficial, and ecologically feasible. Although this scenario may be plausible, it is not compelling because current evidence is too fragmentary to allow us to specify exactly when sexual dimorphism was reduced within the hominid lineage. As new evidence emerges, the plausibility of speculative scenarios like this one can be evaluated more fully.

Sexual dimorphism, mating systems, and male–female behavior among contemporary humans

In contemporary human populations, the ratio of female weight to male weight is 0.84 (Abbie 1975), and the ratio of female height to male height is 0.93 (Gray and Wolfe 1980). When humans are placed on the same graph with other primates (Fig. 10.3), it seems quite clear that we are less dimorphic than species living in one-male groups or multi-male groups, but somewhat more dimorphic than species that form monogamous pair bonds. If this were any other primate species, we would predict that it would be characterized by either monogamous pairs or multi-male groups.

Do contemporary human mating systems conform to this prediction? Cross-cultural surveys of human marriage practices indicate that nearly all human societies are either monogamous or polygynous; as in other primates, polyandry is very rare. Monogamy is consistently practiced in approximately 30 percent of all societies, while polygyny is practiced in the remainder. Polygyny is apparently common in only half of these societies (Murdock 1967).

The number of human societies in which polygyny is permitted may provide a misleading estimate of the extent of reproductive competition among males. These data tell us very little about the mean number of wives per man, or the variance in the number of wives each man marries. This omission is a crucial one because the intensity of sexual selection upon males is proportional to the variance in their fitness (Wade 1979; Wade and Arnold 1980).

In non-human primate groups, we can make qualitative comparisons of the magnitude of the variance in male mating success in monogamous, multi-male, and one-male groups. In monogamous primate groups almost all males have a single mate, although a few males probably have none, and a few males may have more than one mate (Fig. 10.4a). In this case, the variance in male reproductive success will be very low. In one-male groups, a few males will be associated with groups of females, while the remainder will form bachelor parties or remain solitary. If there are five females in each one-male group, four out of every five males will have no mates (Fig. 10.4b). The variance in male reproductive success in one-male groups will be considerably greater than in monogamous groups. In most multi-male groups, males do not mate randomly with receptive females. In many species, males form dominance hierarchies, and in some of these species male dominance rank is positively correlated with reproductive success (Fedigan 1983; Silk 1987). This means that in multi-male groups, a few males will have many mates, and many males will have none. Most males, however, will achieve intermediate mating success (Fig. 10.4b). In multi-male groups, the magnitude of the variance in reproductive success will depend upon the size of the slope of the regression between male dominance rank and reproductive success.

The same logic can be applied to human marriage practices. In monogamous human societies most men are married, and no man has more than one wife at a time (Fig. 10.5a). There are probably some men who marry more than once during their lifetimes, and some men who never marry. Nonetheless, variance in male reproductive success is probably

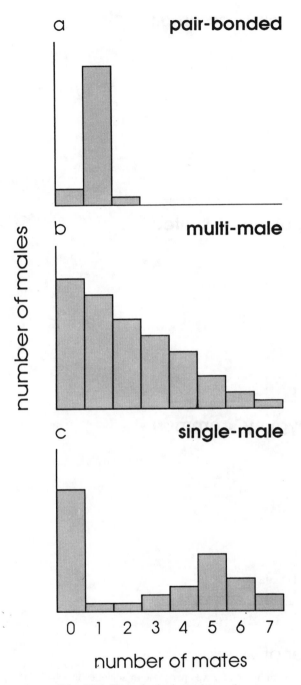

Fig. 10.4 Hypothetical numbers of mates per male in (a) pair-bonded, (b) multi-male, and (c) single-male groups

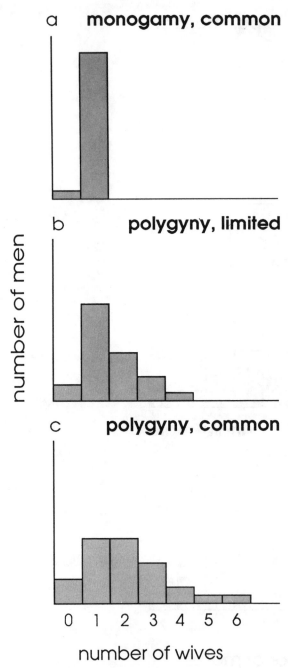

Fig. 10.5 Expected number of wives per male in societies in which (a) monogamy is common, (b) polygyny is limited, and (c) polygyny is common

very low. In polygynous human societies, the range of variation in male reproductive success is potentially much greater. It is possible for one man to marry dozens of women, but such cases are probably rare. In Murdock's sample (1967), polygyny was common in only half of the societies that permitted it. Thus, in many polygynous human societies, most men may actually have only one wife (Fig. 10.5b). In the remaining polygynous societies, men may have multiple wives (Fig. 10.5c), but it is unlikely that many men have more than a few wives. It seems reasonable to conclude that the magnitude of the variance in male reproductive success is likely to be quite low in at least two-thirds of all human societies, those in which monogamy is practiced or polygyny is uncommon.

These rough estimates of the variance in male reproductive competition are consistent with the observation that humans are considerably less sexually dimorphic than non-human primates living in one-male groups or multi-male groups. It would be tempting to conclude that reduced sexual dimorphism is the product of relaxed intra-sexual competition among men. However, such a causal conjecture would be premature for several reasons. First, there may be considerably more variance in male reproductive success than I have supposed. Second, the reduction of sexual dimorphism does not necessarily imply a reduction of male–male competition. Since men use weapons in competition with other men, the extent of sexual dimorphism may not accurately reflect the intensity of competition among them. Finally, the focus of male competition may have shifted. Competition among men may center on the differential abilities to acquire resources which can be offered to women, rather than the ability to dominate physically other men.

Cross-cultural variation in sexual dimorphism

There has been considerable interest in the variation in sexual dimorphism among contemporary human populations. Alexander and his colleagues (1979) attempted to demonstrate that the extent of sexual dimorphism in human societies is associated with marriage practices within societies. Their cross-cultural analysis suggests that societies with the lowest amounts of polygyny are least sexually dimorphic, so the pattern of variation is consistent with predictions derived from comparative studies of other taxonomic groups. These data have been cited as one of the primary examples that variation among contemporary human populations may be adaptive. But Alexander et al.'s results have been challenged on methodological grounds. Gray and Wolfe (1980) raise a number of questions regarding the procedures used to classify the marriage practices that characterize societies, and they report that when a more consistent categorization scheme is used, differences in the extent of sexual dimorphism among monogamous and non-monogamous societies become vanishingly small. They argue that cross-cultural variation in the extent of sexual dimorphism can be explained by other variables, particularly latitude, which Alexander *et al.* do not control for in their analysis.

Even more compelling problems with the empirical data are considered by Gaulin and Boster (1985). They calculate the regression between male height and female height within populations and find that there is very little scatter of points around the slope of the computed regression line. They thus conclude that there is little variation in sexual dimorphism among populations, and that the variation in dimorphism that does exist is likely to be a statistical artifact since the values that deviated most from the slope of the regression line were drawn from the smallest and least carefully collected samples. Therefore, Gaulin and Boster (1985) argue that it is cross-cultural consistency, rather than cross-cultural variation, in the extent of sexual dimorphism that needs to be explained.

Sexual dimorphism and gender hierarchies among contemporary humans

In other primate species, the extent of sexual dimorphism is related to the kinds of social relationships that males and females form. Given the limited amount of sexual dimorphism among contemporary humans and the fact that there is considerable overlap in size and strength among individual men and women, we might expect to find limited differentiation in dominance status and power between men and women. The ethnographic data do not seem to fit this prediction. Although it is extremely difficult to quantify precisely the distribution of power in human societies (Sanday 1981), there is little doubt that in many societies men monopolize political, legal, and economic power. This is not to say that human women are powerless in such societies, or that this description fits all societies. Women in food foraging societies (Lee 1982) and matrilineal horticultural societies (Schlegel 1972) do have considerable autonomy and social influence. However, the generalization of male dominance seems to fit a good number of societies, far more than a naïve primatologist would predict from human morphology or marriage practices alone.

Why do gender hierarchies exist among contemporary human societies? If humans were simply another primate species, they would seem to be very unlikely candidates for pronounced asymmetries in dominance and power. It might be argued that such asymmetries are the relic of a more dimorphic evolutionary heritage. This cannot be the whole explanation, because it does not account for the fact that these differences have been maintained in human populations for thousands of generations. Moreover, it ignores the fact that gender hierarchies are more pronounced in some societies than others. I suspect that gender hierarchies may be the by-product of cultural traits that set us apart from most other primates, such as the prevalence of warfare, the sexual division of labor, common female exogamy, and unilineal inheritance patterns. This conclusion does not mean that exploration of the evolutionary roots of gender hierarchies in early hominids and other primates is a fruitless endeavor. We gain insight about the magnitude and complexity of the puzzle of gender hierarchies by identifying the contradictions as well as the consistencies between ourselves and other primates.

NOTE

A number of people have shared their expertise with me during the preparation of this chapter. I would like to thank Henry M. McHenry, J. Patrick Gray, Steve Gaulin, Richard Potts, Barbara Smuts, and Wenda Trevathan for discussing their work and providing me with expert guidance through the literature. I also thank Sarah Blaffer Hrdy and Robert Boyd for several careful readings of the manuscript. Adrienne Zihlman also commented helpfully on an earlier draft. I gratefully acknowledge support received from the Harry Frank Guggenheim Foundation and National Science Foundation (BSR 8219127).

REFERENCES

Abbie, Andrew A. 1975 Metric Characteristics of Adult Aborigines. *Studies in Physical Anthropology* 2:76–103.

Alexander, Richard A. 1979 *Darwinism and Human Affairs*. Seattle: University of Washington Press.

Alexander, Richard A., John L. Hoogland, Richard D. Howard, Katherine M. Noonan, and Paul W. Sherman 1979 Sexual Dimorphism and Breeding System in Pinnipeds, Ungulates, Primates, and Humans. In *Evolutionary Biology and the Evolution of Human Social Behavior: An Anthropological Perspective*. Napoleon A. Chagnon and William Irons, eds., pp. 402–35. North Scituate, MA: Duxbury Press.

Axelrod, Robert and William D. Hamilton 1981 The Evolution of Cooperation. *Science* 211:1390–6.

Bearder, Simon K. 1987 Lorises, Bushbabies, and Tarsiers: Diverse Societies in Solitary Foragers. In *Primate Societies*. Barbara B. Smuts, *et al.*, eds., pp. 11–24. Chicago: University of Chicago Press.

Bernstein, Irwin S. 1981 Dominance: The Baby and the Bathwater. *Behavioral and Brain Science* 4:419–58.

Boyd, Robert and Peter J. Richerson 1985 *Culture and the Evolutionary Process*. Chicago: University of Chicago Press.

Brown, F., J. Harris, Richard Leakey, and Alan Walker 1985 Early *Homo erectus* Skeleton from West Lake Turkana, Kenya. *Nature* 316:788–92.

Campbell, Bernard G., ed. 1982 *Humankind Emerging*. Boston: Little, Brown, and Co. 3rd edition.

1985 *Human Evolution: An Introduction to Man's Adaptations*. New York: Aldine Publishing. 3rd edition.

Chase, Ivan P. 1980 Social Process and Hierarchy Formation in Small Groups: A Comparative Perspective. *American Sociological Review* 45:905–24.

Cheney, Dorothy L. 1983 Intergroup Encounters among Old World Monkeys. In *Primate Social Relationships: An Integrated Approach*. Robert A. Hinde, ed., pp. 233–41. Sunderland, MA: Sinauer Associates.

Clutton-Brock, Timothy H. and Paul H. Harvey 1976 Evolutionary Rule and Primate Societies. In *Growing Points in Ethology*. Patrick P. G. Bateson and Robert A. Hinde, eds., pp. 190–238. New York: Cambridge University Press.

1977 Primate Ecology and Social Organization. *Journal of Zoology* 183:1–39.

1984 Comparative Approaches to Investigating Adaptation. In *Behavioural Ecology, an Evolutionary Approach*. John R. Krebs and Nicholas B. Davies, eds., pp. 7–29. Oxford: Blackwell Scientific Publications.

Clutton-Brock, Timothy H., Paul H. Harvey, and B. Rudder 1977 Sexual Dimorphism, Sex Ratio, and Body Weight in Primates. *Nature* 269:797–800.

Darwin, Charles 1871 *The Descent of Man, and Selection in Relation to Sex*. New York: D. Appleton and Company.

Eisenberg, John 1981 *The Mammalian Radiations: An Analysis of Trends in Evolution, Adaptation, and Behavior*. Chicago: University of Chicago Press.

Fairbanks, Lynn A. 1984 Predation by Vervet Monkeys in an Outdoor Enclosure: The Effect of Age, Rank, and Kinship on Prey Capture and Consumption. *International Journal of Primatology* 7:27–38.

Fedigan, Linda M. 1983 Dominance and Reproductive Success in Primates. *Yearbook of Physical Anthropology* 26:91–129.

Fisher, Ronald A. 1958. *The Genetical Theory of Natural Selection*. New York: Dover Publications.

Gaulin, Steven J. C. and James Boster 1985 Cross-Cultural Differences in Sexual Dimorphism. Is There Any Variation to be Explained? *Ethology and Sociobiology* 6:193–9.

Gaulin, Steven J. C. and Lee D. Sailer 1984 Sexual Dimorphism in Weight among the Primates: The Relative Impact of Allometry and Sexual Selection. *International Journal of Primatology* 6:515–35.

Gray, J. Patrick 1985 *Primate Sociobiology*. New Haven, CT: Human Relations Area File Press.

Gray, J. Patrick and Linda D. Wolfe 1980 Height and Sexual Dimorphism of Stature among Human Societies. *American Journal of Physical Anthropology* 53:441–56.

Hamilton, William D. 1964 The Genetical Evolution of Social Behaviour. *Journal of Theoretical Biology* 7:1–52.

Harvey, Paul H. and P. M. Bennett 1985 Sexual Dimorphism and Reproductive Strategies. In *Human Sexual Dimorphism*. J. Ghesquiere, R. D. Martin, and F. Newcombe, eds., pp. 43–59. Philadelphia: Taylor and Francis.

Harvey, Paul H., Michael Kavanagh, and Timothy Clutton-Brock 1978 Sexual Dimorphism in Primate Teeth. *Journal of Zoology* 186:475–86.

Hrdy, Sarah Blaffer 1979 Infanticide among Animals: A Review, Classification and Examination of the Implications for the Reproductive Strategies of Females. *Ethology and Sociobiology* 1:13–40.

1981 *The Woman that Never Evolved*. Cambridge, MA: Harvard University Press.

Hrdy, Sarah Blaffer and Glenn Hausfater 1984 Comparative and Evolutionary Perspectives on Infanticide: Introduction and Overview. In *Infanticide: Comparative and Evolutionary Perspectives*. Glenn Hausfater and Sarah Blaffer Hrdy, eds., pp. xiii–xxxv. New York: Aldine.

Jolly, Alison 1985 *The Evolution of Primate Behavior*. New York: Macmillan. 2nd edition.

Lande, Russell A. 1981 Models of Speciation by Sexual Selection on Polygenic Traits. *Proceedings of the National Academy of Sciences, USA* 78:3721–5.

Lee, Richard A. 1982 Politics, Sexual and Non-sexual, in an Egalitarian Society. In *Politics and History in Band Society*. Richard A. Lee and Eleanor Leacock, eds., pp. 37–60. New York: Cambridge University Press.

Leutenegger, Walter and James Cheverud 1982 Correlates of Sexual Dimorphism in Primates: Ecological and Size Variables. *International Journal of Primatology* 3:387–402.

Leutenegger, Walter and Bettina Shell 1987 Variability and Sexual Dimorphism in Canine Size of *Australopithecus* and Extant Hominoids. *Journal of Human Evolution* 16:359–67.

Lumsden, Charles J. and Edmund O. Wilson 1981 *Genes, Mind, and Culture: The Coevolutional Process*. Cambridge, MA: Harvard University Press.

McHenry, Henry M. 1982 The Pattern of Human Evolution: Studies on Bipedalism, Mastication, and Encephalization. *Annual Review of Anthropology* 11:151–73.

1988 New Estimates of Body Weight in Early Hominids and their Significance to Encephalization and Megatontia. In *Evolutionary History of the "Robust" Australopithecines*. F. E. Grine, ed., pp. 133–48. New York: Aldine.

Murdock, George Peter 1967 *Ethnographic Atlas*. Pittsburgh, PA: University of Pittsburgh Press.

Post, David G., Glenn Hausfater, and Sue Ann McCuskey 1980 Feeding Behavior of Yellow Baboons (*Papio cynocephalus*): Relationships to Age, Gender, and Dominance Rank. *Folia Primatologica* 34:170–95.

Potts, Richard 1984 Hominid Hunters? Problems of Identifying the Earliest Hunter/Gatherers. In *Hominid Evolution and Community Ecology: Prehistoric Human Adaptation in Biological Perspective*. Robert Foley, ed., pp. 129–66. Orlando, FL: Academic Press.

1985 Evidence of Social Life from Early Hominid Archaeological Sites. Paper presented at the annual meeting of the American Anthropological Association, Washington, DC.

Pusey, Anne E. and Craig Packer 1987 Dispersal and Philopatry. In *Primate Societies*. Barbara B. Smuts *et al.*, eds., pp. 250–66. Chicago: University of Chicago Press.

234   *Joan B. Silk*

Richard, Alison F. 1987 Malagasy Prosimians: Female Dominance. In *Primate Societies*. Barbara B. Smuts *et al.*, eds., pp. 25–33. Chicago: University of Chicago Press.

Richards, S. M. 1974 The Concept of Dominance and Methods of Assessment. *Animal Behavior* 22:914–30.

Rowell, Thelma E. 1974 The Concept of Social Dominance. *Behavioral Biology* 11:131–54.

Sanday, Peggy R. 1981 *Female Power and Male Dominance: On the Origins of Sexual Inequality*. New York: Cambridge University Press.

Sarich, Vincent M. and John E. Cronin 1976 Molecular Systematics of Primates. In *Molecular Systematics of Primates*. Morris Goodman and Richard E. Tashian, eds., pp. 141–70. New York: Plenum.

Schlegel, Alice 1972 *Male Dominance and Female Autonomy: Domestic Authority in Matrilineal Societies*. New Haven, CT: Human Relations Area File Press.

Selander, Robert K. 1972 Sexual Selection and Dimorphism in Birds. In *Sexual Selection and the Descent of Man, 1871–1971*. Bernard Campbell, ed., pp. 180–230. Chicago: Aldine Publishing Company.

Seyfarth, Robert M. 1977 A Model of Social Grooming among Adult Female Monkeys. *Journal of Theoretical Biology* 65:671–98.

　1980 The Distribution of Grooming and Related Behaviors among Adult Female Vervet Monkeys. *Animal Behaviour* 28:798–813.

Silk, Joan B. 1987 Social Behavior in Evolutionary Perspective. In *Primate Societies*. Barbara B. Smuts *et al.*, eds., pp. 318–29. Chicago: University of Chicago Press.

Silk, Joan B. and Robert Boyd 1983 Cooperation, Competition, and Choice in Matrilineal Macaque Groups. In *Social Behavior of Female Vertebrates*. Samuel K. Wasser, ed., pp. 315–47. New York: Academic Press.

Smuts, Barbara B. 1984a Dynamics of "Special Relationships" between Adult Male and Female Olive Baboons. In *Primate Social Relationships*. Robert A. Hinde, ed., pp. 112–16. Sunderland, MA: Sinauer Associates.

　1984b Special Relationships between Adult Male and Female Olive Baboons: Selective Advantages. In *Primate Social Relationships*. Robert A. Hinde, ed., pp. 262–7. Sunderland, MA: Sinauer Associates.

　1985 *Sex and Friendship in Baboons*. New York: Aldine Publishing Company.

　1987 Gender, Aggression, and Influence. In *Primate Societies*. Barbara B. Smuts *et al.*, eds., pp. 400–12. Chicago: University of Chicago Press.

Terborgh, John and Anne W. Goldizen 1985 On the Mating System of the Cooperatively Breeding Saddle-Backed Tamarin (*Saguinus fuscicollis*). *Behavioral Ecology and Sociobiology* 16:293–9.

Trevathan, Wenda R. 1985 Readjustments in Birth and Mother–Infant Bonding throughout Hominid Evolution. Paper presented at the annual meeting of the American Anthropological Association, Washington, DC.

Trinkaus, E. 1980 Sexual Differences in Neanderthal Limb Bones. *Journal of Human Evolution* 9:377–97.

Trivers, Robert L. 1972 Parental Investment and Sexual Selection. In *Sexual Selection and the Descent of Man, 1871–1971*. B. Campbell, ed., pp. 136–79. Chicago: Aldine Publishing Company.

Wade, Michael J. 1979 Sexual Selection and Variance in Reproductive Success. *American Naturalist* 114:742–6.

Wade, Michael J. and Stevan A. Arnold 1980 The Intensity of Sexual Selection in Relation to Male Sexual Behavior, Female Choice, and Sperm Precedence. *Animal Behaviour* 28:446–61.

Walker, Alan, M. R. Zimmerman, and Richard E. F. Leakey 1982 A Possible Case of Hypervitaminosis A in *Homo erectus*. *Nature* 296:248–50.

Watts, David 1985 Relations between Group Size and Composition and Feeding Competition in Mountain Gorilla Groups. *Animal Behaviour* 33:72–85.

Whitten, Patricia L. 1983 Diet and Dominance among Female Vervet Monkeys (*Cercopithecus aethiops*). *American Journal of Primatology* 5:139–59.

Wolfe, Linda D. and J. Patrick Gray 1982 A Cross-Cultural Investigation into the Sexual Dimorphism of Stature. In *Sexual Dimorphism in* Homo sapiens: *A Question of Size*. Roberta L. Hall, ed., pp. 197–230. New York: Praeger.

Wood, B. 1985 Sexual Dimorphism in the Hominid Fossil Record. In *Human Sexual Dimorphism*. J. Ghesquiere, R. D. Martin, and F. Newcombe, eds., pp. 105–23. Philadelphia: Taylor and Francis.

Wrangham, Richard W. 1975 The Behavioural Ecology of Chimpanzees in Gombe National Park, Tanzania. Ph.D. dissertation, Cambridge University.

1981 Drinking Competition in Vervet Monkeys. *Animal Behaviour* 29:904–10.

11   Conjugal power in Tokugawa Japanese families: a matter of life or death

G. William Skinner

This chapter argues that the precise combination of husband's and wife's age at marriage can provide a valid index of conjugal power and demonstrates the analytical utility of such an index for studying the family demography of Tokugawa Japan. The two empirical arguments pursued here illustrate distinctive causal flows. In the first, I show how differential conjugal power shapes reproductive decisions, in particular those concerning infanticide, abortion, and early stopping of childbearing. Whether or not a neonate is allowed to live for instance, is partly a function of the balance of power between husband and wife within differently constituted households. In the second argument, I show that the relative power of husband and wife in the conjugal relationship affects their respective longevity, and I interpret the results to imply that the experience of wielding effective power as an adult within the family increases longevity. The data also support the obverse argument that unrelieved powerlessness and structural vulnerability to oppression are in the long run life-negating.

I base these arguments on preliminary findings from a larger research project entitled "Family System and Demographic Process in Rural Japan, 1702–1872." The inclusive project treats eight villages situated in a compact and homogeneous area near the castle town of Ogaki in central Japan. For each of these villages there survives a long run of annual household registers that provide detailed, accurate records of both family and demographic processes. The present analysis, based on data for only two of the eight villages, is provisional in at least three ways. First, some of the relationships reported here may fall short of statistical significance when tested with the enlarged data base. Second, the limited number of cases supplied by two villages cannot support a longitudinal analysis. Thus, how the relationships reported here vary through historical time – with economic conditions and environmental stress, for example – can be explored only with the enlarged data base. And, third, how family and demographic process in this particular locale relate to patterns within internally differentiated regional systems cannot even be broached at this stage of the research. Generalization to Japan as a whole is unwarranted.

The two villages under analysis, Nishijo (Hayami 1980, 1985, 1988) and Nakahara (Smith 1977) are situated on adjacent polders in the delta of the three major rivers that traverse the Nôbi Plain. The general area, one of sparsely populated fens at the beginning of the Tokugawa period (1600–1868), was reclaimed in the seventeenth century and, during the eighteenth, transformed through massive water-control projects into productive paddy fields on which cotton, rapeseed, and other cash crops were also cultivated. In these villages, as in most of Japan, a corporate stem family system obtained (Nakane 1967; Bachnik 1983), which means, among other things, that a spouse was brought in for only one offspring in each generation and succession was to the couple married within the household (Foster 1978; Hammel and Wachter 1977). The non-heirs in each generation normally left their natal household prior to or shortly after the marriage of the heir. Some entered other households as spouses of the heir, a few established new corporate households within the village, and many left the village unmarried to serve as apprentices or servants in nearby villages and towns or to migrate to one of the large cities.

Data for the present analysis were drawn largely from the basic register of village population, the *shûmon-aratame-chô*, as supplemented, checked, and/or corrected by reference to other, more specialized registers for years when they are available (Cornell and Hayami 1986; Smith 1977:Chapter 2). The data base is a reconstructed household-by-household record of life-cycle events that covers uninterrupted periods of 97 years for Nishijo and 114 years for Nakahara. For the analysis of reproductive behavior, the sample consists of the 360 couples for whom the span of years from marriage to the end of the childbearing period is completely covered by the registers.[1] The subsequent analysis of mortality treats the 342 ever-married persons for whom data are available on the entire span of years from marriage to death.

Family system, gender differentiation, and conjugal power

Conjugal power, that is, the relative power of husband and wife within the conjugal unit, is a major analytical focus of family sociology and a matter of growing concern within anthropology and demography. That portion of the theoretical literature treating cross-societal variation in normative systems appears to be seriously marred by a preoccupation with developmental stages and by generalization to overinclusive and/or improperly specified categories of societies. A prime example of the former is the four-stage typology of societal development presented by Rodman (1972:63–5). Examples of the latter are arguments that the very process of peasantization "lead[s] to the patri-oriented family system" (Goldschmidt

and Kunkel 1971:1070) or that beneath the public façade of male dominance that characterized agrarian societies the balance of real power in
peasant households resided with women (Rogers 1975). These examples
and many others gloss over the wide range of family systems that obtain
in agrarian societies prior to the onset of modernization and construct a
single story about changes in the norms of conjugal authority from a
homogenized past to a modern future, whether from patriarchy to egalitarianism (Rodman 1972; Scanzoni 1975) or from a position of dignity and
authority for women in their separate domestic sphere to a position of
subordination in families reshaped to meet capitalist imperatives (Bossen
1975; Rogers 1975). My view is that normative regimes of conjugal power
are most usefully typologized according to family system and that the
trajectory of modern change ought, on first principles, to be distinctive for
each type of family system.

Family system refers to the customary, normative manner in which
family process unfolds – to the usual preferred pattern of household
dynamics. It incorporates marriage form(s), succession, the transmission
of property, the normal sequence of coresidential arrangements, and the
customary bias by gender and relative age (if any) that informs these other
dimensions. The term family *system* is used because these various
elements of customary family life are contingently related in a systematic
fashion (complete, in many cases, with feedback, feedforward, and an
internal dialectic) such that a given family system can be captured in a
single processual model. Anthropologists generally distinguish three
broad classes of family systems: conjugal, stem, and joint. Conjugal
family systems are characterized by neolocal marriage (both bride and
groom leaving their natal household on marriage to establish a new
family), by equal inheritance among offspring and an absence of succession *per se*, and by a usual sequence of coresidential arrangements in
which an extended phase of the fully fleshed-out conjugal family is
preceded by an initial phase when the young couple is childless and
followed by the empty-nest phase, when all offspring have departed.

Stem and joint family systems are distinguished from conjugal family
systems, in the first instance, by the fact that a spouse is brought in for at
least one of the offspring in each generation. It follows directly that in
stem systems households are potentially corporate – that is, they may
persist indefinitely irrespective of the life spans of particular members –
and that at least a portion of the domestic cycle will be characterized by a
family structure comprising two or more conjugal units. (The three
elements of an intact conjugal unit are husband/father, wife/mother, and
child. It is now standard practice to count as a conjugal unit any coresiding
two of these three elements.) Within the more inclusive category of

potentially corporate family systems, stem family systems may be distinguished as follows: a spouse is brought in for only one offspring in each generation; succession is to the offspring who was married within the household or to the married couple; inheritance, which is unequal, favors the single successor/heir; and the domestic cycle is characterized by an alternation between a conjugal phase and a stem phase in which the junior and the senior conjugal units coreside. By contrast, in joint family systems, spouses are brought in for all of a category of offspring (usually those of one gender); inheritance is partible and equal among those within the favored category of offspring; succession is absent, variable, or fudged; and the domestic cycle is characterized by conjugal, stem, and joint phases, not necessarily in that sequence.

Gender bias informs these three types of family systems in contingent fashion. In general, structural bias is pronounced in joint family systems and minimal in conjugal family systems, with stem family systems intermediate. Without attempting to ring the gender-related changes among joint family systems, let it be said (by way of establishing a useful foil) that patrilineal joint family systems present the extreme examples of consistent, thoroughgoing male bias. They are characterized by patrilineally organized extra-familial kin groups, by virilocal marital residence (whereby the bride moves to the groom's household), by inheritance norms favoring sons, by descent through the male line, and by kinship terminologies that distinguish agnates from other kinsmen at the same genealogical distance. And the patriarchy of patrilineal joint family systems is normatively stark, if only because of its reinforcement by every other structural feature of the system.

Stem family systems present a very different picture, in that kinship is cognatic or bilateral and unilineal kin groups are normally absent. These structural features alone greatly restrict the scope for gender bias in comparison with joint family systems. Whether in Western Europe, Southeast Asia, or Japan, the kinship terminologies associated with stem family systems group together relatives at the same genealogical distance without regard to patrilaterality or matrilaterality. In the absence of patrilineages or matrilineages, the scope of unilineality is limited to the ongoing corporate family itself. And, in fact, the gender bias of any stem family system is expressed with neat consistency in terms of marital residence and the lineality of the family stem. If the preferred sex of the single heir is female, then marital residence is uxorilocal (whereby the groom moves on marriage to the bride's household) and the family stem is matrilineal. If the preferred sex of the single heir is male, then marital residence is virilocal and the family stem is patrilineal. If the normative preference is indifferent as to sex (taking the form, for instance, of primogeniture or ultimogeniture regardless of gender), then marital residence is ambilocal and the family stem is ambilineal. While a degree of normative patriarchy may be present in any of these variants, on first principles one expects male authority to be hedged if not mitigated by the absence of agnatic privilege and by the gender-balancing ideologies normally associated with cognatic kinship.

Conjugal norms in Japan: an attenuated patriarchy

In considering the norms of conjugal power among Tokugawa peasants, one must break free of two analogies that can mislead the unwary with respect to the degree and nature of patriarchy. One analogy suggests that conjugal relations in Tokugawa Japan were similar to those in Qing China. After all, the rhetoric of Japanese family ideology was, for the most part, borrowed wholesale from China. Along with the neo-Confucian interpretation of the ancestral cult and of filial piety came, it has been inferred, a full-blown patriarchy: authority was concentrated in the hands of the senior male, and wives were to submit to their husbands as subjects submitted to the emperor. In fact, the Japanese family system was little affected by the Sinicization of terminology and concepts, which, in any case, scarcely penetrated to the peasant level of society. Despite the cultural influence – and in accordance with the generic discussion in the previous section – the cognatic stem family system of Tokugawa Japan contrasts sharply with the patrilineal joint family system of Qing China. As a corollary, female autonomy was greater among Tokugawa peasants and conjugal relations considerably less skewed in favor of husbands.

The second misleading analogy supposes that conjugal relations in Tokugawa times were at least as patriarchal as those of the post-Restoration era (say, 1900–45). After all, the greater part of the sociological literature on marital power assumes the inevitability of a linear historical trend from patriarchy to egalitarianism. For instance, Scanzoni's well-known scheme (1975) identifies the dimensions of gender norms along a continuum ranging from traditional to modern. "Traditional" characterizes situations in which the interests of the wife are subordinate to those of the husband, and "modern" characterizes situations in which the interests of the wife are equal in significance to those of the husband. While it may be apparent today that such "modernization" paradigms are logically flawed, their recent hegemony has made it difficult for non-specialists to recognize the curvilinear trajectory of family history in modern Japan. In fact, the "Japanese family system" of the early twentieth century was a social construction of the Meiji era, propagated by a modernizing state intent on strengthening the family, tying it more closely to the state, and bringing the variety of local customs into accord with norms of the erstwhile samurai class. Male primogeniture was universalized, and the peasantry was required to adopt patronymic surnames comparable to those previously used only by the samurai and a favored fraction of the rural elite. The authority of the patriarch within the *ie* (corporate household) was reinforced by new laws taken seriously by a modernized police force and by a court system imbued with a familistic ideology. Women were exhorted to be "good wives and wise mothers," properly submissive to their menfolk and dedicated to the transcendental goals of the *ie* and higher-order collectivities in the newly rationalized hierarchy culminating in the imperial state.[2]

Prior to this Meiji endeavor in social engineering, however, the situation was quite different. Most of the peasantry lacked surnames altogether, and in many localities succession and inheritance were unbiased as to gender. In one common system the first-born child was the putative heir, regardless of gender, a son-in-law being brought in for a daughter just as a daughter-in-law was brought in when the firstborn was a son (Suenari 1972; Takeda 1970:27–33). Even where the preferred heir was customarily male, adopting a son-in-law for a daughter was a common alternative form of marriage. In formal terms the sex of the single heir was irrelevant. That is, the rights and duties extended by the natal family (*jikka*) to the family of a son who married out as an adopted husband were the same as those extended to the family of a daughter who married out as a bride (Brown 1988).

To be sure, as in most agrarian societies, the household headship was normally reserved for males,[3] men largely monopolized positions of authority within the village, and public deference of women to men was customary. It is likely that even in the privacy of the home, a wife usually spoke to her husband with a certain degree of respect, whereas a husband would find it unnatural to say please when addressing his wife (Smith and Wiswell 1982: Chapter 8). However, as Stephens points out in his cross-cultural study of the family, it does not follow that deference, "a ritual expression ... of an unequal power relationship" reflects the actual power relationship between spouses, that is, "who dominates and who submits; who makes family decisions ... who gets his (or her) way in case of disagreements; who is catered to; who commands and who obeys ..." (1963:296). And, indeed, a plausible argument can be made that in Tokugawa villages, especially those in the core areas of regional economies, women generally wielded effective power on a par with men.

In a provocative article, Rogers (1975) argues that in certain societies (of which more below) the male monopolization of household and community authority and the deference accorded men by women constitute a cover for "a non-hierarchical power relationship" between the sexes. Male dominance is, according to Rogers, a kind of myth that paradoxically serves to order social relationships in a non-hierarchical system:

The perpetuation of this "myth" is in the interests of both peasant women and men because it gives the latter the *appearance* of power and control over all sectors of village life, while at the same time giving to the former *actual* power over those sectors of life in the community which may be controlled by villagers. The two sex groups, in effect, operate within partially divergent systems of perceived advantages, values, and prestige, so that the members of each group see themselves as the "winners" in respect to the other. Neither men nor women believe that the "myth" is an accurate reflection of the actual situation. However, each sex group believes (or appears to believe, so avoiding confrontation) that the opposite sex perceives the myth as reality, with the result that each is actively engaged in maintaining the illusion that males are, in fact, dominant. (Rogers 1975:729) (Reproduced by permission of the American Anthropological Association from *American Ethnologist* 2(4), November 1975. Not for sale or further reproduction.)

Rogers' fieldwork was conducted in a French village, and the ethnographic literature she cites is almost entirely limited to Western Europe and the Mediterranean. Nonetheless, she presents her model as applying to peasant societies everywhere, a claim that sits poorly with specialists on agrarian societies with patrilineal joint family systems. Male dominance was hardly a myth in premodern China or India. But Rogers' formulation does resonate with the (premodern/historical) ethnographic record of much of Western Europe, Southeast Asia, and Japan, and I would therefore propose three necessary conditions for the phenomenon she describes in peasant communities, that is, for an approximate balance of power between the sexes beneath the public façade of male dominance: a gender division of labor in which females control the domestic sphere, a cognatic kinship system, and a gender system in which men and women are approximately equally dependent on each other in meeting both individual and collective goals.[4] While these conditions were essentially met in the Japanese villages under analysis, it is difficult, given the constraints of historical ethnography, to take the next step and demonstrate that the dynamic Rogers has described actually obtained in Nishijo and Nakahara. My purpose here is more modest: to document a number of structural features that enhanced the potential power of wives *vis-à-vis* their husbands. I wish to establish the plausibility that, despite the rhetoric and rituals of patriarchy, wives in these Tokugawa villages may well have prevailed over their husbands on certain issues at least some of the time.[5]

Gender division of labor

The ethnographic record indicates that the gender division of labor was fairly rigid in rural Tokugawa Japan. Farm households could not function properly without at least one adult member of each sex, and they functioned best when there was a balanced number of male and female adult workers. Child care, food preparation, and the manufacture and care of clothing were all women's work. Women managed the household's consumption economy and assumed responsibility for establishing and maintaining relations with kinsmen on both sides (Wakamori 1964:98). In the cultivation of rice, the principal crop in both villages, men prepared the paddy fields (including plowing, fertilizing, and irrigation) and carried the bundles of rice seedlings to the paddy fields, but the critical and meticulous tasks of transplanting and weeding were women's work (Kumatani 1970:68; Wakamori 1964:72). Night work was common throughout the year, and here, too, chores were strictly gender-linked. In the early fall, men worked at husking rice, women at grinding flour. In the late fall and winter, women spun and men made items of straw and fiber: rope, mats, sacks, sandals, and straw raincoats. Men continued these evening activities into the spring, while women turned to dyeing, weaving, sewing, and other needlework (Sakurada 1974:223–4; Andô 1975:215; Nakamichi 1974:453). Throughout the agricultural year both men's work and women's work were essential to the household's well-being, and necessary labor inputs in the women's sphere were at least as great as those in the men's sphere.[6]

Commensurate spheres

Just as the spheres of men and women were roughly equivalent with respect to the household's productive activities, so a certain symmetry characterized externally derived power: if men gained power and strategic information from their links to formal administrative institutions, women were linked to an exclusively female gossip network that provided information of strategic value in tempering and constraining male behavior. Writing about the first Japanese village studied by Western anthropologists, Suye-mura in the 1930s, Smith and Wiswell (1982:2) describe a situation that can, I think, be projected back to the nineteenth century: "There can be no doubt, on the basis of the evidence, that gossip was one of the pleasures of the women in Suye, and a powerful weapon in their hands." In the area of Nishijo and Nakahara, the paddle-shaped rice server symbolized authority within the domestic sphere, and its transfer from the senior woman to her daughter-in-law was a significant ritual within the *ie*. The autonomy of the women's domestic sphere is underscored by the fact that this ritual was not necessarily synchronized with the devolution of authority (the headship) from father to son and could in practice be delayed for years (Wakamori 1964:106; Nakamichi 1974:97; compare with Dore 1958:101).

Gender interdependence

It follows from the complementary nature of women's and men's productive work and from the interdigitation of their respective commensurate spheres that within the *ie* the sexes were closely interdependent. The loss of either spouse posed a serious existential crisis, but, interestingly enough, one that wives were apparently better positioned to weather than husbands. The contrast emerges clearly from the household registration data for the two villages: widowers living alone seldom survived for more than a year or two, whereas (controlling on age) widows in the same situation often lived on for a decade or more. Rogers (1975:745–6) notes a similar phenomenon in the French village she studied: "While men and women are obviously interdependent, women seem to maintain themselves alone more successfully than men do." She attributes this advantage to the greater security and independence women enjoy by virtue of their being anchored in the "fundamentally important" domestic unit. Whatever the reason, husbands in Nishijo and Nakahara appear to have been more dependent on their wives than vice versa.

This situation is but one of several reasons for supposing that wives had considerable bargaining power in their conjugal relationships. Both game theory and exchange theory suggest that the better one's alternatives outside a relationship, the better one's bargaining position within it (England and Farkas 1986:54–6). Were the alternatives outside of a current conjugal relationship better or worse for Tokugawa Japanese wives than for their husbands? The widowhood alternative was somewhat better for women, but what about divorce and remarriage? Without spelling out the details, we may summarize the evidence from household registration data for the two villages. Divorce was quite common, with high rates during the first few years of marriage, declining steadily after the fifth year of marriage duration. Remarriage was common for widowers and divorced men, with rates remaining high up to ages 50–5 years. Up to age 40, remarriage was no less common for widows and divorcees, but thereafter the remarriage rate sharply declined. The gender difference in age-specific remarriage rates might be thought to reflect the "double standard of aging," whereby men prefer younger women while women prefer men either their age or older (England and Farkas 1986:57), but it could be a simple consequence of the fact, suggested by most ethnographies of Japanese villages, that older widows and divorcees, especially those with surviving children in the *ie*, found the prospect of remarriage unattractive, whereas the reverse held for older widowers and divorced men, especially when there were no daughters coresiding.

Alternatives outside a specific conjugal relationship also turn on differences in the kind of investment wives and husbands make in the marriage. It may be argued that a wife normally makes more relationship-specific investments than does her husband, not only in her spouse and children, but also in her spouse's kin (England and Farkas 1986:55–8). In the context of Japanese virilocality, this factor reduces the attractiveness to a wife of alternatives outside the particular marriage and hence her bargaining power within it. What good are the kin links she has forged with the current husband's family once she has divorced or when she is remarried? And what of her investment in rearing children, who, as was customary, would remain after divorce in the *ie* into which they were born? This factor unquestionably diminished the wife's bargaining power within marriage and, in all probability, depressed the incidence of wife-initiated divorce in Japanese villages, but its overall importance is weakened by the husband's concern for the continuity and well-being of his *ie*. First, the carefully cultivated links to the *ie*'s kin forged by the current wife constituted an asset of the household that could be difficult to reconstruct. Second, the well-being of the children of the marriage, on whom hopes for the *ie*'s future devolved, could easily be jeopardized by a stepmother who failed to fit into the "ways of the household" and/or could not win the confidence or overcome the initial resistance of her stepchildren. In short, stepmothers were generally second-best as mothers, and the risks of replacing the children's mother had implications for the quality of the heir.

The *shûmon-aratame-chô* provide no clue as to which partner instigated particular divorces, but once again the situation in Suye-mura as of the 1930s is instructive: "[T]he women of Suye displayed a remarkable and quite unexpected degree of independence in the matter of marriage and divorce. Many of them had been married more than once, and what is astonishing is that it was not at all uncommon for the woman herself to terminate the marriage, whether it had been formalized or was a common-law one" (Smith and Wiswell 1982:149).

Sexual autonomy

It remains to discuss here one more factor that has been shown by comparative studies to be an important determinant of conjugal power, namely, women's sexual autonomy. Caldwell and Caldwell emphasize

the control by a woman of her own sexuality and of her right to decide on behavior which might be thought to have sexual implications. Our own working definition of female autonomy is whether a single woman is in danger if it is found that she has had premarital sexual relations or if she becomes pregnant. In the countries of North Africa and the Middle East she is still quite likely to be killed. In South Asia she is likely to commit suicide ... The real issue is whether a woman's sexual morality is largely her own business or whether it is chiefly the concern of her male relatives ... (1988)

The evidence I have indicates that in Tokugawa villages a woman's sexuality was largely the woman's own business – both before and after marriage. For starters, the very notion of secluding adolescent girls and women was alien to Tokugawa village society. This feature alone sets off Japan, along with most of Southeast Asia, from what Caldwell and Caldwell term "the great peasant societies of the Old World" – the Middle East, South Asia, and China.

Premarital sex appears to have been commonplace in village Japan and may well have been the normative expectation prior to the Meiji "reforms." Suye-mura in 1935 is instructive on this point, for the Embrees' informants explicitly recognized that changes had taken place in the past generation. A woman of 45 maintained that when she was young

all girls lost their virginity about the age of eighteen. "That is the best age," she confided, "for the later one loses it, the worse it is." Defloration usually happened during some secret meeting, when the young couple wandered off from a gathering or went out strolling at night. But nowadays girls are different, she says, and are told that they must keep their virginity until marriage ... Formerly the marriage ceremony was extremely simple and did not mean much in itself, so if a girl disliked something or other in her new home, she could go back to her family and start over again. Virginity in a bride did not seem important. That is why you find so many old women who have been married so many times. But now weddings have become elaborate affairs, and so girls take them less lightly and do not seek divorce so readily." (Smith and Wiswell 1982:130)[7] (Reproduced by permission of The University of Chicago Press; © 1982 by The University of Chicago.)

Yobai, nocturnal visits by young men to the sleeping mats of girlfriends, appear to have been customary in Tokugawa villages. Even in Suye-mura in 1935, "young men were assumed to have a go at slipping into a house at night with a view to having intercourse with a daughter of the house or a female servant" (Smith and Wiswell 1982:115).[8] That the custom expresses female as well as male sexual autonomy is suggested by the admission of one young lady to Ella Embree that "men will come in at night if the door is left open for them."[9] Ella Embree's journal, which faithfully records what Smith delicately terms the "candid discussions" she had with married women about sex, makes it clear that extra-marital affairs and the sexual activity of widows were, if not instigated or orchestrated by the women involved, then gladly tolerated. There is no hint of sexual intimidation of women by men (Chapters 4 and 8). It is difficult to imagine any reason why peasant women of the Tokugawa era would have exercised less control over their own sexuality.

To sum up, within the *ie* women controlled the domestic sphere of activity, which was essential to the household's production as well as its reproduction and continuity. In the later phases of the life cycle husbands were more likely to be dependent on their wives than the other way around. Moreover, wives no less than husbands enjoyed *de facto* sexual autonomy, and their alternatives outside a particular marriage were very nearly as good as their husbands'. For these and other reasons, the bargaining power of women within marriage should have been considerable and their domestic power potentially on a par with that of their husbands. It is less certain whether the forms and rhetoric of male dominance that also characterized Tokugawa village society should be seen as tipping the balance of conjugal power in favor of men or as providing a culturally acceptable framework whereby the wife realized her power potential by allowing her husband to be the overt decision-maker.

Nuptial configuration and conjugal power

The discussion to this point has skirted one important determinant of conjugal power, namely, the relative ages of the spouses at marriage. A pattern whereby husbands are normally older by a sizeable margin is, of course, congruent with patriarchal authority, and (as Japanese informants are quick to point out) brides are more readily socialized to the ways of the household when they are young. The distribution of marriage ages in our two villages is instructive in this regard. It will be seen from Table 11.1 that in general men married at considerably older ages than women and that the variance in marriage age was far greater for men than for women. Both patterns are characteristic of Japan as a whole (Hayami 1987) and of virtually all of the developing countries covered by the World Fertility Survey (Casterline, Williams, and McDonald 1986).[10] The mean ages at marriage shown, 20.6 for women and 28.4 for men, indicate that on average husbands were seven to eight years older than their wives. In less than 6 percent of the couples were women as old or older than their husbands, whereas in over a third of all couples men were at least ten years older than their wives.

Nuptiality can be viewed as a customary norm in any society; it can be shown, in fact, that cultural preferences operate not only with respect to the ages at which women and men ought to marry but also to the

Table 11.1. *Age at first marriage, by sex, Nishijo and Nakahara*

Age at first marriage	Females		Males	
	No.	Cum. %	No.	Cum. %
–14	19	5.3	2	0.6
15–18	135	42.9*	17	5.3
19–23	140	81.9	64	23.1
24–30	52	96.4	174	71.6
31–39	13	100.0	79	93.6
40–	0		23	100.0
Total	359		359	
Mean	20.6		28.4	
Standard deviation	4.85		6.76	
Maximum	39		62	

acceptability of particular age differences (Casterline, Williams, and McDonald 1986). However, the variation of concern here is not among societies but rather among couples within the same society. The factors influencing marriage age are many and varied, with specifically cultural norms playing only a part, but whatever the complex of causes that determine the marriage ages of a couple, the effect of that marriage-age configuration is systematic. I would argue, in fact, that the configuration of spousal ages is such a strong and systematic determinant of conjugal power that the former can be taken, within limits, as an index of the latter. The rationale for such an index is worth spelling out in detail.

Conjugal power is likely to vary systematically according to both the wife's absolute age at marriage and the age difference between her and her husband. A 16-year-old girl is, almost by definition, shy, self-effacing, and inexperienced by comparison with a 26-year-old woman.[11] In the context of a Tokugawa village, moreover, a 16-year-old will have had few occasions to leave her natal village, whereas any woman marrying as late as 26 is likely to have worked for a time outside the village as a servant or weaver or waitress. Holding the absolute age difference between the spouses constant (at six years, say, so that the 16-year-old marries a man of 22 and the 26-year-old marries a man of 32), it is clear that the former is more likely than the latter to be dominated by her husband in the early years of marriage.

At the same time, varying the age difference between the spouses also has an independent effect. If each of our two brides confronts a groom of 26 (so the 16-year-old marries a man ten years her senior and the

26-year-old marries a man of the same age), then the contrast between the couples would be sharpened, for the authority of the husband would be further enhanced in the eyes of the younger bride but considerably diminished in the eyes of the older bride. Thus, in couples formed through the marriage of absolutely young women to men relatively much older, the husband is likely to overpower his wife. But in couples formed through the marriage of absolutely older women to men of roughly the same age, the wife is likely to stand up for her own interests and defend her preferences.

A reference to Fig. 11.1 will situate this argument and point us toward the weighting to be used in constructing an index. The marriage-age matrix show wife's age at marriage in rows and husband's age at marriage in columns. The first component of the proposed index, the absolute age of the wife at marriage (WAGEMAR), is displayed at the top. The second component, the age difference between the spouses (DIFAGE), is displayed at the bottom. These dimensions represent only two of the many possible ways of slicing the marriage-age matrix.[12] The various slices that might be made intermediate between DIFAGE and WAGEMAR would represent different weightings of the two components, and two of these are diagrammed in Fig. 11.1. With DIFAGE specified as H-2W (husband's age minus wife's age), the dimension H-2W will be seen as exactly halfway between DIFAGE and WAGEMAR, and, indeed, H-2W gives equal weight to the two components. The dimension formalized as H-3W gives greater weight to wife's age at marriage (WAGEMAR) than to spousal age difference (DIFAGE).

I have used both of these indexes in my initial analyses, and it is clear that the empirical data "favor" the latter. That is, the statistical associations between conjugal power on the one hand and both reproductive behavior and adult morality on the other are higher when conjugal power is indexed by H-3W, the dimension that gives greater weight to WAGEMAR than to DIFAGE.[13] Accordingly, I have adopted as the index of conjugal power the dimension of H-3W, which I call HUSPOWER rather than, say, CONPOWER, so that its directionality will be clear: high values indicate that the husband is dominant, low values that the wife is dominant (Fig. 11.1).

It is probably correct to say, echoing an earlier formulation, that in couples high on the HUSPOWER index the husband's domination in practice conforms fully to the patriarchal rhetoric, whereas in couples intermediate on the index the wife would carry her weight without arousing the husband's anxiety about his authority. In couples still lower on the HUSPOWER index, we might expect the actual power of wives to match or even exceed that of their husbands despite the public façade

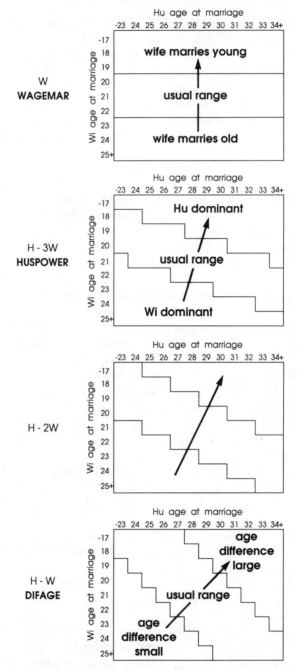

Fig. 11.1 Dimensions of the marriage-age matrix: HUSPOWER in relation to WAGEMAR and DIFAGE

of male dominance. In this range of the index Rogers' notion of a "probably unconscious" exchange between power and image would be particularly apt: "I'll give you credit for making the decisions here, if you'll make the ones I tell you to" (Rogers 1975:747). Couples in which husbands are not allowed even the façade of authority would, presumably, fall at the low extreme of the HUSPOWER index.[14]

A number of contingencies compound the significance of the HUSPOWER dimension. On the demographic side, for instance, women with husbands much older than themselves are more likely to be widowed, and to be widowed at an early age, than are women married to men of nearly the same age. On the side of social dynamics, spouses close together in age are likely to be more solitary *vis-à-vis* other members of the household than are those separated by many years. On the psychological side, since mothers tend to encourage the emotional dependence of eldest sons in particular, we may expect men who marry late to have been closely bound emotionally to their mothers, whereas men who marry young may have signified their independence of their mothers by insisting on an early marriage. While these are strictly speaking concomitants of DIFAGE, they cannot be overlooked in explaining variation along the closely related HUSPOWER dimension of the marriage-age matrix.

Conjugal power and infanticide

Abundant qualitative evidence from the Tokugawa period indicates that both infanticide and abortion were commonplace throughout Japan (Taeuber 1958:31–2; Chiba and Ōtsu 1983; NSS:162–9; Washino 1977:170). Many of the reasons given imply objectives that could be achieved by either means, namely, to terminate illegitimate pregnancies, to space out births in the interests of the mother's health and the quality of child care, to match offspring-set size to household resources, and to annul pregnancies of the senior couple in a stem family after the junior couple have begun childbearing. Although these objectives could be achieved by abortion as well as infanticide, the latter appears to have been favored. The very term for infanticide – *mabiki*, "thinning" – points to its use in spacing out offspring and limiting their number. The chief apparent reason for preferring infanticide to abortion as a means of annulling pregnancies is that it was less harmful to the mother (NSS:171). A common abortifacient was a mercurial compound that almost certainly had harmful side effects. A technique favored by midwives after the mid-seventeenth century was to insert a stick-like object into the head of the uterus (Hanley and Yamamura 1977:233–4). Not only was infanticide less dangerous to the mother, it was also simpler in its technical requirements and, as Smith (1977:151) has argued, "actually more efficient in controlling fertility owing to the much longer period of sterility associated with a full-term pregnancy."

Other objectives of family planners could be met only by infanticide, for they required selection on the basis of observable characteristics of the live infant(s). Literature and lore are explicit about twins. They were an unnatural abomination and one of them must be killed. The sources agree that the choice was made in terms of sex preference or, if the same sex, the relative health or robustness of the infants (Kuzutani 1977:227; NSS:161). Weak, sickly, and deformed infants appear to have been routinely killed (Muraoka 1972:227; NSS:160). Selection according to sex was, of course, possible only through infanticide. A major advantage of infanticide compared to abortion, then, was that it could be used to shape the sex configuration of the offspring set as well as its size and spacing.

From the earlier discussion of the gender division of labor, we saw that farm households functioned best when there was a balance in the gender of adult workers. In addition, the absolute balance between male and female tasks was such that each spouse had a roughly equal claim to timely assistance from a maturing offspring of the same gender. These considerations had direct relevance for family planning in the two villages. If a household consisted of a married couple plus a relatively young widowed grandmother, one might expect parents to have preferred a son as the firstborn child in order to rectify as soon as possible the gender imbalance. Similarly, with a relatively young widower in the household, a daughter might be preferred as the firstborn. If the husband in a conjugal family were older than his wife by a decade or more, or the grandfather in a stem family considerably older than his wife, one might expect a preference for the son to precede the daughter. In the case of intact conjugal and intact stem households, in which a gender balance obtained among the married adults, parents might well strive for sex balance in their first two children.

In any case, the most common form of strategizing via infanticide with respect to the sex configuration of offspring sets in Nishijo and Nakahara is that which favored both an overall balance and a regular alternation between the sexes.[15] This pattern is reflected in the tabulation shown in Fig. 11.2 which depicts all births beyond the first for a majority subset of couples defined in terms of nuptial configuration. It is clear that both balance and every-other alternation were being pursued simultaneously.

The most astonishing of my findings is that a sizeable proportion of all couples, perhaps as high as one-third, had recourse to infanticide at first birth. The very possibility that a firstborn child might be "returned" has seemed remote to analysts of Tokugawa demographic history. A source-

Sex balance of all preceding births	Sex of last preceding birth				Total	
	Male		Female			
	No. of births	%Male	No. of births	%Male	No. of births	%Male
M>F	274	43	42	48	316	44
M=F 1+F	123	46	270	56.	393	53
2+F	6	67	104	60	110	60
TOTAL	403	44	416	56	819	50

Fig. 11.2 All registered births of second and later parity arrayed according to characteristics of existing offspring at time of each birth

book on Japanese folk customs (NSS:162) tells us that in the Kantô region "parents considered three children as the limit, and the midwife took care of the rest at the time of birth." In her study of Japanese population Taeuber (1958) concludes: "All the observations of the late Tokugawa and the early Meiji eras indicate that the eldest son was subject to no hazard of willed death; that furthermore, the first two or three children were relatively secure." Thus, it has seemed probable that infanticide and abortion were being used, as contraception so often is in the modern world, only to stop childbearing after the couple's family-size objectives had been attained. Sex ratios of first births in most Japanese populations offer no clue that sex-selective infanticide might have been practiced. In the combined sample of Nishijo and Nakahara, for instance, the percentage of males at first birth is 51.8, a sex ratio of 107, only slightly above the normal sex ratio at birth for human populations of 105. Smith (1977:65) concludes that "there seems to have been no general sex preference for the first two births."

My analysis shows otherwise. Sex ratios of first registered children appear nearly normal for the simple reason that couples who killed female infants were roughly balanced in number by other couples who killed male infants. But why, in a population where male primogeniture was customary, would many couples deliberately kill firstborn males?

Ethnographic data point to a culturally preferred daughter-first strategy that was generally pursued when circumstances minimized its inherent risks. This strategy is sanctioned by a saying that had (and still has) widespread currency in Japanese society: *ichihime nitarô* – "first a girl, then a boy" (see, for example, Ôto 1950:191; SOS:126, 143). What lies behind this well-known bit of folk wisdom? The ethnographic literature provides two clues. The first comes from Harada Kiyoshi (1936:45), an ethnographer who interviewed intensively in one locality of the Nôbi region. The reason for the preferred girl-boy sequence, he was told, is that "the girl can help care for the boy, and the parents need not hire a nursemaid." The implication is clear: an older sister but not an older brother could help the mother in tending the infant. And indeed, as noted above, in the prevailing gender division of labor child care was the responsibility of females. Daughters were cast in the role of little mothers. If the firstborn were a girl, the mother could count on help in rearing the second and subsequent children, but such help would be postponed several years if the firstborn were male. There is the additional consideration that with their first child mothers lack experience and assurance; if the chances of botching the job are greater with the firstborn, better it should be a girl than a boy. Since we are dealing with a system in which the putative single heir is the eldest son, providing him with an older sister may be seen as improving his "quality" on two counts: not only a less harried mother, assured of help in child care, but also a more experienced mother.

The second clue to the preference for an initial female–male sequence is lore predicting dire consequences for the father should the sequence be reversed. If the firstborn was a boy, the infant and his father were said to be in competition such that one or the other would sicken and die early (Ôto 1950:191; NSS:143). This formulation can only be a metaphor for the intergenerational conflict, between father as household head and eldest son as heir presumptive, inherent in stem family systems with male primogeniture (Cornell 1983). In the ideal domestic cycle, the son and heir should be ready to take over management of the farm and begin having children at about the time his father is ready to cease heavy farm labor and acquiesce in the transfer of authority. In a system with a normative retirement age of 60 *sai* (a Western age of 59), a son born when his father was still in his twenties might be expected to challenge his father's authority prematurely. If the female–male sequence were pursued via infanticide, the age of the father at the heir's birth would be increased on average not only by the spacing between two normal births, but also by the time lost through killing unwanted male firstborns and unwanted female secondborns. Fathers who married young would thus favor girls as firstborns in the interests of unchallenged authority in middle age. One folk explanation of *ichihime nitarô* (NSS:126) is explicit on this point: if the firstborn is male, then the father will become *shûto* (retired household head) prematurely and "face much difficulty."

In light of these advantages, the daughter-first strategy was generally pursued insofar as the risk could be minimized that among subsequent births no son would survive. Data for the two villages treated here generally support the specific hypotheses that may be derived from these considerations. First, the daughter-first strategy was more likely to be followed when the wife married early, for the risk involved was minimized by the long prospective period of childbearing. Conversely, when the wife married exceptionally late, in her early thirties, the couple might be prepared to kill a daughter in order to hasten the arrival of a son. Second, the daughter-first strategy was more likely to be followed by the rich than the poor, in part because couples strategized to match offspring-set size to resources (so that couples in rich households planned to, and did, have relatively large offspring sets, thereby minimizing the risk of missing out on a male heir) and in part because the consequences of sonlessness were less than drastic for households with the resources to attract a high-quality son-in-law. Third, the daughter-first strategy was favored when the husband married at an early age, presumably in order to postpone the birth of the first son and thereby avoid a premature challenge to paternal authority. Conversely, men who married exceptionally late, in their late thirties, would probably desire a son as soon as possible both to ensure an heir and to relieve themselves of heavy farm work before old age overtook them.

We are now in a position to understand how conjugal power affects the decision to keep or return a newborn child. We shall consider a comparative analysis of couples in two different phases of the domestic cycle at the onset of childbearing and focus on first registered births. Fig. 11.3 displays data on the sex of first registered births in the marriage-age matrix for couples in conjugal families (the charts to the left) and for those in grandmother-only stem families (the charts to the right), both categories being limited to cases where the marriage form was virilocal.[16]

Focusing first on virilocal conjugal families (the left-hand charts), we see that high-HUSPOWER couples apparently practice female infanticide to achieve a male firstborn, whereas low-HUSPOWER couples apparently practice male infanticide to achieve a female firstborn. This inference from the unnatural sex ratios, summarized at the bottom of Fig. 11.3, is strongly supported by the analysis of preceding intervals.

The presumed dynamic within conjugal families is straightforward. With only two "players," there is no scope for coalition formation, and the results can be interpreted as a simple outcome of the respective desires

(a)

VIRILOCAL CONJUGAL

POOR (0–0.4 <u>koku</u>)

husband's age at marriage

-22 23 24 25 26 27 28 29 30 31 32 33 34 35+

wife's age at marriage

$\frac{11}{13}$ 85%

$\frac{11}{19}$ 58%

$\frac{5}{15}$ 33%

N=47

GM-ONLY STEM

POORER (0–4.9 <u>koku</u>)

husband's age at marriage

-22 23 24 25 26 27 28 29 30 31 32 33 34 35+

wife's age at marriage

$\frac{3}{10}$ 30%

$\frac{7}{11}$ 64%

$\frac{9}{10}$ 90%

N=31

INTERMEDIATE (0.5–12.9 <u>koku</u>)

husband's age at marriage

-22 23 24 25 26 27 28 29 30 31 32 33 34 35+

wife's age at marriage

$\frac{5}{5}$ 100%

$\frac{5}{11}$ 45%

$\frac{4}{10}$ 40%

N=26

RICHER (5.0 <u>koku</u> and more)

husband's age at marriage

-22 23 24 25 26 27 28 29 30 31 32 33 34 35+

wife's age at marriage

$\frac{1}{5}$ 20%

$\frac{5}{12}$ 42%

$\frac{8}{10}$ 80%

N=27

RICH (13.0 <u>koku</u> or more)

husband's age at marriage

-22 23 24 25 26 27 28 29 30 31 32 33 34 35+

wife's age at marriage

$\frac{11}{14}$ 79%

$\frac{2}{7}$ 29%

N=21

(b)

VIRILOCAL CONJUGAL					GM-ONLY STEM				
Sex of firstborn					**Sex of firstborn**				
HUSPOWER	M	F	T	%M	HUSPOWER	M	F	T	%M
Low	11	21	32	34	Low	17	3	20	85
Intermediate	16	14	30	53	Intermediate	12	11	23	52
High	27	5	32	84	High	4	11	15	27
TOTAL	54	40	94		TOTAL	33	25	58	

Fig. 11.3 (a) Sex of first registered birth by HUSPOWER, controlling landholdings and comparing two household types at the onset of child-bearing: virilocal conjugal v. grandmother-only stem; (b) summary of data presented in (a)

and power of husband and wife. Husbands prefer a male firstborn, and they prevail when HUSPOWER is high; wives prefer a female firstborn, and they prevail when HUSPOWER is low; when neither prevails, no infanticide occurs.

Why, in this context, do husbands prefer sons and wives prefer daughters? First of all, in the absence of grandparents, the force of the daughter-first logic outlined above is strengthened for wives but weakened for husbands. The anxiety of a young bride concerning her inexperience as a mother would be sharpened by the absence of anyone with child care experience. Her need for help in child care sooner rather than later could be met only through rearing a daughter. Hence, for the wife the attractiveness of the daughter-first strategy is enhanced by her isolation. At the same time, the husband's fear of a precocious challenge from an early-born heir, though still present, would be less salient than in stem households since the issue had been experientially muted through his own father's early death. Second, the constraints of the gender division of labor take on particular salience in a household consisting solely of a conjugal couple. Just as daughters would eventually lighten mothers' domestic chores, so sons could eventually relieve some of their fathers' back-breaking field work. Since men were generally much older than their wives, it would seem only fair that help in their domain should come first. By virtue of their greater age, husbands more than wives would be concerned to ensure a surviving son (and heir) soon and less inclined to run the risk in this regard of pursuing the female-first strategy. It is telling that both of these considerations would weigh more heavily on husbands high in HUSPOWER (that is, on those who succeeded in forcing female infanticide), for by definition such husbands were both absolutely old and relatively much older than their wives.

Let us now contrast the findings for virilocally formed conjugal families with those for virilocally formed stem families in which the grandfather has died. The only difference in household composition between the two cases, then, is the presence of the widowed grandmother. First-birth data for such households, set out on the right side of Fig. 11.3 contrast diametrically with those for conjugal households: high-HUSPOWER couples, who annul girls to attain male firstborns in conjugal families, annul boys to attain female firstborns in grandmother-only stem families. Low-HUSPOWER couples practice male infanticide in conjugal families but female infanticide in grandmother-only stem families. Why?

When three "players" are present, as in the grandmother-only stem family, three coalitions are theoretically possible, but a coalition between the father's mother and her daughter-in-law is improbable given the psychodynamics of the situation in the first few years of the marriage. My argument is that the conjugal coalition (husband and wife contra the husband's mother) prefers sons and that it prevails when HUSPOWER is low, and that the filial coalition (the mother and her son contra the daughter-in-law) prefers daughters, and that it prevails when HUSPOWER is high. Why might coalition formation be expected to vary systematically in this way? First, spouses are close together in age when HUSPOWER is low but far apart when HUSPOWER is high, which circumstance favors conjugal solidarity in the former but not the latter. Second, in low-HUSPOWER couples, the bride is older and more mature and thus better positioned to stand up to her mother-in-law. Third, since the widowed mother would have had a major say in the timing of her son's marriage, high-HUSPOWER (late-marrying) husbands are likely to have been closely bound emotionally to their mothers, whereas low-HUSPOWER (early-marrying) husbands may have been self-selected for emotional independence.

The situation in the grandmother-only stem family is different from that in a conjugal family on two counts. First, the presence of the grandmother to assist in the domestic sphere and to help rear the heir serves to reduce the mother's reasons for desiring a girl. Second, with two adult women but only one adult man in the household, the gap to be filled first should logically be on the male side of the division of labor. These circumstances resolve the conflicting interests of the spouses that obtain in conjugal families so that solidary couples in grandmother-only stem families can readily agree that their best interests would be served by a son. Note that in households with low-HUSPOWER couples, the grandmother is likely to be relatively young at the time of the marriage (for her son married early), so that the couple could reasonably expect her to remain active in the domestic sphere until a female secondborn would be old enough to take on domestic chores.[17]

Conjugal power and longevity

I now turn to an analysis of adult mortality and ask now the relative power of husband and wife in the conjugal relationship affects their respective longevity. It is apparent from other analyses with the same data set that mean age at death is in general a sensitive indicator of the relative hardship and stress associated with different family-life experiences.[18] For instance, our data show that married women lived longer when registered births were widely spaced, and the first registered birth was female – as one might expect since both factors ease a mother's lot. That the prover-bial oppression of brides by their mothers-in-law had demographic effects appears likely from Nishijo and Nakahara mortality data for women in ordinary virilocal stem families in which the mother-in-law was present during the first eight years of marriage. In cases where the mother-in-law was widowed and also served as family head, the daughter-in-law died early, at a mean age of 52 years. But when the father-in-law was also present (that is when the stem family was intact) the mean age at death for the junior woman was 63 years when her father-in-law retained the headship and 66 years when the headship had passed to her husband. Thus, it appears that a woman fared better when the mother-in-law was held in check by the father-in-law and better still when the husband was positioned to protect her. A not unrelated pattern appears in the mortal-ity of *mukoyôshi* (the married-in-son-in-law). The mean age at death was much earlier when the father-in-law retained the headship than when the son-in-law assumed the headship on marriage.

These findings are suggestive of a more general argument, namely, that unrelieved powerlessness and structural vulnerability to oppression – and, we must assume, to the consequent overwork and physical hardship – are in the long run life-negating. The data presented below on conjugal power may be interpreted as supporting not only this proposition but also its converse, namely that the experience of wielding effective power within the family is life-enhancing.

In Fig. 11.4 we see that longevity for ever-married men is a direct function of HUSPOWER. Husbands who dominated the conjugal couple lived long, those who were dominated by their wives died young. Since no controls have been made, we can be sure that this interpretation is only part of the story.[19] Still, in a society where familial authority patterns are

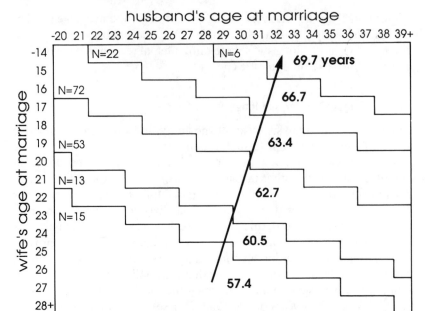

Fig. 11.4 Mean age at death, ever-married men, according to the HUSPOWER dimension of the marriage-age matrix, couples in land-holding households only

Huspower Index	N	Mean Age at Death
- 13	15	57.4
14 - 19	13	60.5
20 - 29	53	62.7
30 - 38	72	63.4
39 - 45	22	66.7
46 -	6	69.7
	181	

supposed to be patriarchal, it is not implausible that in general men thrive on power and that dominated husbands die early (compare Fox *et al.* 1979:126).

The data on female mortality also point to the experience of power within the family as favoring longevity, though in a more complex way.

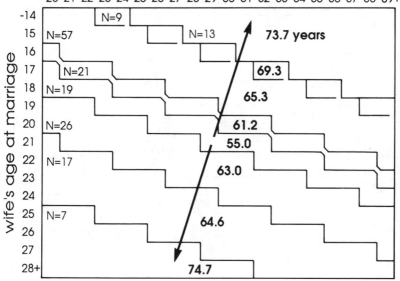

husband's age at marriage

Huspower Index	N	Mean Age at Death
- 06	7	74.7
7 - 16	17	64.6
17 - 24	26	63.0
25 - 28	19	55.0
29 - 31	21	61.2
32 - 39	57	65.3
40 - 41	9	69.3
42 -	13	73.7
	169	

Fig. 11.5 Mean age at death, ever-married women, according to the HUSPOWER dimension of the marriage-age matrix, couples in land-holding households only

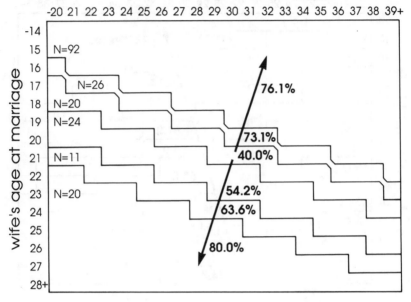

Huspower Index	Widowed	Total	% Widows
- 14	16	20	80.0
15 - 18	7	11	63.6
19 - 24	13	24	54.2
25 - 28	8	20	40.0
29 - 31	19	26	73.1
32 -	70	92	76.1
	133	193	

Fig. 11.6 Proportion of ever-married women who died as widows, according to the HUSPOWER dimension of the marriage-age matrix, couples in landholding households only. The total includes twenty-four women still alive in the year of the last extant register whose husbands had already died.

As shown in Fig. 11.5, longevity for women is a curvilinear function of HUSPOWER. In low-HUSPOWER couples, where men are exceptionally short-lived, women are long-lived. In couples intermediate on the HUSPOWER scale, women are short-lived and, more often than not, predecease their husbands. But at the high extreme of the HUSPOWER scale, women as well as men live to a ripe old age. It is in high-HUSPOWER couples, where age differences are large, that men may be expected to predecease their wives by 10 to 20 years. We may hypothesize, then, that these long-lived women had extensive experience as effective powerholders in the family after their husbands had died.[20]

This proposition is tested in Fig. 11.6, which displays the proportion of ever-married women who died as widows, according to the HUSPOWER dimension of the marriage-age matrix. A comparison with Fig. 11.5 shows that women who died as widows are distributed in the marriage-age matrix in rough accordance with the distribution of women's age at death. It appears, then, that wives thrived on the power that fell to them as their husbands grew old and passed away. Women who died young were disproportionately those in the middle range of the HUSPOWER index, benefiting neither from considerable conjugal power at the onset of marriage nor from early widowhood. Unrelieved powerlessness was associated with an early demise.

Altogether, these findings suggest that the experience of wielding power within the household favors longevity for both sexes.

Conclusions

On the methodological side, I have attempted to show that the precise configuration of wife's and husband's age at marriage can provide a valid index of conjugal power. Spousal age difference alone, despite its use for this purpose (for example, Blood 1967:143–5), does not do the trick, for the absolute age of the wife accounts for about three times the variance. HUSPOWER, the dimension of the marriage-age matrix that expresses this weighting, has been shown here to discriminate sharply among couples with respect to family demography. On theoretical grounds we may suppose that in societies with patrilineal joint family systems, say, the range of variation in conjugal power among couples might be constricted to the point where the HUSPOWER index would not prove very discriminating in practice. But the logic of the index is social structural rather than cultural, and there is no theoretical reason why, within the wide range of societies with stem and conjugal family systems, it could not usefully be introduced as an analytical variable in studies of family process. Its potential utility for the historical study of the family is great, for the precise marriage ages of husband and wife are usually available in parish records as well as household registers, and, in permitting inferences about behavior and motivation, the HUSPOWER index can provide some sociological flesh for the bare bones of demographic events.

This demonstration that conjugal power matters – that it shapes family-planning decisions and alters the mortality risks of married adults – also carries a weighty caveat for those who would bring HUSPOWER into their research designs. The conjugal relationship is embedded in the more inclusive structure of the household, and the operational significance of conjugal power is dependent on the configuration of all coresident adults. The man who dominates his wife in a high-HUSPOWER couple may be dominated in turn by his mother, who calls the shots in the winning coalition. We have seen that the presence or absence of the senior woman reverses decision-making with respect to infanticide. Without controls on household structure – on phase in the domestic cycle – the countervailing relationships would have been erased. The ultimate moral is that demographic process is inextricably intertwined with family process, and since both are multivalent, sophisticated analytical controls are essential.

On the substantive side we may conclude that the distribution of power within the Tokugawa Japanese family was a matter of great importance for its members. Given the cognatic structure of kinship, and despite the male bias in family succession and the cultural norm of patriarchy, men did not always rule the roost. They were able to do so consistently only when they had married relatively late to absolutely young brides. The normative gender hierarchy that obtained in Tokugawa villages masked a wide range in the balance of conjugal power within households, a range that epitomized the patriarchal norm at one extreme but mocked it at the other. Nonetheless, how it went in any given family – whether the husband or the wife was on top – could be and often was a matter of life or death.

NOTES

I am grateful for the support provided by Stanford University's Center for East Asian Studies, the Rockefeller Foundation's Research Program on Women's Status and Fertility, and the National Science Foundation under Grant No. 8718451. Mariko Fujita and Satomi Sato provided research assistance. Philip L. Ritter assisted with the programming. The research reported here owes much to the encouragement, generosity, and cooperation of Akira Hayami and Thomas C. Smith.

1 The 360 cases include a dozen "ongoing conjugal units" that involve successive marriages. An "ongoing conjugal unit" tracks the build-up of an offspring set within the same household. A conjugal unit is considered to continue beyond the death or divorce of a spouse so long as at least one child survives to the marriage that brings in a "replacement" spouse.

2 Compare Dore 1958: Chapter 8, and Sievers 1983: Chapter 5. The critical event was the promulgation of the Meiji Civil Code in 1898.

3 Female household heads were typically widows with no coresiding son as old as, say, 15 years. I have shown elsewhere (Skinner 1988:35) that, within the Nôbi region, the proportion of household heads who were female increased steadily from 3.6 percent in the far periphery to 6.9 percent in the inner core. Nishijo and Nakahara are situated in the northwestern sector of the region's inner core.

4 At one point in her paper, Rogers (1975:729–30) backs off from her generalizing stance toward "peasant society" and considers the "components" or "fundamental characteristics" of societies where male dominance may be expected to operate as a myth. While her components overlap with the criteria suggested here, they notably exclude any reference to family or kinship.

5 Useful summary treatments of conjugal power as an analytical issue within family sociology include Cromwell and Olson 1975; Lee 1977:229–42; Scanzoni 1979; McDonald 1980; and England and Farkas 1986:54–9.

6 Ella Embree observes that in Suye-mura, "Refusal of either spouse to do his or her share of the work will cause a row in most farm families" (Smith and Wiswell 1982:170). Would it have been much different in villages of the late Edo period?

7 Kawashima and Steiner (1960) document a dramatic decline in divorce rates during the course of Japan's modernization, a trend that was eventually reversed after World War II. Both Kawashima and Steiner and Smith and Wiswell discuss the traditional trial marriage, *mikka kasei*, a custom that had not entirely died out as of the 1930s.

8 Whereas in certain Southeast Asian and Polynesian societies, premarital affairs often led eventually to a stable pairing and marriage, in Japan girls normally did not marry a man with whom they had had a previous affair (compare Smith and Wiswell 1982:133–5). Marriages were generally arranged by the parents, but "young women could and did refuse marriages when they were not pleased with the prospective husband" (Smith and Wiswell 1982:156).

9 One can only speculate about historical trends in the rate of premarital pregnancies and of registered illegitimate births. Prima facie, the household registers for Nishijo and Nakahara show a negligible number of illegitimate registered births. This could mean that unwanted bastard infants were usually victims of infanticide. It is no less plausible, however, that a birth out of wedlock was registered as a child of the girl's mother or of her married brother, depending on the household's phase in the domestic cycle. Bastards were not uncommon in Suye-mura in the 1930s, but one interpretation of a passage from Ella Embree's journal is that in previous generations fewer illegitimate infants were allowed to live. After describing premarital sexual activity as virtually universal when she was young, a middle-aged informant noted that "in her day ... few babies resulted from such encounters," to which Embree adds "I wonder how correct this information is, considering the number of local bastards [in Suye today]" (Smith and Wiswell 1982:130). The Embrees appear to have been unaware that infanticide was commonplace in the nineteenth century.

10 It is no less true of Tokugawa Japan than of contemporary developing countries that "observed distributions of the age difference are not simply the coincidental by-product of the random matching of separately determined distributions of men's and women's ages at marriage. Certain age differences

are avoided; others chosen more frequently" (Casterline, Williams, and McDonald 1986:374). It would appear that demographic determinants of the age difference (age structure constraints on the pool of possible matches) are less important in explaining variation among societies than sociocultural factors, particularly kinship and gender differentiation.

11 Smith and Wiswell (1982:xviii) observe that in Suye-mura "girls and young women, especially new brides, exhibited paralyzing degrees of shyness."

12 Other cardinal dimensions, not shown, are husband's age at marriage, with the arrow pointing eastward, and the sum of spousal marriage ages, with the arrow pointing southeast.

13 This suggests, of course, that the absolute age of the wife at marriage is more important than spousal age difference in shaping conjugal power, which in turn implies that the conjugal patterns established in the initial year or two of marriage have considerable staying power.

14 That conjugal relationships in one Japanese village ran the gamut covered by the HUSPOWER index is clear enough from the vignettes in Ella Embree's Suye-mura journal. At one extreme are the many wives who do "nothing but cook, sew, wash, and wait on the men of the house all day long." But certain "husbands sometimes helped out with domestic chores" and "one formidable woman ... was said to be waited on by her husband" (Smith and Wiswell 1982:177). "Certainly some husbands were extremely tolerant of their wives' shortcomings," whereas others "exercised decisive control over the domestic arrangements at whatever cost to their wives' happiness or peace of mind" (pp. 183–4). Conjugal relationships were variously described as congenial, companionable, and even romantic, on the one hand, or as distant, detached, and cool. And "there were men known to mistreat their wives physically" (pp. 177, 184).

15 The methods used to detect infanticide cannot be fully described here. It should be emphasized that infanticide can only be inferred from data in the *shūmon-aratame-chô*. Vital events were recorded once a year at a fixed time, so that a child born and put to death during an elapsed year would never be entered in the record. Nor is it possible to determine sex-selective infanticide for any particular couple: whatever the combination of births by sex and interval, it could not be said to fall outside the expected range of variation. My strategy, therefore, is to work with homogeneously defined categories of couples and with homogeneously defined subsets of births. The assumption is that couples whose objective circumstances are similar in certain crucial respects (form of marriage, nuptial configuration, household structure, household landholdings) are likely to follow similar reproductive strategies. If we then analyze births subset by subset (each defined homogeneously in terms of parity, configuration of preceding siblings, mother's age at the time of birth), evidence of sex-selective infanticide will be revealed so long as a sizeable proportion of the couples had in fact killed an infant of the same sex before the registered birth so categorized. An unnatural sex ratio is, of course, the critical evidence of sex-selective infanticide, but I accept a skewed sex ratio as reliable evidence only when the patterning of intervals for those births is compatible with infanticide of the sex that would have produced the skewing.

16 The data have been controlled on landholding because in wealthier families the significant range of HUSPOWER differentiation is higher up on the scale;

thus the sharp distinction that obtains within each landholding class is blurred when the test is not controlled.

17 In contrasting infanticide decisions in these two distinct family types, I have held headship constant in the sense that the family head is the father-to-be in the grandmother-only stem case as well as in the conjugal case. But headship, by definition a critical element in the family's power structure, also affects decision outcomes. For instance, when the headship is in the senior generation the daughter-first strategy is generally favored (with males constituting only 39 percent of first registered births), whereas when the headship is in the junior generation the son-first strategy is favored (with males accounting for 82 percent). It is the precise configuration of power among all the adults present in the household that counts in infanticide decisions.

18 Mean age at death is used here as a simple measure for exploring various hypotheses. While the patterns indicated are most probably generally correct, given the context of the analysis and the magnitude of the differences, mean age at death may yield a distorted picture when a population is growing. In the eight-village study I shall use life-table methods to control for the various biases inherent in the mean-age-at-death statistic.'

19 As a component of HUSPOWER, spousal age difference should reveal a congruent association with longevity, and, indeed, the three studies known to me that investigate the effect of spousal age difference on longevity all find that husbands with younger wives live longer. Rose and Bell (1971) studied 500 white men in the greater Boston area who died during 1965 of natural or age-related causes. They found that having a younger wife was conducive to male longevity, and surmised that the chief causal factor was enhanced nurturance and care: "a younger wife was less apt to be lost by death, and the benefits of a wife's care, with their implications for favoring the husband's longevity, would be less likely to be lost" (p. 20).

Fox et al. (1979) investigated spousal age difference and age at death of both men and women aged 15–74, using data from death certificates for a 10 percent sample of the 1971 English census. The statistic used, standardized mortality ratios (SMR), was adapted so that the ratio would be 100 for all combinations of spousal ages. A summary of their empirical data for males shows a progression of SMRs from 93 for all husbands with younger wives, to 104 for husbands with wives of the same age, to 118 for husbands with older wives. (Their more detailed analysis reveals, however, that the overall relationship is curvilinear, with SMRs rising with spousal age difference when husbands were *very* much older than their wives. Although their data do not permit analytical controls on marriage duration, Fox et al. present evidence to suggest that the "unexpec-ted" high SMRs at the extreme may be "the result of a tendency for the sick and lonely to marry young 'nurses,' or for the young to marry in the hope of inheriting wealth" [Fox et al. 1979:131].)

Foster et al. (1984) studied white men aged 50–79, using data from the 1980 National Mortality Followback Survey and the 1970 US Census. They showed that for husbands of all ages over 50, those married to younger wives lived longer than expected on average. In their interpretation, Foster et al. called attention to premarital selection as a possible causal factor, hypothesizing that healthier, wealthier, or more vigorous men select, or are selected by, younger women. (It should be possible to test this hypothesis with the eight-village dataset, but the numbers involved in the present two-village study are too small for this purpose.) For the most part, however, the social psychological literature on the relation between spousal age difference and male longevity seeks explanations in terms of psychological, physiological, or social benefits that marriage to a younger woman affords. That literature fails to mention one factor that presumably affects *joie de vivre*, namely, that men with much younger wives are more likely to remain sexually active into old age. And nowhere in the literature linking spousal age difference to longevity is there any explicit mention of conjugal power.

20 In their study of mortality in England, Fox *et al.* (1979) found that the longevity of married women was enhanced when husbands were the same age or younger, but depressed when husbands were older. Expressed as standard mortality ratios (SMR), their empirical data, by sex, may be aggregated as follows:

	Husbands	Wives
Husband older, wife younger	93	107
Spouses same age	104	96
Husband younger, wife older	118	98

The relatively low mortality of women who were the same age as or older than their husbands fits the hypothesis presented above concerning conjugal power. Since the English data were limited to women who were still married at death, they exclude widows and hence cannot speak to my hypothesis concerning the liberating effects of widowhood.

REFERENCES

Andô Masuo, ed. 1975 *Wajû: Sono tenkai to kôzô (The Development and Structure of Polders in the Nôbi Delta)*. Tokyo: Kokon shoin.

Bachnik, Jane M. 1983 Recruitment Strategies for Household Succession: Rethinking Japanese Household Organization. *Man* 18:160–82.

Blood, Robert O., Jr. 1967 *Love Match and Arranged Marriage: A Tokyo–Detroit Comparison*. New York: Free Press.

Bossen, Laurel 1975 Women in Modernizing Societies. *American Ethnologist* 2:587–601

Brown, Keith 1988 Consanguinity, Descent, Affinity, and Ethnicity: A Cultural Analysis of Family-Based Kinship Systems in Northeastern Japan. Unpublished paper, Department of Anthropology, University of Pittsburgh.

Caldwell, Pat and John Caldwell 1988 Kinship Forms, Female Autonomy, and Fertility. Paper prepared for the Rockefeller Workshop on Women's Status in Relation to Fertility and Mortality, Bellagio.

Casterline, J., L. Williams, and P. McDonald 1986 The Age Difference between Spouses: Variations among Developing Countries. *Population Studies* 40:353–74.

Chiba Tokuji and Ôtsu Tadao 1983 *Mabiki to mizuko – kosodate no fôkuroa (Infanticide and Abortion: Folk Customs Concerning Child Rearing)*. Tokyo: Nôsangyôson bunka kyôka.

Cornell, Laurel L. 1983 Retirement, Inheritance, and Intergenerational Conflict in Preindustrial Japan. *Journal of Family History* 8:55–69.

Cornell, Laurel L. and Akira Hayami 1986 The *shûmon aratame chô*: Japan's Population Registers. *Journal of Family History* 11:311–28.

Cromwell, Ronald E. and David H. Olsen 1975 Multidisciplinary Perspectives of Power. In *Power in Families*. R. E. Cromwell and D. H. Olson, eds., pp. 15–37. New York: Wiley.

Dore, Ronald P. 1958 *City Life in Japan*. Berkeley: University of California Press.

England, Paula and George Farkas 1986 *Household, Employment, and Gender*. New York: Aldine.

Foster, Brian L. 1978 Domestic Development Cycles as a Link between Population Processes and Other Social Processes. *Journal of Anthropological Research* 34:415–41.

Foster, Dorothy, Laurel Klinger-Vartabedian, and Lauren Wispé 1984 Male Longevity and Age Differences between Spouses. *Journal of Gerontology* 39:117–20.

Fox, A. John, Lak Bulusu, and Leo Kinlen 1979 Mortality and Age Difference in Marriage. *Journal of Biosocial Science* 11:117–31.

Goldschmidt, Walter and Evalyn Jacobson Kunkel 1971 The Structure of the Peasant Family. *American Anthropologist* 73:1058–76.

Hammel, Eugene A. and Kenneth W. Wachter 1977 Primonuptiality and Ultimonuptiality: Their Effects on Stem-Family-Household Frequencies. In *Population Patterns in the Past*. Ronald D. Lee, ed., pp. 113–34. New York: Academic Press.

Hanley, Susan B. and Kozo Yamamura 1977 *Economic and Demographic Change in Preindustrial Japan, 1600–1868*. Princeton: Princeton University Press.

Harada Kiyoshi 1936 Kikitorichô (Interview Notes). *Shitara* 14:447–57.

Hayami Akira 1980 Class Differences in Marriage and Fertility among Tokugawa Villagers in Mino Province. *Keio Economic Studies* 17:1–16.

1985 Rural Migration and Fertility in Tokugawa Japan: The Village of Nishijo, 1773–1869. In *Family and Population in East Asian History*. Susan B. Hanley and Arthur P. Wolf, eds., pp. 110–32. Stanford: Stanford University Press.

1987 Another *Fossa Magna*: Proportion Marrying and Age at Marriage in Late Nineteenth-Century Japan. *Journal of Family History* 12:57–72.

1988 *Edo no nômin seikatsushi – Shûmon aratame chô ni miro Nôbi no ichi nôson (Peasant Livelihood in the Edo Period: A Nôbi Village as Seen through Household Registers)*. Tokyo: Nihon hôsôhuppan kyôkai.

Kawahashi Takeyoshi and Kurt Steiner 1960 Modernization and Divorce Rate Trends in Japan. *Economic Development and Cultural Change* 9(2):213–39.

Kumatani Tsutomu, ed. 1970 *Mikawa-koku Hôi chihô minzoku shiryô (Sources on Folk Customs of the Hôi Area, Mikawa Province)*. Tokyo: Kokusho kankôkai.

Kuzutani Toshiharu 1977 Gifu-ken no iwaigoto (Folk Customs and Rites in Gifu Prefecture). In *Minani Chûbu no iwaigoto (Folk Customs and Rites in the Southern Chûbu Area)*. Ozawa Hideyuki, ed., pp. 217–71. Tokyo: Meigen shobô.

Lee, Gary R. 1977 *Family Structure and Interaction: A Comparative Analysis*. Philadelphia: Lippincott.

McDonald, Gerald W. 1980 Family Power: The Assessment of a Decade of Theory and Research, 1970–1979. *Journal of Marriage and the Family* 42:841–54.

Muraoka Asao, ed. 1972 *Kankon-sôsai to ie no mondai (Rites of Passage and the Analysis of Corporate Households)*. Hiroshima: Hiroshima minzoku no kai.

Nakamichi Sakuji 1974 Tôtômi Sekishi-mura minzokushi (Folk Customs of Sekishi Village, Tôtômi Province). In *Nihon minzokushi taikei*, vol. 5, *Chûbu (Complete Gazetteer of Japanese Folklore*, vol. 5, *Chûbu)*, pp. 399–501. Tokyo: Kadokawa shoten.

Nakane, Chie 1967 *Kinship and Economic Organization in Rural Japan*. London: Athlone Press.

NSS 1975 *Nihon saniku shûzoku shiryô shûsei (Japanese Folk Customs on Births: A Sourcebook)*. Onshi zaidan boshi aiiku-kai, ed. Tokyo: Dai-ichi hôki shuppan.

Ôto Yuki 1950 *Ko yarai (Folk Beliefs on Births and Infants)*. Tokyo: Giipusha.

Rodman, Hyman 1972 Marital Power and the Theory of Resources in Cultural Context. *Journal of Comparative Family Studies* 3:50–69.

Rogers, Susan Carol 1975 Female Forms of Power and the Myth of Male Dominance: A Model of Female/Male Interaction in Peasant Society. *American Ethnologist* 2:727–56.

Rose, Charles L., and Benjamin Bell 1971 *Predicting Longevity: Methodology and Critique*. Lexington, MA: Heath.

Sakurada Katsunori 1974 Mino Tokuyama-mura minzokushi (Folk Customs of Tokuyama Village, Mino Province). In *Nihon minzokushi taikei*, vol. 5, *Chûbu (Complete Gazetteer of Japanese Folklore*, vol. 5, *Chûbu)*, pp. 210–72. Tokyo: Kadokawa shoten.

Scanzoni, John 1975 *Sex Roles, Life-Style, and Childbearing: Changing Patterns in Marriage and Family*. New York: Free Press.

1979 Social Processes and Power in Families. In *Contemporary Theories about the Family*, Vol. 1. Wesley R. Burr *et al.*, eds., pp. 293–316. New York: Free Press.

Sievers, Sharon L. 1983 *Flowers in Salt: The Beginnings of Feminist Consciousness in Modern Japan*. Stanford: Stanford University Press.

Skinner, G. William 1988 Nôbi as a Regional System. Paper presented at the Second Workshop of the Nôbi Regional Project, Nagoya.

Smith, Robert J. and Ella Lury Wiswell 1982 *The Women of Suye Mura*. Chicago: University of Chicago Press.

Smith, Thomas C. 1977 *Nakahara: Family Farming and Population in a Japanese Village, 1717–1830*. Stanford: Stanford University Press.

SOS 1968 *Shinshu Ôgaki-shi shi*, vol. 1 *(History of Ôgaki Municipality*, vol. 1*)*. Ogaki-shi, ed. Gifu: Ôgaki-shi.

Stephens, William 1963 *The Family in Cross-Cultural Perspective*. New York: Holt, Rinehart and Winston.

Suenari Michio 1972 First-Child Inheritance in Japan. *Ethnology* 11:122–6.

Taeuber, Irene B. 1958 *The Population of Japan*. Princeton: Princeton University Press.

Takeda Akira 1970 *Ie o meguru minzoku kenkyû (Folk Customs Concerning the Corporate Household)*. Tokyo: Kobundo.

Wakamori Taro 1964 *Onna no issho (The Life Cycle of Women)*. Tokyo: Kawade shobô.

Washino Madaaki 1977 Aichi-ken no iwaigoto (Folk Customs and Rites in Aichi Prefecture). In *Minami Chûbu no iwaigoto (Folk Customs and Rites in the Southern Chûbu Area)*. Ozawa Hideyuki, ed., pp. 167–216. Tokyo: Meigen shobô.

Part 3

Complexity and change in gender hierarchies

12   Skeletal evidence for sex roles and gender hierarchies in prehistory

Mark Nathan Cohen and Sharon Bennett

Comparisons among human societies provide recognition of cross-cultural regularities in the relationship between gender roles or gender hierarchies and other aspects of society such as the mode of production (see review articles by Lamphere 1977; Quinn 1977; Rapp 1979; Atkinson 1982; Mukhopadhyay and Higgins 1988). Such studies enable us to move outside the cultural stereotypes of our own society, to see something of the range of cultural variations on gender themes, and to begin to discern the degree to which gender differences are grounded in biology or defined by cultural roles.

Despite the importance of these contributions, cross-cultural studies on contemporary human groups are limited in several respects. Contemporary societies represent only a fraction of the cultural variations with which human beings have experimented; moreover by the time they are witnessed by contemporary observers such societies are often heavily influenced by participation in the world market or by Western values and role expectations (Leacock 1978 and this volume; Anderson 1985). At least until 1970, such societies have been represented to anthropologists primarily by male informants and witnessed and interpreted primarily by male Western observers who not only were accustomed to visualizing relations between the sexes from a male perspective but were often excluded in the field from areas of female activity and power. Rosaldo (1980) has argued that modern ethnographers (of either sex), who come from a culture in which attention focuses on male activities, simply have not known what questions to ask about women. Sacks (1976) warns that observers familiar with state-level societies may be blind to sexual equality in other contexts.

The problem is further complicated by the fact that the meaning of the concept of "gender hierarchy" is diffuse, embracing a number of measures including prestige, power, access to and control of economic goods, and "gender ideology" which are not necessarily congruent with one another (see chapters by Nelson and Spiro, this volume). Measurement problems abound. As Rapp (1979) and Lamphere (1977) point out, we do not readily distinguish gender "asymmetry," gender "complementarity," and gender "subjugation." We lack consistent measures of status or of hierarchy which are valid across cultures and can be applied in a comparative manner from case to case.

The appeal to archaeological information can help resolve some of these problems. Archaeological samples expand the range of cultures which can be considered, and they help to guarantee that we witness cultures which are uninfluenced by Western values. Skeletons of prehistoric individuals provide some of the most useful archaeological data for gender studies.[1] Well-preserved adult skeletons can be sexed with an accuracy in excess of 95 percent, and even fragmentary human remains can often be sexed with an accuracy of 85 percent or more (Buikstra and Mielke 1985). Sex is more difficult to determine in children's skeletons, but since the adult skeleton records childhood events in a number of ways it is theoretically possible, even in the absence of associated artifacts, to make significant statements about sex-related differences in the experience of childhood. Furthermore, skeletal data are comparatively immune to distortion by the gender-role expectations of the observer, since much of the analysis can be done in testing procedures that are sex-blind (the known sex of the skeleton can be withheld from individuals making other analyses).

Information on gender roles and hierarchies provided by the sketetal record can be acquired in two ways. The first is to look at the design and construction of tombs and cemeteries as overt clues to social status of the individuals studied (see Nelson, this volume). Differences in the quality of artifacts accompanying individuals in death, in the construction of tombs, or in the spatial placement of tombs afford clues to the overt social rules which govern hierarchies of all kinds including gender hierarchy. Such patterns of burial have been used not only to identify upper-class individuals and royalty but also – in combination with types of skeletal analysis described below – to determine whether status is ascribed or achieved, whether or not high status is associated with genetic or ethnic distinctions, and whether it results in differential access to basic resources. Patterning of skeletons in cemeteries along with studies of genetic traits in the skeleton may even reveal which sex leaves home at marriage (Haviland 1967; Swedlund and Armelagos 1976; Chapman, Kinnes, and Randsborg 1981; Buikstra 1976, 1984; Goldstein 1976; Blakely and Beck 1982; Koch 1983; Cook 1984; Konigsberg 1986, 1987).

In this chapter, we bypass the wealth of information available from spatial and contextual analysis of burial patterns and focus instead on analysis of the skeletons themselves, noting techniques summarized by various authorities (Brothwell 1981; Steinbock 1976; Ubelaker 1978;

Ortner and Putschar 1981; Buikstra and Cook 1980; Huss-Ashmore *et al.* 1982; Cohen and Armelagos 1984; Gilbert and Mielke 1985). Information in large quantity from skeletal analysis is relatively new and is less familiar and intuitively less accessible to non-specialists than burial data. Moreover, the skeletal information is directly revealing of health, nutrition, activity, physical stress or workload, risk, and mortality – aspects of status and hierarchy which analysis of formal and overt social markers may miss. At the same time, the skeletal data may challenge conclusions about hierarchy derived from more symbolic modes of analysis. Analysis of skeletons provides data about biological well-being which can be objectively measured and compared across cultures, thus bypassing the problem of definition and comparability that plagues studies of gender hierarchy cross-culturally. The same point must also be put in a more negative way, however. Measures of health and activity may not provide direct clues to "power" or "authority" or other more symbolic aspects of hierarchy. At the very least, however, the juxtaposition of explicit measures of health and activity with other measures of hierarchy and status raises issues about the definition of the latter.

The major problem or limitation of skeletal data is that few such data are yet available. Quantitative or population-based work in paleopathology that has been done involves samples unevenly distributed in time and space. There is a particular paucity of samples from mobile hunter-gatherers who often do not collect their dead in a single location. Nevertheless, even the available data are richly indicative of gender hierarchies in the distant past.

Applications of skeletal data to gender issues

This chapter presents a "sampler," based on a review of the literature, of applications of skeletal analysis to issues of gender inequality. We divide the presentation into seven sections: physical injury, trauma, and violence; physical stress and workload; infection and disease; nutrition; childhood stress; reproduction; and mortality. Examples are provided for prehistoric populations as well as for some twentieth-century groups.

Physical injuries, trauma, and violence

Paleopathologists[2] can assess the nature of physical health risks experienced by members of each sex through the analysis of wounds, fractures, and dislocations observable in skeletal populations. Such analysis provides a picture of the overall frequency of trauma, its distribution by age and sex, and the pattern of limbs at risk. In many cases the cause of injury can be determined and the distinction made between accidental injury and interpersonal violence. As a result, hypotheses about the distribution of gender-related violence can theoretically be tested. For example, an analysis of the large American Indian population from the Late Woodland Libben site (*c* AD 800–1100) in Ohio, revealed a high incidence of fractures – 45 percent of skeletons had at least one. But most fractures appeared to have resulted from accidents, predominantly falls. The authors discovered no significant sex-related differences in the distribution of fractures, except that males were more likely to have fractured a femur than were females. Fractures were extremely rare among small children. Apparently neither domestic violence nor traumatic child abuse was characteristic of the culture. The incidence of fractures was instead a simple function of age or years at risk, suggesting that fracture was a random risk not associated with specific activities of different age groups.

The early colonial period Mayan population of Tipu, comprising about 600 individuals who died in the sixteenth and early seventeenth centuries, displays a much lower rate of trauma; fewer than 10 percent of individuals display a fracture (Armstrong 1985). Here, too, most traumas appear to be accidental in origin and random in distribution through the population, although there are two clear cases of violence directed toward children. In contrast, Eisenberg (1986), working with a prehistoric Mississippian period American Indian population from the Averbuch site (AD 1275–1400), suggests that most traumas were intentionally inflicted and that traumas show a different age distribution and a different skeletal distribution in males and females. Swedlund and Armelagos (1976) report a disproportionate increase in fractured bones in female skeletons dating to the Christian period (after AD 550) in Nubia which they consider indicative of the comparatively low status of women at the time.[3]

These isolated examples tell us little about the factors which govern the frequency of pathology. Until the examples become far more numerous, a more promising approach is the comparative analysis of sequential populations at one archaeological site or a collection of closely related sites in the same area. Ideally such comparisons enable us to evaluate changes in sex roles and gender status, associated with defined changes in economy or politics, with other aspects of culture held relatively constant. Cohen and Armelagos (1984) recently collected studies on the changes in skeletal pathology in archaeological series spanning the transition from hunting and gathering to intensive farming in different parts of the world in an attempt to gain a cross-cultural perspective on the impact of farming on human health. Few of the studies, however, or other sources of data, provide good comparative, quantitative evidence on the frequency of trauma, and trauma data differentiated by sex are even more unusual.

In one case, Goodman *et al.* (1984) analyzed the archaeological sequence from the Dickson Mounds site in Illinois (AD 950–1300) where the frequency of fractures in adults increased as a hunting and gathering population adopted and intensified its agriculture and became increasingly involved in a larger political network. The trend toward increasing trauma was more pronounced for adult males, suggesting that the new economic/political regime intensified physical risk for men more than for women. Similarly, Perzigian, Tench, and Braun (1984) discovered an increase in intentional trauma to males, presumably due to an increase in warfare, during the intensive agricultural Fort Ancient period in Ohio (after *c* AD 1000).

Physical stress and workload

Paleopathologists can assess the quality and quantity of the physical stress imposed on individuals by different lifestyles and thus assess the distribution of the workload by sex. The skeleton provides two major clues to physical stress and workload: degenerative arthritis (Jurmain 1977; Steinbock 1976) and the robusticity of the skeleton (Larsen 1984). Degenerative arthritis or degenerative joint disease (DJD), which reflects the wear on particular joints, is displayed either as the polishing of joint surfaces through friction or as the development of extra bony growths on joint margins. Robusticity reflects the response of bone shafts to biomechanical stress as well as the enlargement of muscle attachment areas and joint surfaces associated with use. The pattern of either DJD or robusticity in the skeleton can provide clues to the activities in which individuals engaged; and quantitative changes in frequency and severity of DJD can provide clues to changing distribution of the workload.

In their analysis of twentieth-century black Americans from Arkansas, Rose and co-workers (1985) discovered markedly high rates of arthritis for adults of both sexes, compared even to prehistoric populations with which they had worked. They suggest that the pattern of work was different for the two sexes: men were likely to display arthritis of the long bones, while women seem to have made particularly strenuous use of their hands. At the prehistoric Mississippian period Averbuch site in Tennessee, American Indian males had much higher rates of arthritis than females as well as a higher frequency of back injuries (Eisenberg 1986).

The attempt by Cohen and Armelagos (1984) to establish patterns of change in physical stress and workload associated with the origins of agriculture and thus to assess theories about the evolution of human workload incorporates only a few studies with explicit reference to gender-specific patterns. Goodman *et al.* (1984) report that at Dickson Mounds both DJD and osteophytosis (arthritic changes in the spine) increased through time, suggesting an increase in physical stress with the adoption of agriculture, and they note that these forms of arthritis, like trauma, displayed more severe increase for males than for females. This finding suggests that it was primarily males at this site who bore the brunt of the increased workload. Cassidy (1984), however, contrasting hunter-gatherers with later farmers in Kentucky (the Archaic period Indian Knoll population, *c* 2500 BC, and the Mississippian period Hardin Village site, *c* AD 1550) found that vertebral arthritis was less pronounced for men in the later group, suggesting that they enjoyed a reduced workload. But the same condition increased or remained steady, depending on the age of individuals, among women. Arthritis of the joints also increased more consistently among women than among men with the adoption of agriculture. In this population farming seems to have resulted in a significant redistribution of the workload by sex.

Cook (1984) also reports changing patterns of arthritis with the adoption of agriculture in Illinois (a sequence of populations from 6000 BC to AD 1200). Arthritis became more severe in women in the later populations, but there was no change in the pattern of arthritis in the skeleton. Men displayed no increase in the severity of arthritis, but displayed a change in the pattern of arthritic joints. The evidence suggests that women may have experienced an intensification of their existing activity pattern, men a change in activities. Hamilton (1982), cited by Cook (1984), reports a disproportionate increase in deltoid tuberosity (an area of muscle attachment on the upper arm) in women associated with the intensification of food production in these same populations. Similarly, Bridges (1982, 1983), working with populations from Alabama spanning roughly the same periods and the same economic transition, found robusticity to increase through time particularly in female skeletons. Larsen (1984) reports that in Georgia arthritis was reduced after the adoption of agriculture (*c* AD 1150), but the greater reduction in arthritis occurred among male skeletons.[4]

Infection and disease

Paleopathologists can assess patterns of infection in prehistoric populations. Most analysis of infection deals with undifferentiated infection – infection of unspecified etiology – which is referred to as periostitis when it afflicts only the surface of the bone or as osteomyelitis when it invades the bone cortex. The most frequent causes of such infection are common staphylococcus and streptococcus bacteria. In addition, several diseases, most notably treponemal infection (yaws and/or syphilis) and tuberculosis can be diagnosed specifically in the skeleton (Steinbock 1976; Ortner and Putschar 1981). When mummies are available for analysis a much larger range of specific infections can be identified. Unfortunately, mummified specimens – although they may enable us to make comparisons of health among sequential populations in some specific locations (see, for example, Allison 1984) – are not yet common enough to be useful for identifying cross-cultural patterns.

The relationship between patterns of infection and gender hierarchy is less obvious than with other classes of pathology. The distribution of an infectious agent within a population is less subject to conscious or even unconscious cultural control than are other forms of stress, so the link between disease distribution and cultural patterns may not be self-evident. As with other types of pathology some attention must also be paid to possible sex differences in natural susceptibility to specific diseases as well as differences in behavior. A number of known diseases are associated with specific human activities and their distribution is therefore a good index of the sexual division of labor. For example, a number of human diseases, such as toxoplasmosis and tularemia, are associated with handling animals or meat. Unfortunately, few of these diseases leave diagnostic scars on the skeleton.[5]

Rates of infection, however, may tell something else about the sexual division of labor. There is a clear positive association between rates of infection and sedentism and/or large population aggregates (Cohen and Armelagos 1984). To the extent that their activities were more domestic, hence more closely tied to sedentary living, members of one sex might well display higher rates of "village" diseases.[6] There is evidence from skeletal populations for sex-differentiated rates of infection although as yet the meaning of most of these data is not clear. For example, men were significantly more infection prone than women in the agricultural Fort Ancient population from Kentucky (Cassidy 1984). In Georgia, females experienced a slightly greater increase in frequency of infection than did males with the adoption of agriculture – a pattern which suggests that women were more sedentary than men in the new economy (Larsen 1984).

Nutrition

Paleopathologists and bone chemists can assess the quality and quantity of the nutrition available to individuals. Several specific vitamin and mineral deficiencies can be at least tentatively identified, including shortage of iron (anemia), zinc (anemia), calcium (poor bone mineralization), vitamin C (scurvy), and vitamin D (rickets) (see Steinbock 1976; Ortner and Putschar 1981). Protein calorie malnutrition is evident in bone cortical area and bone remodeling (Martin, Goodman, and Armelagos 1985). In addition a number of different aspects of the skeleton – stature and robusticity of the skeleton, diameter of the pelvic inlet, and the height of the base of the cranium – provide clues to the overall adequacy of nutrition, particularly the adequacy of protein and calorie intake (Angel 1984).

Assessing sex-related differences in nutrient intake through skeletal analysis can be tricky. We know on the one hand that the two sexes differ in some degree in their utilization of nutrients: for example, women lose more iron than men. Similarly, there is clearly sexual dimorphism in bone cortical maintenance based on demand for calcium through pregnancy and lactation, and on levels of estrogen, but we do not know to what extent those differences are universal and constant in a quantitative sense across cultures.

It is not surprising that porotic hyperostosis and cribra orbitalia, the skeletal symptoms of anemia, are often more common in adult female than male skeletons just as anemia is more common in contemporary women than men. For example, 13 percent of adult women but only 5 percent of adult males in an early historic period population from British Columbia display cribra orbitalia (Cybulski 1977). Signs of anemia are more common in female skeletons than male skeletons in prehistoric cultures in Iran (Rathbun 1984). What is surprising is that male/female differences are often not as pronounced as contemporary clinical experience would suggest. Walker (1985), for example, finds no significant differences between the sexes in prehistoric populations from the American Southwest. Stuart-Macadam (1985), citing the rather small difference between the sexes in most prehistoric populations, argues that the visible scars may be primarily the unremodeled remains of childhood malnutrition.

It is also difficult to determine whether such differences as do occur reflect the better quality of the male (adult or child) diet, the greater susceptibility of women to iron loss, or even different experience with parasites since parasitization of one form or another can be an important factor in the observed anemias.[7] Our best clues, therefore, will lie not so much in the uncorrected quantitative comparison of male and female skeletons within a particular population, but in an assessment of changes in sex-related differences which occur as cultures change. In assessing the pattern of nutritional changes associated with the transition from hunting and gathering to agriculture in various parts of the world, Cohen and Armelagos (1984) demonstrated that various skeletal indicators most commonly suggested a decline in nutrition as a concomitant of incipient or intensified agriculture. The frequency of anemia increased almost universally. Where reported, bone cortical area often declined at least temporarily. And retarded growth in childhood became more common.[8]

Where the data are appropriately broken down, sex-related differences in nutrition are often apparent as are sex-specific trends in the quality of nutrition over time. Cassidy (1984) reports that anemia was more pronounced in the agricultural Fort Ancient population in Kentucky than in an earlier hunting and gathering group, but symptoms of anemia were more pronounced in adult women than in adult men during the later period, suggesting that women (or perhaps female children?) had suffered a disproportionate decline in the quality of the diet. Martin *et al.* (1984), reporting on the archaeological sequence from Nubia, note that young females in agricultural societies displayed nutritional problems evidenced by pathological bone loss to a degree which they considered not simply a function of aging. Smith and co-workers (1984) found premature osteoporosis in populations in the Levant, particularly concentrated among women, but also particularly concentrated among women of later (Roman and Arab) periods. Early paleolithic and mesolithic populations in the Levant showed no such pattern of bone loss or showed significantly less loss. Apparently changes in diet and/or fertility associated with later agricultural economies exerted a disproportionately negative effect on the nutritional status of women in this part of the world.

Dental caries rates also provide a clue to changes in diet. Caries are rare in early human populations and increase almost universally with the adoption of agriculture and the preparation of soft sticky foods (Turner 1979; Powell 1985). The sexes may be affected unequally by the transition because they obtain a different dietary balance. Larsen (1983, 1984) reports that among Indians in Georgia women suffered a greater increase in dental caries than men as a result of the adoption of agriculture, a pattern which he believes represents economic and dietary specializations similar to those reported for some ethnographic groups.[9]

The proportions of meat and vegetables, and of seafood in the diet can also be assessed through trace element analysis, particularly the analysis of strontium and the ratio of strontium to calcium, and the analysis of stable isotopes, particularly those of carbon and nitrogen (see Sillen and Kavanaugh 1982; Norr 1984; Nelson *et al.* 1986; Klepinger 1984; Gilbert 1985; Schoeninger 1979, 1982). Several studies have attempted to use strontium analysis to suggest gender differences in access to meat – roughly speaking, a high strontium content translates as a low meat diet, other things being equal. Schoeninger (1979) suggests that the higher strontium levels of women in a prehistoric Mesoamerican population indicate women's low status and low meat consumption. Similarly Angel (1984) reports that at the bronze age Karatas site in Greece women had lower zinc levels than men which might indicate lower meat intake. It has now been recognized, however (by Schoeninger herself among others; see also Gilbert 1985), that we must first factor-out sex differences in skeletal utilization of strontium and perhaps other elements. Women may store more strontium than men in their skeletons on the same diet. Pregnant and lactating women screen their infants from normal strontium intake, storing the excess in their own skeletons. So, absolute differences in levels of strontium or other trace elements between men and women may not be socially meaningful.

In the terminal Woodland period in the Illinois Valley (AD 800–1000), during the transition to agriculture, strontium analysis shows a greater sex differential than in earlier periods, possibly reflecting a relative decline in women's access to animal protein (Buikstra 1984; Lambert, Szpunar, and Buikstra 1977). Conversely, at Dickson Mounds (referred to above) the difference in trace element content between male and female skeletons declined through time suggesting that the adoption of agriculture tended to make male and female diets more equal (Gilbert 1985).

Changes in body size, particularly in stature, may be indicative of changes in nutrition, although changes in activity patterns may also be implicated. Changes in sexual dimorphism – the ratio of average male to average female dimension – provide clues to the relative nutrition, and activity patterns, of the two sexes.[10]

Haviland (1967) reported some years ago that Mayan stature declined through the Classic period of Mayan civilization, a pattern that has been observed also by Saul (1972) and Nickens (1976). Declining nutrition is implicated, but Haviland also noted that female stature was less affected than male stature by the trend.

Frayer (1980, 1981) and Mieklejohn *et al.* (1984) document a decline in sexual dimorphism associated with declining stature for both sexes during the European mesolithic period. This trend may be indicative of a decline in nutrition which had a greater impact on men than on women. Frayer, however, interprets this pattern as reflecting declining physical demands on the male with the decline of big game hunting. He argues that the greater similarity of male and female dimensions indicates the increasing similarity of their workloads.

Angel (1984) also reports a decline in stature from the paleolithic through the neolithic periods in the region of the Mediterranean, but one shared by both sexes. Combining stature with other measures, Angel suggests that the trend reflected a decline in nutrition. Smith, Bar-Yosef, and Sillen (1984) found that Levantine populations had similar percentage dimorphism throughout the sequence, except that they displayed slightly lower dimorphism in the Natufian terminal hunting and gathering phase, now thought to be a period of nutritional stress, and a time of very short stature for both sexes. In Ecuador there were parallel trends in stature for the two sexes through the known archaeological sequence (Ubelaker 1984). On the other hand, in Nubia, females showed less variation over time in femur length (an estimator of stature) than did males (Martin *et al.* 1984). In the Caddoan region of the south-central United States the adoption of agriculture resulted in increased size (measured on the head of femur) for both males and females – but females in particular increased dramatically in size, suggesting that they participated disproportionately in an improvement in nutrition which accompanied the transition (Rose *et al.* 1984). Conversely, in the Mississippi Valley, sexual dimorphism increased with the origins of agriculture because both males and females got smaller but women decreased in size more dramatically than men. In the latter case, not only did nutrition apparently decline but women's share in available nutrients also was reduced. In Georgia, both sexes became smaller with the adoption of agriculture, but females showed the greater size reduction (Larsen 1981, 1984). Larsen suggests that there was a greater reduction in female workload with the adoption of agriculture as noted above, but also a relative as well as absolute decline in women's access to protein. Conversely, Bridges (1985 cited in Frayer and Wolpoff 1985) reports that sexual dimorphism declined over the transition to agriculture in Alabama because female body size increased more than male as a function of a greater increase in their workload.

Childhood stress episodes

Paleopathologists can provide a quantitative assessment of episodes of stress in childhood. The human skeleton records episodes of stress or growth disturbances during the growth period of the child in two major ways: in the formation of Harris lines in the shafts of long bones (lines of high bone density that appear as opaque lines in radiographs) and in macroscopic or microscopic lines of irregular enamel formation in teeth referred to as enamel hypoplasia and Wilson bands. Harris lines are thought to reflect relatively transient stress episodes while macroscopic hypoplasia are considered to represent more severe or long-lasting stresses (Martin, Goodman, and Amelagos 1985). Of the two indicators, Harris lines are the more controversial since many authorities consider them an indication of the ability to recover from stress rather than of the frequency of stress *per se* (Murchison, Owsley, and Riopelle 1983; Cohen and Armelagos 1984). Defects of tooth enamel are now widely used as indicators of comparative stress frequency. Because both Harris lines and enamel defects occur at age-specific positions on bones and teeth, the pattern of defects can be used to determine both the age at which stress occurs and the time-pattern of stresses. It is possible, for example, to distinguish between annual, seasonal, and irregular stresses (Cassidy

1984; Goodman *et al.* 1984). Because these indicators, particularly those in teeth, survive into adulthood in the skeleton it is possible to identify patterns of childhood stress in individuals whose sex can be determined. As a result it is possible to identify sex-specific rates of stress or sex-related differences in the age distribution of stresses.

Danforth (1988) reports that microscopic dental defects of teeth (Wilson bands) are far more common among males than females in the Tipu colonial period Mayan population. In the Late Woodland Libben population from Ohio (referred to above) males and females typically display different ages of formation of Wilson bands which are tentatively interpreted as indicative of different weaning patterns for male and female children (Rose, Boyd, and Condon 1981; Rose, Condon, and Goodman 1985).

The interpretation of sex differences, however, is complicated by the possibility that the sexes may be inherently different either in the degree to which the body buffers stress episodes or in the manner in which stress is recorded. Some authorities consider the female body to be more resilient (less prone to growth disruption) than the male body. As a result, there is some tendency to view lower stress rates in females as natural, and lower stress rates in males as a reflection of disproportionate cultural protection to male children. It is also possible that the sexes differ in the periods of growth during which they are more or less resilient. Clearly much more work is needed before we can establish the "natural" background pattern of sex differences in stress markers against which culturally induced patterns of stress can be measured. As with other indicators already discussed, absolute differences between the sexes for these stress markers in any one culture are less important than evidence of changes in relative frequency of stress.

The two indicators commonly yield conflicting patterns when hunter-gatherers are compared with farmers in any one region (Cohen and Armelagos 1984). Harris lines were often more common in hunter-gatherers; enamel hypoplasia and Wilson bands were almost universally more common in farming populations. Cohen and Armelagos conclude (following a suggestion in Cassidy 1984) that the pattern might be interpreted as showing that the neolithic revolution represented a trade off of one kind of stress for another, such as bouts of seasonal hunger traded for periodic starvation and epidemics. They also note that, since Harris lines denote healthy recovery rather than stress *per se*, the two indicators together might point to a greater frequency of stress among farmers, better recovery from stress among hunter-gatherers, in accordance with other signs that hunter-gatherers were comparatively well nourished.

Unfortunately, few studies have differentiated the data by sex. Goodman *et al.* (1984) do report differences in the frequency of Harris lines by sex at Dickson Mounds, and they also found differences between the sexes in the age distribution of lines. Females were commonly more stressed during the adolescent growth spurt; males more often in ages one to seven years. Goodman, Armelagos, and Rose (1980) report that women in the earliest hunting and gathering population at Dickson Mounds showed more enamel hypoplasia than men although rates of hypoplasia for the two sexes were equal in the later Mississippian farming population at the site. They suggest that male children received preferential treatment in the earlier population but not in the later. Cook (1984) found that Harris lines showed different trends in the two sexes, associated with the transition from hunting and gathering to agriculture in Illinois, suggesting that the transition had very different effects on the health of male and female children. Cook also discovered that microscopic dental indicators of stress occurred with similar frequency in the two sexes in the earlier Woodland period hunting and gathering population but were significantly more frequent in men than in women during the later Mississippian period farming population. This result suggests a relative decline in the protection afforded male children at the later site.

In the burials of children, and particularly those skeletons retaining their deciduous teeth, it is possible to identify periods of stress which occurred *in utero* or in the first few months of life, during which time nursing would have been nearly universal in prehistoric cultures. Such stress markers provide indirect evidence about maternal health and nutrition. Cassidy (1984), for example, reports that children in the agricultural Fort Ancient sample (but not in her Archaic hunter and gatherer sample) displayed significant numbers of enamel defects of deciduous teeth suggesting severe stress both *in utero* and during the first months of life – a pattern which may represent severe maternal malnutrition in the later population. Working with prehistoric populations from Ohio, Sciulli (1977) has also found more enamel defects of deciduous teeth in agricultural groups than in hunter-gatherer groups. Storey (1985), reporting on the population from one ward of Teotihuacan, the urban metropolis in prehistoric Mesoamerica, similarly has identified a high frequency of deciduous tooth enamel hypoplasia, as well as of still birth, late fetal death, and late fetal growth retardation (bones whose lengths are below expectations based on aging the infant by the development of its teeth). She suggests this pattern is indicative of severe maternal malnutrition.

Reproduction

Paleopathology offers a number of approaches to identifying changes in parity and maternal behavior in prehistory. This work bears on the interpretation of the interaction between reproductive behavior and gender hierarchies. It may be possible to estimate directly the number of children that a given woman has borne or at least the number of pregnancies that she has experienced by identifying and quantifying "parturition scars" on the pelvis (Angel 1969, 1971, 1984). The method is controversial and not widely accepted (Buikstra and Mielke 1985; Green, Suchey, and Gokhale 1979). Since, as discussed below, the quantitative representation of children in prehistoric cemeteries is also suspect, attempts to determine changing rates of fertility directly have proved unsatisfactory. Charles *et al.* (1987) have proposed that it may be possible to identify the effects of pregnancy on annular rings of tooth cementum which are now known to form throughout life – a technique which, if successful, may permit us to identify individual patterns of reproduction including an individual's age at first pregnancy, number of pregnancies, and interval between pregnancies.

Sillen (Sillen and Smith 1984) has pioneered a method of estimating the average age of weaning or, more precisely, the average age of cereal or vegetable food supplementation of children's diets in prehistoric populations. The method is based on the fact that breast milk is very low in strontium content, cereals very high. Sillen suggests that once correction is made for changes in the growing child's own systemic discrimination against absorption and deposition of strontium, this difference in diet can be recognized. Identification of the age at which a shift in levels of strontium occurs when a number of infants in a cemetery are compared can provide an estimate of the average age of supplementation in a population. This technique potentially can help sort out the controversy surrounding interpretation of the impact of the neolithic revolution on nursing patterns and fertility (Lee 1980) and can also bear on the hypotheses of Kolata (1974) and Draper (1975) relating nursing and fertility to men's workload and women's status.[11]

We are currently working on a technique to evaluate changes in strontium content along the axis of growth of a single tooth which should permit us to identify the age of weaning (Cohen and Bennett 1987). Since this technique can be applied to adult teeth, whose formation spans the range of probable weaning ages, it should be possible to determine whether male and female infants were treated differently in any given population.

Mortality

The most controversial area of skeletal analysis concerns the determination of age at death and the construction of mortality profiles and other descriptive statistics about mortality experience. Everyone involved in skeletal analysis recognizes that cemetery populations may not be complete or representative samples of the living population from which they have been culled. All agree that the methods of determining the age at death, particularly among adults, are imprecise, although whether the imprecision is sufficient to call the results into question is a matter of debate (Van Gerven and Armelagos 1983; Bocquet-Appel and Masset 1982, 1985). Finally, there is growing recognition that even when cemeteries are complete death assemblages, they can provide a misleading picture of the living population from which they are derived (see especially Sattenspiel and Harpending 1983).

Where gender issues are concerned there are further potential sources of error. First, sex is an obvious potential bias in the selection of people for burial in a cemetery. Second, at least two of the most reliable aging techniques now employed – age estimation from the auricular surface of the pelvis and from the pubic symphysis – involve areas of the body in which sexual dimorphism is an obvious and large, but imperfectly measured, source of error. Hence, for the time being, conclusions about lifespan need to be made with caution. Cementum annulation of teeth, briefly mentioned above, may provide a more accurate means of assessing age at death (Condon et al. 1986; Charles et al. 1986, 1987). These caveats notwithstanding, skeletal data may offer some useful observations. Particularly of interest are cases in which a single investigator or team sees changes in the relative ages at death between the sexes. Such comparisons within the work of individual scholars minimize the risk that apparent differences reflect differences in the techniques of age determination that are applied.

One common pattern in prehistoric groups is that, contrary to contemporary Western experience (but like the experience of some non-industrial nations, see United Nations 1978), men often appear to have had higher average ages at death than women (Acsadi and Nemeskeri 1970; Angel 1984; Owsley and Bass 1979; Rathbun 1984; Blakely 1971; Buikstra and Mielke 1985 who cite also Milner 1982). The explanation frequently cited is that women experience higher mortality during childbearing years. An alternative finding is that of Lovejoy et al. (1977) who suggest that higher young-adult mortality among males at the Libben site results from warfare. It is clear that the relative life expectancy of the two sexes is at least partially a culturally controlled variable which can be used as one measure of gender hierarchy. Demographic profiles can also determine how the patterns of death differ between the sexes, displaying different modal ages at death (Owsley and Bass 1979; Owsley and Bradtmiller 1983).

As is true of other skeletal indicators, the most interesting results involve change in relative levels of mortality when sequential populations are compared. Cassidy (1984), for example, argues that life expectancy at all ages was higher for men than for women in the Archaic period culture in Kentucky. In the agricultural Fort Ancient population, female life expectancy was higher than male life expectancy for all ages, suggesting that the adoption of agriculture and associated social and political changes had a more profound negative effect on male lifespan than on female lifespan.

Mortality profiles in a cemetery may also contribute indirectly to the interpretation of other social patterns. Benfer, working with the Paloma site in Peru (*c* 6000 to 2500 BC), suggests that the distribution of ages at death may permit the identification of marital patterns. Starting with the assumption that the peak of adult female mortality represents death in childbirth, and noting that the peak of female ages at death at Paloma is comparatively late, Benfer suggests that the Paloma data indicate a pattern of delayed marriage and late childbirth.

Cemetery profiles may also yield information on socially induced patterns of mortality. Cassidy (1984) concludes explicitly that the overall distribution of health and death in the Archaic population in Kentucky points to a sexually egalitarian society. In contrast, Benfer (1984) suggests that gender-specific age distributions at death point to socially induced mortality among female infants at Paloma in Peru.

Summary

Although skeletal data are scant and scattered, their study can contribute powerfully to the elucidation of gender issues. These data provide evidence of changing sex-associated differentials in workload, physical risk, disease, nutrition, reproductive patterns, childhood stress, and mortality. They provide fairly concrete indices of relative biological status and health which should help to refine our measurement of gender hierarchy – and to which other, more symbolic measures of status and gender hierarchy must always be compared. The data supplement ethnographic studies and enlarge the observed range of cultural variation. They permit us to observe the effects of specific economic or social transitions on the relative well-being of the two sexes in contexts clearly removed from Western influence. And they allow expanded tests of hypotheses generated by studies of the ethnographic present. Substantial additional information of the type reviewed in this chapter can be obtained by increased attention to existing skeletal populations and by continued excavation.[12] Future studies will help cut through some of the complexities and controversies involved in the interpretation of gender hierarchy.

NOTES

1 The major difficulty with many archaeological data from the perspective of gender studies is that individual actors are difficult to identify. Despite numerous attempts by archaeologists to identify gender-associated activity spheres in archaeological refuse, usually through ethnographic analogy, actual gender distinctions underlying or implied by refuse patterns cannot be precisely identified, an inability which may result in reading Western role expectations into the archaeological record.

2 Paleopathology refers to the analysis of pathology in prehistoric populations of skeletons or mummies.

3 Working with an early twentieth-century black American population, Rose and coworkers (1985) found signs of interpersonal violence to be much more common among men than among women.

4 There is some danger of facile over-interpretation of these data using Western cultural stereotypes. Bridges (1987) has recently evaluated a series of Archaic and Woodland populations from Alabama for the phenomenon known as "atlatl elbow" – a pattern of arthritis of the elbow joint once thought to be diagnostic of use of the spear thrower, a presumed male activity. She provides the interesting observation that the pattern is as well developed among women as men in her Archaic period (spear throwing) sample, suggesting either that women hunted in the same pattern as men or that some other activity is responsible for the reported arthritis.

5 A possible exception of this generalization is a form of arthritis secondary to infection by Erysipelothrix bacteria from handling animals including hunted animals such as deer (Hubbert, McCulloch, and Schurrenberger 1975; Wood 1975; Hudson et al. 1975).

6 Many diseases associated with crowding are not transmitted directly from person to person so that they may not be shared by all members of a family even if family members spend every night together. Diseases carried by organisms associated with human feces, accumulated garbage, or household pests, and caught from those sources rather than from other people, might be greater risk factors for individuals with more sedentary habits. A person spending a day in the village and using the village defecating grounds is much more susceptible to a heavy dose of hookworm than a person living in the same house but working (for example, hunting) away from camp and defecating in the wild.

7 There has been some recent discussion about whether anemia is primarily of dietary origin or the result of secondary nutrient loss to parasites (Walker 1986; Stuart Macadam 1985). Stuart-Macadam summarizes reported differences between male and female skeletons in rates of porotic hyperostosis in several populations and argues that the differences between the two sexes are neither as large nor statistically as significant in most prehistoric populations as we might expect from contemporary rates of anemia. She suggests that the skeleton primarily records anemia in childhood which often persists, only partly healed or remodeled, in adults.

8 A review of the world paleopathological literature suggests that most serious nutritional diseases did not become common in Europe until Roman times or later and were particularly evident only in the medieval period (Cohen 1989).

9 On the other hand, it is common for women to display more caries than men in caries-prone populations as Larsen notes.
10 Moreover, the sexes may differ in the degree to which the body resorbs or "remodels" Harris lines after they are formed. Enamel defects are not remodeled.
11 Sillen and Smith (1984) have applied this method to a population in the Middle East, but to our knowledge no other applications have so far been made.
12 Unfortunately both existing collections and future excavations are now at risk because of the issue of forced reburial.

REFERENCES

Acsadi, Gyorgy and J. Nemeskeri 1970 *History of Human Lifespan and Mortality.* Budapest: Akademei Kiado.

Allison, Marvin 1984 Paleopathology in Peruvian and Chilean·Populations. In *Paleopathology at the Origins of Agriculture.* Mark N. Cohen and George J. Armelagos, eds., pp. 515–30. New York: Academic Press.

Anderson, Karen 1985 Commodity Exchange and Subordination: Montagnais-Naskapi and Huron Women 1600–1650. *Signs* 11:48–62.

Angel, J. Lawrence 1969 The Bases of Paleodemography. *American Journal of Physical Anthropology* 30:427–37.

   1971 Early Neolithic Skeletons from Çatal Hüyük: Demography and Pathology. *Anatolian Studies* 21:77–98.

   1984 Health as a Crucial Factor in the Changes from Hunting to Developed Farming in the Eastern Mediterranean. In *Paleopathology at the Origins of Agriculture.* Mark N. Cohen and George J. Armelagos, eds., pp. 51–74. New York: Academic Press.

Armelagos, George J. and Dennis P. Van Gerven 1980 Sexual Dimorphism and Human Evolution: An Overview. *Journal of Human Evolution* 9:437–46.

Armstrong, Carl 1985 Pathology and Measure of Robusticity in the Long Bones of the Tipu Population. Paper presented at the annual meeting of the Northeast Anthropological Association.

Atkinson, Jane M. 1982 Anthropology. *Signs* 8:236–58.

Benfer, Robert 1984 The Challenges and Rewards of Sedentism: The Preceramic Village of Paloma, Peru. In *Paleopathology at the Origins of Agriculture.* Mark N. Cohen and George J. Armelagos, eds., pp. 531–58. New York: Academic Press.

Blakely, Robert 1971 Comparison of the Mortality Profiles of Archaic, Middle Woodland, and Middle Mississippian Skeletal Populations. *American Journal of Physical Anthropology* 34:43–54.

Blakely, Robert and Lane Beck 1982 Trace Elements, Nutritional Status, and Social Stratification at Etowah, Georgia. *Annals of the New York Academy of Sciences* 376:417–31.

Bocquet-Appel, J. P. and C. Masset 1982 Farewell to Paleodemography. *Journal of Human Evolution* 11:321–33.

   1985 Paleopathology: Resurrection or Ghost. *Journal of Human Evolution* 14:107–11.

Bridges, Patricia S. 1982 Postcranial Dimensions in the Archaic and Mississippian Cultures of Northern Alabama: Implications for Prehistoric Nutrition and Behavior. *American Journal of Physical Anthropology* 57:172–3.

1983 Subsistence Activities and Biomechanical Properties of Long Bones in Two American Populations. *American Journal of Physical Anthropology* 60:177.

1985 A Biomechanical Analysis of Two Prehistoric Amerind Groups: Changes in Habitual Activities and the Division of Labor with the Transition from Hunting and Gathering to Agriculture. Ph.D. dissertation, University of Michigan.

1987 Osteological Correlates of Prehistoric Activities. Paper presented at the annual meeting of the American Anthropological Association.

Brothwell, Don R. 1981 *Digging Up Bones: The Excavation, Treatment and Study of Human Skeletal Remains.* 3rd edition. Ithaca, NY: Cornell University Press.

Buikstra, Jane 1976 *Hopewell in the Lower Illinois Valley: A Regional Study of Human Biological Variation and Prehistoric Mortuary Practices.* Northwestern University Archeological Program Scientific Papers 2. Evanston, IL: Northwestern University.

1984 The Lower Illinois River Region: A Prehistoric Context for the Study of Ancient Diet and Health. In *Paleopathology at the Origins of Agriculture.* Mark N. Cohen and George J. Armelagos, eds., pp. 217–36. New York: Academic Press.

Buikstra, Jane and Della C. Cook 1980 Paleopathology: An American Account. *Annual Review of Anthropology* 9:433–70.

Buikstra Jane and James Mielke 1985 Demography, Diet and Health. In *The Analysis of Prehistoric Diets.* Robert I. Gilbert, Jr and James H. Mielke, eds., pp. 359–422. New York: Academic Press.

Cassidy, Claire M. 1984 Skeletal Evidence for Prehistoric Subsistence Change in the Central Ohio River Valley. In *Paleopathology at the Origins of Agriculture.* Mark N. Cohen and George J. Armelagos, eds., pp. 307–46. New York: Academic Press.

Chapman, Robert, Ian Kinnes, and Klaus Randsborg, eds. 1981 *The Archaeology of Death.* New York: Cambridge University Press.

Charles, Douglas K. *et al.* 1986 Cementum Annulation and Age Determination in *Homo sapiens.* I. Tooth Variability and Observer Error. *American Journal of Physical Anthropology* 71:311–20.

1987 Age Estimation and Differential Diagnosis. Paper presented at the annual meeting of the Northeast Anthropological Association.

Cohen, Mark N. 1989 *Health and the Rise of Civilization.* New Haven, CT: Yale University Press.

Cohen, Mark N. and George J. Armelagos, eds. 1984 *Paleopathology at the Origins of Agriculture.* New York: Academic Press.

Cohen, Mark N. and Sharon Bennett 1987 Analysis, Seriation and Age-Determination of the Maya of Tipu. Proposal to the National Science Foundation.

Condon, Keith, Douglas Charles, James Cheverud, and Jane Buikstra 1986 Cementum Annulation and Age Determination in *Homo sapiens.* II. Estimates and Accuracy. *American Journal of Physical Anthropology* 71:321–30.

Cook, Delia C. 1984 Subsistence and Health in the Lower Illinois Valley: Osteological Evidence. In *Paleopathology at the Origins of Agriculture.* Mark N. Cohen and George J. Armelagos, eds., pp. 237–70. New York: Academic Press.

Cybulski, Jerome S. 1977 Cribra Orbitalia, a Possible Sign of Anemia in Early Historic Native Populations of the British Columbia Coast. *American Journal of Physical Anthropology* 47:31–40.

Danforth, Marie 1988 Comparison of Health Patterns in Late Classic and Colonial Mayan Populations Using Enamel Microdefects. Ph.D. Dissertation, Indiana University.

Draper, Patricia 1975 !Kung Women: Contrasts in Sexual Egalitarianism in the Foraging and Sedentary Contexts. In *Toward an Anthropology of Women.* Rayna Reiter, ed., pp. 77–109. New York: Monthly Review Press.

Eisenberg, Leslie 1986 The Pattern of Trauma at Averbuch: Activity Levels and Conflict During the Late Mississippian Period. Paper presented at the annual meeting of the American Association of Physical Anthropologists.

Frayer, David 1980 Sexual Dimorphism and Cultural Evolution in the Late Pleistocene and Holocene of Europe. *Journal of Human Evolution* 9:399–413.
    1981 Body Size, Weapon Use and Natural Selection in the European Upper Paleolithic and Mesolithic. *American Anthropologist* 83:57–73.

Frayer, David and Milford Wolpoff 1985 Sexual Dimorphism. *Annual Review of Anthropology* 14:429–74.

Gilbert, Robert I. Jr. 1985 Stress, Paleonutrition and Trace Elements. In *The Analysis of Prehistoric Diets.* Robert I. Gilbert Jr and James H. Mielke, eds., pp. 339–58. New York: Academic Press.

Gilbert, Robert I. Jr and James H. Mielke, eds. 1985 *The Analysis of Prehistoric Diets.* New York: Academic Press.

Goldstein, Lynne 1976 Spatial Structure and Social Organization: Regional Manifestations of Mississippian Society. Ph.D. dissertation, Northwestern University.

Goodman, Alan, George J. Armelagos, and Jerome Rose 1980 Enamel Hypoplasias as Indicators of Stress in Three Prehistoric Populations from Illinois. *Human Biology* 52:515–28.

Goodman, Alan, Debra Martin, George J. Armelagos, and George Clark 1984 Health Changes at Dickson Mounds, Illinois (A.D. 950–1300). In *Paleopathology at the Origins of Agriculture.* Mark N. Cohen and George J. Armelagos, eds., pp. 271–306. New York: Academic Press.

Gray, J. Patrick and Linda D. Wolfe 1980 Height and Sexual Dimorphism of Stature among Human Societies. *American Journal of Physical Anthropology* 53:441–56.

Green, Richard, Judy M. Suchey, and D. Gokhale 1979 Analysis of Dorsal Pitting on the Pubis in an Extensive Sample of Modern American Females. *American Journal of Physical Anthropology* 51:317–40.

Hamilton, Margaret E. 1982 Sexual Dimorphism in Skeletal Samples. In *Sexual Dimorphism in* Homo sapiens: *A Question of Size.* Roberta L. Hall, ed., pp. 107–63. New York: Praeger.

Haviland, William 1967 Stature at Tikal: Implications for Ancient Maya Demography and Social Organization. *American Antiquity* 35:316–25.

Hubbert, William T., William F. McCulloch, and Paul Schurrenberger 1975 *Diseases Transmitted from Animals to Man*. Springfield, IL: Thomas.

Hudson, Charles, Ronald Butler, and Dennis Sikes 1975 Arthritis in the Prehistoric Southeastern United States: Biological and Cultural Variables. *American Journal of Physical Anthropology* 43:57–62.

Huss-Ashmore, Rebecca, Alan Goodman, and George J. Armelagos 1982 Nutritional Inference from Paleopathology. *Advances in Archaeological Theory and Method* 5:395–474.

Jurmain, Robert D. 1977 Stress and the Etiology of Osteoarthritis. *American Journal of Physical Anthropology* 46:353–65.

Klepinger, Linda 1984 Nutritional Assessment from Bone. *Annual Review of Anthropology* 13:75–96.

Koch, Joan K. 1983 Mortuary Behavior Patterns and Physical Anthropology in Colonial St. Augustine. In *Spanish St. Augustine: The Archaeology of a Spanish Creole Community*. Kathleen A. Deagan, ed. with contributions by Joan K. Koch, pp. 187–226. New York: Academic Press.

Kolata, Gina Bari 1974 !Kung Hunter-Gatherers: Feminism, Diet, and Birth Control. *Science* 185:932–4.

Konigsberg, Lyle 1986 Skeletal Lineages and Biological Distance. Paper presented at the annual meeting of the American Association of Physical Anthropologists.

1987 A Formal Basis for the Analysis of Osteological Indicators of Residential Practices. Paper presented at the annual meeting of the American Association of Physical Anthropologists.

Lambert, Joseph, Carol Szpunar, and Jane Buikstra 1977 Chemical Analysis of Excavated Human Bone from Middle and Late Woodland Sites. *Archaeometry* 21:115–29.

Lamphere, Louise 1977 Anthropology. *Signs* 2:612–17.

Larsen, Clark 1981 Functional Implications of Post-Cranial Size Reduction on the Prehistoric Georgia Coast, USA. *Journal of Human Evolution* 10:489–502.

1983 Behavioral Implications of Temporal Change in Cariogenesis. *Journal of Archaeological Science* 10:1–8.

1984 Health and Disease in Prehistoric Georgia: The Transition to Agriculture. In *Paleopathology at the Origins of Agriculture*. Mark N. Cohen and George J. Armelagos, eds., pp. 367–92. New York: Academic Press.

Leacock, Eleanor 1978 Women's Status in Egalitarian Society: Implications for Social Evolution. *Current Anthropology* 19(2):247–75.

Lee, Richard B. 1980 Lactation, Ovulation, Infanticide and Women's Work: A Study of a Hunter-Gatherer Population. In *Biosocial Mechanisms of Population Regulation*. Mark N. Cohen, R. S. Malpass, and H. G. Klein, eds., pp. 321–48. New Haven, CT: Yale University Press.

Lovejoy, C. Owen, and K. G. Heiple 1981 The Analysis of Fractures in Skeletal Populations with an Example from the Libben Site, Ottowa Co., Ohio. *American Journal of Physical Anthropology* 55:529–42.

Lovejoy, C. Owen, R. S. Meindle, T. R. Pryzbeck, T. S. Barton, K. G. Heiple, and D. Kotting 1977 Paleobiology at the Libben Site, Ottowa Co., Ohio. *Science* 198:291–3.

Martin, Debra, George J. Armelagos, Alan H. Goodman, and Dennis Van

Gerven 1984 The Effects of Socioeconomic Change in Prehistoric Africa: Sudanese Nubia as a Case Study. In *Paleopathology at the Origins of Agriculture*. Mark N. Cohen and George J. Armelagos, eds., pp. 193–216. New York: Academic Press.

Martin, Debra, Alan Goodman, and George J. Armelagos 1985 Skeletal Pathologies as Indicators of Diets. In *The Analysis of Prehistoric Diets*. Robert I. Gilbert Jr and James H. Mielke, eds., pp. 227–79. New York: Academic Press.

Meiklejohn, Christopher, Catherine Schentag, Alexander Venema, and Patrick Key 1984 Socioeconomic Changes and Patterns of Pathology and Variation in the Mesolithic and Neolithic of Western Europe: Some Suggestions. In *Paleopathology at the Origins of Agriculture*. Mark N. Cohen and George J. Armelagos, eds., pp. 75–100. New York: Academic Press.

Milner, G. 1982 Measuring Prehistoric Levels of Health: A Study of Mississippian Period Skeletal Remains from the American Bottom, Illinois. Ph.D. dissertation, Northwestern University.

Mukhopadhyay, Carol C. and Patricia J. Higgins 1988 Anthropological Studies of Women's Status Revisited: 1977–1987. *Annual Review of Anthropology* 17:461–95.

Murchison, M. A., Douglas Owsley, and A. J. Riopelle 1983 Transverse Line Formation in Protein Deprived Rhesus Monkeys. Paper presented at the annual meeting of the Paleopathology Association.

Nelson, David R., Malcolm McCulloch, and Shen-su Sun 1986 Effects of Diagenesis on Strontium, Carbon, Nitrogen and Oxygen Concentrations and Isotopic Composition of Bone. *Geochemica et Cosmochemica Acta* 50:1941–9.

Nickens, Paul 1976 Stature Reductions as an Adaptive Response to Food Production in Meso America. *Journal of Archaeological Science* 3:31–41.

Norr, Lynette 1984 Prehistoric Subsistence and Health Status of Coastal Peoples from the Panamanian Isthmus of Lower Central America. In *Paleopathology at the Origins of Agriculture*. Mark N. Cohen and George J. Armelagos, eds., pp. 463–90. New York: Academic Press.

Ortner, Donald J. and Walter G. Putschar 1981 *Identification of Pathological Conditions in Human Skeletal Remains*. Smithsonian Contributions to Anthropology 28. Washington, DC.

Owsley, Douglas and William Bass 1979 A Demographic Analysis of Skeletons from the Larson Site (39ww2), Walworth County, South Dakota: Vital Statistics. *American Journal of Physical Anthropology* 51:145–54.

Owsley, Douglas and Bruce Bradtmiller 1983 Mortality of Pregnant Females in an Arikara Village: Osteological Evidence. *American Journal of Physical Anthropology* 61:331–8.

Perzigian, Anthony J., Patricia Tench, and Donna J. Braun 1984 Prehistoric Health in the Ohio River Valley. In *Paleopathology at the Origins of Agriculture*. Mark N. Cohen and George J. Armelagos, eds., pp. 347–66. New York: Academic Press.

Powell, Mary L. 1985 Dental Wear and Caries in Dietary Reconstruction. In *Analysis of Prehistoric Diets*. Robert I. Gilbert Jr and James H. Mielke, eds., pp. 307–38. New York: Academic Press.

Quinn, Naomi 1977 Anthropological Studies on Women's Status. *Annual Review of Anthropology* 6:181–225.

Rapp, Rayna 1979 Anthropology. *Signs* 4:497–513.

Rathbun, Ted A. 1984 Skeletal Pathology from the Paleolithic through the Metal Ages in Iran and Iraq. In *Paleopathology at the Origins of Agriculture*. Mark N. Cohen and George J. Armelagos, eds., pp. 137–68. New York: Academic Press.

Rosaldo, Michelle Zimbalist 1980 The Use and Abuse of Anthropology: Reflections on Feminism and Cross Cultural Understanding. *Signs* 5:389–417.

Rose, Jerome, Barbara A. Barnett, Michael S. Nassaney, and Mark W. Blaeuer 1985 *Gone to a Better Land*. Research Series 25. Fayetteville: Arkansas Archaeological Survey.

Rose, Jerome, L. F. Boyd, and Keith W. Condon 1981 Enamel Microdefects and Subadult Infections. *American Journal of Physical Anthropology* 54:270.

Rose, Jerome, Keith W. Condon, and Alan H. Goodman 1985 Diet and Dentition: Developmental Disturbances. In *The Analysis of Prehistoric Diets*. Robert I. Gilbert Jr and James H. Mielke, eds., pp. 281–305. New York: Academic Press.

Rose, Jerome *et al.* 1984 Paleopathology and the Origins of Maize Agriculture in the Lower Mississippi Valley and Caddoan Culture Areas. In *Paleopathology at the Origins of Agriculture*. Mark N. Cohen and George J. Armelagos, eds., pp. 393–424. New York: Academic Press.

Sacks, Karen 1976 State Bias and Women's Status. *American Anthropologist* 78:565–9.

Sattenspiel, Lisa and Henry Harpending 1983 Stable Populations and Skeletal Age. *American Antiquity* 48:489–98.

Saul, Frank P. 1972 *The Human Skeletal Remains of Altar de Sacrificios*. Papers of the Peabody Museum of Archaeology and Ethnology 63(2). Cambridge, MA.

Schoeninger, Margaret J. 1979 Diet and Status at Chalcatzingo: Some Empirical and Technical Aspects of Strontium Analysis. *American Journal of Physical Anthropology* 51:295–310.

1982 Diet and Evolution of Modern Human Form in the Middle East. *American Journal of Physical Anthropology* 58:37–52.

Sciulli, Paul W. 1977 A Descriptive and Comparative Study of the Deciduous Dentition of Prehistoric Ohio Valley Amerindians. *American Journal of Physical Anthropology* 48:71–80.

Sillen, Andrew and Maureen Kavanaugh 1982 Strontium and Paleodietary Research: A Review. *Yearbook of Physical Anthropology* 25:69–90.

Sillen, Andrew and Patricia Smith 1984 Weaning Patterns are Reflected in Strontium–Calcium Ratios of Juvenile Skeletons. *Journal of Archaeological Science* 11:237–45.

Smith, Patricia, Ofer Bar-Yosef, and Andrew Sillen 1984 Archaeological and Skeletal Evidence for Dietary Change during the Late Pleistocene/Early Holocene in the Levant. In *Paleopathology at the Origins of Agriculture*. Mark N. Cohen and George J. Armelagos, eds., pp. 101–36. New York: Academic Press.

Steinbock, R. Ted 1976 *Paleopathological Diagnosis and Interpretation: Bone Diseases in Ancient Human Populations*. Springfield, IL: Thomas.

Stini, William 1969 Nutritional Stress and Growth: Sex Differences in Adaptive Response. *American Journal of Physical Anthropology* 31:417–26.

1985 Growth Rates and Sexual Dimorphism in Evolutionary Perspective. In *The Analysis of Prehistoric Diets*. Robert I. Gilbert Jr and James H. Mielke, eds., pp. 191–226. New York: Academic Press.

Story, Rebecca 1985 An Estimate of Mortality in a Pre-Columbian Urban Population. *American Anthropologist* 87:519–35.

Stuart-Macadam, Patty 1985 Porotic Hyperostosis: Representative of a Childhood Condition. *American Journal of Physical Anthropology* 66:391–8.

Swedlund, Alan and George J. Armelagos 1976 *Demographic Anthropology*. Boston: William C. Brown.

Tanner, Nancy and Adrienne Zihlman 1976 Women in Evolution. Part I: Innovation and Selection in Human Origins. *Signs* 1:585–608.

Turner, Christy 1979 Dental Anthropological Indicators of Agriculture among the Jomon People of Central Japan. *American Journal of Physical Anthropology* 51:619–35.

Ubelaker, Douglas H. 1978 *Human Skeletal Remains: Excavation, Analysis, Interpretation*. Chicago, IL: Aldine Publishing Company.

1984 Prehistoric Human Biology of Ecuador: Possible Temporal Trends and Cultural Correlations. In *Paleopathology at the Origins of Agriculture*. Mark N. Cohen and George J. Armelagos, eds., pp. 491–514. New York: Academic Press.

Ullrich, H. 1975 Estimation of Fertility by Means of Pregnancy and Childbirth Alterations of the Pubis, Ilium, and Sacrum. *Ossa: International Journal of Skeletal Research* 2:23–39.

United Nations 1978 *Statistical Yearbook 1977*. New York: United Nations.

Van Gerven, Dennis and George J. Armelagos 1983 Farewell to Paleodemography: A Reply. *Journal of Human Evolution* 12:352–66.

Walker, Philip 1985 Anemia among Prehistoric Indians of the American Southwest. In *Health and Disease in the Prehistoric Southwest*. Charles F. Merbs and Robert Miller, eds., pp. 139–64. Arizona State University Anthropological Research Papers 34. Tempe: Arizona State University.

1986 Porotic Hyperostosis in a Marine Dependent California Indian Population. *American Journal of Physical Anthropology* 69:345–54.

Wood, Richard L. 1975 Erysipelothrix Infection. In *Diseases Transmitted from Animals to Man*. William T. Hubbert, William F. McCulloch, and Paul Schurrenberger, eds., pp. 271–81. Springfield, IL: Thomas.

13   Gender hierarchy and the queens of Silla

Sarah M. Nelson

Recent scholarship has exposed some of the "self-evident" truths of the anthropology of the last century as being products of cultural blinders which prevent a clear view of the evidence (Fee 1974; Tiffany 1979). Assumptions about the origins of gender hierarchy and the relationship of male dominance to the formation of states need to be re-examined in this light (Gailey 1985). While feminists have explicitly discussed these topics, sometimes using archaeological data in their discussions (Rohrlich 1980; Lerner 1986), mainstream archaeology has not often examined the gender assumptions implicit in their arguments (see the critique by Conkey and Spector 1984, as well as Zagarell 1986 for a recent exception). Theories of cultural evolution have been derived more from ethnographic than archaeological examples, since the major variables were thought to be difficult to retrieve archaeologically. Theoretical problems with universal explanations regarding the origin of the state include overgeneralizing and a lack of attention to kinship structures (Rapp 1977). A combination of archaeological and ethnohistoric evidence can help to reveal our own cultural assumptions in formulations of cultural evolution.

The school of thought that perceives gender hierarchies in all societies (Rosaldo and Lamphere 1974:3) has largely been replaced by an awareness of variation in women's autonomy, power, and authority in prestate societies (Leacock 1978; Draper 1975; Ortner 1981:359; Sanday 1981:132). However, the more specific thesis that state-level societies are inevitably characterized by gender hierarchy, and indeed that other hierarchies are built on the model of inequality by sex and age (Flannery 1972; Service 1975; Sagan 1985; Rousseau 1985), has received less attention.

Rohrlich not only assumes that the formation of the state is based on inequality of women (1980:98), but asserts that the "critical factor in state formation is the emergence of patriarchy" (1980:76). Historical analyses of the antecedents of Western society also indict "patriarchy" and the "patriarchal family" as the source of gender stratification in archaic states (Lerner 1986:212). It is interesting to note that the equation of hierarchies with the state is not limited to Western writers. For example, in *Kuan-tzu*, a Chinese document written around the fourth century BC:

In antiquity, before there was a distinction between prince and minister, superiors and inferiors, and before there was a union of husband and wife, consort and mate, people lived like beasts and lived in herds, and attacked each other by means of force ... When superiors and inferiors had been established, the people formed an organization, and the state was founded (Duyvendak 1928:103).

Archaeologists, on the other hand, tend to ignore gender stratification in their analyses of state formation, assuming that males are in "the competitive public arena vying for external power in contrast to the private arena of females" (Earle 1987:299), even in chiefdom-level societies.

Universality of female subordination at any stage is a proposition that should be scrutinized. Ruling women in chiefdoms and early states are not as uncommon as general theories about the origin of states would suggest. Women were eligible to rule in Celtic society (Muller 1987), in early Sumer (Rohrlich 1980), in early Japan (Wheatley and See 1978), and in the Silla state of Korea, to name a few. The actual rule by these women is more often acknowledged with reference to documents. Archaeologists tend to discount finds associated with women which, if male, would be considered evidence of very high status (Gilman 1981). Focusing on the high status of some women allows us to examine the supposed necessary connection between the origin of states and "patriarchy," between the formation of elites and the hierarchization of gender relationships (Service 1975; Sagan 1985), between militarism with territorial expansion and the lowered status of women (Harris 1977; Divale and Harris 1976), and to focus on the kinship group as a preservator of women's status (Sacks 1979).

An example of apparent gender equality in the Silla state on the Korean peninsula during the first to seventh centuries may shed some light on these questions. The discovery in 1973 that the largest and most elaborate of the Silla royal tombs in Korea contained a woman as its major occupant, complete with all the accoutrements of power of that early kingdom (Kim W. Y. 1981), has raised major questions about Silla history and society. Have the symbols been misinterpreted, and was not this queen the head of government? If she did rule, why is she missing from the king lists in both of the major Korean documents relating to this time[1] although later ruling queens are included?[2] How does this discovery fit into the social structure as it has been understood, with endogamous "bone ranks" each having its own appointed range of occupations, and sumptuary laws to keep individuals and families from rising above their own class? What was the position of women *vis-à-vis* the class hierarchy and the bureaucracy?

Clearly, wherever there are ruling queens, or even figurehead queens, the principle of royal descent overrides any gender hierarchy that might be present, demonstrating that there are hierarchies of hierarchy, that class may be more important than gender in many cases (Ortner 1981). Regarding the Silla example, we need to know whether there is any necessary relationship between gender hierarchy and the social, economic, and political systems, and whether gender equality applies to the lower classes as well as to the nobility.

Old Silla in documents and archaeology

The Old Silla kingdom was centered on the city of Kyongju, in southeastern Korea. The traditional dates for this kingdom are 57 BC to AD 668, although the earlier half of this period is generally not considered to be a state-level society. Old Silla ended when it conquered Paekche and Koguryo, the other competing states of the Korean Three Kingdoms period, forming United Silla. In this chapter "Silla" refers to Old Silla.

From 108 BC to AD 313 there was a significant Chinese presence on the Korean peninsula north of the developing Silla state, in the form of commanderies established by the Former Han dynasty expansion. With various border changes and revolts the Lolang colony, with its capital near present day Pyongyang, continued until it was extirpated finally by the Koguryo kingdom on its northern border in AD 313. Comments about the oddities of the unconquered regions of southern Korea are extant in Chinese documents, especially a section of the *Wei Shu*[3] regarding the "Eastern Barbarians" from the third century AD. Neither the Silla nor the Paekche kingdom is named in that document; rather we read of the Three Hans,[4] Ma-Han, Pyon-Han, and Chin-Han, of which the last is usually identified with Silla (Joe 1972:25). Chin-Han contained twelve "*guo*," a character that now is translated as "state," but is thought to refer to some less organized form, such as walled villages or towns protected by hill forts. One of these *guo* was Saro, a confederation of six villages, whose capital was at the present site of Kyongju in southeastern Korea. Saro expanded by the conquest of neighboring states and ultimately became Silla.

The formation of the Silla kingdom was less influenced by China than the other two Korean kingdoms of the Three Kingdoms period. It is clearly an example of a secondary state, but the concept of "peer policy interaction" (Renfrew 1982) is also relevant, for Silla's interactions with the other kingdoms of Korea and Japan were probably as critical as those with China in its early development. One of Silla's own traditions, recorded in the *Wei Shu*, is that some of its founders were Ch'in refugees from the harsh laws of the Chin dynasty of China, who came to the Korean peninsula "to escape the misery of forced labor" (Parker 1890:209). Their dialect was said to be like that of northwest China. Chinese sources additionally relate that in AD 37 a great many ("five thousand") refugees from the Lolang colonies fled to Silla and were apportioned among the villages (Kim C. S. 1965:160).

Archaeological discoveries suggest an intrusive population in the third to first centuries BC, with a new form of pit burial replacing the stone cist graves under dolmens of the Bronze Age.[5] In the pit graves iron implements accompanied the dead, along with bronze weapons (Kim W. Y. 1982:26). Differentials of wealth are evident in these burials. The region around Kyongju, later Silla's capital, is one of two areas in South Korea with extensive early Iron Age sites. It is probably significant that both these areas are near outcrops of iron ores. In the Han river basin, semisubterranean dwellings and Mumun (Bronze Age) pottery are found associated with early iron artifacts, while in the southeast, iron has so far only been found in pit graves associated with Wajil and Kimhae (Iron Age) pottery. The techniques of iron working have been found to include both cast iron and steel, with technology equal to that of Han China. The technology may have been imported, but the metal was locally worked (Lee 1982).

Perhaps as early as the first century AD, a new variant appeared in the burial system. Stone cairns were raised over cobble-lined tombs, instead of simple earthen pits. The tradition of mounded tombs was long established in China, and was also practiced in the Lolang commandery in Korea. Thus, an inspiration for this new burial style is to be found close at hand.

Excavations in Choyadong, Kyongju, have been dated to the early centuries AD. One of the burials contained four mirrors in the style of the Former Han dynasty, helping to date the graves as well as demonstrating connections with China. Another set of graves, excavated in the vicinity of King Michu's tomb in Kyongju, is believed to date from the second and third centuries AD (Kim W. Y. 1974). Long-distance trade and human sacrifice were already evident. Round pits with horse skeletons were found outside human burials, along with multi-chambered tombs, which appeared to contain human sacrificial victims. Tomb 4 in Area C contained an elaborate glass bead of Roman type, with a round-eyed face in the bead. The excavators consider this to be evidence that long-distance trade was carried on at this early date (Kim and Yi 1975). At about this time in China, poems were being written celebrating foreign glass objects (Engle 1976:35), making it likely that China was the mediator of this trade.

Choi (1981) has seriated the Silla wooden chamber tombs under cobble and earth mounds, which date from about AD 350–720. These tombs show increasing amounts of high-status grave goods, although craft specialization can be inferred from the artifacts from much earlier times. Great artistry and technical sophistication in fabricating artifacts are hallmarks of this period. Glass vessels from the Western world are not uncommon in the high-status tombs, but only one Chinese artifact has been unearthed – a glazed brown ceramic bottle. This suggests the possibility of later trade not mediated by China, but how and by what route is not clear. Perhaps the paucity of Chinese goods merely indicates that they were not exotic enough for royal burials. Regardless of the source of trade goods, Sillan contact with China is attested to in various documentary sources.

Chinese manners and customs began to be adopted during the period of the mounded royal tombs. Chinese and Korean records concur that in the reign of King Chinji in the fourth century Korean rulers began to use the Chinese code of mourning and the custom of posthumous names for rulers. But not until the early sixth century did Silla begin to use the Chinese calendar instead of the native lunar reckoning, and to call the kings "wang" after the Chinese fashion, instead of using native Korean titles. By this time Buddhism was well established, literacy in Chinese was the rule in the court, and the Korean language was being written in Idu, using Chinese characters for their phonetic value to represent the sounds of Korean words. Alongside this sinicization, the Sillans maintained many of their ancient customs.

Silla society

The social system is the most thoroughly recorded subsystem of Silla. Class stratification was the basic building block of society. A system called *kolpum*, "bone ranks" (bone being the Korean metaphor for kinship), kept everyone in the same social position into which they were born. The highest group was the *songgol*, or Holy Bone, a quality required for the ruler until this group became extinct in the seventh century. Neither primogeniture nor patriliny was a necessary category in selection of the ruler, but *songgol* status was *sine qua non*. It appears that there was a rule of hypodescent in which both parents had to be *songgol* for the children to enjoy this status, but given *songgol* birth, "the holders of the highest status . . . were eligible for the throne regardless of sex" (Kim C. S.

1977). Only three families (Pak, Sok, and Kim) comprised the *songgol*, but not all branches of these families were among the Holy Bone. Endogamy within the *songgol* became ever more pronounced, with not only cousin marriages but marriages between niece and uncle occurring commonly in royal families, according to the lists of kings and queens.

Below the *songgol* were the *chin'gol*, the True Bone. Each rank in the government could be held only by a person of the appropriate social rank, and members of each wore robes of a distinctive color. The highest five ranks of the government could be filled only by *songgol* who wore purple, or *chin'gol* in red robes. The *ryuktupum*, "six head rank," were eligible to hold the four government ranks below those held by *chin'gol*; they were distinguished by blue robes. The next two state ranks could be filled by the "fifth head rank" wearing yellow robes, and the lowest four groups were *pyongmin*, commoners, not eligible for government service (Kim C. S. 1977). Under this system, "every individual in Silla was by birth assigned a specific status from which it was virtually impossible for him [sic] to escape" (Kim C. S. 1977:4).

Strict sumptuary laws also enforced the *kolpum* ranks. For example, male *chin'gol* were prohibited from wearing "embroidered trousers made of fur, brocade or raw silk," while among the prohibitions for female *chin'gol* were "hairpins engraved and inlaid with gems and jades" (Kim C. S. 1977:59). Wrinkled purple reindeer leather was not allowed as a material for boots for male *ryuktupum*, while male *odupum* were limited to cotton cloth for their underwear, and female *sadupum* could not use underskirts at all. *Chin'gol* were forbidden to hang carved wooden fish from the eaves of their houses, and the largest stable permitted commoners would accommodate only two horses.

Although there are champions for an interpretation of either matrilineality (Kim C. S. 1965) or patrilineality (Choi 1971:32) in early Silla, the relationships demonstrated by the king lists cannot be described by simple linearity. For instance, it was common for a ruler's daughter's husband to succeed to the kingship, and about equally common for the past ruler's brother or son to succeed, or both in no necessary order. Groups of endogamous families appear to have formed corporate descent groups without a unilineal principle at all, descent being reckoned bilaterally. Examining these patterns of succession, Grayson (1976:38) concludes that "women play important connective roles in [royal] succession. A new king will have as wife a close female relative of the former king." There is another possible way to view this pattern which I discuss in the conclusion.

While archaeology cannot confirm all the details of the social structure, excavated tombs from the Silla period show a great disparity in quality and quantity of burial goods, size of grave mound, and elaboration of tomb construction, even within the city of Kyongju itself. Some unexcavated mounds are connected with specific kings in popular lore, but not all the mounds have attributed occupants, nor do all rulers have an ascribed mound. Thus, the folklore of the tombs cannot be used to argue for or against tomb size alone as an indicator of prestige and the ability to mobilize labor.

The political system

Silla grew from a confederation of six villages which joined together because of "strong enemies nearby" (Ilyon 1972 [1281]), eventually to rule the entire peninsula. Not surprisingly, this change in scale was accompanied by changes in the structure of the government. Although the precise organization is unknown, glimpses of the original pattern are possible in the various historical texts. The foundation legend of Silla recounts the selection by the village elders of an exceptional individual as leader. This council of elders seems to have persisted throughout Silla's history, institutionalized as the *hwabaek*. In this body, all important matters had to be settled by unanimous consent. Although the council originally met at four sacred outdoor localities, in the mountains or by streams, eventually a hall was constructed next to the royal palace where the deliberations of this group took place.

According to the *Samguk Sagi*, the office of chief minister was established in AD 10, and the seventeen official ranks in AD 32. While these dates may be anachronistic, there is other evidence of centralized power, and hierarchies of power, even in the first three centuries. For example, there is the use of the word *guo*, "state," in the Chinese annals. The larger *guo* comprised more than 10,000 households, and even the smallest contained 600–700 families (Parker 1890:207). These units were composed of a capital, surrounding villages, and a special village with a religious function. In each capital there was a leader, a standing army, and an official house called *kwanga* (Kim C. S. 1965:48), whose function, according to the *San Guo Chih*, was to organize corvée labor to construct forts and other public works. While we have no specific data from Korea on the gender of the various officials, Japanese chronicles indicate female court officials in a system imported from the Korean Paekche Kingdom (Barnes 1987:87). Approaching the problem of what the Chinese meant by *guo* from the vantage point of early Japan, Wheatley and See (1978:20) conclude that "generally speaking, the chroniclers of Han times seem not to have used it in connection with societies totally without manifestations of hereditary inequalities and territorially defined institutions."

We do know that Silla (or its predecessor Saro) had organized armies which invaded other native *guo*, as well as the Chinese commanderies. It is recorded that in AD 104 the state of Silchikkok, which had previously been conquered by Saro, revolted. Not only was it crushed militarily, but the population was forcefully removed to another location, a feat which requires strong central power. Perhaps the date is wrong, but archaeology suggests endemic warfare even earlier than the first century. Details of the conquest of other small states by Silla abound in the *Samguk Sagi* and *Samguk Yusa*.

Corvée labor is also evidence of state power. An edict of AD 144 ordered the extension of irrigation works to increase the amount of land under cultivation and forbade the conscription of farm workers for public works during the agricultural season. In AD 231 the office of *Taejanggun*, chief military leader, was created and at about the same time a principal administrator was installed. The *Hou Han Shu*[6] gives the titles of five ranks of village heads. Thus, the political system became increasingly centralized, with more and more differentiation of leadership positions, between the first and fifth centuries.

Symbols of power in the form of pure gold crowns hung with tinkling gold and jades, and gold belts with multiple pendants shaped as golden fish or made of curved jade jewels, have been unearthed in Silla tombs. Gilt-bronze crowns are sometimes found in lesser graves, but only the royal graves[7] have sheet-gold crowns. The shapes used in the crowns are thought by scholars to be shamanic symbols, especially the uprights in the form of stylized trees and antlers. Inscriptions on objects in the Silla tombs are rare, and none found so far names the occupant of the tomb. The traditional ascription of certain mounds to particular rulers is the only clue to the identity of the interred, other than approximate dates inferred from imported objects which can be compared against the dates in the king lists.

Tomb 98 in Kyongju is an example of a royal burial. It is unusual in being a double mound, with one major burial in each half. One of the largest of all Silla tombs, it measures 23 m high, and the diameter of each mound is about 80 m, for a combined length of 120 m. This mound is so large that before excavation it was used as a natural hill, having houses built on its flanks with alleys between them.

The south mound, containing the burial of a male, is the earlier. Only a few teeth and a mandible remained at the time of excavation, from which the occupant's age was estimated at about 60 years. He was interred wearing a small gilt-bronze crown and "other personal ornaments were also of rather poor quality" (Kim W. Y. 1976:6). A separate pit beside the coffin contained over 2,500 artifacts, including a silver crown, two gilt-bronze crowns, weapons, pottery, and glass vessels identified as of Mediterranean manufacture. The iron weapons included 30 swords, 543 spears, 380 battle axes, and more than 1,000 arrowheads. Armor was included as well, even his silver leggings.

The person buried in the north mound was female, identified by an inscription on a silver ornament on one of her ceremonial belts. She was laid to rest wearing one of the most magnificent gold crowns yet found in Korea, as well as a gold belt with pendants of the type found only in royal graves. She wore five pairs of gold bracelets, gold earrings, and three necklaces. The total weight of her gold jewelry was nearly 4 kg. A Chinese brown-glaze pottery bottle buried with her is similar to examples unearthed from Chinese graves dated to the mid-fourth century. A Sassanian-style chased silver bowl was also found with the queen, possibly one of the silver wine cups noted by the *Samguk Sagi* as a gift to Silla from China (Kim W. Y. 1981).

Assignment of Tomb 98 to a specific ruler in the king list is a matter of controversy. The earliest time estimate is by Choi (1981), who places the south mound at around AD 400. This placement implies that the male occupant was King Naemul (reign 356–402); with a 46-year reign, he would have been elderly at death. Queen Poban, the consort, as the daughter of King Michu, was eligible to rule in her own right, by the rules as they have been inferred. Kim Won-Yong (1981) selects King Nulji (reign 417–58) as the likely occupant. Nulji died at age 56 and was likewise married to a king's daughter eligible to rule. Kim and Pearson (1977) suggest King Soji (reign 479–500), but this possibility seems unlikely, since his queen predeceased him. The problem of who are the occupants of Tomb 98 continues to be a matter of controversy.

The economy

The Silla state was largely agrarian, although its foundation was probably related to trade in iron and gold (Kim W. Y. 1982). The Chinese chronicles report that "the country produces iron, and the Wei, Wa, and Mahan[8] all go to buy it; for purposes of barter the sole money exchange is iron" (Parker 1890:210). The early Chinese observed that "the land was fat and fair, and suited to the five cereals; they understand mulberry and sericulture, and the making of cloth fabric; they use oxen and horses in riding and carts" (Parker 1890:209). The arable land was considered to belong to the state itself and not to any individual, and thus a feudal system did not develop. Certain villages were expected to produce particular products, including various grades of cloth, metals, basketry, and paper (Choi 1971:66; Sohn, Kim, and Hong 1970:66). The farmers were taxed in both grain and labor, and the state kept grain warehouses from which grain was allocated in years of famine. Farmers' associations, called *ture*, are believed to date back to the Silla period (Shin 1985). Women's cooperative weaving may also have been organized into *ture* (Joe 1972). This suggestion is based on a tale about King Yuri (reign AD 24–57), who divided each *guo* into two teams, each headed by one of his daughters. A competition lasted for a month, after which the winning team was treated to a feast by the losers, followed by singing, dancing, and games (Shin 1985:6).

A thriving economy can be deduced from the sumptuary laws. Many kinds and qualities of cloth, blankets, saddles, shoes, and other manufactured products are prohibited for lower groups. However, reports of famines and floods appear in the chronicles frequently, indicating intermittent problems with the agricultural base.

The *Samguk Sagi* names "more than 90 occupational titles in the central government [among them] historians, mathematicians, doctors, astronomers, gardeners, tax collectors, metallurgists, leather and shoe specialists, butchers, sorcerers, guards, cotton and hemp specialists, wardens, druggists, warehouse keepers, sickle makers, temple officials, sewing and laundry girls, bookkeepers" (Kim C. S. 1974:36). Except in a few cases, gender is not specified, so we do not know how many of these occupations were gender-marked.

A census from the eighth century has survived, showing that the state kept careful records on all the villagers by sex and age groupings, as well as all the livestock and trees. Land was allocated with a constant amount for each adult, and was conceptualized as belonging to the state (Kim C. S. 1965). Division of labor by sex is alluded to in terms of women's weaving, but other documents make it possible to infer that both males and females were expected to work on the public labor projects.

Religion

Many important local deities were female, including the goddess of agriculture (Chee 1974:144). *Changsung*, representations of village guardian spirits, are still occasionally found in Korea (Kim T. G. 1983). They were always carved in male and female pairs, suggesting equality in the spirit world.   .

Ceremonies by and for the lower classes were conducted at the village level, and there are several reasons to suppose that women participated equally with men. In remote villages ceremonies to bless and purify the village are still conducted, presided over by a shaman, usually a woman called a *mudang* or, more politely, *manshin* (Kendall 1985). Not only could women become shamans, but women in Silla represented the majority of those who could deal with the supernatural (Kim Y. C. 1977:14), as they do at the present time. In fact female *mudang*s thrive in modern Korea. Several writers have seen in the *mudang* the reflection of a time in the past when women's roles had not been debased by Confucianism. Whether or not this is so, at the very least it can be said that women even at present are in no way excluded from ceremonial roles or contact with the supernatural on behalf of individuals or groups. Traditionally, *mudang*s even "presided in national ceremonies" (Kim Y. C. 1977:14). Even in Buddhism, women were relatively equal to men (p. 19).

Archaeological evidence of religion in Silla is limited by the fact that large ceremonial buildings did not become a part of the system until the advent of Buddhism in the sixth century. Sacred precincts called *sodo* were set aside, marked by a tall pole on which were hung a bell and a drum. Some of the same ideas may survive today in village sacred trees, and the bell and drum towers of Buddhist temples. Unfortunately, in terms of archaeology these places are invisible. Various bronze bells and bronze "ritual objects" of uncertain date have been discovered in caches, and they are often considered probable shaman's equipment (Kim W. Y. 1981). The archaeological record gives no hint as to the gender of their owner.

Gender stratification

The *Wei Chih* records disapprovingly that the people of Chinguk[9] "drew no distinctions of age and sex" (Parker 1890:209). Confucian values, strongly male dominant, date from the fifth century BC (Joe 1972:97), and influenced Chinese foreign policy at least as early as the unification of all China by the Chin. The severe laws which helped the Chin dynasty conquer all of China in the third century BC are credited to a Lord Shang, who boasted about his accomplishments. Regarding the Chin conquest of their neighbors, he reported, "Formerly, the Jung and Ti barbarians of Ch'in, in their teaching knew no difference between father and son, and they lived together in the same room. Now I have altered and regulated their moral teaching and have made distinctions between men and women" (Duyvendak 1928:214). Some of these same Ch'in barbarians might have helped populate early Chin-Han as their own traditions suggest.

Another indication of the status of women in early Silla is found in the poorly understood society of the *wonhwa*, an association of girls, which later was transformed into the male institution of the *hwarang*. Even the *hwarang*, about which much is written, is not easy to understand. It had both a military and a moral training function, as well as esthetic activities and excursions to the mountains. Meaning "flower youth," it has been seen as having a homosexual base and as shamanistic (Rutt 1961), or as basically military. It is recorded that the *wonhwa* preceded the *hwarang*, but the girls quarreled, so its functions were turned over to boys. Each of the *wonhwa* were selected by the ruler for service to the state, and had "thousands" of followers.

Although the assumption of later scholarship and the language of the translators often seem to present the government bureaucrats as men only, the institution of *wonhwa* suggests that women were also involved in the government, for the *hwarang* was seen as a training ground for government leaders. Court functionaries from the more sinicized Paekche state included women (Barnes 1987:87) which may reflect a widespread pattern in southern Korea.

The extant portion of the eighth-century census previously discussed reveals a considerably greater number of females than males at each age level, especially adult. The total population in four villages was 884, of which 194 were adult males and 248 adult females (Kim C. S. 1965). This ratio could reflect a high military death rate for males, or might result from deception in reporting. The fact that there are more females than males in all age categories may indicate that the later Korean tendency toward preference for sons had not taken root at this late date, at least not to the extent of female infanticide.

The movement of women was not restricted. Prescriptions concerning certain kinds of saddles according to a woman's rank indicate that all women rode horses. In various tales, women are described as moving around the countryside independently. At least some women were educated, for we learn that the famous general Kim Yusin was "taught and instructed by his mother." Women were accorded respect in the family: the majority of examples of filial piety concern mothers, not fathers (Kim Y. C. 1977:44). The most compelling data concern the social system: "Women must have played an important role in the Silla social system, as it is through them that males could establish their claim to the throne. In addition, three women became ruling queens in their own right" (Grayson 1976).

Archaeological finds reinforce the interpretation of relative gender equality. Many burials are in male-female pairs in the regions surrounding Kyongju, with each person receiving roughly equal treatment in separate but overlapping mounds. In an extensive study of the artifacts from 155 excavated mounds, it was concluded that 52 percent of the burials were male, based on the presence of weapons and armor (Ito

1971:25), further suggesting a lack of gender stratification. The excavated mounds may be skewed in favor of the nobility, but only a few are royal tombs.

The nature of Silla hierarchies

Although rigidly hierarchical in terms of social rankings, the structure of the Silla state is revealed as relatively simple. The social system was composed of strata to which each person was assigned at birth and from which there appears to have been no escape. Presumably the uppermost social level contained the fewest people, and the lowest level formed the bottom of a broad-based pyramid. The highest-ranking *songgol* must have been a small group to begin with, for they diminished in numbers over the centuries and died out in 654.

The political system was a reflection of the social system, and dependent upon it. One's place in the social system determined one's potential place in the political system, although there must have been fewer government offices than there were *songgol* and *chin'gol* to fill them.

The social/political system was so rigid and so well-established that it did not allow wealth to be used to usurp the place of status by birth. No incipient merchant class was permitted to develop. There were few means of becoming wealthy, because the economy was totally subservient to the state. Agricultural land was allotted by the state, and care was taken to extract the taxes and labor owed by each individual directly to the state. The mechanism for trade is unknown, but the exotic items from great distances found in high-status burials were probably limited to royalty and acquired in the form of gifts to the head of state. Sumptuary laws regulated everything from roofs to saddles, preventing persons from rising above their station in life, even if they could find the means to do it. The color-coded robes within the government must have helped to keep officials in their proper places as well. Until the extinction of the *songgol* the system seems to have maintained itself. *Chin'gol* factionalism then held sway (Kim C. S. 1969), but this was not class struggle. It was jockeying for power within the social group, not between classes. In the ninth century when the famous Chang Pogo, a commoner, created a trading empire extending to bases in China, his bid for political and social power in Korea was firmly crushed (Han 1970:115).

The shamanistic religious system had no separate hierarchy which could interfere with the power of the state. Each mountain and stream had its local deity, each village its guardian spirits. As long as there were *songgol*, the rulers may have performed rites on behalf of the state, since they were believed to be descended from gods. But there were no national

deities. The local gods were worshipped by local people in local ceremonies, a decentralized system presenting no potential threat to the state.
The power of Buddhism as an organized religion came later to Silla than
to Koguryo and Paekche. It was not until the succeeding Koryo dynasty
(936–1491) that Buddhist temples became large enough landholders to
challenge the power of the state.

Sex and age as models of hierarchy

Let us return to the notion that "egalitarian societies" may have inequalities by sex and age, and the common assumption that the model for
state-level inequality derives from the family, well articulated by Service:
"All families, of course, have internal dominant-subordinate relationships, based primarily on age and sex differences" (Service 1975:71). The
essential question is not how hierarchies came to be formed, but whether
states necessarily entail gender inequality, using pre-existing gender hierarchy as a model for other kinds of inequalities. The Silla example
suggests that gender inequality may arise well after the formation of a
state.

A parallel question can be asked regarding age hierarchy. Trigger
considers the extension of hierarchical patterns as deriving from the state.
"Another unanswered question is whether the concept of relations based
on inequality began with the state and only later was projected into family
life and the activities of other small groups or whether such relations first
developed within the nuclear or extended family and later were utilized in
the construction of the state" (Trigger 1985:59). Examining patterns of
physical punishment of children in early Egypt, Mesopotamia, and the
Aztec state, he concludes that "the specific types of relationships found
within the family in early civilizations were ones that were only possible
within the broader context of inequality of the whole society and ultimately depended on the sanctions of the state."

Although Sacks (1979) finds the rise of the state destructive to women's
positions in her African examples, she demonstrates that women could
have equality in emerging complex societies. She sees corporate kinship
groups as the protectors of "sisterly prerogatives," including partial
control of group resources. Perhaps there is an analogy here with the Silla
endogamous groups.

A basic problem with any analysis of the Silla case is the reification of
the state in the literature on cultural evolution. A typical definition of the
state includes a strong, centralized government, a ruling elite which
controls the economy, and a monopoly on force, allowing the state to
"draft soldiers, levy taxes, and exact tribute" (Flannery 1972:403). States

also involve the shift from the principle of kinship to that of territory. How, then, do we understand the Silla state? All the defining characteristics of a state were present, *except* that kinship, having become identical with the stratification system, was still an important organizational principle. (Perhaps we should think of this as an Asiatic Mode of Reproduction.)

Is Silla, then, not a state? The exercise of pigeonholing societies into typologies seems to be fruitful only in revealing anomalies, which may help to show variation in the processes of human social and political evolution. Theory suggests that ruling classes destroy kin groups. This destruction did not occur in Silla as long as the ruling classes were kin groups. If we accept Silla as a state, this example suggests that analyses which find the source of female inequality in surplus extraction (Gailey and Patterson 1987), in the elite control of production (Muller 1987), in militarism (Rohrlich 1980), or even in "generalized coercion" (Trigger 1985), are not sufficient. State-level political and economic power can coexist with relative gender equality, as long as kinship is the basic organizing principle of the elites.

Theories about state formation have been closely entwined with supposed male activities: warfare, the managerial system, and long-distance trade. Archaeology has compounded this bias by interpreting finds differentially according to gender and making unwarranted assumptions, as Shennan (1987:372) points out regarding the exchange of women. Trigger (1984:292) reminds us that "archaeological interpretations are subtly influenced by social and personal preconceptions of reality that preclude an awareness of alternative explanations which might encourage formal testing or of the actual limits within which a generalization holds true."

And what of the enigmatic burial in the north mound of Tomb 98? Based on the archaeological evidence alone, it would seem that this woman was the ruler, and the male in the south mound was merely a military leader. One could argue that they were corulers with complementary positions, or that the woman alone was the political/religious head of the state. Later Confucian (*Samguk Sagi*) and Buddhist (*Samguk Yusa*) scholarship, especially in the context of the Koryo dynasty, would both have preferred to suppress the fact of women rulers in earlier times.[10] The three queens that *were* recorded in the king lists had no husband to whom the kingship could be ascribed. Genealogies of the relevant period – variously placed from the mid-fourth to the mid-fifth centuries – show that kings' daughters almost always became queens. For example, the wife of Nulji, the nineteenth king (reign 417–58), was the daughter, granddaughter, and great-granddaughter of ruling kings (and queens), and her daughter's son became the twenty-second king. Interpreting the queens as reigning themselves, or as corulers, is consistent with these data.

The specific puzzle of the queen in Tomb 98 may never be solved, but it is evident that Silla had found a way to create a stable state with a single hierarchical system. Women had always had a place in society equal to men, and there was no room in the structure for social climbing. Adding gender stratification might have upset the balance.

NOTES

I would like to thank the Academy for Korean Studies and the International Cultural Society of Korea for grants in 1983 and 1986 which allowed me to do some of the research for this chapter.

1   *Samguk Sagi* (History of the Three Kingdoms) and *Samguk Yusa* (Memorabilia of the Three Kingdoms) were compiled in the twelfth and thirteenth centuries respectively on the basis of more nearly contemporary documents which have since been lost. *Samguk Sagi*, by Kim Pu-sik, is strongly influenced by the Confucian tradition of history writing in China, and is full of moralizing lessons. Buddhist influences on *Samguk Yusa* by Ilyon, the monk, are just as clear, with an entire section dedicated to Buddhist miracles. However, the latter is accepted by Korean historians as more accurate and more "Korean" (Joe 1972:207).

2   The recorded ruling queens are Sondok (reign 632–47), Chindok (reign 647–54), and Chinsong (reign 887–97).

3   The *Wei Shu* contains a section on the Three Kingdoms, *San Guo Chih*, which is the earliest written record about the southern part of the Korean peninsula. It was written by the Chinese historian Chen Shou in AD 297 (Kim Y. C. 1977:40). It was translated by Parker (1890), but no distinction is made between the translation and the author's comments.

4   The Han dynasty of China is written with a different character than the Han of the Korean Three Hans. The two should not be confused.

5   The pit-burial people are sometimes associated with refugees from Ko-Chosun, the state centered on the Taedong river which was conquered and replaced by Lolang (Sohn, Kim, and Hong 1970:40).

6   The *Hou Han Shu* is a Chinese historical work about the Later Han dynasty (AD 25 to 220), written by Fan-yeh.

7   Graves with sheet-gold crowns are considered "royal" by definition. So far ten such graves have been excavated.

8   The *Wei* were northern Chinese, the *Wa* were from the Japanese archipelago, and the *Mahan* occupied the southwestern part of the Korean peninsula.

9   Chinguk was on the southern border of the Chinese colonies in Korea.

10 "The tradition of the sociology of knowledge mandates two ears, a first to hear what the authors of texts want to tell you, a second to hear what they do not want to tell you" (Rudolph 1987:735).

REFERENCES

Barnes, Gina 1987 The Role of the *Be* in the Formation of the Yamato State. In *Specialization, Exchange, and Complex Societies*. E. M. Brumfiel and T. K. Earle, eds., pp. 86–101. Cambridge: Cambridge University Press.

Chee, Changboh 1974 Shamanism and Folk Beliefs of the Koreans. In *Traditional Korea, Theory and Practice*. A. C. Nahm, ed., pp. 141–57. Kalamazoo: Center for Korean Studies, Western Michigan University.

Choi, Byung-hyan 1981 The Evolution and Chronology of the Wooden Chamber Tomb of the Old Silla Period. *Hanguk Kogo Hakbo* 10–11:137–228. (In Korean.)

Choi, Hochin 1971 *The Economic History of Korea*. Seoul: The Freedom Press.

Conkey, Margaret and Janet Spector 1984 Archaeology and the Study of Gender. *Advances in Archaeological Method and Theory* 7:1–38.

Divale, William and Marvin Harris 1976 Population, Warfare and the Male Supremacist Complex. *American Anthropologist* 78:521–38.

Draper, Patricia 1975 !Kung Women: Contrasts in Sexual Egalitarianism in Foraging and Sedentary Contexts. In *Toward an Anthropology of Women*. Rayna Reiter, ed., pp. 77–109. New York: Monthly Review Press.

Duyvendak, J. J. L. 1928 *The Book of Lord Shang*. Chicago: University of Chicago Press.

Earle, Timothy 1987 Chiefdoms in Archaeological and Ethnohistorical Perspective. *Annual Review of Anthropology* 16:279–308.

Engle, Anita 1976 Glass Making in China. *Readings in Glass History* 6–7:1–38.

Fee, Elizabeth 1974 The Sexual Politics of Victorian Social Anthropology. In *Clio's Consciousness Raised*. M. Hartman and L. Banner, eds., pp. 86–102. New York: Harper Books.

Flannery, Kent V. 1972 The Cultural Evolution of Civilizations. *Annual Review of Ecology and Systematics* 3:399–426.

Gailey, Christine W. 1985 The State of the State in Anthropology. *Dialectical Anthropology* 9(1–4):65–90.

  1987 Culture Wars: Resistance to State Formation. In *Power Relations and State Formation*. Thomas C. Patterson and Christine W. Gailey, eds., pp. 35–56. Washington, DC: American Anthropological Association.

Gailey, Christine W. and Thomas C. Patterson 1987 Power Relations and State Formation. In *Power Relations and State Formation*. Thomas C. Patterson and Christine W. Gailey, eds., pp. 1–26. Washington, DC: American Anthropological Association.

Gilman, A. 1981 The Development of Social Stratification in Bronze Age Europe. *Current Anthropology* 22:1–8.

Grayson, James H. 1976 Some Structural Patterns of the Royal Families of Ancient Korea. *Korea Journal* 16(6):27–32.

Han, Woo-keun 1970 *The History of Korea*. Lee Kyng-shik, trans. Grafton K. Mintz, ed. Seoul: The Eul-Yoo Publishing Company.

Harris, Marvin 1977 *Cannibals and Kings: The Origins of Cultures*. New York: Random House.

Ilyon 1972 *Samguk Yusa: Legends and History of the Three Kingdoms* (1281). Tae-hung Ha and Grafton Mintz, trans. Seoul: Yonsei University Press.

Ito, Akio 1971 *Zur Chronologie der Frühsillazeitlichen Gräber in Südkorea*. Munich: Bayerische Akademie der Wissenschaften. New Series, Vol. 71.

Joe, Wanne 1972 *Traditional Korea: A Cultural History*. Seoul: Chungang University Press.

Kendall, Laurel 1985 *Shamans, Housewives, and Other Restless Spirits*. Honolulu: University of Hawaii Press.

Kim, Chae-kuei and Eunchang Yi 1975 *A Report on the Excavation of the Tombs at Hwangnam-dong, Kyongju.* Yongnam, Korea: Yongnam University Museum, Monograph 1.

Kim, Chong-Sun 1965 The Emergence of Multi-Centered Despotism in the Silla Kingdom: A Study of the Origin of Factional Struggles in Korea. Ph.D. Dissertation, University of Washington.

1969 Sources of Cohesion and Fragmentation in the Silla Kingdom. *Journal of Korean Studies* 1(1):41–72.

1974 Slavery in Silla and Its Sociological and Economic Implications. In *Traditional Korea, Theory and Practice.* A. C. Nahm, ed., pp. 29–43. Kalamazoo: Center for Korean Studies, Western Michigan University.

1977 The Kolp'um System: Basis for Sillan Social Stratification. *Journal of Korean Studies* 1(2):43–69.

Kim, T'ae-gon 1983 A Study on the Rite of *Changsung*, Korea's Totem Pole. *Korea Journal* 23(3):4–19.

Kim, Won-Yong 1974 *Archaeology in Korea, An Annual Review of Korean Archaeology 1.* Seoul: Seoul National University, Department of Archaeology and Anthropology.

1976 *Archaeology in Korea 3.* Seoul: Seoul National University, Department of Archaeology and Anthropology.

1981 *Recent Archaeological Discoveries in the Republic of Korea.* Tokyo: UNESCO.

1982 Kyongju: The Homeland of Korean Culture. *Korea Journal* 22(9):25–32.

Kim, Won-Yong and Richard Pearson 1977 Three Royal Tombs: New Discoveries in Korean Archaeology. *Archaeology* 30(5):302–13.

Kim, Yung-Chung 1977 *Women of Korea: A History from Ancient Times to 1945.* Seoul: Ehwa University Press.

Leacock, Eleanor 1978 Women's Status in Egalitarian Society: Implications for Social Evolution. *Current Anthropology* 19(2):247–75.

Lee, Nam-kyu 1982 A Study of Early Iron Age Culture in South Korea. *Hanguk Kogo Hakbo* 13:39–59. (In Korean with English summary.)

Lerner, Gerda 1986 *The Creation of Patriarchy.* New York: Oxford University Press.

Muller, Viana 1987 Kin Reproduction and Elite Accumulation in the Archaic States of Northwest Europe. In *Power Relations and State Formation.* Thomas C. Patterson and Christine W. Gailey, eds., pp. 81–97. Washington, DC: American Anthropological Association.

Ortner, Sherry B. 1981 Gender and Sexuality in Hierarchical Societies: The Case of Polynesia and Some Comparative Implications. In *Sexual Meanings: The Cultural Construction of Gender and Sexuality.* Sherry B. Ortner and Harriet Whitehead, eds., pp. 359–409. New York: Cambridge University Press.

Parker, E. H. 1890 On Race Struggles in Korea. *Transactions of the Asiatic Society of Japan* 18(2):157–228.

Rapp, Rayna R. 1977 The Search for Origins: Unraveling the Threads of Gender Hierarchy. *Critique of Anthropology* 3(9–10):5–24.

Renfrew, Colin 1982 Socio-economic Change in Ranked Societies. In *Ranking, Resource, and Exchange.* Colin Renfrew and Stephen Shennan, eds., pp. 1–8. New York: Cambridge University Press.

Rohrlich, Ruby 1980 State Formation in Sumer and the Subjugation of Women. *Feminist Studies* 6(1):76–102.

Rosaldo, Michelle Zimbalist and Louise Lamphere, eds. 1974 *Women, Culture and Society*. Stanford, CA: Stanford University Press.

Rousseau, Jerome 1985 The Ideological Prerequisites of Inequality. In *Development and Decline, the Evolution of Sociopolitical Organization*. H. Claessen, P. van de Velde, and M. S. Smith, eds., pp. 36–45. South Hadley, MA: Bergin and Garvey Publishers.

Rudolph, Susanne Hoeber 1987 Presidential Address: State Formation in Asia – Prolegomenon to a Comparative Study. *Journal of Asian Studies* 46(4):731–46.

Rutt, Richard 1961 The Flower Boys of Silla. *Transactions of the Korea Branch of the Royal Asiatic Society* 37:1–61.

Sacks, Karen 1979 *Sisters and Wives: The Past and Future of Sexual Equality*. · Westport, CT: Greenwood Press.

Sagan, Eli 1985 *At the Dawn of Tyranny: The Origins of Individualism, Political Oppression and the State*. New York: Alfred A. Knopf.

Sanday, Peggy Reeves 1981 *Female Power and Male Dominance: On the Origins of Sexual Inequality*. New York: Cambridge University Press.

Service, Elman 1975 *Origins of the State and Civilization: The Process of Cultural Evolution*. New York: W. W. Norton.

Shennan, S. J. 1987 Trends in the Study of Later European Prehistory. *Annual Review of Anthropology* 16:365–82.

Shin, Yong-ha 1985 Social History of the Ture Community and Nongak Musik (I). *Korea Journal* 25(3):4–17.

Sohn, Powkee, Chol-choon Kim, and Yi-sup Hong 1970 *The History of Korea*. Seoul: UNESCO.

Tiffany, Sharon 1979 Woman, Power and the Anthropology of Politics: A Review. *International Journal of Women's Studies* 2:430–42.

Trigger, Bruce 1984 Archaeology at the Crossroads. *Annual Review of Anthropology* 13:275–300.

1985 Generalized Coercion and Inequality: The Basis of State Power in Early Civilization. In *Development and Decline, the Evolution of Sociopolitical Organization*. H. Claessen, P. van de Velde, and M. S. Smith, eds., pp. 46–61. South Hadley, MA: Bergin and Garvey Publishers.

Wheatley, Paul and Thomas See 1978 *From Court to Capital: A Tentative Interpretation of the Origins of the Japanese Urban Tradition*. Chicago: University of Chicago Press.

Zagarell, Allen 1986 Trade, Women, Class and Society in Ancient Western Asia. *Current Anthropology* 27(5):415–30.

14   Gender hierarchy in Burma: cultural, social, and psychological dimensions

Melford E. Spiro

Introduction

This chapter[1] addresses the question of how we determine the shape of a social hierarchy in any domain when, instead of sustaining a relationship of structural homology, the relevant dimensions of social relations in that domain – cultural, social, and psychological – are either orthogonal to, inconsistent with, or in opposition to each other. That is the case, as we shall see, with respect to gender hierarchy in Burma.[2]

Among the many cultural propositions that govern the Burmese domains of sex and gender relations, two subsets are distinguishable by the fact that they are seemingly anomalous. One is anomalous because although many of its propositions are inconsistent with the social system of gender relations they are nevertheless held by the male actors with strong conviction. The second subset is anomalous because although most of its propositions are highly threatening to the male actors, nevertheless they too are held by them with strong conviction and also motivate their behavior, even though they are either empirically undemonstrable or else demonstrably false.

The propositions comprising the first subset proclaim the innate superiority of males over females; collectively, these propositions comprise a cultural system which I shall designate as the "Ideology of the Superior Male." The propositions comprising the second subset claim that in many ways females are highly dangerous for males; collectively, they comprise a second cultural system which I shall designate as the "Ideology of the Dangerous Female."[3]

I shall now proceed as follows. First, I shall describe the Ideology of the Superior Male. Second, I shall describe the social system of gender relations. Third, I shall describe the Ideology of the Dangerous Female. Finally, I shall pose (but not resolve) the problem which this sociocultural configuration presents for the determination of gender hierarchy.

A cultural system of gender hierarchy: the Ideology of the Superior Male

According to this cultural system males are superior to females in virtue both of their sexual anatomy and a psychospiritual entity known as *hpoun*. As for the first, the penis is a "noble" organ, a "golden flower," while the vagina is an "ignoble," polluting organ. It is for that reason that "Even a male dog," as the traditional maxim puts it, "is superior to a human female." We shall return to the issue of sexual anatomy in some detail when we examine the second cultural system.

Hpoun, the second mark of male superiority, is an ineffable essence which, except for a famous female disciple of the Buddha, is possessed only by males. Although usually translated as "glory," *hpoun* is perhaps more accurately glossed by that overworked word, "charisma." In either event, since males alone are born with *hpoun*, they are innately "higher" than females in three important ways: intellectually, morally, and spiritually.

That males are *intellectually* superior to females is attested to by Burmese ethnopsychology. Intelligence is determined by (among other things) the size of the intestine; and whereas the male intestine is 32 m in length, the female intestine is only 28 m. The lower intelligence of women is perhaps best summed up in the well-known proverb, "If a woman had no nose, she would eat excrement."

The *moral* superiority of males is evidenced by the prevalence among females of three moral defects: greed, "evil practices," and lust. In respect to greed, a columnist for the Burmese paper, *Bahosi* (1961), expressed the ideology very well when he commented that "women are never satisfied with their gold and silver ornaments, however valuable they may be. Although they may be worth hundreds of thousands of *kyat*, they still want more. This is the nature of women. They are full of greed."

That females are prone to "evil practices" is taught by a variety of traditional texts. To take but one example, according to the *Dhammathat* (a compendium of Burmese customary law) these practices include their consumption of intoxicating liquor, gadding about the entrance to the house, habitual visiting of others, causing their husbands to become angry, neglecting their domestic duties, and taking lovers (Maung Maung 1963:50).

Taking lovers is not only an "evil practice," but it is also an expression of another of the three moral defects of females – lust. Although, on the one hand, the libido is regarded as the most powerful of all biological drives, on the other hand it is regarded, in accordance with Buddhist teachings, as a "base" drive. Hence, just as Buddhist monks are moral virtuosi because of their ability to control their sexual passion, females are morally defective because theirs is virtually insatiable.

The latter proposition is taught by a variety of traditional texts, both Buddhist and secular. Among the former, the "Culla-Paduma Jataka" is perhaps the most prominent not only because the Jatakas (tales of the previous rebirths of the Buddha, see *The Jataka* 1957) are the most popular of the Buddhist texts, but also, and more especially, because this particular tale forms the basis for a famous drama in the repertoire of the classical Burmese theater. The drama recounts the story of a princess who falls passionately in love with and seduces a male who has no arms, legs, nose, or ears. One of the characters accounts for this seemingly bizarre behavior of the princess by observing that the strength of the female libido is "as wide as the ocean and as intense as a roaring fire" (Htin Aung 1937:appendix v). *The Lokaniti* (a popular compendium of Burmese secular lore) is equally insistent on this point, claiming that a woman's sexual passion is eight times as strong as a man's (*The Lokaniti* 1962:355).

The third mark of male superiority, *spiritual* superiority, is attested to by men's special place in Buddhist teaching and practice. Thus, the Buddhist initiation ceremony (*hsimbyu*) and induction into the monastic order are both restricted to males, and rebirth as a male is a *sine qua non* for the attainment of the highest levels of spiritual achievement: saint-hood, Buddhahood, and nirvana.

Having now summarized the major tenets of the Ideology of the Superior Male, it may be remarked that this cultural system draws a practical moral from the putative fact of male superiority. Since males are "nobler" than females, it is only proper that they should have authority over them. In particular, husbands should have authority over wives, whose duty it is to serve and obey them. The duties of the wife are summarized by the *Dhammathat*:

Rising from bed before her husband rises; retiring to bed after he has done so; taking his instructions for her day's work; carrying out his behests according to his wishes; speaking to him in a pleasant and affectionate way; and providing against the inclemencies of weather for the husband's comfort. (Maung Maung 1963:50)

As was already mentioned, this cultural system is strongly internalized by males as a personal belief system. The most important measure of its internalization is, perhaps, the readiness with which they embrace what is, to our minds, its *reductio ad absurdum*. Thus, if I would challenge the notion of male superiority, the males would quote the maxim mentioned above: "Even a male dog is superior to a female human." This maxim, it might be added, is accepted by many women as well.

Less dramatically, if more frequently, evidence for the internalization of this cultural system is demonstrated whenever males are asked to explain some difference between their behavior and that of females. Thus, for example, men observe that women rarely engage in political and religious discussions because, given their lower intelligence, their knowledge of such matters is limited. The same explanation, they say, accounts for the fact that so many more women than men firmly believe in witches, spirits, shamans, and other practitioners of the occult. As the *Bahosi* columnist mentioned above put it, "a woman is a woman after all. However developed she may be mentally, she cannot escape the snare of deception." Evidence for the internalization of the other descriptive propositions of this system, those regarding female lust, will be presented below in the discussion of the second system.

The normative dimension of this cultural system – the males' authority over females – is internalized just as strongly as its descriptive dimension. In interviews, men repeatedly stressed that the paramount duty of a woman is to serve her husband and to satisfy his needs. Thus, she should have his meals prepared when he returns from the fields, see that his clothes are washed and fresh when he needs them, and more generally make his welfare her own concern. Above all, she should respect him and obey his wishes. Moreover, many men say (though I never saw it practiced) that if necessary, a husband may beat his wife in order to guarantee his authority.

Gender hierarchy in the social system

Burmese women, it is probably accurate to say, enjoy a higher social status than any other group of women in Asia. Indeed, until the recent dramatic changes in the status of women in the West, Burmese women arguably enjoyed a greater degree of economic, legal, and social equality than Western women as well.

In the village productive economy – mostly wet rice agriculture – the sexual division of labor is more or less equal: males do the planting, females the transplanting, and both do the harvesting. In the non-agricultural economy, in which achievement rather than ascription is the basis for recruitment to economic statuses, males are predominant in craft occupations, females in retail trade – village hawkers and the proprietors of the stalls in urban bazaars being preponderantly female. Moreover, some women are highly successful entrepreneurs in both the manufacturing and importing sectors of the urban economy, and others are equally successful in such professions as medicine and university teaching.

In the legal system, too, females are the equals of males. Thus, for example, women may own property in their own name, the family estate is inherited both by sons and daughters, husband and wife own all property jointly, and so on. Similarly, girls (like boys) may enter freely into marriage, and wives as well as husbands may initiate divorce. Indeed, in some respects, women have the "upper hand," as the Burmese say, in these matters. Thus, it is the bride, not the groom, who receives a marriage payment, and it is the girl's hand, not the boy's, that is sought in marriage.[4]

But that is not all. Burma is remarkably free from the antagonism between the sexes that characterizes many societies with similar ideologies of sex and gender (cf. the marked sexual antagonism found in New Guinea, Poole and Herdt 1982; Herdt, this volume). Moreover, social interaction between males and females is marked by a degree of freedom and joviality, including sexual banter (Spiro 1977:216–18) that is rare in many, perhaps most, societies. Finally, Burmese women are free from the numerous disabilities suffered by women both to the west of Burma, in India and the Middle East, and to the east, in China. Thus, the veil, purdah, child betrothal, female infanticide, footbinding, suttee, the prohibition of widow remarriage, and the like are all absent from Burma.

This picture of sexual equality does not, however, hold for three other domains – government, family, and religion[5] – not at any rate in their formal dimensions. Let us now examine the formal (structural) gender hierarchy in each of these domains, beginning with the first.

Since by cultural prescription the exercise of authority (*awza*) is a male prerogative, any status that is endowed with authority is, by cultural ascription, a male monopoly. Thus, in the macro-social system, all political offices, from chief of state to village headman, are typically open only to males.[6] For the same reason, in the microsocial system of the family, authority is invested in the status of husband, not of wife, a point to which we shall return.

The structural subordination of females is just as marked in Buddhism which, both as a social institution and a cultural system, is of overriding importance in Burmese society (Spiro 1982). Within Buddhism, the most honorific status, and the one with the highest prestige (*goun*) in the entire social system, is that of monk. A monk is called a *hpoungyi*, "a [person with] great *hpoun*." Since by cultural attribution males alone possess *hpoun* (charisma), recruitment to the Buddhist monastic order, the very embodiment of what might be called "institutionalized charisma," is restricted to males. Women can become nuns, but the status of nun is one of very low prestige.

The subordinate position of females both in the formal political system and in the normative religious system does not, however, tell the whole story. Although, because they are typically barred from office, women rarely exercise authority in the political system, they may nevertheless wield considerable influence and power. First, they often exert influence on the behavior of their office-holding husbands. This pattern may occur both at the highest level of government – thus, Supayalat, the last queen of Burma, exerted considerable power over her consort, King Thibaw – and at the lowest, as in the case of wives of village headmen. Second, because of their husbands' structural position, wives of government officials may exercise considerable extra-structural power (*ana*) in their dealings with their husbands' subordinates. It is well known, for example, that judicial decisions often depend on the size of the "gift" that a claimant offers the wife of a magistrate or judge. In short, as a result of the wife's assumed influence over her husband, she has considerable (albeit extra-structural) power, as the deferential manner and demeanor of ordinary citizens indicate.

Returning now to the religious domain, it may be remarked that there is at least one magico-religious status, that of shaman (*nat kadaw*), in which females enjoy considerable structural influence. An achieved status, the shaman is the ritual specialist in the Burmese spirit (*nat*) cult, a religion which exists side by side, if somewhat uncomfortably, with Buddhism. As an otherworldly religion, Buddhism does not specialize in the mundane problems of human life – illness, cattle loss, barrenness, and a host of others – and this gap is filled by the spirit cult, which attributes these problems to the action of a certain class of spirits (*nats*).

By trafficking with the offended spirits who cause the above-mentioned problems, shamans (so it is believed) not only can prevent their occurrence, but also can remove them after they occur. In consequence, although shamans have low, if not negative, prestige (*goun*), they have considerable influence on laymen in respect of such matters. In principle a shaman may be either male or female, but in fact almost all are female. Even small villages have at least one shaman, and the reputation of some of them may extend to many parts of the country.[7]

In the domestic domain, as in the political domain, the distinction between the formal and informal structure is again crucial. As has already been noted, authority in the family is invested in the husband. His authority is manifested both instrumentally and symbolically.

Instrumentally, the husband's authority is manifested in the wife's waiting upon him: she cooks and serves his food, washes and irons his clothes, obeys his commands, and so on. Symbolically, too, the husband's authority is manifested in a variety of ways. Thus, for example, the husband is designated as "the lord (*nat*) who lives in the front part of the house," and although he may not actually reside in the front, his authority (as well as his *hpoun*) is symbolically represented in other spatial and architectural forms. Thus, the eastern, or "noble," side of the house – the side where the shrine for the Buddha is kept – is reserved for the husband (and other males), while the western, or "ignoble," side is reserved for the wife (and other females). Similarly, if a house has more than one room, the floor of the eastern room is made of long (superior) planks, while that of the western room is made of short (inferior) ones.

The husband's authority (and *hpoun*) is symbolically expressed most importantly in the ritual in which the wife pays him homage by physical prostration, kneeling before him and touching her forehead to the ground. Known as *shikkhou*, this ritual is otherwise performed only by commoners for royalty, religious devotees for the Buddha and his representatives (monks and pagodas), and children for parents and teachers.

It must now be emphasized that despite their domination in the *formal* structure of the family, males are typically subordinate to females in the *informal* structure. In short, although in virtue of his status as a male it is the husband who has authority (*awza*) and consequently prestige (*goun*), in virtue of her influence over him it is the wife who most frequently has power (*ana*). This generalization rests on three kinds of data: informants' reports, behavioral observations, and psychological findings. Let us examine each in turn.

Informants of both sexes view the wife, not the husband, as the dominant partner in the marriage. When villagers were asked to identify the dominant partner in their own marriage, they usually (and not unexpectedly) affirmed the ideology of male superiority by naming the husband. But when they were asked to name the dominant spouse in other marriages, they mostly (though not unanimously) named the wife. This finding was replicated when, in two other villages, the elders were asked to name the dominant spouse in the marriages in their villages; and it was replicated yet again when a four-member panel from Yeigyi (two males and two females) were asked to identify the dominant spouse in a randomly selected sample of marriages. Since in the latter case, however, the wife was identified as the dominant partner in only a small majority of the marriages, some additional comment is required.

In Burmese marriages, including those characterized by informants as "husband dominated," the wife literally holds the purse strings, as she does in most of southeast Asia (Geertz 1961:123; Blanchard 1958:436; Steinberg 1959:79), and if the husband needs or wants spending money he must request it from her. Although by Western, let alone Middle Eastern, standards, such a marriage would be characterized as "wife dominated," that is not the case according to Burmese standards. In short, most of the marriages designated by the village panel as "husband dominated" would, by the cultural standards of many other societies, by judged as "wife dominated."

It is useful to tarry over the wife's control of the disposable family income because it offers important insights into the relationship between Burmese spouses. As the men view it, the women hold the purse strings because a man expects his wife to assume the financial responsibility in their marriage. The women, however, view this arrangement as a mark of the husband's dependency on the wife. Men, so the women claim, are irresponsible, somewhat like children, and were it not for the wife's control of the family income the husband would squander their resources on women, gambling, and drink. In short, it is from her enlightened self-interest that the wife holds the purse strings.

But the wife's control of the family finances is not motivated by self-interest alone; it is also motivated, so some women claim, by compassion for the husband. For if, they explain, the husband squandered the family's financial resources, he would then have to work all the harder to support his family, and the wife wishes to spare him that burden. It is hardly necessary to comment on the wife's condescension toward the husband implicit in such an attitude, or on her perception of him as dependent upon her. The condescension is not as strong, however, as that of the Javanese wife of her putatively financially irresponsible and incompetent husband (Jay 1969:92).

That the wife is the dominant partner in most Burmese marriages is the view not only of the Burmese themselves, but also of foreign observers, both early and late. Thus, one nineteenth-century commentator holds that "women rule the roost in Burma" (Forbes 1878:56), while an early twentieth-century commentator claims that the wife "is the predominant partner" in the marriage (Hall 1913:239). These comments are echoed in the observations of a contemporary ethnographer: "In theory and in public," Nash (1965:253–4) writes of two villages in Upper Burma, "the husband is supposedly dominant, but this dominance is so tenuous, so indefinite and ambiguous that its social visibility is virtually nil." My observations are entirely consistent with these commentators. In addition to controlling the purse strings, the wife is also the controlling influence in many other aspects of her husband's behavior including the type of clothing he wears, the kind of food he eats, the friends he brings home, where and how often he spends his time away from home, and the like.

Even more important perhaps is that these (and other) behavioral manifestations of female dominance are expressions of deep-seated underlying emotional attitudes. This is shown, in the first place, by the emotional salience of the Ideology of the Morally Dangerous Female, an ideology whose basic thesis is the female domination of males, including that of wives in their relationship with their husbands. It is shown in the second place by the findings of psychological (projective) tests, both the Rorschach and the TAT (Thematic Apperception Test). In the case of the TAT, males and females alike tell stories in which men have little control over women, and the men perceive women as difficult to control or please, and they perceive themselves as relatively helpless to cope with female infidelity or desertion (Steele nda:4). Similarly, the male Rorschach protocols suggest that males are especially anxious about mothers and other females, and show a "lack of independence from female or maternal figures" (Steele nda:5). Conversely, "females appear in many ways to be psychologically more powerful than males" (Steele ndb: 6).

The wife's dominance is, however, almost always subtle. A blatantly dominant wife is intolerable for most men – it is a sign that he has lost his authority – and such behavior almost invariably leads to divorce. Publicly, and even privately, the wife shows the husband the deference that his structural authority and *hpoun* require. Subtle or not, however, the wife's dominance reflects the fact that the husband is dependent upon her, both instrumentally and emotionally. As one female informant put it, the husband expects the wife to be sister, friend, and mother all in one, and in her role as "mother" he expects her to be nurturant, thereby permitting him to be dependent. Her observations are consistent with the TAT results which indicate that males possess strong "oral dependent and nurturant needs."

Hence, what from one perspective may be viewed as the husband's domination *by* the wife, may from another perspective be viewed as his dependence *on* the wife. It is not that the dependency needs of Burmese males are stronger than those of other males – and they are probably less strong than those, for example, of Japanese (Doi 1973) or Javanese (Geertz 1961; Jay 1969) males – but they are strong enough, and, as in the case of many other societies, it is the wife who importantly satisfies, or is expected to satisfy, those needs.

Let us now summarize this discussion of gender hierarchy in the Burmese social system. First, across all domains, males are structurally superior to females in respect of ascribed status marked by authority or charisma. Second, in the case of other ascribed statuses, females are more or less the structural equals of males. Third, across all domains, when status recruitment is a function of achievement, females are frequently the equals of males, and sometimes they surpass them. Fourth, in some domains, most notably politics and religion, females have considerable power and influence, structural in the latter domain, extra-structural in the former. Finally, in the domestic domain, females typically control males through their extra-structural power and influence, usually because the males are psychologically dependent upon them.

A cultural system of gender hierarchy: the Ideology of the Dangerous Female

If now we consider both the cultural system described in the previous section (the Ideology of the Superior Male), as well as the social system, it should be apparent that the shape of the Burmese gender hierarchy is not unilinear, but curvilinear or U-shaped. That is, its shape can be delineated by a scale which, based on the cultural system and one structural dimension of the social system, proceeds from a relationship of male superiority and dominance; thence, based on a second structural dimension of the social system, to a relationship of more-or-less sexual equality; followed, based on the informal dimension of the social system, by a relationship of female dominance and control, determined in large measure by male emotional dependency on females.

But the delineation of that scale is not yet complete, for we have still to describe its end point, a second cultural system – the Ideology of the Dangerous Female – which is the polar opposite of the first system. This system comprises two subsystems: the Morally Dangerous Female and the Sexually Dangerous Female.

First, we consider the subsystem of the Morally Dangerous Female. Although not explicitly mentioned in the *Dhammathat*, an especially dangerous moral defect of females is their treachery. Women, according to a well-known proverb, are one of the "four things [together with thieves, rulers, and the boughs of trees] that cannot be trusted." According to another proverb, women, together with Brahmans and rivers, are one of the "three crooked things." And according to *The Lokaniti* (1962:279) women, like fire, water, serpents, and royal kinsmen, "should be approached with great circumspection; for they may take life in an instant." These secular traditions are supported by the sacred tradition of Buddhism. The following quotation from the "Andabhuta Jataka" is typical of the genre:

> 'Tis nature's law that rivers wind;
> Trees grow of wood by law of kind;
> And, given opportunity,
> All women work iniquity.

> A sex composed of wickedness and guile,
> Unknowable, uncertain as the path
> Of fishes in the water, – womankind
> Hold truth for falsehood, falsehood for the truth!
>
> (*The Jataka* 1957)

Female treachery is dangerous for males because it is deployed to usurp the males' right of domination and control. If they cannot achieve power over males by fair means, females use devious techniques, including witch-craft. Although males may also practice witchcraft, there is less to fear from them because although very few males are witches, one out of every seven households is said to contain a female witch (Spiro 1974: Chapter 2).

While witchcraft is particularly dangerous, females more frequently employ other treacherous techniques to achieve control over males. Most especially, they may exploit their sex and sexuality for that end. One tech-nique by which, according to this ideology, a woman may dominate her husband is to insert a betel nut in her vagina, grinding it up after it has absorbed her vaginal secretions, preferably menstrual blood, and feeding it to him together with his food. Since the husband thereby loses much of his power, her control over him is assured.

Most often, however, a woman does not resort to such an extreme measure for she can usually achieve the same result by means of her sexual allure. Thus, a woman need only employ "sexual wiles" – tradition enumerates no less than forty (!) (Maung Maung 1963:11–12) – to entice her husband into subjugation. That being the case, it is prudent for any man to heed such proverbs as, "Don't show affection to your wife, lest she take advantage of you," or "A woman is like an ox; one should not display affection to either."

The epitomization of the sexually enticing, male-subjugating female is represented by a class of female spirits known as *ouktazaun*. Because of sins committed in a previous existence, these spirits must guard the buried treasure of the future Buddha. Some of them, however, attempt to escape their lonely fate by assuming the guise of an alluring woman and enticing a man to fall in love with them. Should the victim of such a spirit, unable to resist her attraction, have sexual intercourse with her, he dies and must then share her task (Spiro 1974:165–7). Even, however, if he resists her allure, he leads a living death because his sexual obsession with her drives him mad (Spiro 1974:174–94).

But female sexuality may be harmful to men not only because immoral women may intentionally employ sexual techniques as a means to control and dominate them, but also, and perhaps more important, because female sexuality, regardless of a woman's intentions, is intrinsically dangerous for men. That at any rate is the message of the ideology of the Sexually Dangerous Female. According to the latter subsystem, women possess three sexual characteristics – an extraordinarily powerful libido, a polluting vagina, and sexual allure – any one of which is dangerous for men. Let us examine each of these characteristics in turn, beginning with the first. Since, however, the intensity of the female libido was already described in the previous section, here we shall deal only with the threat which it poses for the males.

That threat, allegedly, consists in the fact that their powerful libido drives the females to sexual infidelity, yet another expression, albeit unintentional, of their threat to male authority and control. This proposition is enunciated by many traditional texts, including the drama of Paduma described previously. Thus, for example, in reflecting on the fact that his wife seduced a physically grotesque lover, Paduma proclaims that the libido of women is so strong that "they will [even] kill their rightful husbands the moment they want a new lover. Their lust blinds them ... They receive all, just as a roaring fire receives all rubbish ... One is more certain of one's ability to drink up all the waters of the ocean, than of the faithfulness of one's wife" (Htin Aung 1937:231).

Buddhist teachings are no different. Consider, for example, the following quotation from the "Andabhuta Jataka":

You couldn't be certain of a woman, even if you had her inside you and always walked about with her. No woman is ever faithful to one man alone. As greedily as cows seek pastures new, women, unsated, yearn for mate on mate. (*The Jataka* 1957)

Females are sexually dangerous for males not only because of their sexual physiology, but also because of their sexual anatomy. Briefly, the vagina is a polluting organ, and any contact with it is a threat to a male's physical strength, his sexual potency, and his spiritual power. Vaginal discharges, particularly menstrual blood, are especially polluting. Although direct contact with the vagina is necessary to endanger a man's physical strength and sexual potency, even indirect contact is sufficient to endanger his spiritual power (*hpoun*). Thus, since a man's head is the most sacred part of his body, should a woman's genitalia chance to be higher than his head – should a woman, for example, stand while the man is sitting, or should she be in the upper room of a house while he is in a lower room – his *hpoun* can be seriously diminished. Nor is that all. Since his *hpoun* is located in the man's right shoulder, it may be diminished merely by a woman standing to his right, let alone should she touch his shoulder.

Any object that has been in contact with the vagina is also dangerous. For example, it is dangerous for a man to use a toilet or a bathroom that is used by a woman, to touch a woman's sarong, or to walk beneath a clothes line on which a woman's sarong is hanging. Similarly, a man is endangered if his sarong is laundered together with a woman's, or ironed with a woman's, or if it is placed on a shelf or in a closet with a woman's.

Females are dangerous, finally, because of their sexual allure. Since females are sexually desirable, and since sex is perhaps man's strongest desire, males wish to have sexual intercourse with them. But if even indirect contact with the vagina is harmful for males, direct contact is all the more harmful. Penile penetration of the polluting organ is the most harmful of all, constituting a threat to a man's physical strength, his sexual potency, and his spiritual power (*hpoun*) all at once.

As in the case of the Ideology of the Superior Male, this ideology is also strongly internalized by the males (and in some cases by the females, as well). In respect to the first subsystem, that of the Morally Dangerous Female, the most dramatic evidence consists of "actual" cases of bewitchment and of enticement by an *ouktazaun*. That some males believe that their wives have intruded themselves inside their bodies from whence they are working witchcraft upon them, that other males believe that they have been seduced by life-threatening spirits in the guise of sexually enticing women, and that their fellows, males and females alike, believe that their experiences are real and their reports veridical (Spiro 1974:Chapters 9–10) – all of this shows how very deep-seated is the internalization of the cultural propositions regarding female treachery and its power.

Evidence for the internalization of the second subsystem, that of the Sexually Dangerous Female, though not as dramatic, is just as abundant. That males internalize the propositions regarding the intensity of the female libido is perhaps most importantly evidenced by their conviction that females are virtually insatiable. Thus, while they themselves, they say, are satisfied after one act of intercourse, females require at least three, and even then they are not satisfied. That is why, immediately following a wedding, the groom's friends "strengthen" his penis by feeding him eggs and milk.

Males' internalization of the propositions regarding the dangerous vagina is perhaps best evidenced by the males' anxious compliance with all the culturally prescribed avoidances. Thus, they avoid sex with a menstruating woman, they do not touch, indeed they will not even look at, the vagina, they make sure to be above and to the left of females, etc.

Finally, the males' conviction that intercourse is dangerous is evidenced by their sexual behavior. According to their self-reports foreplay is brief and coitus is rapid. Moreover, exorcists, whose traffic with the supernaturals is a dangerous business at best, curtail their sexual activity altogether so that they might have the power to cope with those dangers. Again, the males' conviction regarding the dangers of semen loss is evidenced by their taking of "medicine," especially as they grow older, to replenish their semen supply.

The males' internalization of the Ideology of the Dangerous Female is especially interesting because in some important respects it is the opposite both of the Ideology of the Superior Male, as well as the social system of gender relations and other "facts on the ground." Thus, while the former ideology claims that males are superior to females and that, as a consequence, it is their right to dominate them, the latter ideology claims that females not only constitute a formidable threat to male dominance, as well as to their very being (their vital powers), but also that the superior attributes of males are virtually incapable of overcoming that threat.

The discrepancy between this ideology and the "facts on the ground" is equally pronounced. Thus, the claim that females employ magic, witchcraft, and other forms of "treachery" to usurp the male right of dominance does not seem to correspond to the actual behavior of the females, although admittedly the evidence is still out because, according to that proposition, female "treachery" is hard to detect. As for their alleged infidelity, however, it can be stated with confidence that the latter claim bears no correspondence to the actual behavior of the females for, as has already been noted, female adultery is very infrequent. Similarly, none of the dangers that this ideology attributes to the vagina, menstrual blood, semen loss, and the like bear any correspondence to their "objective" properties.

It is now perhaps clear why I claim that this cultural system is the end point of a complex scale of gender relations, one in which the two cultural systems occupy the polar ends of the scale, and various aspects of the social system are distributed along a U-shaped curve, some of which are closer to the first cultural system, others to the second.

Conclusions

Although we sometimes tend to view social hierarchies as fairly clearcut – one social group, social category, or social status being unambiguously superordinate to another – I have attempted to show that this is not the case in respect to the gender hierarchy in Burma. This conclusion probably holds for most other complex societies, as well.

The difficulty in arriving at an unambiguous judgment concerning a social hierarchy – of gender or any other – is twofold. First, any social relationship can and should be described in terms of three dimensions: cultural, social, and psychological. Hence, unless all three descriptions yield one and the same "graded series" (as *Webster's Collegiate Dictionary*, 1942, puts it) concerning the groups, statuses, or categories in question, it is difficult to arrive at a *reliable* judgment regarding their "true" hierarchical rank, unless there were a consensus among social theorists regarding the relative weights to be assigned to each of these dimensions. Unfortunately, such a consensus does not exist. And even if there were a consensus, it would be difficult to arrive at a *valid* judgment regarding the true hierarchy when, as is so often the case, each of these dimensions is itself internally differentiated and internally inconsistent.

Thus, it would be simple to arrive at a valid and reliable judgment regarding the gender hierarchy in Burma if gender relations in that society were accurately described as follows. According to the cultural system, males are superior to females morally, intellectually, and spiritually. Consistent with the cultural system, males are structurally superior to females – in authority, power, and charisma – across all the domains comprising the social system. Moreover, at the psychological level, males both believe and feel that they are superior to females. Given such a description, one that applies not only to Burma but also to most other human societies, we could hardly doubt that the judgment that males are superordinate to females in the Burmese gender hierarchy would be both valid and reliable, despite the fact that jurally females are more or less the equals of males, and, moreover, they sometimes surpass them in achievement.

The problem with such a judgment is that this description of the gender hierarchy in Burma (and many other societies), though not inaccurate so far as it goes, does not go far enough. Thus, in respect of the cultural dimension of Burmese gender relations, although one cultural system claims that males are superior to females, a second system (one which is as strongly internalized as the first) claims that females are a threat to males. Again, although structurally males are superior to females across most domains comprising the social system, in the domestic domain, females dominate males – not, to be sure, in the formal system, but in the informal one.[8] Similarly, while at the psychological level males claim to be superior to females, there is much evidence to indicate that, consciously and unconsciously, they both fear them – their power, their sex, and their sexuality – and are emotionally dependent upon them.

Confronted, now, with this second, more accurate, description of Burmese gender relations, a valid and reliable judgment of the gender hierarchy in Burma is much more difficult, and perhaps impossible, to arrive at. For those theorists for whom the social structure, but more especially the social structure in the extra-domestic domain, is the crucial dimension of hierarchy, there would be little doubt that males are superordinate to females in the Burmese gender hierarchy. Considering, however, that the domestic is the one in which most of life (at least in peasant societies) is lived, and the one in which males and females encounter each other not in the abstract, but one on one, other theorists would deem such a judgment questionable, given that in Burma females dominate males in the domestic domain.

That judgment would be even more questionable for those theorists for whom the psychological dimension of social relations must also be taken into account. For these theorists, the structural subordination of the females must be balanced by the males' fear of the dependency upon them. If, in addition, the males' psychological claim to superiority, as well as their internalization of the Ideology of the Superior Male, are interpreted as a defense against their (unconscious) feeling of inferiority to females, then for these theorists the judgment that males are superordinate in the Burmese gender hierarchy would be highly questionable. In any event, my purpose here is not to resolve the problem, but to raise it. And I raise it not only in the case of Burma, but also in the case of all other societies in which the cultural, social, and psychological dimensions of gender relations are characterized by an absence of structural homology.[9]

NOTES

1 This chapter is one section of a larger manuscript addressed to two theoretical problems, the problems of sociocultural integration and of cultural internalization, in the service of which the domain of gender relations in Burma is a particularly useful (because complex) case.

2 Fieldwork was conducted in villages in Upper Burma in 1961–2, and was abruptly terminated as a result of a military coup. Consequently, I worked with Burmese, mainly urban, refugees in Thailand in the summers of 1972–5. Because my investigations focused on religion, kinship, and social structure, the data on gender were collected in passing. A more detailed and systematic study cannot be undertaken until the military regime is replaced or overthrown.

3 Since the cultural propositions were culled piecemeal both from traditional Burmese texts and from informants' statements, their combination into two separate and internally integrated "systems" is my own construction. If they also comprise systems for the Burmese, it is perhaps only at an unconscious level; "unconscious" not in the Freudian sense, but in the sense that a grammar is said to be "unconscious."

4 For an analysis of the Burmese system of marriage payments and its sociological entailments, see Spiro 1976.

5 By "religion" I refer to Buddhism, the normative religion of the Burmese, not the spirit cult which is addressed separately.

6 Although typically the son succeeded the father to the hereditary office of village headman, in the absence of a son a daughter could succeed him (Mya Sein 1938). Moreover there is one recorded case in the fifteenth century in which a daughter, the famous Shinsawbu, succeeded her father to the throne (Harvey 1925:117ff.).

7 For an extended discussion of shamans and the spirit cult, see Spiro 1974.

8 The discrepancy between male dominance in extra-domestic domains and female dominance in the domestic domain is not unique to Burma. Although this phenomenon has been frequently documented in a wide range of human societies (for example, Friedl 1967; Rogers 1975; Sanday 1981; Ségalen 1983; Whyte 1978), its theoretical implications have yet to be explicated systematically.

9 There are four problems, however, that I believe can be resolved, at least I attempt to do so in the manuscript mentioned in note 1. They are: (a) Why are the two cultural systems the polar opposites of each other? (b) Why are the cultural systems not structurally homologous with the social system? (c) Given the absence of structural homology, why is the first cultural system, the Ideology of the Superior Male, internalized? (d) Given that the second system, the Ideology of the Dangerous Female, is both empirically false and emotionally threatening, why is it internalized?

REFERENCES

Bahosi 1961 (Burmese newspaper, 16 October.)

Blanchard, Wendel 1958 *Thailand*. New Haven, CT: HRAF Press.

Doi, Takeo 1973 *The Anatomy of Dependence*. Tokyo and New York: Kodansha International.

Forbes, C. J. F. S. 1878 *British Burma and Its People*. London: John Murray.

Friedl, Ernestine 1967 The Position of Women: Appearance and Reality. *Anthropological Quarterly* 40:98–105.

Geertz, Hildred 1961 *The Javanese Family*. Glencoe, IL: The Free Press.

Hall, H. Fielding 1913 *A People at School*. London: Macmillan.

Harvey, G. E. 1925 *History of Burma*. London: Longman Green.

Htin Aung, Maung 1937 *Burmese Drama*. London: Oxford University Press.

The Jataka 1957 (edited by E. B. Cowell). London: Luzac.

Jay, Robert R. 1969 *Javanese Villagers*. Cambridge, MA: MIT Press.

The Lokaniti 1962 (translated by U. Sein Tu). Mandalay: University Research Council Publication No. 9.

Maung Maung, U. 1963 *Law and Custom in Burma and the Burmese Family*. The Hague: Martinus Nijhoff.

Mya Sein, Daw 1938 *Administration of Burma*. Rangoon: Zabu Meitswe Pitoka Press.

Nash, Manning 1965 *The Golden Road to Modernity*. New York: John Wiley.

Poole, Fitz John P. and Gilbert H. Herdt, eds. 1982 *Sexual Antagonism, Gender, and Social Change in Papua New Guinea*. Special Issue, *Social Analysis* 12.

Rogers, Susan Carol 1975 Female Forms of Power and the Myth of Male Dominance: A Model of Female/Male Interaction in Peasant Society. *American Ethnologist* 2:727–56.

Sanday, Peggy 1981 *Female Power and Male Dominance: On the Origins of Sexual Inequality*. New York: Cambridge University Press.

Ségalen, Martine 1983 *Love and Power in the Peasant Family: Rural France in the Nineteenth Century*. Chicago, IL: University of Chicago Press.

Spiro, Melford E. 1974 *Burmese Supernaturalism*. Philadelphia, PA: ISHI.

1976 Marriage Payments: A Paradigm from the Burmese Perspective. *Journal of Anthropological Research* 31:89–115.

1977 *Kinship and Marriage in Burma*. Berkeley: University of California Press.

1982 *Buddhism and Society*. Berkeley: University of California Press.

Steele, James nda Burmese TAT Analysis. Mimeo.
  ndb An Analysis of the Burmese Rorschachs. Mimeo.
Steinberg, David J. 1959 *Cambodia*. New Haven, CT: HRAF Press.
Whyte, Martin K. 1978 *The Status of Women in Preindustrial Society*. Princeton,
  NJ: Princeton University Press.

15　Turning the tables? Male strippers and the gender hierarchy in America

Maxine L. Margolis and Marigene Arnold

Anthropologists have long asserted that all societies differentiate their members by gender. Some activities and occupations are defined as "masculine," others as "feminine." That these definitions are largely arbitrary is suggested by the fact that what is obviously a masculine activity to one group is just as obviously a feminine one to another group. Thus, among the Pueblo Indians of the American southwest only men weave, while their Navaho neighbors insist that women are the superior weavers. Societal ideologies justify such divisions of labor by appealing to sexual stereotypes. Women are said to be "naturally" better than men at whatever tasks a given society assigns to the feminine realm, while men's "innate" talent is said to be just as unambiguously displayed in tasks that society defines as masculine.

The United States has not been exempt from ideologies that rationalize the sexual status quo. In American society of the 1950s, for example, the "ideal" family was synonymous with the "ideal" gender hierarchy. Thus, men were to be breadwinners, women housewives and domestic consumers, with a clear cultural preference for the male role. Moreover, the woman who dared to cross over the sexual boundary line and seek a career was decried and labeled a "feminist neurotic" (Margolis 1984:218–25).

In a classic article the anthropologist Jules Henry neatly summarized the gender hierarchy in the United States: A "man validates himself by working and supporting," Henry wrote, "a woman validates herself by getting a man. A man does, a woman is. Man performs, woman attracts" (1973:135).

While there have been significant social and economic changes in American society since the rebirth of the feminist movement in the late 1960s, elements of the traditional gender hierarchy are still very much with us. Sey Chassler, former editor of *Redbook Magazine* writes:

The women's movement has made some remarkable changes in our lives, but it hasn't changed the position of the male much at all. Men still make the moves. They are the ones who, in their own good time, move in. And in their own good

time, move out. Someone makes the rules, someone else does as she is told ... As
men we are surely in charge. It comes with the territory. (1988:173)

The gender hierarchy is expressed in diverse realms. In many societies,
and America is no exception, sexual activity is symbolic of men's control
over women. One anthropologist writes that "the essential formal characteristic of the sex act ... is the exploitation of women by men"
(Kemnitzer 1977:294). Men are expected to initiate sex and women are
expected to submit. Men are the consumers, women the providers. In
America even the right to ogle the opposite sex has been, until recently,
the exclusive province of men. As Laura Mulvey, a film editor and
director, puts it:

In a world ordained by sexual imbalance, pleasure in looking has been split
between active/male and passive/female. The determining male gaze projects its
fantasy onto the female figure, which is styled accordingly ... Women displayed as
sexual object is the leitmotif of erotic spectacle; from pinups to striptease, from
Ziegfeld to Busby Berkeley, she holds the look, plays to, and signifies male desire.
(1977:418)

This chapter examines what appears to be a reversal of this aspect of the
traditional gender hierarchy in America by describing the role of male
striptease dancers who play to female audiences. Here men would appear
to be the sexual objects, the passive caterers to women's needs. In such
performances, it is male, rather than female bodies that are put on display
and judged. Our aim is to analyze the male strip show within the broader
context of gender hierarchies in the United States. In order to do this we
compare male strip shows with the more traditional ones that feature
female dancers. Female strippers are said to be symbols of the sexual
objectification of women (Lewin 1984). Moreover, their jobs have a
tendency, in the words of one feminist historian, "to reproduce in the
cruelest possible way the structure of patriarchal power and female
dependence" (Kessler-Harris 1985:12).

If this interpretation is true, and we believe that the few studies of
female strip shows support it, our question then is, are male strip shows in
any way analogous to their female counterparts? We focus primarily on
the issue of control during the men's performance because we see control
as an important clue to power relations and, therefore, to gender hierarchy. We ask what, if any, are the differences between audience–performer interaction in shows featuring male and female strippers? Our
assumption is that if the male strip show does indeed represent a true
inversion of the traditional gender hierarchy, it should be a mirror image
of the female strip show with only the sex of the performers and the
audience reversed.

The male strip show

Before presenting our findings, which are based partly on participant observation in a discothèque featuring male strip shows, we provide some background on the phenomenon itself. Bars and nightclubs featuring male strippers were first established some time during the mid to late 1970s. While their total number in the United States is impossible to estimate, they appear to be widespread. They are not limited to the sophisticated metropolitan centers of the two coasts or to big cities in general (*Time Magazine* 1979:69). Male strip shows have mushroomed in suburban areas and small cities in the Midwest and the South including University City, a town of about 100,000, where we conducted our research.[1] Patrons of these establishments are of all ages, although our own study is heavily weighted toward college-age women because of the makeup of University City's population.

As a general rule, the owners of bars and nightclubs that feature male strippers restrict their clientele to women. A number of explanations are given for this policy. Some club owners say they want to avoid attracting male customers who are gay, while others claim that the all-woman policy serves to keep out straight men who make their female clientele uncomfortable and who occasionally become violent (Brackley 1980:70). Then, too, some women customers argue that because of the absence of men in the audience they feel safer and more relaxed in these establishments than they do in regular bars (*Chicago Tribune* 1980:1).

Through zoning ordinances and license challenges a few communities have attempted to shut down businesses featuring male strippers, although it is not clear if these efforts are greater than those to control the more traditional female strip joints and topless bars (Brackley 1980:69). It is true, however, that in one small city in the Northeast male strippers were arrested for "disseminating obscene materials" while the city fathers have made no similar attempt to limit the right of female performers to remove their clothes in public or the right of male customers to watch them (*New York Times* 1980). In a Chicago suburb a male strip joint was closed less than two weeks after opening purportedly because it lacked a "special use permit." Yet, according to the city manager the true reason was that the nightclub did not "offer the type of show generally identified with our hometown atmosphere." "I don't know," he said, "maybe there's some male chauvinism behind this. We say belly dancers are okay but when men do the same thing, we say it's obscene" (*Chicago Tribune* 1980:2).

The show at Ginnie's

Our research was conducted at Ginnie's, a discothèque that features a male strip show one night a week. It strictly enforces an all-female policy during the two-hour show, but permits men in immediately following the performance. Its advertisements, in fact, invite men "to come dance and romance with the ladies who have just experienced the ultimate Male Review."

Ginnie's charges $5.00 admission for the show itself which includes the cost of unlimited quantities chosen from a list of alcoholic beverages and soft drinks. In addition, customers are expected to tip the male dancers as well as the waiters, an expectation of which they are reminded constantly by the disc jockey.

Most women come to the show in groups of threes and fours. We observed no lone women customers at Ginnie's, a point to which we will return later. Attendance is often in celebration of the birthday of one of the women. There have been reports that friends of a recently divorced woman will invite her to a male strip show to mark her new status (*Time Magazine* 1979:69).

The performance at Ginnie's takes place on a small dance floor lined on two sides by banquettes on which patrons may sit. These are the seats of choice for some customers who arrive up to an hour before the doors open so that they may dash in and reserve them for themselves and their friends. There are also small tables on one side of the dance floor as well as on two balconies overlooking it.

As the sixty or seventy patrons are seated and place their drink orders against the din of loud rock music, a disc jockey begins to work the audience. "This is ladies' night out," he proclaims. "You deserve a night out." The refrain, "ladies, this is *your* night," is repeated throughout the performance. We agree with other researchers that the "equal time for women" theme is a salient feature of the male strip show (Petersen and Dressel 1982:189). Following the popular media's portrayal of the male strip show as part of the feminist movement's demand for women's equality, Ginnie's female audience is obliquely told that attendance at such a show is a liberating experience (*Time Magazine* 6 August 1979; Snider 1980).

The show is presented by five male performers collectively known as the "Feelgood Dancers." Each show begins with the same scenario: four of the five dancers, wearing white tuxedos and top hats and carrying long-stemmed carnations, enter the bar area and begin distributing flowers and kisses to patrons. The four work their way to the dance floor where they proceed to dance and strip. This opening number sets the stage for the rest of the performance. An aura of romance and chivalry is created which will be mixed throughout the evening with more overt sexuality and male aggressiveness.

After the opening number each dancer returns twice, dressed in a variety of elaborate costumes – a sailor, a construction worker, an explorer, a fireman, an American Indian, Charlie Chaplin, Conan the Barbarian, and a Kung Fu in leather. Each dancer is introduced by the disc jockey, makes his way to center stage, and does a bump and grind performance while stripping off layers of clothes until he is wearing only a G-string. Total nudity is not a feature of the show.[2]

These performances take place against a backdrop of loud frenzied music and the non-stop encouragement of the disc jockey. "The more you scream, the more you see," he urges his audience over and over again. Customers are told they must continually yell and clap to show their appreciation of the performers. The message is that the audience must behave in a certain way in order to get the desired results – presumably having the dancers strip down to their G-strings.

Sexual banter and *doubles entendres* are constant. The audience is told that the explorer "has a large animal which he is going to show us tonight." When two dancers appear in striped uniforms, the deejay warns: "Watch out, ladies, these guys have been in prison for twenty years!"

A central feature of the performance is the dancers' singling out women in the audience for attention. Once a dancer has completed his strip and is wearing only a G-string he will start to "work" the crowd, moving from table to table where he accepts dollar bills which the patrons stuff into his G-string. Each tip is followed by a kiss. Some women in the audience hold up dollar bills and the dancer will usually move to their tables. However, each dancer also singles out patrons by leaping on a table or the railing around the balcony and focusing his gyrations at a particular woman who is sometimes embarrassed into making a physical and monetary response as the only way to be left alone. The finale features all of the performers simultaneously going from table to table to pick up additional tips, and by the end of the show their G-strings are overflowing with dollar bills.

Gender and control in the female strip show

Earlier we suggested that the male strip show, in which women as consumers take the active role and men as providers take the passive one, appears to be a reversal of the traditional American gender hierarchy. Before analyzing this point, however, the male strip show can be put into sharper focus by comparing it to the traditional female strip show with particular attention being paid to the interactions between the performers and the audience.

Despite its ubiquitous and long-term presence on the American scene, relatively little social science research has been done on the female strip show. Moreover, with few exceptions, most work has focused on stripping as a "deviant" profession (Boles and Garbin 1974b, 1974c; Carey, Peterson, and Sharp 1974; McCaghy and Skipper 1972; Skipper and McCaghy 1970). Aside from an article by Boles and Garbin (1974a) and a personalized account of Boston strip joints by Lewin (1984), no researchers have investigated the actual performances in bars with female strippers or the patterns of dancer–customer interactions in these establishments.

It is clear from the few studies of behavior in nightclubs featuring female strippers that one of the principal functions of the performers is to encourage customers, most of whom are men, to buy drinks. In some clubs there is a distinction between "featured strippers" who draw customers because of their abilities as performers and "house girls" who also dance, but whose main responsibility is to mingle with customers and get them to buy drinks. House girls may help tend bar, wait on tables, and seat customers. They are also expected to interact with the audience on a personal level, particularly if requested to do so by a customer (Boles and Garbin 1974a).

Female strippers often adopt distinctive personae in their acts – the vamp, the baby doll, the ice queen – donning elaborate costumes and exaggerated face make-up. They also almost invariably use stage names appropriate to their chosen persona – Cleopatra, Lolita, Crystal, and so on. Nevertheless, according to Boles and Garbin, "the very image strippers are attempting to create may be destroyed in the process of sitting with members of the audience" (1974a:139). A number of the dancers indicated that they found this requirement disturbing because it breaks down the social and physical distance that usually exists between performer and audience and interferes with their self-image as entertainers.

This lack of distinction between performer and audience seems to be a problem endemic to female strip shows. In *Naked is the Best Disguise* (1984), a study of bars featuring such shows in Boston, Lewin describes how female strippers try to keep their sense of dignity and self-esteem by setting limits on their interactions with male patrons. Here too, the stripper is expected to entertain male clients when she is not performing and her success is, in part, judged by the number of drinks clients buy for her. In fact, this feature is so central to the job that strippers were warned that if they "couldn't please customers," as measured by how many drinks were bought, they would be let go (1984:37).

While strippers are expected to joke and banter with their customers, the degree to which touching and other sexual activities take place between stripper and customer seems to vary with the type of establishment. In the clubs studied by Boles and Garbin the strippers rarely permitted men to touch them (1974a), while in one of the "combat zone"[3] bars Lewin investigated, a private back room was available for sexual trysts. But even here the strippers attempt to set limits, or need to have what one of them called "a gimmick." One stripper, for example, permitted male customers to touch her, but refused to touch them, while another touched the men but would not allow them to fondle her. Still another would engage in a variety of sexual activities but drew the line at sexual intercourse claiming (falsely) that she had a venereal disease (1984:43).

The men who attend female strip shows appear reluctant to show any appreciation for the performance. They must be shamed into applause either by the establishment's manager or by other dancers. An overt display of appreciation might demonstrate the female dancers' power over the male audience.

Perhaps because of the problematic nature of the relationship between audience and performer in bars featuring female strip shows, any action by a member of the audience, no matter how inadvertent, that appears hostile may provoke the stripper's wrath. This is particularly true of female customers. At the slightest sign of hostility or rejection, the stripper will immediately react with a verbal assault, often making a disparaging remark about some inadequacy in the customer's anatomy. At times strippers have to contend with customers who leap on the stage either because they want physical contact with the dancer or are inebriated and want to be part of the show (Boles and Garbin 1974a:140). In either case, the performer–audience distinction is breached and the dancer loses at least temporary control over the show.

The question of control – who has it and how it is maintained – seems to be a recurrent issue in the context of female performers playing to (largely) male audiences. Lewin sees the stripper retaining control over her performance, at least in her own mind, by deciding how explicit her "floor show" will be. After stripping, the dancer sits on the floor and exposes her genitals. By varying the degree and length of exposure, she sees herself as being "in control" (1984:73–4). Whatever one thinks of this feeble attempt at control, in other circumstances the audience clearly has the upper hand. A waitress in a University City establishment featuring a "mini-skirt contest" – which is actually an amateur strip show – noted that "the strippers do what the crowds want. Every time one girl shows a little, the next one has to show more." And since this is a contest, those who show the most receive the most applause and are the most likely to win. According to the same informant, men watching the mini-skirt contest "are not easily satisfied and usually try to get the contestants to show more" (Schultz 1985:1, 8).

In some respects the audience controls the female stripper, but control over the audience in these establishments is exerted by male bouncers (Lewin 1984:173). The owner of the mini-skirt contest bar claims that bouncers are essential for restraining unruly men in the audience who try to touch the dancers, behavior that is forbidden by house rules (Schultz 1985:8). Thus, in the female strip show some members of the male audience try to have their way with the performers and audience behavior is kept in check only by muscular male bouncers.

The permeable boundary between audience and performer and the issue of control are not the only problematic aspects of the female strip show. According to Boles and Garbin, the main complaint of the female strippers they studied was that they were "objectified" by their audience, that they were "treated as instruments rather than as persons valuable in themselves" (1974a:141). Dancers are propositioned indiscriminately by men in the audience under the assumption that strippers are, by definition, prostitutes. The same negative stereotypes hold for contestants in the mini-skirt contest, many of whom are college students. According to the owner of the club which holds the contests, these attitudes have presented problems: "We've had the girls out getting something to eat and because they dance in the mini-skirt contest the guys treat them like some sleazy whore" (Schultz 1985:8). Performers bridle at these attitudes and even those who do accept money for sex resent the lack of "courting behavior" on the part of male customers (Boles and Garbin 1974:141). "I'm not a sleaze bag or a slut," protested one mini-skirt contestant who said that although she entered the contests only in hopes of winning money, she always felt reservations when she performed (Schultz 1985:8).

The belief that female strippers are available sexually is related to the general denigration of stripping as an occupation (Bryant 1982:151–2). The dancers deeply resented the question: "What's a nice girl like you ...?" and mini-skirt contestants previously acquainted with men in the audience often heard the refrain: "I thought you had more class than that ... " (Boles and Garbin 1974a:141; Schultz 1985:8).

Given these tensions it is not surprising that researchers have described the atmosphere in bars with strip shows as suffused with hostility and even violence. Dancers will routinely insult members of the audience who act uninterested in their performance or who offend them in some other way. Lewin (1984) describes many violent incidents between strippers and customers as well as between customers and bouncers. Boles and Garbin (1974a) note that the level of violence varies from club to club and that the greatest displays of anger are between customers and performers. In fact, most clubs serve drinks in plastic glasses so as to lessen the chance of serious injury during fights.

It is evident that the context and structure of the stripper's job replicates the external gender hierarchy of male dominance and female submission in a number of ways. Male club owners and managers maintain tight control over the female performers. "Club rules" which dictate the strippers' behavior are strictly enforced. For example, pay is withheld if strippers are unable to convince customers to buy a specified number of drinks. Strippers are expected to do nothing that will displease customers and to use their "womanly wiles" to get them to spend as much money as possible. It is a stripper's duty to cajole her customers into buying drinks; a common strategy is to evoke the male client's sympathy and plead for support. Lewin notes that no matter how old, sickly, or unattractive they are, male customers can still "buy illusions of power," while female performers generally feel powerless and exploited (Lewin 1984:36, 122, 124, 145).

Gender and control in the male strip show

We now return to our analysis of the male strip show. Briefly put, we found that the purported role reversal in the male strip show is illusory. The male strip show is not a mirror image of the female strip show with an inversion of the sex of the audience and the performers.[4] Moreover, because the male strip show contains elements reminiscent of traditional gender hierarchies in the United States the popular media's widely touted interpretation of it as a symbol of women's liberation rings false.

A number of factors contribute to our conclusion that the structure and content of the contemporary male strip show is characterized by antiquated sex role expectations. Most important is how, through a variety of mechanisms, both the male dancers and the other employees of Ginnie's direct and manage the female audience in such a way as to recreate the traditional gender hierarchy of male dominance and female subservience.

The first indication to Ginnie's female customers that their behavior is subject to external control is the requirement that they line up in a public corridor to await the door's opening at 9 p.m. After they enter and are seated the disc jockey takes command. First, he repeatedly reminds the audience to tip the waiters. While this may be a response to the stereotype that women do not tip, it is a patronizing gesture. The deejay also enjoins the audience to behave in a certain way in order to get the dancers to strip. Again and again he says, "they won't take it off if you don't scream." Then, too, by emphasizing the male dancers' sexual starvation (in the case of escaped convicts and sailors returning after years at sea) or their sexual endowments, and, by extension, prowess (a sheriff with a six-shooter and a lion tamer with a large animal) the disc jockey verbally creates scenarios in which the male dancers would be expected to be the sexual assailants. Thus, the image of the dancers, rather than being sexual providers as implied in gender role reversal, are instead depicted as sexual aggressors.

The dancers themselves add to this sense of control. One performer indicated this when he said, "Compared to most topless nightclubs we put more emphasis on costumes and choreography. You can control your audience by the way you present yourself" (Schultz 1985:1). As we have seen, the male dancers choose the women they play to and some women are embarrassed into making a monetary response to the dancer's attentions. Quite unlike the cajoling stance of the female stripper, the male stripper seems to be demanding payment for his performance.

There are still other aspects of their performance that enhance the feeling that the male dancers are in charge of the action. First, they are all well-muscled. This fact contributes to the sense that they are stronger than the clients and could presumably overpower them at will. In addition, they enhance their size by dancing on tables and balconies, thus, positioning themselves above the female audience for much of the performance. A dancer often gets a woman from the audience to remove a piece of his clothing; when this is done he invariably stands on a chair and towers above her. In one instance a woman who got up from her chair to kiss a dancer was taller than the dancer; he immediately hopped on a chair before he kissed her. While this incident may have been merely a whimsical moment in the show, it, along with the other behaviors we have described, may be taken as symbolic of differential male and female power.

Nowhere is this differential more apparent than in the "dive bomb" method of tipping the dancers. From the start of the show the deejay extols patrons to be creative in their tipping and cajoles them to be the first to "dive bomb." Early in the show women stuff tips into the sides and back of the dancers' G-strings; later in the evening, and presumably with the assistance of alcohol, dive bombing begins. To dive bomb, a woman puts a dollar bill in her mouth, gets down on the floor on her knees and sticks the bill into the front of the dancer's G-string. This action, which mimics fellatio, is symbolic not only of women's subservience, but of their sexual availability and vulnerability.

Audience control, then, does not seem to be a major problem for the male strippers at Ginnie's.[5] Perhaps because command of the situation is not in doubt, the deejay encourages women in the audience to touch the male dancers, behavior that is strictly forbidden in establishments featuring female strippers. In other words, physical contact with the dancers is not seen as threatening because it is not likely to be disruptive as it might be were the sexes of the customers and performers reversed. This interpretation is supported by the comments of the owner of another University City nightclub that features male strippers who work the audience in the manner described above. When asked why he does not have an equivalent show with female dancers, he replied that "a woman going out into the crowd is going to get abused. We can intercede but if some guy in the audience grabs [her], it may take four bouncers to get him off, and by that point the damage has been done" (Schultz 1985:8).

Then, too, the audience/performer dichotomy is far better defined in the male strip show than in the female strip show because the male dancers interact with the female clientele only as performers. They do not wait on tables, nor do they sit with female customers after the show and encourage them to buy drinks. Unlike many female strippers, male strippers are not obliged to wait in attendance on an audience of the opposite sex. It is assumed that they can please the female clientele with the artistry of their performances; they are not called on to interact with members of the audience on a more personal level.

Distinctive patterns of attendance at the male and female strip shows also are related to the issue of control. As mentioned earlier, we observed no lone women at Ginnie's. Similarly, Petersen and Dressel (1982) note that during eight months of visiting the male strip club in which they conducted their research they never once observed a woman attending the show alone. This pattern is in marked contrast to the bars featuring topless waitresses or female strip shows. In these establishments the lone male customer seems to be the norm. Although Lewin (1984) provides no specific figures in her description of the audience in bars featuring female strippers, she gives the strong impression that most of the men come to the bars alone.

There are several possible interpretations of the phenomenon of "group female" versus "solitary male" attendance at these performances. Perhaps it is simply the relative novelty of male strip shows that induces women to go to them with their friends; attendance in a group lessens an individual's feeling of discomfort in a new situation. Conversely, because female strip shows have been around for years, the lone male attending a performance is likely to find himself in familiar surroundings. We believe, however, that there are more profound social and psychological explanations for this pattern of attendance. Given the norm of male control, women who go to male strip shows seeking a reversal in erotic roles may feel more at ease in a setting of group solidarity than of individual liberation. The "safety in numbers" dictum may well apply here as a logical outgrowth of traditional patterns of female socialization in the United States. Then, too, perhaps women go to these performances accompanied by their friends because of the hoary notion that a sexually assertive woman is "out of control." By attending a performance alone, a woman may fear that she would be making a social statement that she "needs" more satisfaction than the vicarious sexual expression obtained from the male strip show itself.

We are on more tentative ground in trying to explain the lone male pattern of attendance at female strip shows. Men may worry that attending a strip show sullies the ideal of the macho American male as a sexual dynamo capable of seducing women at all times. In line with this idealized image of masculinity, why should the vicarious eroticism of viewing nude or semi-nude female performers be necessary for a "man's man"? Is going to a strip show an activity best concealed from (male) friends? The question also arises of how a man would react to a friend getting comparatively more attention from a female dancer. Is the solitary male unwilling to share the attention of the dancers *qua* sexual beings? While we are uncertain as to which of these interpretations is the most accurate one, we are convinced that the marked gender differences in patterns of attendance at these performances are not random.

The self-images of the male strippers and their profession also diverge significantly from those of their female counterparts. Unlike the negative feelings expressed by the female strippers, the male dancers seemed to enjoy their work. "I love what I'm doing," said a male stripper in a Chicago club. "You see, I really love the ladies" (*Chicago Tribune* 1980:2). Said another, "It's basically a man's dream ... The opportunities come fast and furious" (quoted in Petersen and Dressel 1982:194). Nor do they appear ashamed of their jobs: "Everybody I know knows what I do and most of them have seen the show, including my mother," boasted yet another (quoted in Schultz 1985:8). Moreover, the job seems to evoke interest because of its novelty. "When I tell people I'm a dancer, they say 'How interesting, tell me about it,'" according to one of the Feelgood Dancers.

These attitudes are reflections of the American gender hierarchy. Why are similar activities judged so differently when they are performed by males and females? Why is comparable behavior admired in men and denigrated in women? Why are women strippers characterized as "sluts" and "sleaze bags," while men strippers are seen as artistic and sexy? Why are the male dancers not "fair game" to the audience like the female dancers are? If the male strip show were really an analogue of the female strip show we would not see such a marked contrast in attitudes toward the performers and the job itself.

There is also the issue of economic compensation. While it is difficult to come up with accurate figures for the earnings of male and female strippers, there is some evidence that the men, on average, earn much more than the women do. One of the Feelgood Dancers said that he never earned less than $120 a night and could earn up to $200 when he performed on a "hot night" in a club in a larger city (Campbell 1985). These figures are comparable to those cited by other male strippers (Bryant 1982:197).

The pattern of compensation in one nightclub that features both male strippers and a mini-skirt contest is illuminating. The male dancers earn $600 from salary and tips for four shows, while the female contestants, in what amounts to an amateur strip show, get $10 for entering the contest and compete for first, second, and third prizes of $200, $50, and $25 respectively (Schultz 1985:8). Although both men and women provide the night's entertainment, the women are not compensated for their performance, aside from a token payment, unless they win one of the prizes.

Lewin (1984) explains what female strippers must do for their earnings. In addition to a salary of $40 a day, they receive a commission on the drinks they induce customers to buy for them. They earn $1 on every $6 drink, but only if they fill their quota of twelve drinks for the evening; no commission is paid if less than twelve drinks are sold. Moreover, she makes it clear that in some establishments the size of a stripper's "tips" is proportional to her willingness to be fondled by male customers (1984:36–7).

Finally, there is a very telling theme in some of the print and broadcast advertising for male strip shows, a theme that would be nearly unimaginable in ads for their female counterparts. The advertisement that Ginnie's directs at potential male customers is illustrative. It urges men "to come dance and romance with the ladies who have just experienced the ultimate Male Review." A radio spot for Dazzles, another club that features a male strip show and allows men in afterward has a similar, albeit more explicit, come on: "Men, you have two things to look forward to: a most sophisticated nightclub and some *very* excited women."

The common leitmotif here is that witnessing a performance by male strippers "readies" women sexually for other men. One interpretation of this message is that male strip shows ultimately benefit men by making women who view the shows more sexually available to them. The salience of this point in terms of the perpetuation of the gender hierarchy becomes explicit if we imagine the likelihood of a similar advertisement being directed at women. What are the chances that the print or broadcast media would run ads that try to induce women "to dance and romance the [gentlemen] who have just witnessed the ultimate [Female] Review"?

Thus, although the media paints the male strip show with an "equal time for women" motif, this is a deceptive commentary on a phenomenon that, in fact, symbolically recreates traditional gender roles. It is true that the shows contain a reversal in the sense that women are encouraged to look at and enjoy male bodies – a recent innovation. Nevertheless, the male dancers adopt an active, aggressive stance throughout the performance. It is they who select female members of the audience for attention, an audience that is kept in check by constantly being told how to behave through the patronizing and infantilizing prattle of the disc jockey.

Then, too, male dancers are seen in an entirely different light from their female analogues. Their status is not degraded through participation in the strip show and their jobs are even viewed as novelties. They earn more money than female strippers and they are never required to wait on and socialize with members of the audience. Finally, they are responsible, at least in a symbolic way, for "turning on" the client for the ultimate benefit of her boyfriend or some other male. And so despite a surface appearance of the male strip show as a "liberating" experience for women, role reversal is illusory and the deeply embedded gender hierarchy is reenacted and upheld.

Turning the tables?

This description and analysis forces us to conclude that the male strip show is yet one more example of the traditional American gender hierarchy in action. Nevertheless, Ginnie's is always packed, many of the women attend time and time again, and the crowd appears to enjoy itself tremendously. What explains the disparity between our interpretation of the show and the audience's evident enjoyment of it?

Several elements of the male strip show help explain the enthusiasm of Ginnie's patrons. One analyst claims that while "men watching [female] strip shows tend to be aroused ... women tend to treat the whole thing [i.e., male strip shows] as a joke" (Faust 1980:37). While our informal interviews with patrons do not indicate that the show at Ginnie's is seen as a joke, it certainly is perceived as fun. Moreover, there is the novelty of women being encouraged to enjoy viewing scantily clad male bodies.

Then, too, the environment during the show, though meant to be erotic, is perfectly safe. The sense of security, in fact, has been cited as an explanation for why the "new erotica" is so popular with women; they can rent x-rated, romance-oriented movies and watch them on their VCRs in the privacy of their own homes (Leo 1987:63).

There is also the question of whether Ginnie's show would have succeeded had it actually featured a true gender role reversal. Beginning with Kinsey, research indicates that men and women, at least in the United States, respond to very different sexual stimuli (Faust 1980; Whitehurst and Booth 1980; Frayser 1985; Weatherford 1986; Leo 1987). Keith McWalter expressed the difference best: "Men's sexual response is triggered predominantly by visual stimulation [but] ... women are creatures of gestalt, aroused by the full range of the senses and the heart and brain besides" (1987:138). Another analyst claims that "most erotica fits into our cultural stereotypes of men and women and reinforces the conventional elements of such scripts" (Gagnon cited in Whitehurst and Booth 1980:144). This statement aptly describes the show put on by the Feelgood Dancers. The performance plays up gender stereotypes, reinforces "conventional elements" and is more reminiscent of a Harlequin Romance novel than of a female strip show.

Like the male strip show, the issue of control also arises in women's magazines, romance novels, and the like. They portray

sex and violence in such a way that heroines are often raped, but 'never ruined'; their experiences explore a wide range of sexual activities for women but only in contexts over which the women have no control ... they absolve women from the responsibility of choice in sexual relationships and provide vicarious satisfaction for women who have no intention of being permissive in "real" life. (Frayser 1985:421)

Thus, the successful formula for the romance novel and other entertainment directed at women also works well for the male strip show. A similar point is driven home if we try to conceive of a true gender role reversal in a sexual context:

Imagine two doors: in front of each door is a line of people; behind each door is a room; in each room is a bed; on each bed is a person. The line in front of one room consists of beautiful women, and on the bed in that room is a man having intercourse with each of these women in turn. One may think of any number of things about this scene. One may say that the man is in heaven, or enjoying himself in a bordello; or perhaps one might wonder at the oddness of it all. One does not think that the man is being hurt or violated or degraded – or at least the possibility does not immediately suggest itself ...

Now consider the other line. Imagine that the figure on the bed is a woman and that the line consists of handsome, smiling men. The woman is having intercourse with each of these men in turn. It immediately strikes one that the woman is being degraded, violated, and so forth – "that poor·woman." (Baker 1988:293)

Although sexual behavior in America has changed since the sexual revolution,[6] attitudes toward active female sexuality have not kept pace. The male strip show, like the fun-house mirror, distorts the fact that, sexually, women still live in a "man's world."

NOTES

We appreciate the helpful suggestions of the participants in the Wenner-Gren Symposium on Gender Hierarchies as well as the insightful comments of Professor David Suggs of Kenyon College.

1 University City is a pseudonym as is Ginnie's, the club featuring male strip shows in which we did our research. The research was conducted during the spring and winter of 1985.

2 Total nudity also was not a feature of the strip shows observed by Petersen and Dressel (1982). However, there are shows in which the male dancers completely strip. It is our impression that the latter are confined to large cities.

3 The "combat zone" in Boston is an area of the city so designated because it has been zoned for bars featuring strip shows, pornographic book shops and other forms of "adult" entertainment. It is also a center of prostitution and drug traffic.

4 The role of gigolo would also seem to be a role reversal but, for the combat zone in Washington, DC, Weatherford reports that "[in] the terminology of the street ... these men were pimps rather than gigolos because the word *pimp* implied control over the woman rather than just serving her. According to this distinction, the man who took a woman's money was 'pimping' her ... " (1986:179).

5 Audience control did present more of a problem in the club featuring a male strip show that was studied by Petersen and Dressel. They note that some female customers were verbally and physically aggressive toward the dancers, pinching or scratching them, pulling at their G-strings, and insulting the dancers' physical attributes (1982:201). We never witnessed any comparable behavior at Ginnie's.

6 The AIDS scare may be reversing these changes.

REFERENCES

Baker, Robert 1988 Pricks and Chicks: A Plea for Persons. In *Racism and Sexism: An Integrated Study*. P. S. Rothenberg, ed., pp. 280–95. New York: St Martin's Press.

Boles, Jacqueline and Albeno P. Garbin 1974a The Strip Club and Stripper–Customer Patterns of Interaction. *Sociology and Social Research* 58:136–44.

1974b The Choice of Stripping for a Living. *Sociology of Work and Occupations* 1:110–23.

1974c Stripping for a Living: An Occupational Study of the Night Club Stripper. In *Deviant Behavior: Occupational and Organizational Bases*. C. D. Bryant, ed., pp. 312–35. Skokie, IL: Rand McNally.

Brackley, Judith 1980 Male Strip Shows: What Women See in Them. *Ms. Magazine* 9 November:68–70, 84.

Bryant, Clifton 1982 *Sexual Deviancy and Social Proscription: The Social Context of Carnal Behavior*. New York: Human Sciences Press.

Campbell, Lori 1985 You've Come a Long Way Baby: Three Men Who've Turned the Table on Female Roles. *The Independent Florida Alligator* February:5.

Carey, Sandra H., Robert A. Peterson, and Louis K. Sharpe 1974 A Study of

Recruitment and Socialization in Two Deviant Female Occupations. *Sociology Symposium* 11 (Spring):11–24.

Chassler, Sey 1988 Listening. In *Racism and Sexism: An Integrated Study*. P. S. Rothenberg, ed., pp. 167–75. New York: St Martin's Press.

Chicago Tribune 1980 Girls' Night Out: A Bump and Grind. 20 April:1–2.

Faust, Beatrice 1980 *Women, Sex and Pornography: A Controversial and Unique Study*. New York: Macmillan.

Frayser, Suzanne G. 1985 *Varieties of Sexual Experience: An Anthropological Perspective on Human Sexuality*. New Haven: HRAF Press.

Henry, Jules 1973 *On Sham, Vulnerability and Other Forms of Self-Destruction*. New York: Vintage.

Kemnitzer, David S. 1977 Sexuality as a Social Form: Performance and Anxiety in America. In *Symbolic Anthropology: A Reader in the Study of Symbols and Meanings*. J. L. Dolgin *et al.*, eds., pp. 292–309. New York: Columbia University Press.

Kessler-Harris, Alice 1985 Selling Sex, Buying Power? *The Women's Review of Books* 2 (February):12.

Leo, John 1987 Romantic Porn in the Boudoir. *Time* 30 March:63–5.

Lewin, Lauri 1984 *Naked is the Best Disguise*. New York: Morrow.

McCaghy, Charles H. and James K. Skipper, Jr 1972 Stripping: Anatomy of a Deviant Life Style. In *Life Styles: Diversity in American Society*. S. D. Feldman and G. W. Thielbard, eds., pp. 362–73. Boston: Little, Brown.

McWalter, Keith 1987 Couch Dancing. *New York Times Magazine* 6 December:138.

Margolis, Maxine L. 1984 *Mothers and Such: Views of American Women and Why They Changed*. Berkeley: University of California Press.

Mulvey, Laura 1977 Visual Pleasure and Narrative Cinema. In *Women and the Cinema: A Critical Anthropology*. Karyn Kay and Gerald Peary, eds., pp. 412–28. New York: Dutton.

New York Times 1980 Banned in Lawrence. 27 March:A29.

Petersen, David M. and Paula L. Dressel 1982 Equal Time for Women: Social Notes on the Male Strip Show. *Urban Life* 11(2):185–208.

Schultz, Annette 1985 Skin Shows: The Double Standard. *The Independent Florida Alligator* 6 September:1, 8.

Skipper, James K., Jr and Charles H. McCaghy 1970 Stripteasers: The Anatomy and Career Contingencies of a Deviant Occupation. *Social Problems* 17:391–404.

Snider, B. 1980 Girls' Night Out. *Oui* 9:107–10, 112, 128.

Time Magazine 1979 And Now, Bring on the Boys. 6 March:69.

Weatherford, Jack McIver 1986 *Porn Row*. New York: Arbor House.

Whitehurst, R. V. and G. V. Booth 1980 *The Sexes: Changing Relationships in a Pluralistic Society*. Agincourt, Canada: Gage.

Eleanor Leacock

In great part as a result of active Third World scholarship, it is now widely accepted that adequate cultural analysis requires delineating a society's changing relations with the world system, economically and politically. Hundreds of studies since the mid 1970s have analyzed the nature of culture change, either ethnohistorically, in relation to Western colonization, or ethnographically, in relation to "development" and "modernization." During the same period intensive inquiry into the activities and attitudes of women cross-culturally has made it abundantly clear that a full understanding of a culture requires analysis of its structure of gender relations. Much rethinking about the nature of culture itself, and its relation to individual and group behavior and action, has been generated by these two developments.

This chapter examines the case of women in Samoan history and thereby points to two major shortcomings in Derek Freeman's book, *Margaret Mead and Samoa: The Making and Unmaking of an Anthropological Myth* (1983) – its ignoring of both historicity and the structure of gender relations.[1] Despite his claim of advancing anthropology as a scientific discipline, Freeman seems unaware of these important foci in contemporary cultural anthropology and their theoretical and methodological significance. In Freeman's book, history is absent as a dynamic factor. He writes that there is no reason to suppose

that Samoan society and behavior changed in any fundamental way during the fourteen years between 1926, the year of the completion of Mead's inquiries, and 1940, when I began my own observations of Samoan behavior. In the refutation that follows, in addition to making use of the rich historical sources that date from 1830 onward, I shall draw on the evidence of my own research in the 1940s, *the years 1965 to 1968, and 1981.* (1983:120, emphasis added)

As a major part of his refutation of Mead's findings of a relatively carefree adolescence, Freeman cites police records on violence and delinquency among youth in the 1960s (Chapter 17). He does not even discuss the possibility that these data may tell us something of the problems of contemporary Samoa. Instead to Freeman, the data reveal the "darker

351

side" (p. xvii), the "grim realities" (p. 85) of an unchanging Samoan culture. And he buttresses his argument with examples of violence in the ethnohistorical record but without any reference to their context.

His account of rape, and of suicide among youth, is similarly ahistorical and contextless. Nowhere does Freeman make any reference to the kinds of problems people I talked with in Samoa discussed: the disjunction and distortion of traditional mores in the contemporary life of a poor and economically dependent Third World island nation (contrasts between American and Western Samoa are relevant here and Freeman lumps both); the problem of youth unemployment (meaningless in a subsistence economy but a major problem throughout the Third World today); the tragedy of a rising rate of youth suicide (a problem of concern throughout the South Pacific as well as in many other parts of the world); the new phenomenon of teenage vagrancy (impossible in Samoa of the past) and of teenage prostitution (a logical spin-off of vagrancy in a port town and a concern in Pago Pago). Nor does Freeman make any reference to the dilemma of young people who would strive to fulfil both old and new goals – parental and kin expectations, where much was expected of them but where the rewards were predictable and certain, and expectations for their success at school and in employment, where competition is intense, particularly in Western Samoa, and where effort may well result only in failure.

As for women, they were certainly not ignored by Freeman. They are prominent as guarded virgins and, consequently, as potential victims of rape. They are also presented as punitive mothers. In Freeman's view these roles are old in Samoan culture. To him church teachings on female chastity and on the importance of corporal punishment for children fitted with traditional Samoan culture and were easily integrated into it in the latter nineteenth century. Subsequently *fa'aSamoa* – the Samoan way – has changed little. Elsewhere I have criticized Freeman's static portrayal of Samoan culture and shown how it distorts his analysis of the problems of contemporary youth (Leacock 1986a). Here I draw on my ongoing ethnohistorical research and on the recent work of Schoeffel (1977, 1978, 1979) to address the issues of sexual practices and gender relations which Freeman raises. I do so by offering an analysis of the structure of Samoan gender relations as they have changed during the past 150 years.

Historical outline of Samoan–Western relations

The profound changes that have been taking place in Samoan culture and in the structure of Samoan gender relations can be most conveniently analyzed in terms of four major phases in relations between Samoa and

Western nations. These four periods are: an initial phase of sporadic contacts, followed after 1830 by a "trade and mission" stage, a "colonial" phase beginning in the 1880s, and a "modernization" phase starting around World War II.

During the phase of sporadic contacts, Samoan interest in the new trade with Europe led to the movement of interior villages to the coast and to the stepping up of inter-village warfare. Occasional sailors who had jumped ship and other castaways settled in Samoa. Sometimes they posed as missionaries, and their teachings (such as the assertion of one particularly colorful character that God had not one, but many sons, and he was one of them) were a bane to the teachers of the gospel who followed.

The second "trade and mission" phase followed the establishment of permanent mission stations after 1830. Developments associated with this phase were unevenly distributed among villages in contact with mission stations. They included: mission schools and the introduction of literacy; the institution of the village pastor – at first European or Tongan, then Samoan – as a basic part of village life; the introduction of European norms as ideals for gender relations and family life; and production of coconut oil for trade and for mission station collections. As counter-models to the missionaries, there were heavy drinkers and anti-clerics who formed part of the small European settlements on the islands.

Third, the "colonial" phase commenced in the early 1880s with the establishment of permanent European-run plantations and commercial centers sustained by secondary enterprises and services. European-owned plantations typically employed labor imported from China, Fiji, or elsewhere in the South Pacific, since Samoans usually refused to work on others' lands, especially under the harsh conditions that prevailed on the plantations. Formal outside rule was established at the turn of the century: the American Navy administered the small islands of American Samoa (which were later turned over to the Department of the Interior), and Western Samoa became German territory (after World War I it came under the control of New Zealand). European men involved in plantation and commercial enterprises often married high-status Samoan women, and an elite of mixed Samoan and European descent became established.

Last, the phase of "modernization" and "development" can be said to have begun by World War II, at least for American Samoa where the number of soldiers that passed through exceeded the local population, and where, as a consequence, the goals of young people were profoundly influenced. This phase brought the usual innovations associated with development – national school systems, hospitals and other health services, and island-wide networks of roads. It also brought self-rule to

American Samoa and independence to Western Samoa. At the same time, however, it brought new problems of trade deficits and economic dependency. The small islands of American Samoa are heavily subsidized, but the export of copra and lumber does not support Western Samoa's import of new "necessities" including food itself. Outmigration has become an established pattern, and there are more Samoans living in New Zealand, Hawaii, California, and other parts of the United States than there are living in Samoa. Remittances from overseas relatives constitute half of Western Samoa's GNP. The modern period has also brought with it the frustration of unemployment which was impossible in the former subsistence economy; the environment of port cities which, although small, nonetheless afford the setting for juvenile delinquency; and the sharpened conflict between Samoan and Western goals and ideals, between extended kin ties and the nuclear family, and between individual professionalism and the habits and attitudes associated with collective work.

The changing structure of gender relations and ideologies

In Samoa, as elsewhere in the world, the introduction of European trade and market relations, and the missionary activity that accompanied it, initiated fundamental changes in the structure of gender relations and ideology (Etienne and Leacock 1980). Some of these changes were matters of conscious policy as missionaries sought to replace broad kin-based socio-economic structures with an individualized work ethic of the West and a nuclear family form of kinship and marriage. In good part, however, changes were the indirect consequences of new and compelling economic and political forces unleashed by Samoa's increasing involvement in the "world capitalist system" and its transition from a subsistence to a largely market economy.

Missionary politics ranged over the gamut of Samoan cultural practice. The traditional hair style was not tolerated (men wore their hair long in Samoa, women short), nor was the clothing style. The introduction of Victorian ideals concerning female chastity, marital fidelity, monogamy, and the abolition of divorce were major missionary concerns. Christian converts were banned from attending the public defloration of the ceremonial village maiden, the *taupou,* and missionaries were suspicious of the *auluma,* the work and social group of girls and unmarried women. They tried to have young girls live at the mission (Roach 1984:99–100). They also tried to ban the "night dances" with their open ritualized celebration of sexuality, as well as the *malaga,* the visiting party that was (and long remained) a major form of recreation. The missionary Stair, writing of his experiences in Samoa, can serve as an informant. He described how people would plant their taro crop, and while allowing it to grow, would go from village to village feasting at each one:

Many evils were attendant upon this system. In the olden days it led to much dissipation and immorality, as well as fostered lazy and dissolute habits to such an extent that very few young men cared to settle down and work so as to provide for the family wants unless compelled to do so for dependence upon a chief, but spent their time roving from place to place in careless indolence. Of late years this system has been greatly modified, as the natives have become more chary of their property and learned to depend more upon their own individual efforts. (Stair 1983 [1897]:129–30)

Another missionary commented astutely on the conflict between the redistributive structure of the Samoan economy and the market orientation desired by the missionaries:

The people require more artificial wants before they will be induced to imitate foreign customs. They prefer their own houses to plastered cottages and certainly the Samoan homes are neat, strong and clean. There is little inducement for any individual to make any unusual efforts to improve his condition owing to what might be called a community of goods amongst them. The man who works the hardest seems to be imposed upon by his relatives. He has only the pleasure of distributing what he gets amongst them. (Sonderland 1854).[2]

The conflict between market and kin-based relations has been repeated at different times and in different contexts in societies around the world (Childe 1951; Wolf 1982). Although the precise course it has taken in each instance has been shaped by the particularities of a people's history and traditions, the overall unity of the process is clear. On the one hand, the roots of the conflict in relatively egalitarian societies can be traced to the increased importance of producing for exchange rather than direct consumption by the local group. This change led to the creation of new interest groups, the possibility of differential access to basic resources, and to the emergence of social ranking. With its corollary challenge to the principle of total equity, social ranking began to affect relations both within and between the genders (Leacock 1986b).[3] On the other hand, the transformation of kin relations and the subversion of women were both far from automatic processes. As the African data well attest, strong kin ties can coexist with a good measure of stratification and political centralization, and where women are involved in marketing and trade, they may maintain publicly recognized and responsible roles paralleling those of men. Using African data on societies ranging from the egalitarian Mbuti to the Dahomean state, Sacks (1979) examines the implications for women of the conflict between kin and market-based production relations. She analyzes the contrast between women's high status as wives when conjugal ties begin to supersede consanguinal ties in economic importance.

A focus on the sister/wife contrast is also apt for Samoa where, according to Shore: "a distinction between sisters and wives ... is central to a Samoan concept of the feminine" (Shore 1981:211).[4] Gailey's study of women in Tonga (1987) is historically oriented and defines conflicting trends at differing points in time. She treats women as people acting in their own interests. Instead of lumping women into a single category, she distinguishes between chiefly and non-chiefly statuses. Chiefly women in seventeenth-century Tonga were "engaged in the production and distri-bution of valuables, in the arrangement of strategic marriages, and directly and indirectly in contention for chiefly titles" while "Nonchiefly women produced valuables for their bilaterally integrated kin groups and for the chiefly groups" (Gailey 1980:304). Both chiefly and non-chiefly women "could rely on their brothers and maternal uncles for support regardless of their marital status." She continues:

All people had complexly balanced roles of authority and deference. For women, the two key roles were those of wife and sister, entailing deference and authority respectively. The content of each role varied with rank, chiefly women's marital and sibling relations being far more charged politically than those of nonchiefly women. With European contact and gradual colonization, the relative importance of sisterhood for both chiefly and nonchiefly women diminished, and, at the same time, women – especially nonchiefly women – became dependent on hus-bands. (1980:304–5)

Chiefly hierarchies were more firmly established in Tonga than in neigh-boring Samoa, and Tonga became – and remains – a monarchy. However, broad similarities between the two islands with respect to both pre-contact and post-contact culture history are strong. The above quotation could readily apply to Samoa as well, with the qualification that in Samoa *aiga* (kin group) ties are still too strong for women as wives to have become fully "dependent" upon their husbands.

Outline of the changing Samoan gender system

The following reconstruction of broad changes that have taken place in the Samoan gender system over the past century and a half, as these have affected women, includes some tentative postulates along with more conclusive statements. I am as yet midway in my ethnographic and ethnohistorical research.

The trade and missionary phase

Organization of work and distribution of products In keeping with the Polynesian patterns, Samoan women produced tapa cloth, coconut oil, and fine mats, valuables that were essential for exchanges that marked important occasions – marriages, achievement of titles, retribution for wrongs. The *auluma* was the social organization of unmarried and untitled women, and wives of untitled men. Its work was allocated by the *faletua ma tausi*, the organization of titled women and wives of titled men who participated in the distribution of valuables. Thus, the *faletua ma tausi* shared in the responsibility of the *fono*, the council of titled men, for negotiating inter-village relations. The *aumaga* was the organization of youth and untitled men that was responsible for most of the cooking and farm labor.

Coconut oil was an important product to Europeans, both missionaries and traders. The major change in women's work in the mid-nineteenth century lay in the stepped-up demand for this product. I am as yet unclear about the extent to which this led to the development of individualized ties, primarily through men in those villages near ports and mission stations, thus bypassing the role of the *faletua ma tausi*.

Sociopolitical activities In Samoan politics, chiefly titles were by no means a set hereditary affair, and the preoccupation of Samoan adults with jockeying for position has been dealt with extensively by Goldman (1970) and Keesing (1934) as well as Mead and Freeman. Although Sahlins (1958) designated Samoan society as stratified, the historical data point to strong and active conflict between egalitarian principles of sharing and of achieved status and emergent hierarchical principles of institutionalized differences in access to trade and its resources, to valuables, and to followers.

Ambitious women, as well as ambitious men, were involved in manipulating goods and people to enhance the position of their *aiga* and their villages, and their own status within both. Adult women operated in their *aiga* (as "sisters"), as wives of chiefly men, and occasionally as regional and national title holders in their own right. In the nineteenth century, the four highest titles in Samoa were held by a woman, Salamasina, the only person in Samoan history to achieve this national status. Coincidentally, Salamasina is also the name of the highest-ranking person in contemporary Western Samoa. She is the sister of the traditional head of state (an honorific status similar to the British crown). Interestingly enough, the present-day Salamasina has never married.

While the missionary attempt to break up the *auluma* initiated the process of downgrading its status (Schoefel 1977, 1979), it was too central to the Samoan organization of production to be disbanded. Instead women moved into the new institution of the village church as an additional arena for activity (Roach 1984). What began to happen in this context, however, was a blurring of the distinction between the chiefly women and wives of titled men on the one hand, and non-chiefly women on the other. Thus, the female hierarchy was weakened at the same time as the male hierarchy was strengthened.

Gender ideology and sexuality While missionary households served as models for the Victorian ideals of female chastity and marital fidelity, the fact that missionary wives were active teachers and workers with women's groups and in girls' schools meant that the Samoan expectation that women would be active in the "public" arena was left unchallenged. Furthermore, the staffing of the missionary households with Samoan youth was in keeping with the Samoan practice of assigning daily routine tasks to young people. However, the mission expectation that young women would do the cooking did contradict the Samoan division of labor according to which this was a male task. What appears to have happened is that indoor cooking with stoves and pots became women's work, while outdoor *umu* (stone oven) cooking remained men's work. But today, young women complain that they often find themselves having to do the latter, while their brothers will not do the former.

With respect to sexuality and Western ideologies of femininity, missionary letters reveal an expectable range of Samoan responses to mission teachings. A small number of converts, for whatever personal reasons, became deeply involved in church teachings. One letter, for example, recounts the case of a young woman fleeing to the mission for protection from sexual advances made to her and from other temptations to desert church teachings. At the other end of the spectrum were people interested in the small colony of Europeans around the ports with their passing ships, a setting that offered drinking and festivity along with the opportunity to trade. In this context, as happened so commonly the world around, the relative sexual freedom of non-elite women could be transformed into virtual prostitution.

In between the two extremes was the majority of people who were interested in the new activities opened up by the church in a range of areas – the dramatic performance of the pastor, the mastery of literacy and chance for philosophical discourse on Christian dogma, new forms of music and song, and the possible access to trade and other relations with outside countries. Some converts became backsliders as the novelty of the new activities wore off, or as their expectations were not met, or as

Western teachings posed too great a conflict with cultural traditions. But over the course of the latter part of the nineteenth century the Samoans took over the church and made it their own.

Perhaps its function as a physical center for village activity was the church's main attraction. In her ethnohistorical study of the church's impact on women, Roach (1984) points out that, by contrast with the political and economic structures that were beginning to emerge, the church was open to women's full participation, and they moved as a body into the opening. The missionaries' wives worked with the women, but unfortunately their letters are not filed in the mission archives, so we have only hints of Samoan women's attitudes at the time.

The missionaries occasionally expressed concern that, despite church attendance and activity, Western beliefs were not being fully adopted. Christianity, a missionary complained, "instead of bursting the bonds of the old life, has been eaten up by it" (Keesing 1934:410). Indeed, so assertive were the native pastors that they went on strike in an attempt to become salaried, as were the foreign missionaries, rather than be supported directly by their parishioners. Nonetheless, Victorian moralism, which was also being taught in the new boarding school, had to be outwardly espoused to some degree. Night dancing had to be muted, not paraded; the ban against divorce somehow dealt with; clothing styles altered, at least on formal occasions; adolescent affairs made more secretive. While much of this might be a matter of practicing discretion, nonetheless the die was cast.

The colonial phase

Organization of work The last two decades of the nineteenth century saw the full establishment of local commercial centers in Samoa and the opening up of some white-collar jobs to educated Samoans. At the same time a new method of drying copra for shipment was adopted on the plantations, and women's production of coconut oil lost its economic importance. The period was one of considerable cultural change, not stasis as Freeman argues. It saw the Samoan subsistence economy and the entire social fabric based upon it become increasingly and systematically undercut as it was being incorporated into the world economy.

Sociopolitical activities From the 1870s on, natural *fono*, chiefly councils of men, were set up in order to deal with new administrative problems and with relations to the European powers who were competing for control of the Pacific island nations. In 1899, by agreement among the United States, Britain and Germany, as Captain Gray (1960:101) discreetly puts it, "The United States accepted Tutuila, Aunu'u and Manu'a and all the rest of Samoa became a German responsibility."

Thus, on both economic and political fronts, Samoa came under Western centers of power and control. Samoan women, however, were not easily pushed into the domestic arena, as happened among indigenous populations in the West. Already active in the church, women's committees, comprised of the *auluma* and the *faletua ma tausi*, moved into public health and sanitation. These committees cooperated with authorities in introducing needed health and sanitation programs into the villages, thereby continuing to play active and publicly recognized roles of importance and responsibility. Yet in an economy that was rapidly becoming monetized, women were taking on this new responsibility as volunteers rather than paid workers.

Gender ideology and sexuality In contrast with the free-drinking and free-thinking European settlement of the mid-nineteenth century, the newly established Samoan elite was, with some exceptions, deplored by the missionaries, church-going and firmly supportive of Victorian moralism. The fact that this elite was made up in part of European men married to high-status Samoan women meant that many direct ties were maintained between it and chiefly village elites. Active reciprocal exchanges involved subsistence goods and various services on the one side, and on the other, cash and access to schooling, jobs, and help in emigrating. These ties were further strengthened by the fact that the port towns of Apia in Western Samoa and Pago Pago in American Samoa developed as an amalgam of the villages that were strung along the harbor shore and that continued to maintain their separate identities with their separate *fono* and women's committees.

The elite community, then, with its nuclear families and enclosed homes (contrasting with the unwalled Samoan *fale*), provided an alternative model of family life. Following Western upper-class mores, young unmarried women were chaperoned to protect their chastity, a practice which meshed with the chastity required of the Samoan high-status village *taupou*. As Shore has written: "Among distinguished families, which in modern Samoa might refer to possession of wealth, church status, education, part-European parentage as well as traditional rank, female chastity is stressed, a reflection of the enduring power of the *taupou* ideal" (1981:198).[5] The spin-off of the consequent association of female chastity with status became generalized and no longer limited to the *taupou* status.

The phase of "modernization" and "development"

The organization of work Industrial development by definition means the replacement of partially subsistence economies with full capitalist relations and with the individualized labor and nuclear family form that generally accompany it. Although the process is far from complete in Samoa, market relations permeate all corners of the islands. Women's economic activities are usually under-reported, but in 1971, one in every 7.5 women was recorded as earning wages or producing goods for sale.[6] Other women working overseas were sending remittances home. Meanwhile the spread of European housing and furnishings increasingly locks women into housewife and baby-tending roles. Young women may become especially pressured, expected to work hard at school or on the job while still providing the home services traditionally expected of youth (Gerber 1975).

Sociopolitical activities Despite the pace of "modernization," Samoan women maintain active public roles in *aiga* and village. They keep up the ceremonial exchange of fine mats that still figures importantly in social, political, and economic events (Weiner 1986). Women's committees organize maternal and child welfare clinics and take care of village sanitation, beautification, and other amenities, activities that would cost government agencies millions of dollars (Schoeffel 1978:5). However, these activities have become conceptualized as "domestic," and are no longer accorded appropriate public recognition. Women are particularly frustrated by their lack of communication with government bureaucracies (Schoeffel 1978). Meanwhile, they fight actively against discrimination with respect to desirable government jobs, and are presently trying to reinstate the women's commission dissolved by a newly elected prime minister.

Gender ideology and sexuality Schoeffel (1978:9) points out that stereotypes of "traditional" sex roles in Samoa are "a synthesis of Victorian missionary teaching, early 19th century 'traditional' values, and ... other cultural inputs." Among these, in Western Samoa, is the influence of returnees from the middle-class Samoan community in New Zealand, much concerned with preserving its reputation in the face of New Zealand racist stereotypes. Thus, the new feminist consciousness, with its worldwide communication network, faces the paradoxical situation that the freer sex-role mores, once associated with Samoa by the West, are now associated with the West by Samoans. However, in the resulting range of attitudes and behaviors, one can say that now, as in the past, discretion and sensitivity to public deportment are the critical dimensions of social behavior but not necessarily of private practice.

With respect to the alleged prevalence of rape on which Freeman's analysis focused, I found no indication that Samoan women were fearful of rape or saw it as an issue, as has happened in the United States and elsewhere. In fact, Freeman himself notes that many supposed cases are a "ploy" or "ruse" of young people wishing to marry against parental approval, while other cases occur in association with drinking and seaport life. I have argued in this brief account that without a dynamic analysis of the total gender system, the cultural meaning of virginity and rape in Samoa is misrepresented by Freeman's ahistorical and contextless analysis. It conflicts with the ethnohistorical and ethnographic material and with my fieldwork observations.

Samoan women could hardly be regarded as subordinate, dependent victims of male aggression, now or in the past. I was particularly impressed with the ease and assurance with which the women I met dealt with authority – not only older women such as a retired mayor, a *matai*, a high-titled school principal – but also young women who had successfully battled discrimination with respect to good jobs and were managing both work and family. Unlike Western women, Samoan women are not uncomfortable handling authority for they have behind them a long tradition of their own publicly recognized organizations and responsibilities. This tradition has given them, as the brief historical reconstruction presented here indicates, the experience of operating in structured female hierarchies, under female control, and in activity acknowledged to be of vital political, economic, and ritual significance.

EDITOR'S NOTE

Eleanor Leacock died a few months after the Wenner-Gren conference for which a draft version of this chapter was prepared. At the time of her death she was in the field gathering data which would have been incorporated into a revised version of the paper. She never had a chance to revise the chapter, however, to meet her usual high standards. Constance Sutton of New York University kindly offered to assume responsibility for revisions, with the goal of producing a chapter which would present Eleanor Leacock's developing ideas in the absence of having the author's final thoughts and polished views.

NOTES

In the spring of 1985 I went to Samoa to interview professionals working with youth – teachers, counselors, public health workers, administrators, etc. In both American and Western Samoa I attended workshops organized to deal with aspects of youth problems. I also visited Samoan homes, talked with elders, attended festivities, and talked with young people informally. I am indebted to the American Association of University Women for awarding me a Founders Fellowship, and to the Faculty Research Award Program of the City University of New York. I am also grateful to the Laboratoire d'Anthropologie Sociale in Paris for a Visiting Professorship that enabled me to spend time in the French archives and in the archives of the London Missionary Society.

1 So far these issues have not been sufficiently emphasized in reviews of Freeman's book, of which there are so many it would require a separate article to review them. Examples include Schneider (1983), Weiner (1983), Rubin (1983), Strathern (1983), Levy (1983), Holmes (1983), Shore (1983), Bernstein (1983), Shankman (1983), and Ember (1985).

2 Freeman ignores the structure of market relations and the challenge that individualized labor and the nuclear family pose to kin-based relations of production and distribution. Instead he discusses culture change with reference only to the ideological level. Citing Keesing, he writes "during the years from 1830 to 1879, when the Samoans were converted to Christianity and traders became established, a postcontact 'equilibrium of culture' was reached, which persisted virtually unaltered into the 1930s" (1983:120). This equilibrium – the Samoan ethos – Freeman explains later "derives from an admixture of institutions that emphasize rank and the aggressive defense of ancient privilege, with Christianity and its ethic of mutual love and forgiveness ... The stern values of this rank system, though fundamentally unchanged since pagan times, have thus been tempered by a belief in an all-seeing and all-powerful God, who, while he relentlessly punishes those who disobey his commandments, is also a God of love" (1983:273–4). For Freeman, then, market relations did not increasingly augment and add new dimensions to Samoan competition for rank. Instead Western influence, in the form of Christianity, ameliorated and stabilized it. His book gives no hint that the introduction of Victorian norms for gender relations posed a new conflict for Samoan society.

3 By "equity" I do not mean "identity." I have long been impressed by the great latitude for individuality (not individualism) that characterizes egalitarian societies.

4 Working in a structuralist frame, Shore explores the distinction in terms of ideological oppositions – female/male, order/disorder, and culture/nature. His treatment of women's and men's economic activities and social responsibilities are described simply as either "active" or "passive." The same lack of historicity is even more true of Ortner's treatment of the sister/wife dichotomy in Polynesia generally. Ortner notes the lack of essential economic ties between spouses in traditional Polynesian society. (1981:386–8) and its probable relation to the frequency of divorce and adultery noted for the area. But this observation does not lead her to examine the role of kinswomen in economic life, nor to consider that there may have been major changes taking place at the very time ethnographic records were being produced.

5 From a historical-evolutionary viewpoint, the sources of the two traditions are similar. Protecting the virginity of the high-status *taupou* (and its parallels throughout Polynesia) is an interesting example of the concern with legitimacy where the passing on of rank and associated property and other resources is becoming (or is already) institutionalized.

6 The widespread acceptance – at least formally – of Western conventions for gender roles in Samoa, as elsewhere, means that Samoans do not report their work in agriculture, in family business, etc. In Samoa the work of the women's committees is grossly underestimated by everyone with respect to its economic value.

REFERENCES

Bernstein, Richard 1983 Samoa: A Paradise Lost? *New York Times*, 24 April.

Childe, V. Gordon 1951 *Social Evolution*. New York: Henry Schuman.

Ember, Melvin 1985 Evidence and Science in Ethnography: Reflections on the Freeman-Mead Controversy. *American Anthropologist* 87(4):906–10.

Etienne, Mona and Eleanor Leacock, eds. 1980 *Women and Colonization: Anthro-.pological Perspectives*. New York: Praeger.

Freeman, Derek 1983 *Margaret Mead and Samoa: The Making and Unmaking of an Anthropological Myth*. Cambridge: Harvard University Press.

Gailey, Christine 1980 Putting Down Sisters and Wives: Tongan Women and Colonization. In *Women and Colonization: Anthropological Perspectives*. Mona Etienne and Eleanor Leacock, eds., pp. 294–322. New York: Praeger.
    1987 *From Kinship to Kingship: Gender Hierarchy and State Formation in the Tongan Islands*. Austin: University of Texas Press.

Gerber, Eleanor Ruth 1975 The Cultural Patterning of Emotions in Samoa. Ph.D. dissertation, University of California, San Diego.

Goldman, Irving 1970 *Ancient Polynesian Society*. Chicago: University of Chicago Press.

Gray, Captain J. A. C. 1960 *Amerika Samoa, A History of American Samoa and Its United States Naval Administration*. Annapolis, MD: US Naval Institute.

Holmes, Lowell 1983 A Tale of Two Studies. *American Anthropologist* 85(4):929–35.

Holmes, Lowell, ed. 1986 *The Quest for the Real Samoa: The Mead/Freeman Controversy and Beyond*. South Hadley, MA: Bergin and Garvey.

Keesing, Felix 1934 *Modern Samoa: Its Government and Changing Life*. London: George Allen and Unwin.

Leacock, Eleanor 1986a Postscript: The Problems of Youth in Contemporary Samoa. In *The Quest for the Real Samoa: The Mead/Freeman Controversy and Beyond*. Lowell Holmes, ed., pp. 177–88. South Hadley, MA: Bergin and Garvey.
    1986b Women, Power and Authority. In *Visibility and Power, Essays on Women in Society and Development*. Leela Dube, Eleanor Leacock, and Shirley Ardener, eds., pp. 107–35. Delhi: Oxford University Press.
    1986c Postscript: Implications for Organization. In *Women's Work, Development and the Division of Labor by Gender*. Eleanor Leacock and Helen Safa, eds., pp. 253–66. South Hadley, MA: Bergin and Garvey.

Levy, Robert I. 1983 The Attack on Mead. *Science* 220:829–32.

Ortner, Sherry 1981 Gender and Sexuality in Hierarchical Societies: The Case of Polynesia and Some Comparative Implications. In *Sexual Meanings: The Cultural Construction of Gender and Sexuality*. Sherry B. Ortner and Harriet Whitehead, eds., pp. 359–409. New York: Cambridge University Press.

Patience, Allan and Joseph Wayne Smith 1986 Derek Freeman and Samoa: The Making and Unmaking of a Biobehavioral Myth. *American Anthropologist* 88(1):157–62.

Roach, Elizabeth Marchette 1984 From English Mission to Samoan Congregation: Women and the Church in Rural Western Samoa. Ph.D. dissertation, Columbia University.

Rubin, Vera 1983 Review. *American Journal of Orthopsychiatry* 53(3):550–4.

Sacks, Karen 1979 *Sisters and Wives: The Past and Future of Sexual Equality.* Westport, CT: Greenwood Press.

Sahlins, Marshall 1958 *Social Stratification in Polynesia.* Seattle: University of Washington Press.

Schneider, David 1983 The Coming of a Sage to Samoa. *Natural History* 92(6): 4–10.

Schoeffel, Penelope 1977 The Origin and Development of Contemporary Women's Associations in Western Samoa. *Journal of Pacific Studies* 3:1–22.

    1978 The Ladies Row of Thatch: Women and Rural Development in Western Samoa. *Pacific Perspective* 8(2):1–13.

    1979 Daughters of Sina: A Study of Gender, Status and Power in Western Samoa. Ph.D. dissertation, Australian National University.

Shankman, Paul 1983 The Samoan Conundrum. *Canberra Anthropology* 6(1):38–57.

Shore, Bradd 1981 Sexuality and Gender in Samoa: Conceptions and Missed Conceptions. In *Sexual Meanings: The Cultural Construction of Gender and Sexuality.* Sherry B. Ortner and Harriet Whitehead, eds., pp. 192–215. New York: Cambridge University Press.

    1983 Paradox Regained: Freeman's *Margaret Mead and Samoa. American Anthropologist* 85(4):935–44.

Sonderland, J. 1854 Correspondence. In Archives of the London Missionary Society. School of Oriental and African Studies, University of London. South Seas, Samoan Islands, Box 25, Folder 7, Jacket D. Tutuila, June 27.

Stair, J. B. 1983 [1897] *Old Samoa.* London: Religious Tract Society.

Strathern, Marilyn 1983 The Punishment of Margaret Mead. *London Review of Books* 5–18 May:5–6.

Weiner, Annette 1983 Ethnographic Determinism: Samoa and the Margaret Mead Controversy. *American Anthropologist* 85(4):909–19.

    1986 Forgotten Wealth: Cloth and Women's Production in the Pacific. In *Women's Work, Development and the Division of Labor by Gender.* Eleanor Leacock and Helen Safa, eds., pp. 96–110. South Hadley, MA: Bergin and Garvey.

Wolf, Eric 1982 *Europe and the People Without History.* Berkeley: University of California Press.

17 Sanskritization as female oppression in India

Gerald D. Berreman

India has undoubtedly the most complex and rigid system of social hierarchy in the world. It includes examples of virtually every known basis for defining and judging inequalities and for organizing the apportionment of differential power, privilege, well-being, and other valued things and experiences. There we find hierarchies of an astounding variety of social categories: caste, class, ethnicity, estate, lineage and other kin groups, gender, age and more, all of them bases for shared and distinctive, privileged or impaired life chances and life experiences (Berreman 1981).

India is officially a secular nation, but it is dominated by the social organization, culture, and ideology of its Hindu majority. That ideology assigns females to a position distinctly subordinate to males: constrained, dependent, exploited, oppressed, physically and psychically endangered (Kakar 1981; Miller 1981). Muslim society and culture, the principal minority tradition in India, does the same, as do most other great traditional religions in their Indian manifestations.

Combined with female subordination is a deep-seated belief in the power of women (Kakar 1981:52–112). Although they are subordinated, women are not trivialized as they are in the United States, for example (Berreman 1966, 1969). They are controlled, largely by being confined to traditional familial roles in which they are dependent upon and dominated by men. Those who are able or allowed to transcend those roles through such mechanisms as education, familial wealth or influence, organizational or political support, and legal emancipation, are likely to function as respected, capable people in a wide variety of social, political, technical, and occupational roles, where they often prove to be effective leaders and formidable competitors to men.

The manner and extent to which a given social category in Indian society endorses and participates in the dominant Hindu ideology and its behavioral correlates vary. With that variation, there is co-variation in the nature and extent of subordination and suppression of females. Those social categories which characteristically deviate from the dominant ideal of female subordination, collectively constitute a major proportion of the population. Such categories include:

> Groups which are largely or entirely outside the purview of traditional Hindu beliefs, values, and social organization, for example, tribal societies.
>
> Hindus at the bottom of or low in the caste/class hierarchy, for example, "untouchables" and many or most Sudras.
>
> Hindus who are peripheral to the dominant society socio-culturally or geographically in ways that make them peculiar, suspect, or attenuated adherents to the creed, for example Himalayan (Pahari) Hindus (Berreman 1963), or Hindus with matrilineal or bilateral descent systems, unconventional marriage rules, atypical economies, and the like.
>
> Hindus who have fallen out of the bottom of the system economically despite being of respectable caste origin and status, for example people who are poverty-stricken and therefore unable to live up to the requirements of their ascribed status.
>
> Hindus who have transcended or opted out of the traditional value system, at least so far as its criteria for hierarchical status are concerned, through, for example, secularization, modernization, and Westernization (Srinivas 1966:46–146), all of which are processes that entail a shift to economic (class) criteria for status. Others in this category have adopted reformist versions of Hinduism or have converted to non-Hindu belief systems such as Buddhism, Christianity, or Islam.

This chapter addresses two major themes. First is the issue of variation in the repressive subordination of women in India, especially northern India. Female oppression is not a uniform phenomenon throughout Indian society. It is most conspicuously a feature of orthodox, Sanskritic (as prescribed in the sacred Sanskrit texts), Brahmanic (identified with the practices and prescriptions of the elite, priestly category in Hindu society) Hinduism, and its analogues in Indian Islam. Those who are not adherents to the orthodox version of the creed and who do not aspire to acceptance as participants in its traditions or do not seek the approval of participants do not, for the most part, adhere to the beliefs, values, and behaviors which constitute the gender hierarchy of the dominant society. Neither are they subject to the enforcement mechanisms which sustain it.

The co-occurrence of female subordination and the emergence of female power and emancipation has been demonstrated in the context of sociopolitical and economic changes in Indian society. Since the 1970s a surge of organizational activity, much of it militant and far-reaching, has occurred among women and like-minded men in response to female subordination, exploitation of female employees, wife abuse, dowry-deaths, and other damaging and degrading practices against women, with the result that there are now innumerable grassroots voluntary associations and movements throughout the country demanding and achieving female rights and emancipation from male domination. Change in female oppression has also come about as a result of attempts by lower caste and other relatively low-status groups to raise their economic and social status. My research among the Paharis of India's Himalayan region, and more recently with the grassroots environmental movement among them called Chipko, illuminates both of these topics.

Discussion of the issues raised above will be carried out under three basic headings. It will be introduced in the following section with a number of propositions about gender and gender relations in the context of Indian society. These will be followed by observations, examples, and empirical generalizations from the region of my research in Uttarakhand. Finally, some implications of this regionally and situationally specific analysis for the understanding of gender processes at work in contemporary Indian society at large will be suggested.

Status enhancement and female oppression in India: some propositions

1. Status enhancement at the level of caste in traditional India is sought primarily through emulation of high-caste ritual behaviors and other symbolic status markers by groups regarded as having low ritual (caste) status, and sometimes those regarded as outside of the ritual status system. This process is referred to generically as "Sanskritization," a term introduced and elaborated by Srinivas (1952:30, 1956, 1966:1–45, 1977). These status markers include: seclusion and relative circumscription of activities of women, epitomized in the Islamic custom of purdah as it has been incorporated into North Indian society (Jacobson 1982; Papanek 1982; Mandelbaum 1988); patrilocal marriage, wherein the wife joins her husband in the household of his family; dowry marriage, in which the bride's family provides a substantial contribution of money and/or goods to the groom's family at the time of marriage; patrilineal descent and inheritance, wherein children issuing from a marriage are members of their father's kin groups and males inherit all property except some personal possessions of womenfolk; prohibition of wife-initiated divorce while permitting it at the initiative of a husband; prohibition of widow and divorcee remarriage while allowing and in fact encouraging widower and divorce remarriage; female deference to males, especially to the

husband and others in his household after marriage; female economic dependence upon males, especially after marriage; preference and greater concern for male children; multiple wives (polygyny) allowed and multiple husbands (polyandry) prohibited; extra-marital sexual activity strictly prohibited for women, with especially dire sanctions against that with lower-caste men, while extra-marital sexual activity is tolerated for men, especially with lower-caste women (Berreman 1960b). Systematic or routine deviation from any of these norms by members of a caste stigmatizes that caste, condemning its members to low status. Put otherwise, low castes are characterized by such stigmatized behaviors and attributes. Any caste asserting claims to higher status than that generally accorded it must as an initial step demonstrate that it does not tolerate such behaviors among its members and must rigorously avoid other stigmatized behaviors such as violation of dietary rules, ritual requirements, and purity maintenance.

Claims to higher status than that conventionally accorded to them is a common phenomenon among castes in India. In fact, it is probably universal among the two lowest caste categories (varnas), "untouchables" and Sudras. Such claims are rarely successful because status enhancement cannot be achieved by emulation alone, but must be accompanied by the acquisition and exercise of power sufficient to enforce the claim to skeptical higher castes jealous of their prerogatives and ruthless in protecting them. This power may take the form of political influence (votes, patronage), legal recourse (to civil rights legislation), powerful allies (political figures or organizations), social and political education/proselytization, collective action (civil disobedience), physical threats or confrontation, economic coercion, financial power (to hire, bribe), and more. Therefore, traditional status emulation such as Sanskritization succeeds only in conjunction with secular mobility.

2. Status enhancement in India is sought at the levels of the individual, family, lineage, or occupational, neighborhood, regional, ethnic, and linguistic groups, primarily through alternatives to traditional status criteria described by such terms as secularization, modernization, urbanization, Westernization, education, occupational mobility, and economic gain. It therefore constitutes class mobility in most cases. It is achieved to the extent that these endeavors are successful; that is, to the extent that people are able to acquire education, respected and remunerative jobs, and money. Those who are successful are primarily those already of middle class or above.

3. Status enhancement through symbolic emulation (the first proposition above) cannot be realistically attempted by women as such, for they are not an autonomous, exclusive, self-reproducing social, economic, or

political entity, although they certainly are a social category and can be mobilized into a pressure group. Moreover, this route to mobility entails Sanskritization, which initiates or deepens female subordination and is inherently counterproductive for women.

4. The most promising mechanism for status enhancement of females in India is secular mobility as described in the second proposition. It holds the promise of enhanced social, political, and economic power and hence parity with males and emancipation from their domination.

5. Among people who are of low traditional (ritual, caste) status and are poor (low secular, class status), the position of women is often one of a considerable degree of parity with men of their status group, but in that case it is parity in poverty, vulnerability, degradation, and misery, not parity in freedom, autonomy, and a satisfactory quality of life. Parity in poverty is scarcely deserving of the term "equality," and scarcely worth the effort. What is worth the effort, as a first priority, is enhancement of the well-being of all within the group, regardless of gender.

6. Gender inequality or hierarchy is never independent of class, estate, and ethnic hierarchy. In fact, they are inextricably linked: gender hierarchy is an expression of these other hierarchies and they of it. That is, they are various manifestations of an hierarchical ethic. What enhances or degrades one gender ultimately does so for both. It is the fact of hierarchy, of inequality, of privileged and impaired access, which is the source of the iniquities of inequality and which ultimately damages the entire society.

7. Gender hierarchies in India are least developed – females have the greatest autonomy and equality with men – in three types of sociocultural settings: first, in tribal societies (kin based and socially unstratified) which have not been incorporated into the dominant social system of India and its gender hierarchies; second, among the affluent, elite, educated, secularized segments of Indian society which have transcended the gender hierarchy system of the dominant society; and third, among the lowest castes and classes, the poorest and least Sanskritized segments of Hindu society, to which the dominant pattern of gender hierarchy is more or less irrelevant given the overwhelming collective subordination of the group.

8. Gender hierarchies are most developed – females have the least autonomy and equality with men – in Sanskritized, traditional segments of Hindu society. But among elites of this sort, women have the compensatory economic advantage and social respect of the elite caste and class status they share with their menfolk.

9. The most severe gender inequalities of all are found among poor, low-caste groups which are striving for upward mobility in the traditional, ritually defined hierarchy, through Sanskritization. Women there have the worst of all worlds: they do not have gender parity because of the

	Affluence/respect	Poverty/disrespect
Gender parity	1 high caste/class secular status criteria	2 low caste/class static status
Gender disparity	3 high caste/class traditional status criteria (Sanskritic)	4 low caste/class mobility striving (Sanskritizing)

Fig. 17.1 Schematic view of gender hierarchy in India as it intersects with class and caste hierarchies

strictures imposed by Sanskritic status emulation, they do not have economic sufficiency and security because of their class situation (their poverty), and they do not have social respect because of their caste (ritual status). Put another way, they suffer discrimination unique to their gender status as defined by Sanskritic ideology, together with poverty and denigration which they share with their menfolk as a result of their class and caste statuses respectively.

The relationships among these variables can be illustrated with a fourfold table (Fig. 17.1). The principal variables are: gender parity versus gender disparity, and affluence/respect versus poverty/disrespect. The cells represent four social categories which vary by caste/class level; in the case of the affluent categories, by degree to which reference groups are traditional/sacred/Sanskritic versus modern/secular/Western; and in the case of poor categories, by degree to which the status is static (non-Sanskritizing) versus mobile (Sanskritizing). Cell 1 is the most favorable situation for gender categories other than the dominant one, while cell 4 is the least favorable. Cells 2 and 3 are intermediate, the judgment between them involving assessment of the trade-off between poverty and subordination and the trade-off between affluence and parity. That is, is it better to be gender-equal in a group that is poor, disrespected, and dominated, or to be gender-subordinate in a group that is relatively well-off, respected, and independent?

This model provides a schematic view of how gender hierarchy intersects with class/caste hierarchies and traditional/secular value hierarchies. Any single case may fit well or uneasily into any of the four cells, depending on the social dynamics in play.

Gender hierarchy in Uttarakhand: a case study

Uttarakhand is a region occupying 20,000 square miles of the Himalayas immediately west of Nepal, populated by some 4.5 million people most of whom live in the foothills up to an altitude of about 7,500 feet.[1] It is a lightly populated, mountainous, forested, resource-rich appendage to Uttar Pradesh, India's most populous (with over 110 million) and fourth largest state, which is geographically mostly low and flat, economically poor, agricultural, and culturally conservative. The people of the mountains are primarily subsistence farming, Hindu peasants commonly known among themselves and outsiders either by subregional designations, such as Garhwali, or by the generic term Pahari (literally "of the mountains"). They share a regionally distinct version of the major features of culture and social organization found among most rural North Indians (Berreman 1960a, 1962:344–51). That distinctiveness is in part a result of adaptation to their mountainous environment and even more so of their shared history and relative isolation from people of the plains.

One of many significant differences between the Pahari people and people of the plains (whom they term Deshi, literally "of the country"), is in the status of females *vis-à-vis* males. Pahari women are accorded significantly more autonomy and social, economic, and political parity relative to men than is generally the case for plains women. Paharis are aware of, and pleased by, this fact, at least with regard to its manifestations in marriage, family, household, kinship, economy, and religion at the village level.

Aspects of female autonomy

Pahari women are major contributors to agriculture, animal husbandry, and associated activities which are the bases of Pahari livelihood. In addition to doing virtually all of the household work, food preparation, and childcare, they work at least as many hours in the primary tasks of farming as do men, with whom they share nearly every task in animal husbandry and agriculture. Exceptions are that women do the winnowing and mortar-milling of grain, while they are excluded from work entailing animal traction (plowing, harrowing), the transportation and marketing of milk and cash crops (a relatively recent innovation), and construction of houses and implements. Even these tasks they can and will perform in the absence of men, as in "maleless villages" of Garhwal, whose able-bodied men have left to seek employment in cities of the plains (Berreman 1983:296, 313). In fact, the Pahari division of labor is in general flexible, with even caste specialization far less rigid than on the plains (Berreman 1963:69–71).

Pahari women also play a greater role in "public" religious activity than in the plains. Although all Brahman priests are men, Pahari women are prominent among the ranks of shamans and in other non-Brahmanical roles and occasionally as temple-keepers and holy-women. They are active participants in worship at the household, village, and regional temples, but also as central figures in shamanistic activity, curing, exorcism, divination, and a variety of life-cycle, calendrical, and extraordinary rituals. In the Himalayas the lines between traditions that are great and little (Marriott 1955), literate and non-literate, widespread and narrowly spread (Srinivas 1952:213–18), transcendental and pragmatic (Mandelbaum 1964), Sanskritic and vernacular, are blurred and relatively unimportant to those who practice them. The difference between women's and men's participation, as between the nature of low-caste and high-caste religious belief and practice, is therefore comparatively slight.[2]

The high status of Pahari women is revealed in many other ways as well. One example which is important to them as well as to the outside observer is that they can divorce and remarry as freely as can men, which is freely indeed.[3] This practice is startling to plains people, as is the fact that Pahari widows are free to marry (and most do) their deceased husband's brother in accordance with the traditional but not mandatory institution of levirate. Another example is that if a woman feels overburdened with household and agricultural work, she may insist upon her husband taking a co-wife whom she often selects and who is likely to be her relative. Throughout the Pahari area, matrilocality is an alternative to patrilocality. It is disfavored but not infrequently resorted to by landowning families with daughters but no sons so that the son-in-law can assume work and responsibilities of the male head of household.

A distinctive feature of marriage found universally in traditional Pahari society is that bridewealth is given by the groom's family to the bride's at marriage, rather than the dowry being given by the bride's family to the groom's as is characteristic of high-caste plains marriages. In the central Pahari region, Uttarakhand, traditional law made acceptance of bridewealth the single defining criterion for a completed, legitimate marriage (Berreman 1963:129). Those Paharis who aspire to the approval of the dominant plains society, the "plainswardly mobile," have begun since the 1950s to adopt dowry marriage with increasing frequency. Others, however, stoutly defend their Pahari traditions, claiming, for example, that "it is not proper for Rajputs to accept charity ... When we take a girl, we pay for her!" (p. 129). This attitude is reinforced by the pervasive Pahari belief that dowry brides do not live long and/or are likely to prove infertile. Traditional brides, therefore, are not subject to the pressures, abuses and, in extreme cases, "dowry deaths" (murders of brides by in-laws in retaliation for "insufficient" dowry, or to clear the way for a second marriage in order to secure an additional dowry), to which urban plains brides are subjected with apparently increasing frequency (Sharma 1983). The absence of dowry also means that a husband and his family do not have that wealth to hold as ransom to keep the bride from returning home or eloping with another man, should she be so inclined or driven to contemplate by in-laws' threats of abuse. Instead, the Pahari bride need only persuade her family or lover to reimburse her husband and his family the bridewealth in order to effect a divorce. If her interests, wishes, and well-being are important considerations to her family or lover, as they usually are, this transfer can be readily accomplished.

The local exogamy required in the plains is absent in the mountains (Berreman 1962, 1963). Pahari brides and grooms can be of the same village as long as kin and caste relations (of exogamy and endogamy, respectively) are appropriate. Intra-village marriages, which constituted 20 percent of the 377 marriages I recorded in Sirkanda, leave the bride in close proximity to her natal family and kinsmen and their implicit and explicit protection. Even for the majority of marriages, which are extra-village patrilocal ones, the relatively localized marriage networks mean that brides are rarely more than a day's walk from their natal village and its support. Pahari women, wives and daughters-in-law, especially young ones, make annual home visits, often of up to two months' duration. These visits give wives respite from the tensions of life in their husbands' villages and provide an opportunity to air grievances, seek moral support, and even formulate plans for redress, or in extreme cases for escape, with family members or friends. Pahari religion offers support to a bride through the belief that deities of her natal household accompany her to her husband's home upon marriage and remain there, looking after her welfare and ready to wreak punishment on any who would mistreat her.

Another aspect of Pahari women's relative freedom and unusually high status is their participation in recreational and expressive activities. They attend many festive occasions and there participate in folk dancing and singing. These are joyous activities for high-caste women as well as low, but are discouraged by Sanskritic, plainswardly mobile high-caste Pahari elites because of their similarity to the singing and dancing for the entertainment of men by courtesans and prostitutes. Dancing in a state of spiritual possession, especially by high-caste women, is more frequent but even more condemned and concealed by such elites and self-appointed watchdogs on behalf of Sanskritization. This is perhaps because dancing of this kind is less controlled and constrained than folk dancing – in fact is often quite abandoned in nature – and its context of spiritual possession is distinctly non-Sanskritic, although entirely within the folk traditions of all-Indian Hinduism. On occasion, consumption of liquor, sweets, and meat and smoking of tobacco are part of the festive activities in which women as well as men engage on these occasions, sometimes in association with modest displays of public flirtation and affection. These activities, too, are enjoyed by village women and men but are deplored by Sanskritically ambitious elites.

These are important ways in which Pahari women exercise autonomy, self-expression, and fulfilment to a degree rare or unknown among high castes of the plains, and inconsistent with Sanskritic female subordination. It is true that in Uttarakhand women are subordinate to men in many ways, but it is subordination in the context of greater independence, assertiveness, and economic and social participation in public spheres than occurs in the plains. Thus, the henpecked husband, even the cuckolded one, and the divorcing wife are familiar images in Pahari folklore and humor. They seem to be the subject of teasing, good-natured merriment and sly ribaldry more than of hard-edged warning and moralizing as is commonly the case among high-caste people in the plains.

Gender hierarchy and social change

Two major changes have contributed to variability in female status among the Paharis. First, elites have increasingly become educated, some moving to the plains to live as expatriates but with a foothold still in the Himalayas. They often assume the role of spokesmen for and critics of the lifeways of their rural relatives. Others have settled permanently outside, severing all ties with their homeland and becoming assimilated to plains society. In recent years some members of the latter category have reasserted their Himalayan identity but with a new, orthodox, Sanskritic, plains-oriented standard of what Pahari culture and society should be. Some have returned to live in the Himalayas, usually in urban localities (Dhasmana 1982:202–4, has described this "migrant syndrome," see Berreman 1983:298, where he is quoted).

Both kinds of emigrants tend to exhibit a missionary zeal in propounding their puritanical standard, thereby contributing substantially to pressure for Sanskritization in the Himalayas. Such pressure has impelled some rural people of Uttarakhand to aspire to, or adopt, a more Sanskritic division of labor, by gender and caste, than was traditional. They adopt more Sanskritic ritual practices and give up or conceal formerly cherished Pahari ones ranging from buffalo sacrifice to bridewealth marriage. Among the Pahari traditions which have disappeared or threaten to do so are those which have bestowed and perpetuated the relatively high status of Pahari women. They are being replaced by customs of plains orthodoxy, such as dowry marriages, widow celibacy, male-only initiation of divorce and the like, all customs which subordinate and endanger women.

Second, the principal countervailing force to Sanskritic degradation of women in the Himalayas is ironically the devastating impact of environmental degradation imposed under the guise of "development" by entrepreneurs and governmental agencies from the plains. Plainsmen are therefore the source of Sanskritization, which subordinates women while claiming to enhance the status of Pahari society in general, and they are the source of environmental devastation by government and entrepreneurs, which diminishes and jeopardizes the livelihood of all Paharis, disrupting their families, society, and culture while seeking to "modernize" their way of life and "improve" their standard of living. The irony is compounded when one considers that the social and economic disruption which "development" brings, including the emigration of men in search of work, puts into high relief the strength, independence, and skills of Pahari women as they manage their families, farms, and villages in the virtual absence of able-bodied men. That is, economic and social disruption in the Pahari region are survivable because of the high-status attributes of women. The exercise of those attributes is self-enhancing for women even as plains-derived Sanskritic status emulation seeks to constrain and subordinate them. The relative impact of these two counterforces varies according to the circumstances in which they operate, so that the consequences, for women and for the society at large, cannot be predicted or understood in any particular instance without careful investigation of those circumstances.

The sad fact is, however, that material poverty transcends symbolic status, so that even the additional responsibility, authority, and status which social disruption and the departure of men thrusts upon women is more than counterbalanced by the poverty to which the entire population is subject. As a result, everyone regardless of gender or caste suffers from the economic consequences of environmental degradation in ways previously unknown to Pahari people.

In the Himalayas as everywhere else, the position of women and men can be no better than that of the larger social entities to which they belong. This fact accounts largely for the problems elite women have encountered when advocating militant action against men to enhance the status of women in poverty-stricken, and/or oppressed segments of society, be it in India, America, or elsewhere. It is often apparent to women of low-status groups that their men are victims of circumstances –

circumstances of oppression – even as they themselves are, with the result that they define the enemy not as men, the problem not as gender hierarchy, but as the system of caste, class, or ethnic stratification within which both women and men live and suffer. It is yet another difficult step to recognize gender hierarchy as a concomitant or a manifestation of the general problem of hierarchy – of inequality – and to address it, too (perhaps sequentially, perhaps simultaneously), rather than instead or not at all.

Sexual exploitation as gender hierarchy

In Uttarakhand and Himachal Pradesh, and in some regions more than others, women also migrate to the plains in search of income. That these women are primarily of the low castes is attributable to the fact that it is only those castes which have little or no land either to support them (and therefore keep them in their villages) or to require their attention and labor (and therefore tie them down in their villages). Prostitution is too often the source of income these emigrants find, whether or not it was their intent when they embarked. In some areas, such as Jaunsar Bawar, in northwestern Dehra Dun district, prostitution is a major resource in the remittance economy of low castes. Among them the most prosperous low-caste households are often those which include one or more successful urban prostitutes or ex-prostitutes.

Prostitutes may be recruited by high-caste men of the region who profit from their "sale," and who may have told the women they would arrange marriage or concubinage for them with prosperous, generous urban men. The custom of bridewealth is often said to make plausible or at least palatable the claim that the transaction is for marriage rather than prostitution. Intermediaries may earn a regular income from these arrangements (Berreman 1963:74–5). Whether a woman has been kidnapped, misled, unwillingly sold off by her husband or father-in-law, recruited willingly, or has herself sought such employment, prostitution is an inherently exploitative activity. Open to all, it is resorted to almost exclusively by the poor, the exploited, and the desperate.[4] For most Hindu women it is the most degrading and polluting activity possible, although perhaps for some low castes and/or peripheral ethnic groups it may not be.

Equally exploitative are sexual relations imposed or initiated by high-caste men on low-caste women, whose involuntary acquiescence is secured through physical, psychological, or economic coercion (Berreman 1963:233–42, 247–50). Such coercive sex is widespread not only in India but in all rigidly stratified societies of which I am aware (Berreman

1960b). This kind of sexual exploitation is a stark indicator of female subordination wherever it occurs, and a reminder that such subordination is only relatively less in the Himalayas than elsewhere in India. But it *is* less, and that is of great significance to the lives of Pahari women and men.

Categories of women in India who have been traditionally exploited by being denied, or having lost, control over their bodies and themselves in institutionalized ways include: wives in traditional Sanskritic or Islamic marriage and family roles; women of ritually low, oppressed castes whose men are exploited for labor and who themselves are exploited for labor and sex, which they are expected or forced to provide to their employers, masters, or creditors, on demand under threat of loss of livelihood; and women who are occupational providers of sex, both those involved individually and those whose caste or religious roles require it such as entertainer castes and temple prostitutes. The contrast in potential for male exploitation of the various categories of female sexual partners in this gender-stratified society might be summed up in the following way: women of one's own status group (caste) are exploited for their labor in a context (marriage) in which their primary function is sexual (reproduction); women of lower status are exploited for their sexual services (intercourse) in a context in which their primary function is usually labor or personal service; women who provide occupational sexual services to men are paid, but those services are scarcely freely given, for most of those who perform such grievously polluting services do so in a context which defines them as available as a result of low status in the caste, class, or ethnic hierarchy and which defines women as vulnerable providers and men as demanding consumers of such services.[5]

Chipko, women, and the standardization of error

I turn now to discussion of an illustrative instance from my research, of a social movement in which female participation, parity, and assertiveness have been prominent and are frequently identified by observers – erroneously, I think – as a rare instance in India of female domination accompanied by weakness among men.

Chipko is the name for a grassroots environmental movement which originated among rural people of the central Himalayas of India in 1972 and has subsequently attracted worldwide attention (Berreman 1983, 1989). Its participants use non-violent direct action to prevent the destruction of their forests by timber merchants. The word means "to stick to" or "to hug" and refers to the technique of encircling or hugging trees bodily to prevent lumberjacks from felling them. As the founder of the movement, Chandi Prasad Bhatt said recently, "saving the trees is only the first step; saving ourselves is the goal" (*Overseas Hindustan Times* 1986).

Chipko: a women's movement? Chipko is famous as a movement in which rural village women have been prominent both as leaders and as participants. One of the first and most widely publicized of all Chipko actions occurred in the Reni Forest of Chamoli district, in 1974, when a woman named Gauri Devi was reported to have led a successful confrontation which saved a local forest of 2,500 trees that had been sold on government contract to commercial timber merchants (Dogra 1983:45–7). The participation of women at all levels of organization and action has led to widespread characterization of Chipko as a women's movement (Agarwal, Chopra, and Sharma 1982:42–8; Bahuguna 1984; Bahuguna 1975; Bhatt and Kunwar 1982; Jain 1984; Joshi 1981; Kothari 1981; Mishra and Tripathi 1978). Impressive though women's role in the movement has been, this is a misleading characterization, for men originated the movement and continue to be involved in similar ways and to a similar extent as are women. I believe that it is more impressive and more encouraging that the movement is one in which men and women work together, as equals, than if it were one of India's many movements of and for women. The unique promise of Chipko lies in the fact that it is a people's movement that cuts across social and cultural cleavages of many kinds that have so often divided people in India. Under Chipko's banner, people have united across boundaries not only of gender but also of religion, ethnicity, occupation, language, region, class, and even caste,[6] and despite differences of education and rural/urban life styles. This is a rare accomplishment in post-Gandhian India (Berreman 1989).

A combination of factors is responsible for the prominent role of women. First, there is the unusually high status of women in the Himalayas as contrasted with most of India, along with the exceptional freedom of action and movement which is a feature of that status and which accompanies their heavy contribution to the subsistence economy. Second, men have increasingly left their families and villages to pursue employment in the plains in response to decimation of the environment and their traditional sources of livelihood (Berreman 1983:296, 313; *India Today* 1986). Women tend to remain behind as the able-bodied adults responsible for their families and villages in every way. These women, who are by tradition self-confident and active participants in most activities in their society, have become quickly accustomed to further responsibility and leadership in meeting the requirements for community survival in the absence of their menfolk. Moreover, even when men are present in their villages it is often women who do most of the work that entails direct, daily use of the forest environment – collecting fuel and fodder, fetching water, grazing livestock – and who therefore feel most immediately the impact of its destruction. Consequently women are alert to the ecological devastation and respond spiritedly, knowledgeably, and effectively to the need to protect against it.

The image of Chipko as a women's movement is a backhanded manifestation of the kind of androcentrism which permeates elite society of the plains. The fact that women play a substantial and conspicuous role in Chipko, essentially equal to that of men, is alien to the experience and thinking of middle-class, upper-caste urban commentators of the plains, Pahari migrants to the plains and cities, and plains-returned Pahari people whose contact with and knowledge of rural life in the mountains is slight at best. Or, if their knowledge is not slight it may be suppressed or denied as a result of their adoption of Sanskritic plains people as reference groups. In any case, many observers have reported that when they saw Chipko, they had witnessed a female-led and dominated movement.[7] This is not an impression shared by the rural mountain people who are participants in and benefactors of the movement, nor would it be that of any participant-observer familiar with and sympathetic to Pahari society and culture. Beyond that, once this definition of the situation had been purveyed to the broader Indian and world publics as an eagerly awaited sign of effective feminist action based on a reversal of traditional sex roles, the die had been cast. This is so widely taken for granted as truth, that it constitutes what Hughes (1958:354) identified as a "standardization of error." It is difficult to correct because observers have approached Chipko with an "*idée fixe* which is unshakeable," and "as a result gross misinterpretation has occurred" (Hughes 1958:353).[8]

Alcohol: men's problem? The Chipko movement has addressed another gender-related concern, alcohol abuse among Pahari men. Perceptions of male alcohol abuse as a social problem entail some of the same errors of gender stereotyping as those standardized in the view of women's roles in Chipko. This issue deserves brief attention here because attitudes toward women cannot be understood separately from those toward men.

The problems of alcohol abuse and forest destruction are frequently regarded by observers as closely linked. An article on alcohol abuse in the Himalayas asserted that "earlier, liquor virtually dominated the everyday lives of the hill people with 95 percent of the male population being chronic drinkers" (Menon 1984). "Before the movement began, life for women was a virtual hell. With the men unable or unwilling to work because of alcohol addiction ..." In response, an organization was formed and, "reinforced by activists of the ... Chipko movement as well as by large numbers of womenfolk," devoted itself to banning alcohol consumption and "rescuing the hill tribes [*sic*] from the stranglehold that liquor had on their lives." Pahari men were portrayed as irresponsible drunks willing to sell out the forests upon which their livelihood depended in order to get cash to support their addiction, their women as courageous crusaders for sobriety as well as forest protection.[9]

Gross misapprehensions exist among outside observers regarding alcohol consumption in the Himalayas. Even more important is the confusion shared by commentators and reformers concerning the nature of cause and effect in alcohol consumption there. I will describe that process concisely, based on my observations in Sirkanda village (Berreman 1963) where alcohol has not been a problem and in other Pahari regions where it is a problem.

Clearly alcohol abuse is a problem among men in some regions of the Himalayas. Those regions are ones where there is maximum environmental destruction, mainly deforestation of the sort addressed by the Chipko movement. The cause of the alcohol abuse, there as elsewhere, is stress, notably that described by such terms as despair, fear, humiliation, frustration, and boredom. Alcohol affords relief through escape. As a Pahari blacksmith told me, "liquor has one virtue: it lets you forget your troubles for an hour." The cause of the stress is economic and social disruption and their concomitants. Pahari men under these conditions are unable to make a secure living and support a family in the traditional manner – in most cases subsistence farming – by hard work and responsible planning. A major reason the traditional approach no longer works effectively is the environmental devastation resulting from commercial resource extraction, notably by timber interests working with compliant or corrupt government foresters. The results often render farming on the land virtually impossible.

Another cause of economic and social disruption is the intrusion of a market (money-based) economy, making the farmer vulnerable to the vagaries of the national and world markets, thereby eliminating the security and stability of livelihood which a benign climate and farming skills previously provided. Many men leave their villages to seek alternative sources of livelihood in the form of urban employment. This furthers stress by fragmenting the family and isolating men. Others leave in order to escape the increasingly stressful conditions of village life. Still others remain and drink alcohol for that same reason: escape.

The problem with alcohol abuse among men in some regions of the Himalayas is exacerbated rather than resolved by blaming alcohol and the men who drink it. To do so is to mistake the symptom for the cause and therefore to blame the victims as though they were the perpetrators of the problem. Where the environment remains largely intact, capable of supporting its human population, alcohol consumption is an occasional, unabusive recreational activity. But why, where alcohol is abused, is it so largely men who indulge and not women? This puzzle can be explained partly in terms of tradition and values: women are expected not to drink as often, as much, or as openly as men. Drinking is disapproved as especially reprehensible and unsanskritic behavior for women. But the more important reason may be that women's daily lives and sense of themselves are not as grievously disrupted by the changes afoot as are men's. Women have their children and their households to care for, and these remain as important foci of concern, competence, and activity even as the traditional economy crumbles. Women are not as mobile as men because of these responsibilities and because to leave would stigmatize them with the suspicion of immorality. It is men whose work and self-esteem are destroyed first and most completely in the village setting. It is they whose roles are most vulnerable to the changing economy, who are potentially employable in acceptable occupations in cities, and who can most readily leave to seek such employment. And it is men who can most acceptably seek psychic escape in alcohol.[10]

Menon concludes that "the movement [to eradicate alcohol consumption] is now turning its attention to other problems plaguing the hills like deforestation and illegal mining and also the ineffective implementation of development programmes. Says [one of its members] 'It is time people here stopped getting such a raw deal'" (Menon 1984:66). If these problems could be effectively addressed, men and women would have viable roles and reasonable security in their economy and society, and the alcohol abuse could be expected to stop.

Those who view Chipko as a women's movement all too often also view men as its betrayers and alcohol as the vice which leads them in their weakness to that betrayal. That interpretation is factually wrong and tactically counter-productive, and most rural Pahari people of both sexes recognize it as such unless coached to say otherwise. In the long-run, in the Himalayas as elsewhere in India and throughout the world, the well-being of each gender depends upon mutual empathy, support, and respect, and upon the well-being of both.

Social processes as gender process in India

The implications of more general variations in the definitions, circumstances, and social position of gender categories and gender hierarchies in

India can now be adduced. It is worth re-emphasizing that the ideal role
of women is a Brahmanical, Sanskritic one which only those of relatively
high ritual status can attain, and then only if ritual status is accompanied
by relative affluence. It requires that women and men be separated,
ideally with sequestered quarters for women, and that women not be
employed – and preferably rarely venture unaccompanied – outside the
home. It also requires a panoply of occupational specialists, artisans, and
laborers to do for their elite masters or employers the defiling but
necessary tasks which are part of daily living for well-to-do, high-caste
Hindu households. It entails frequent, expensive ritual activities which in
turn require priests, paraphernalia, and supplies and the time and
freedom from conflicting duties to enable observance of the restrictions of
action, interaction, and diet which might jeopardize, or be jeopardized by,
competing obligations and activities. As one high-caste Pahari villager
told me:

We can't observe all of those rules that plains people do. Our women have to
work, they can't bother with seclusion [purdah] or being out of circulation when
they menstruate or for a long time when they give birth. We haven't enough water
nor enough time to waste bathing all the time like plains people do. If a Brahmin
here practiced all the observances a plains Brahmin does, his family would starve.
(Berreman 1963:346)

In their rituals and standards of behavior, to the chagrin of plainswardly
ambitious high-caste Paharis who come to realize it, mountain people do
not differ so much from people of the plains, as from *high-caste* people of
the plains.

Caste differences, dowry, and its abuse

Characterizations of the culture and society of the plains often ignore the
fact that the hierarchical nature of plains society differs from locality to
locality and from varna to varna and caste to caste. Although dowry
marriage has been increasingly widely adopted as an aspect of Sanskritization, it has not been the traditional norm among most low-caste plains
Hindus. Among them bridewealth, modest though it may be in amount,
has long been the custom, as is common among low castes all over India
(Karve 1965:132).

It will take extended research among low castes to ascertain the extent
to which this pattern has changed in rural north India, but a start has been
made (Sharma 1983). Information on caste-differentiated marriage
payments is essential to an understanding of the incidence and distribution of dowry abuses, including dowry deaths, and should be a high

priority for research. This is not to imply that dowry abuses as such are endorsed by orthodox Hinduism. They are no doubt a perversion of Sanskritic marriage prescriptions, and dowry deaths are an obscene manifestation of this perversion. But dowry is their precondition, for they are motivated by demands for greater dowries or the desire to be rid of a wife in order to secure another dowry.

Urbanization and elite secularization

Dowry abuses have reportedly increased drastically in both frequency and severity in India as the traditional matrix of social ties and social controls at local and regional levels has broken down. The breakdown is especially acute in cities where controls are attenuated by the density and heterogeneity of the population, the impersonality, brevity, and fragmentary nature of social interaction, the isolation of families and other kin and caste groupings in the occupationalized, monetized, status-striving, atomized urban environment (Berreman 1972).

The severest abuses of dowry demands occur, then, not only with the adoption of Sanskritic marriages entailing dowry, but with the "secularization of Sanskritization." I use this seemingly self-canceling phrase to refer to a structure that is Sanskritic (in this case the dowry system) and a medium that is secular – money – in a context that is "modern" and secular – the city. Among the social entities (castes, ethnic groups, tribes, classes) where dowry has traditionally not been employed, its adoption is an act of Sanskritization, a claim to high-caste Hindu status. But it is also a preliminary, unintentional step on the path to dowry abuse. A different path with the same endpoint is commonly followed by rural Sanskritic elites who move, often unwittingly and sometimes perhaps unwillingly, toward modernization by migrating from their rural villages to cities. There they adopt urban occupations while retaining and emphasizing many traditional social structures, cultural values, and behaviors associated with the subordination of women. They covet rapid upward economic mobility even as they seek to retain the rewards of society. Dowry is materially and symbolically consistent with the Sanskritic life-style they brought with them or adopted, but in the city it is free of many of the social and economic controls which existed in the village. Abuses follow from this fact. This path seems to be chosen primarily by conservative, traditional, elite, urban migrants.

A contrasting process in elite urbanization is female emancipation involving education, employment, relative autonomy, and secularization. This emancipatory process is an alternative to, or may even grow out of, status-striving in the traditional idiom at the expense of women as described above. It occurs among those who pursue mobility through secular, Western, economic means. Female education, economic independence, and social sophistication are valued as material and symbolic means to that mobility.[11]

Mobility from below, aside, and outside

Low castes, tribal peoples, and many regional and ethnic minorities participate little in the processes of Sanskritization and secularization in cities (Srinivas 1966:46–88, 118–46). They are prevented by poverty, lack of education or other opportunities from reaping or even seeking the benefits of urban economic mobility. From low, peripheral, or alien status, these people come to the city in search of livelihood when opportunities are insufficient to sustain them in the countryside, or when they think they can improve their chances, their standard of living, or the fulfilment of their lives in the urban environment. The push from the village, as distinguished from the pull toward the bright lights, usually takes the form of economic change (occupational displacement by commercialization or technological obsolescence) or population pressure on familial or occupational resources. If they are able to remain and survive in the city they may adopt Sanskritic behaviors in an effort to gain Hindu caste respectability.

These changes sometimes take the form of subordination of women, especially through restriction of their interactions and activities outside the home, including avoidance of employment, if the family can afford these "luxuries." But such isolation and segregation of women are rarely advocated and even more rarely attempted among urban low castes and the poor – who are most often one and the same – simply because their income from outside employment is necessary for survival of the family. Another feature of poverty and low-caste status which affects women's status is that women possess little property, so inheritance is not a major issue. In the absence of land ownership the place of post-nuptial residence has less economic importance and tends to be more variable than among land-owning castes. Ritual prohibitions on public behavior including participation in festival and celebratory activities like singing and dancing are less among the low castes than the high as is the omnipresence of vulnerability to pollution through behavior and contact. Such restrictions are altogether absent among most non-Hindu populations, such as non-assimilated tribal groups, for they do not live by these Hindu concepts.

Tribal peoples as a category are not always distinguishable from low-caste Hindus. Their willing or unwilling absorption into the caste system has been frequently documented and debated with numerous transitional cases cited (Bailey 1960; Ghurye 1943; Sinha 1965). Whatever the definition of "tribal" one adopts, in India it always refers to people outside the dominant society in the sense that they do not, or historically did not, share one or more of its major features. These include features that are economic (plow agriculture or related occupations, for example), social (the caste system or Hindu rules of marriage and kinship), religious ("great tradition" religions of India such as Hinduism, Islam, Sikhism, Buddhism, Christianity – unless by recent conversion), habitat (dwelling in major populated regions rather than in peripheral areas such as mountains, deserts, forests), and settlement patterns (living in villages, towns or farmsteads rather than as nomads, transhumants or itinerants). Any group is likely to be designated "tribal" if it has customs alien or offensive to the dominant population such as polyandry, matriliny, unfamiliar or scanty clothing, unfamiliar rituals or diet. The implicit meaning of the term tribal is *jangli* (literally "of the jungle"), meaning backward and uncivilized. The implicit injunction is that such people should be domesticated, civilized along conventional Hindu (or other great traditional) lines.

A prominent feature of tribal social organization in comparison with that of Hindus is greater social equality. This means the absence of caste, but also more autonomy, higher status for females including such features as matriliny, matrilocality, polyandry, dowry-free marriage, female-initiated divorce, widow remarriage, sexual freedom in parity with males, freedom of casual interaction with males, and a high degree of equality with males in every way. It is doubtless on the basis of some of these criteria of gender-based equality/inequality, together with the mountain environment, that some plains Hindus regard and refer to Paharis as "tribals" to the utter dismay of the latter. Paharis are in fact well within the range of variation of conventional Hindu society.

One of the most urgent tasks faced by an upwardly mobile, Sanskritizing tribe, caste, or other social category in North India is to Sanskritize the behavior and treatment of its females, adopting the definition of female status that is common to elite Hindu populations. This requires that women give up many or most of the prerogatives that they themselves find fulfilling, liberating, satisfying, enjoyable. As the title of this chapter implies, the constraining, exploitative, demeaning, endangering treatment of females, in short their oppressive treatment, is the Sanskritic way. Where that way is not pursued, traditional Hindu society tends to see unorthodoxy, pollution, immorality, and the absence of civilization. Or it sees domination by women which is threatening to men, to society and to Sanskritic values. Only those social entities who reject or ignore the Sanskritic model are in a position to sustain or enhance the autonomy and hence the status of their female members.

Conclusions

That females are subordinated to males in many – even most – segments of Indian society, often with grievous results, is a demonstrable and regrettable fact toward the rectification of which enormous energy, including research energy, must be directed. But women in India are not uniformly oppressed and exploited. India is an extremely complex, multi-ethnic, caste-based, stratified, regionally diverse, and economically differentiated society. It includes large populations which elsewhere in the world might be regarded as curiosities or survivals but which are living components of the nation. In addition to the agricultural and industrial sectors of the economy, there are horticultural, herding, and foraging societies, subsistence as well as market economies, landlords, small landowners, renters, tenants, share croppers, and bonded laborers amounting to slaves, as well as unemployed, unemployables, employees, entrepreneurs, and professionals. There are the very few who are immeasurably rich, the very many who are unimaginably poor, the small but increasing middle class, and the majority who are rural and poor but not poverty stricken in the acute sense. There are tribal peoples of diverse traditions as well as Hindus, Muslims, Sikhs, Christians, Buddhists, ex-untouchable neo-Buddhists, Jains, Parsis, and others. There are patrilineal and patrilocal societies, matrilineal and matrilocal ones, those with bilateral kin reckoning and inheritance, some with neo-local residence, and marriage systems that are monogamous, polygy-nous, polyandrous, and polygynandrous, including those encouraging cousin-marriage of various sorts and those prohibiting it or approving one kind (cross or parallel) and disapproving the other; those wherein the levirate is expected and those in which it is unknown or disapproved. There are sibs, clans, phratries, both ranked and unranked, and there are castes and ethnic groups internally organized in what can best be described as segmentary lineages and those organized as what anthropologists call chiefdoms, composed of ranked kin groups. In short, there is represented in India almost every sort of social organization known to anthropology.

Throughout it all runs another dimension of social organization, gender, and in most cases gender is organized hierarchically. The gender hierarchy varies with the variation in organization of other aspects of society and with the environment and history – economic, political, relig-ious, social – to which the people have been exposed. Whether, to what extent and how females, or any other gender category, are subordinated, can be evaluated only by close examination of the context of the lives of those who make up the gender categories in the society in question. The nature of the gender hierarchy in general can also only be assessed in those terms.

The position of one gender relative to another cannot be understood without reference to the position each occupies relative to non-gender categories in the society. An oppressed population, for example, presents different problems to its women and to its men than does an elite one. A relatively egalitarian economy creates different pressures on women and men than does a highly inegalitarian one, and whether the inequality is kin ranked, caste based, stratified by ethnicity or by class, makes a significant difference in the lives of those who constitute the system (Berreman 1981). Class differences and their concomitants are equal to, if they do not outweigh, gender as well as ethnicity, in their inegalitarian impact. Ratcliffe (1978), in comparing Kerala with other states in India, found that the degree of economic inequality is more highly correlated with quality of life than are measures of economic productivity or overall affluence. Although Kerala has some of the lowest economic indicators in India, it has the highest quality-of-life indicators, and Ratcliffe attributes this to the fact that Kerala has the least inegalitarian economy and social structure in India, and by far the highest rates of female education and literacy. It also has the most pervasive tradition of matrilineality in India. These facts must not be ignored in assessing issues of poverty, inequality, and gender in India.

The dynamic nature of gender inequality in India is driven by two major impetuses, described in this chapter, Sanskritization and economic development. Sanskritization is especially damaging to females because it encourages and enforces patriliny (in both descent and inheritance), patrilocality, early marriage and widow celibacy, limitation of divorce to male initiative, dowry marriage, preference for and favoring of male children, male ownership of virtually all property (especially productive property), low priority to female education, literacy, and even health, earning power restricted to males, isolation and sequestering of females, sexual exploitation of females, limitation of social and physical mobility largely to males, and total economic, political, and social dependence of females on males. Such a process makes women second-class citizens at best, slaves at worst. Economic development is damaging to women because it forces all but the few emancipated elite into astonishingly strenuous, low-paid, low-status occupations (where employment is an issue at all – mainly in cities), and often fragments the family, depriving women even of the rewards of domestic status while making them vulnerable to every kind of exploitation at the hands of their employers.

Female autonomy can be enhanced or (if already substantial) sustained by two contrasting processes. The first is through movements to promote ethnic, tribal, and low-caste traditions and pride, as exemplified by the militant *Dalit* (oppressed) Panthers, the neo-Buddhist conversions, the Santal tribal revitalization movement, and Jarkhand tribal emancipation movement – all of which are essentially counter-Sanskritization movements. The second is through secularization, as in elite movements for female emancipation, programs for elimination or reform of caste as embodied in the Hindu reform sect Arya Samaj, the advocates of casteless religions such as Buddhism and Sikhism, and Ghandian and Marxian egalitarian ideologies. Both of these processes counteract subordination and enhance autonomy in gender hierarchies and other hierarchies as well. Among the societal segments where women are most exploited and oppressed from without, it is because they are poverty-stricken and therefore vulnerable – a condition they share largely with their men and their children. At the broadest level, the hierarchical status of each subcategory within the group is shared by all. The solution for women, therefore, must include abolition of poverty and exploitation for the entire ethnic group, caste, or class to which they belong.

NOTES

1 Since 1957 and most recently in 1990, I have worked periodically in the Himalayan foothills of India between Nepal and Kashmir, primarily in the region known as Uttarakhand, which lies between the Jumna river on the west and the Maha Kali river (the western border of Nepal) on the east. This area comprises two traditional cultural and administrative regions, Garhwal to the west (where I work) and Kumaon to the east. Today these two constitute the eight Himalayan districts of the state of Uttar Pradesh. The village in which I have concentrated my research, "Sirkanda," is located between the mountain towns of Mussoorie and Tehri (Berreman 1963).

2 I may have painted an oversimplified picture of plains-Pahari differences, but if so it errs more in its characterization of plains society than of Pahari society. This is not only because I know the latter better, but also because it is smaller in scale (less populous and less heterogeneous) than the former in its social structure, including its hierarchies, hence more easily described.

3 A strong deterrent, however, is the fact that in this patrilineal, patrilocal society a divorcing woman must move away, leaving her children behind. For a discussion of marriage distance and its implications for women's autonomy in the plains, see Jeffery, Jeffery, and Lyon (1984).

4 For the exceptional case of middle-class call girls in urban India, see Kapur (1979).

5 In the second and third categories, the word "women" should be followed by the phrase, "or other gender categories providing sexual services to men." A discussion of this topic with special reference to male prostitutes and institutionalized transvestitism (*hijira*) in India appeared in the original conference paper upon which this chapter is based, but has been deleted in the interests of brevity (see Nanda 1990).

6 With the deeply disturbing exception of the lowest, poorest, landless castes comprising approximately 20 percent of the population (Berreman 1989).
7 The only exception I have encountered is K. Sharma who notes that "the Chipko movement has given women a strong forum to articulate what obviously are women's concerns. However, their participation has not helped them in their own struggle against oppression although claims have been made that it is a 'feminist' movement" (1984:62).
8 The "standardized error" which Hughes identified and analyzed was a characterization of Eskimo social organization in Greenland.
9 Teetotalism is a tenet of Sanskritic morality, advocated by Gandhi and enacted into law in many parts of India. It is interesting that Chipko women are described as simultaneously crusading for this Sanskritic behavior and against Sanskritic constraints on female roles.
10 The similarity to the relative roles of poor African-American men and women in conditions of acute economic distress is striking (see Liebow 1967; Stack 1974:27, 108–12).
11 The social antecedents which motivate the choice of one or other of these paths to mobility in the urban setting is an important topic for research.

REFERENCES

Agarwal, Anil, R. Chopra, and K. Sharma, eds. 1982 *The State of India's Environment, 1982: A Citizen's Report*. New Delhi: Centre for Science and Environment.
Bahuguna, Sunderlal 1984 Women's Non-Violent Power in the Chipko Movement. In *In Search of Answers: Indian Voices from Manushi*. Madhu Kishwar and Ruth Vanita, eds., pp. 129–30. London: Zed Press.
Bahuguna, Vimla 1975 Contribution of Women to Chipko Movement. *Indian Farming* 25:69–71.
Bailey, Frederick G. 1960 *Tribe, Caste and Nation*. Manchester: Manchester University Press.
Berreman, Gerald D. 1960a Cultural Variability and Drift in the Himalayan Hills. *American Anthropologist* 62:774–94.
    1960b Caste in India and the United States. *American Journal of Sociology* 66:120–7.
    1962 Village Exogamy in Northernmost India. *Southwestern Journal of Anthropology* 18:55–8.
    1963 *Hindus of the Himalayas*. Berkeley: University of California Press. (Second edition, 1972.)
    1966 On the Role of Women. *Bulletin of the Atomic Scientists* 22(9):26–8.
    1969 Women's Roles and Politics: India and the United States. In *Readings in General Sociology*. 4th edition. R. W. O'Brien, C. Shrag, and W. Martin, eds., pp. 68–71. Boston: Houghton Mifflin.
    1972 Social Categories and Social Interaction in Urban India. *American Anthropologist* 74:567–86.
    1981 Social Inequality: A Cross-Cultural Analysis. In *Social Inequality: Comparative and Developmental Approaches*. Gerald D. Berreman, ed., pp. 3–40. New York: Academic Press.

1983 Identity Definition, Assertion and Politicization in the Central Himalayas. In *Identity: Personal and Socio-Cultural*. Anita Jacobson-Widding, ed., pp. 289–319. Atlantic Highlands, NJ: Humanities Press.

1989 Chipko: A Movement to Save the Himalayan Environment and People. In *Contemporary Indian Tradition: Voices on Culture, Nature and the Challenge of Change*. Carla M. Borden, ed., pp. 239–66. Washington, DC: The Smithsonian Institution.

Bhatt, Chandi Prasad and S. S. Kunwar 1982 Hill Women and Their Involvement in Forestry. In *Hugging the Himalayas: The Chipko Experience*. S. S. Kunwar, ed., pp. 84–9. Gopeshwar, Chamoli, India: Dasholi Gram Swarajya Mandal.

Dhasmana, M. M. 1982 Changing Milieu and Development Strategies in Garhwal. In *The Himalayan Heritage*. Manis Kumar Raha, ed., pp. 200–14. Delhi: Gian Publishing House.

Dogra, Bharat 1983 *Forests and People: A Report on the Himalayas*. 2nd edition. New Delhi: Bharat Dogra.

Ghurye, G. S. 1943 *The Aborigines – So Called – and Their Future*. Poona: Gokale Institute of Politics and Economics.

Hughes, Charles C. 1958 Anomie, the Ammassalik, and the Standardization of Error. *Southwestern Journal of Anthropology* 14:352–77.

India Today 1986 Kumaon and Garhwal: The Male Migration. *India Today* 15 December:80–3.

Jacobson, Doranne 1982 Purdah and the Hindu Family in Central India. In *Separate Worlds*. Hanna Papanek and Gail Minault, eds., pp. 81–107. New Delhi: Chanakhya Publications.

Jain, Shobhita 1984 Women and People's Ecological Movement: A Case Study of Women's Role in the Chipko Movement in Uttar Pradesh. *Economic and Political Weekly* 19(41):1788–94.

Jeffery, Patricia, Roger Jeffery, and Andrew Lyon 1984 When Did You Last See Your Mother? Aspects of Female Autonomy in Rural North India. Paper prepared for the IUSSP Working Group on Micro-Approaches in Demography, Australian National University (conference volume in press).

Joshi, Gopa 1981 Protecting the Sources of Community Life: Slandered by the Community in Return. In *In Search of Answers: Indian Voices from Manushi*. Madhu Kishwar and Ruth Vanita, eds., pp. 125–9. London: Zed Press.

Kakar, Sudhir 1981 *The Inner World: A Psycho-Analytic Study of Childhood and Society in India*. 2nd edition. Delhi: Oxford University Press.

Kapur, Promilla 1979 *The Indian Call Girls*. Delhi: Orient Paperbacks.

Karve, Irawati 1965 *Kinship Organization in India*. New York: Asia House. (1st edition, Bombay: Asia Publishing House, 1953.)

Kothari, Ashish 1981 Chipko Andolan: Women Fight for Trees and Justice. *Himmat* 15 April:37–40.

Liebow, Elliot 1967 *Tally's Corner: A Study of Negro Streetcorner Men*. Boston: Little, Brown.

Mandelbaum, David G. 1964 Introduction: Process and Structure in South Asian Religion. In *Religion in South Asia*. Edward B. Harper, ed., pp. 5–20. Seattle: University of Washington Press.

1988 *Women's Seclusion and Men's Honor: Sex Roles in North India, Bangladesh and Pakistan*. Tucson: University of Arizona Press.

Marriott, McKim 1955 Little Communities in an Indigenous Civilization. In *Village India: Studies in the Little Community*. McKim Marriott, ed., pp. 171–222. Chicago: University of Chicago Press.

Menon, Ramesh 1984 Battling the Bottle. *India Today*. 15 September, pp. 64–6.

Miller, Barbara D. 1981 *The Endangered Sex: Neglect of Female Children in Rural North India*. Ithaca, NY: Cornell University Press.

Mishra, Anupam and S. Tripathi 1978 *Chipko Movement: Uttarakhand Women's Bid to Save Forest Wealth*. New Delhi: People's Action for Peace and Justice.

Nanda, Serena 1990 *Neither Man nor Woman: The Hijiras of India*. Belmont, CA: Wadsworth.

Overseas Hindustan Times 1986 Ritual or Remedy. 30 August:12.

Papanek, Hanna 1982 Purdah: Separate Worlds and Symbolic Shelter. In *Separate Worlds*. Hanna Papanek and Gail Minault, eds., pp. 3–53. Delhi: Chanakya Publications.

Ratcliffe, John 1978 Social Justice and the Demographic Transition: Lessons from India's Kerala State. *International Journal of Health Services* 8:123–44.

Sharma, Kumud 1984 Women in Struggle: A Case Study of the Chipko Movement. *Samya Shakti* 1(2):55–62.

Sharma, Ursula 1983 Dowry in North India: Its Consequences for Women. In *Women and Property, Women as Property*. Renée Hirschon, ed., pp. 62–74. London: Croom Helm.

Sinha, Surajit 1965 Tribe-Caste and Tribe-Peasant Continua in Central India. *Man in India* 45(1):57–83.

Srinivas, M. N. 1952 *Religion and Society among the Coorgs of South India*. Oxford: Clarendon Press.

    1956 A Note on Sanskritization and Westernization. *Far Eastern Quarterly* 15:481–96.

    1966 *Social Change in Modern India*. Berkeley: University of California Press.

    1977 The Changing Position of Indian Women. *Man* 12(2):221–38.

Stack, Carol B. 1974 *All Our Kin: Strategies for Survival in a Black Community*. New York: Harper and Row.

Index

see also division of labor by sex/gender, labor force, reproduction of

Yanomami, 64–5, 76 n. 3
yaws, 278

yellow-handed titi (*Callicebus torquatus*), 132
Yoruba, 70–1

Zande, 100–3